THE
COMPLETE WORKS
OF
THOMAS LODGE

THE

COMPLETE WORKS

OF

THOMAS LODGE

[1580-1623?]

VOLUME FIRST

NEW YORK
RUSSELL & RUSSELL · INC
1963

*First Published in 1883 and
Reissued in 1963 by Russell & Russell, Inc.,*

L. C. Catalog Card No: 63–15170

PRINTED IN THE UNITED STATES OF AMERICA

PREFATORY NOTE.

In completing for the Members of the HUNTERIAN CLUB the firſt collected edition of the Works of THOMAS LODGE, the Council begs to thank Mr. S. CHRISTIE-MILLER and Mr. J. PAYNE COLLIER for lending for reproduction or collation the very rare, in ſome caſes unique, originals in their poſſeſſion. A grateful ſenſe of the help which in a ſimilar reſpect the Club received from the late Mr. HENRY HUTH and the late Mr. FREDERIC OUVRY, may alſo here be expreſſed.

The principle ſteadily kept in view in the reproduction of the ſeveral pieces now brought together has been to preſerve the appearance and character of the originals, ſo far as could be done with a uniform type. The typographical ornaments, initial letters, and woodcuts have been given in facſimile, while the ſame exactneſs has been followed in the text, which has been rendered page for page, line for line, and word for word. Miſprints have therefore been retained, but the reader will have no difficulty in correcting theſe for himſelf.

Excepting in one caſe, the tracts have all been reprinted from Firſt Editions, which, as a rule, are conſidered by bibliographers more valuable than later impreſſions.

PREFATORY NOTE.

LODGE tranflated the Works of Jofephus, Seneca, and a French "Summary" of Du Bartas. His own part in the dedications and addreffes which accompanied thefe, as well as his contributions to the "Phœnix Neft," "England's Helicon," and other works, will be found printed with the Mifcellaneous Pieces.

In writing the Memoir it is almoft needlefs to fay that Mr. GOSSE was left entirely free to form his own judgment as to LODGE's place in Englifh literature. The intereft of the Memoir is enhanced by a few points not hitherto known in LODGE's perfonal hiftory.

It has not been thought neceffary to add Notes to the Works of a writer fo purely literary as LODGE: but the appended Gloffary will doubtlefs be found helpful in the perufal of his various pieces, now reprinted uniformly for the firft time.

As a matter of bibliographical intereft, it may be ftated that only Two Hundred copies have been reprinted, exclufively for Members of THE HUN-TERIAN CLUB, with Ten additional copies for prefentation by the Council.

GLASGOW, *March,* 1883.

CONTENTS OF VOL. I.

MEMOIR

OF

THOMAS LODGE.

F a full and continuous biography of
THOMAS LODGE could be recovered,
it would poffefs as much intereft to a
ftudent of Elizabethan manners and
letters as any Memoir that can be
imagined. It would combine, in a
feries of pictures, fcenes from all the principal
conditions of life in that ftirring and vigorous age.
It would introduce us to the ftately civic life of
London City, to Oxford in the firft glow of humanifm
and liberal thought, to the dawn of profeffional
literature in London, to the life of a foldier againft
Spain, to the adventures of a freebooting failor on
the high feas, to the poetry of the age, and then to
its fcience, to the ftage in London and to the
anatomical lecture-room in Avignon, to the humdrum
exiftence of a country practitioner, and to the perilous
intrigues of a fympathifer with Catholicifm trembling
on the verge of treafon. LODGE is therefore in many
refpects a typical figure. His genius, from the purely
literary point of view, is fufficiently confiderable to
make him interefting in himfelf, and to give him a

A

noticeable prefence in the fhifting pageant of the times. But what mainly diftinguifhes him from four or five other compofers of delicate lyrics and amorous romances is the length and picturefque variety of his career. Of this career, unhappily, we poffefs but the outline. A few dates in wills or at the clofe of prefaces, a few nimble conjectures, a page of biography in the *Athenæ* of Anthony à Wood, thefe we have to piece together as beft we may, and to endeavour to recover from them the loft prefence of a man; nor are we without this con-folation, that, for an Elizabethan poet, LODGE ftands out before us at laft with fome meafure of diftinctnefs.

The year of the birth of THOMAS LODGE is a matter of pure conjecture. At the death of his mother in 1579 he was not yet twenty-five, and at the death of his father in 1583 he had almoft cer-tainly paffed that age. The various circumftances of his early career combine to make it probable that he was born in 1557. He was the fecond fon of people in affluent circumftances, his father, Sir Thomas Lodge, a grocer, having been Lord Mayor of London in the plague-year 1563. The poet in after years took care to fign himfelf "Gentleman," and to hold himfelf a little above the crowd of play-wrights. His family pedigree was, or profeffed to be, an ancient one, and he claimed defcent from Odoard di Logis, Baron of Wigton in Cumberland, a nobleman of the twelfth century. The poet's mother, Lady Anne Lodge, was the daughter of a previous Lord Mayor of London, Sir William

Laxton, who died before the poet's birth, in 1556; his grandmother, Lady Laxton, who lived to fee him grown up, feems to have fhown him a particular partiality, and to have felected him for preference among her daughter's children, which were fix in number. According to Wood, THOMAS LODGE made his firft appearance in Oxford about 1573, " and was afterwards fervitour or fcholar under the learned and virtuous Mr. Edward Hobye of Trinity College, where, making early advances, his ingenuity began at firft to be obferved by feveral of his compofitions in poetry." This Edward Hobye was perhaps the fon of that accomplifhed Sir Thomas Hobye, who, a quarter of a century earlier, had Englifhed the *Courtier* of Count Baldaffar Caftilio.

About 1575 there were three diftinct fchools or haunts of polite letters in England, each of them filent to the world, but each preparing to make itfelf widely felt, and each fitting out foldiers for the great conflict of the wits. At the court of Elizabeth, Sidney, Greville and Dyer were turning over the mafter-pieces of Greek and Italian literature, and dreaming, at leaft, of fome form of ftately Englifh emulation. At Cambridge, amid a breathlefs circle of private admirers, Spenfer was tefting his powers of verfifi-cation, as yet with little notion of the direction they would ultimately take. At Oxford, when Lodge went up to Trinity, John Lyly had already been four years at Magdalen, and though ftill only twenty years of age, had attracted confiderable notice by his neglect of purely academical ftudies, and by

3

his proclivities to poetry and romance. Among the youths which were cluftered around him were George Peele, afterwards a famous playwright, and Abraham Fraunce, a writer of more reputation than merit. Probably in the fame year which faw Lodge's advent at the Univerfity, Thomas Watfon came to Oxford, and joined the *cénacle*. It would be very interefting to follow the intellectual development of this fet of Oxford ftudents, who feem, in fome obfcure way, to have found at Cambridge an ardent friend and adherent in Robert Greene. Their early exercifes in verfe and profe have all been loft, unlefs, indeed, as feems not unlikely, fome portion of Lyly's epoch-making *Euphues* was compofed before its author took his degree in 1575. Lodge was beyond queftion deeply influenced by Lyly. To the clofe of his career his ftyle continued to be coloured with Euphuifm, and on two feparate occafions he blazoned the name of Lyly's mafterpiece on a title-page of his own. To his intimacy with Peele he owed, in all probability, his intereft in the ftage, and his zeal for the revival of dramatic art; and Watfon, whom he was deftined to furpafs in every branch of poetry, may have led him firft in a lyrical direction with his amorous and precocious *Hekatompathia*. His own writings fhow that he was deeply read in the claffics, that he had maftered French, Spanifh, and Italian, and that he was familiar with all the learned fubtilties which at that time engaged the leifure of the Univerfities.

All that we pofitively know of Lodge's Oxford career is that he was at college with Edmund and

Robert Carew, fons of Lord Hunfdon, and that he remained at Trinity until he took his degree of Bachelor of Arts, on the 8th of July, 1577, being then probably twenty years of age. He did not remain at Oxford to take the higher degree of Mafter of Arts; but, returning to London, was admitted, on the 26th of April, 1578, into the Society of Lincoln's Inn. His elder brother, William Lodge, had belonged to the Society, in which his father alfo had held office fince 1572. In the winter of 1579 he had the misfortune to lofe his mother, Lady Anne Lodge; in the courfe of that year fhe had drawn out her will, in which fhe makes particular mention of her fon Thomas, bequeathing part of her property towards "his finding at his book at Lincoln's Inn," and the reft to him at the age of twenty-five, with this provifion, that fhould he "difcontinue his ftudies," and ceafe to be what "a good ftudent ought to be," this property fhould, on his father's decifion, be divided among his brothers. It is unfafe to argue from this caution that LODGE was already a youth of unfteady charaᵭer; on the contrary, he .muft have fhown particular powers of intelligence to be thus feleᵭed among fix children as his mother's fole legatee. There was probably fome underftanding on this point entered into between the father and mother, for in Sir Thomas Lodge's will the five other children are provided for, but the poet is not mentioned. It was perhaps recognifed that Thomas had already received his fhare of the family eftate direᵭ from his mother.

The death of his mother feems to have been the occafion of his firft effay in publication. *An Epitaph of the Lady Anne Lodge* was licenfed on the 23rd of December, 1579, and the name of its author was entered as " T. Lodge." This poem, which was probably an unbound pamphlet, has totally dif-appeared. LODGE'S next venture has fhown more vitality, but caufed him at the time great difap-pointment and vexation. In 1579 the Rev. Stephen Goffon, a young divine of more effrontery than talent, publifhed a furious counterblaft againft poetry, mufic, and the drama. This volume, which was named *The School of Abufe*, was in faƈt a puritanical attempt to nip in the bud the whole new bloffom of Englifh literature. It was not infpired, as the attacks of Jeremy Collier were a century later, by the righteous anger of a not very imaginative man who faw the wickednefs of the ftage without noticing its poetry; it was merely the fnarl of a dull cleric who hated all that was urbane and graceful for its own fake. What was perhaps the ftrangeft thing about it was that it abufed poetry, and mufic, and ftage-plays before thefe things had really began to exift in England, fo that its author was forced, in the abfence of aƈtual foes, to fight with fuch phantoms of litera-ture as Webbe and Puttenham. *The School of Abufe* had hardly been publifhed when the *Shepherd's Calendar* appeared, and demonftrated its abfurdity. Young THOMAS LODGE had the want of wifdom to fly in defence of the fine arts againft this lumbering opponent, and to pit his Oxford rhetoric againft the

apparatus of a profeffed pedant. A much greater
honour, and a much more complete difafter, awaited
Goffon in the fact that Sir Philip Sidney was about
to deign to anfwer his attack on the arts in his final
Apology for Poetry. This latter work, not printed
till 1595, was written in the autumn of 1581. It was
probably about a year earlier that LODGE wrote and
hurried through the prefs his reply to Goffon. Of
this reply only two copies have come down to us,
each in a mutilated condition, without title-page or
introduction. There feems to have been a refufal of
publication, for LODGE himfelf fays, in his preface to
the *Alarum againft Ufurers*, in 1584:—

"About three years ago, one Stephen Goffon publifhed a
book, intitled *The School of Abufe*, in which, having efcaped
in many and fundry conclufions, I, as the occafion then
fitted me, fhaped him fuch an anfwer as befeemed his difcourfe, which by reafon of the flendernefs of the fubject,
becaufe it was in defence of plays and play-makers, the
godly and reverend, that had to deal in the caufe, mifliking
it, forbad the publifhing, notwithftanding he, coming by a
private imperfect copy, about two years fince, made a reply."

LODGE'S *Defence of Poetry* need not detain us long.
It is a production of the old inflated type, without a
touch of modern frefhnefs, full of pompous and only
too probably fpurious allufions to the claffics, vague,
wordy, and, in its temper, offenfive. The author's
opponent is "fhamlefs Goffon," a "hypocrite," a
"monftrous chicken without head," and is addreffed
throughout with unmeafured and voluble contempt.
The whole tract confifts, as we poffefs it, of only

twenty-four leaves, and within this fmall compafs all the arts are defended from their clerical affailant. It is illuftrative of the poverty of native literature in 1579, that not a fingle poem or play in the Englifh language is quoted or referred to. That the little tract fhould have been fuppreffed is unaccountable, yet not more fo than fuch an act of purpofelefs tyranny as the extinction of Drayton's *Harmony of the Church* ten years later. We know too little of the circumftances attending the cenforfhip of the prefs under Elizabeth to hazard a conjecture regarding its mode of operation.

During the next few years we have great difficulty in following LODGE's fortunes. According to our conjecture that he was born in 1557, he muft have inherited his mother's fortune in 1582, fince it was to pafs to him when he reached the age of twenty-five. It is poffible that before this he had become alienated from his family, and had even fuffered poverty. In 1581 LODGE revifed for the prefs, and iffued with a commendatory poem of his own, Barnaby Rich's romance of *Don Simonides*. In this poem he fpeaks of his mufe as dulled by his "long diftrefs," and remarks that "a dolefull dump pulls back my pleafant vein." I confefs that thefe phrafes feem to me to fuggeft illnefs rather than material ill-fortune, and I think that this view is juftified by the famous phrafe of Stephen Goffon, who, returning to the attack in 1582, fpoke of LODGE as " hunted by the heavy hand of God, and become little better than a vagrant, loofer than liberty, lighter than vanity itfelf." Here, I think, we may perceive a mixture of fact and fuppofition. Goffon had doubtlefs heard of that "diftrefs" under which Lodge was labouring, and at once proceeded, in the cowardly manner of difputants in that age, to exaggerate it to Lodge's confufion. Goffon knew fo little about his opponent, that he calls him William, fome copies of *Plays Confuted* containing a flip, on which is the word " Thomas," pafted over the " William." Goffon's teftimony is of little value, and if we liften to his vague accufation, we are no lefs bound to remember that, when Lodge found next occafion to take up his pen, he denied the charges of Goffon in a manly and ftraightforward epiftle to thofe who knew him beft, the Gentlemen of the Inns of Court :—

" You that know me, Gentlemen, can teftify that neither my life hath been fo lewd, as that my company was odious, nor my behaviour fo light, as that it fhould pafs the limits of modefty: this notwithftanding, a licentious Hipponax, neither regarding the afperity of the laws touching flanderous libellers, nor the offspring from whence I came, which is not contemptible, attempted, not only in public and reproachful terms, to condemn me in his writings, but alfo to flander me."

Lodge was not fo vagrant a perfon but that he had married by this time, and in 1583 poffeffed property, which he devifed in his will to his wife Joan, and to his daughter Mary. In December of the fame year his father, Sir Thomas Lodge, died and was buried at St. Mary, Aldermary, with civic honours. With this event the early career of the poet clofes, and it is at this point that we muft refer

B

once more to the *Alarum againſt Uſurers*, in which
a number of paſſages occur which have been ſuppoſed,
and not without a ſhow of probability, to be autobiographical. In that work, publiſhed in 1584,
Lodge comes before us as a writer poſſeſſing much
more command over language than he had diſplayed
in his attack on Goſſon. The *Alarum* is a proſe
treatiſe againſt " coney-catching," the firſt of a claſs
in which Greene, and afterwards Dekker, were to
attain a great popularity, in which the temptations
and miſeries of London life were painted in gloomy
colours, and the reſults of diſſolute living were traded
on to produce a literary effect. In Lodge's caſe it has
been taken for granted that the palinode was ſincere
and perſonal, and that in this pamphlet he wore the
white ſheet publicly for notorious offences of his own.
Nothing is more raſh than a ſuppoſition of this ſort,
and nothing more dangerous in biographical criticiſm
than to identify the literature with the man. Lodge
deſcribes a young gentleman from the Univerſity,
whoſe mother tenderly cheriſhed him, and whoſe wit
was praiſed and his preferment ſecured, until his
father brought him to the Inns of Court, where he
fell among evil companions, and ſank into giddy and
debauched habits. His mother is now dead, his
father's allowance to him is inſufficient to meet his
expenſes, and he is deeply involved with uſurers.
There is no doubt a great temptation to the bio-
grapher to diſtribute the incidents of this pictureſque
ſtudy along the ſcanty lines of Lodge's own Memoir,
but a more careful peruſal of the *Alarum* ſhows the

extreme danger of this courfe. The tract is infpired, probably, by fome experience of the evils of which it treats; but it is not poffible that, if the poet had been notorioufly an evil-liver of this boifterous kind, he would have chofen to analyfe his experience in fo full and open a manner, in a book which bore his name, and which was elaborately dedicated to his colleagues of Lincoln's Inn. It is much more likely that his experience as a lawyer opened up to him the abufes that he defcribes, and that the real object of his tract was a diftinctly philanthropic one, a defire to bring the fcandalous tyranny of the money-lenders before the notice of Parliament. Bound up with the *Alarum againft Ufurers*, in 1584, were two other works of a widely different nature. The *Delectable Hiftory of Forbonius and Prifceria* is a romance in profe and verfe, which fhows that LODGE refponded with inftant promptitude to Greene's ftart-word in *Mamillia* the year before. In thefe florid and cumbrous ftories the Englifh novel put forth its firft bud; it is in thefe imitations of Italian romance that our long feries of fiction commences. One or two writers, and particularly Whetftone in his *Promos and Caffandra* in 1578, had given a kind of timid fuggeftion of a ftory; but it is Greene to whom the merit is due of firft writing a book wholly devoted to fictitious adventure in profe. LODGE, on his fide, made an improvement on Greene by introducing into *Forbonius and Prifceria* poetical interludes and a fyftem of correfpondence in fonnets, which were immediately adopted by Greene, and bequeathed by him to his imitators.

Hitherto LODGE's achievements in verfe had been flight and far from promifing, but in this book he begins to exprefs himfelf with that mellifluous fmoothnefs which afterwards characterifed his poems. The profe ftyle of the romance is founded on that of Lyly's *Euphues*, of which LODGE was then, and remained, by far the moft fuccefsful adapter. His memory was no lefs well ftocked, and his fancy no lefs graceful than thofe of Lyly himfelf, and he added to Lyly's rather cold ethical abftraction of ftyle a fouthern glow of feeling. In *Forbonius and Prifceria*, however, we fee rather a fuggeftion of this latter quality than the prefence of it, and the merits of the romance are negative rather than pofitive. The third divifion of the volume is the beft; it is a vigorous fatirical poem in rime royal, intitled *Truth's Complaint over England*. In accordance with prudence, no lefs than the fafhion of the age, the exact meaning of the fatire is concealed under an allegorical narrative. Britain is expoftulated with for her unjuft madnefs, for her prejudice againft truth, and for being "hard-hearted, flinty-minded, and bent to abufe." In the face of LODGE's later relations to the Catholic party, it is difficult to underftand thefe reproaches, otherwife than by fuppofing the fatire to be a prudently concealed proteft againft the anti-Romanift action of Parliament, and the new ftringent laws againft the Jefuits. To have openly attempted to ftem the rapidly increafing flood of prejudice againft the Papacy would merely have been to endanger the poet's own head, and we muft fuppofe *Truth's Com-*

plaint to have been one more of thofe cryptic contributions to politics which the Elizabethan poets
loved to devife, and the only fatisfaction of which
muft have been the pleafure of making an oral com-
mentary to private friends.

As far as I am aware, there is no reafon to fuppofe
that any earlier edition of LODGE's next work, *Scilla's
Metamorphofis*, than that which we now poffefs of
1589, was ever publifhed. Yet I confefs I fhould be
little furprifed if it was found to belong rather to 1585
or 1586. It feems to me to be a product of the poet's
early London life, before the date of his wanderings,
and the tone of the preface, no lefs than the ftyle of the
contents bears out this fuppofition. It is dedicated,
like the *Alarum againft Ufurers*, to the Gentlemen of
the Inns of Court, and the author ftyles himfelf " of
Lincoln's Inn, Gent." The preface, which is written
in a cumbrous and affected ftyle unworthy of LODGE
in 1589, complains of the fpread of poetic compofition,
which enforces him to publifh his verfes and affert
his individuality. This petulance may either have
been provoked by the fuccefs of fuch mifcellanies as
Clement Robinfon's *Handful of Pleafant Delights*,
or may be the expreffion of a paffing irritation at
the fuccefs of LODGE's perfonal friends, Lyly, Greene,
Watfon, and Peele, all of whom had come before the
public with fome prominence during the laft few years.
The rapidity with which Greene, in particular, had
poured forth his romances, might well have fuggefted
to LODGE that " our wits now-a-days are waxed very
fruitful, and our pamphleteers more than prodigal;"

and the eafe and fkill with which the fame writer had
adopted and enriched that manner in poetry, which
Lodge had invented, may have provoked the latter to
irritation. *Glaucus and Scilla*, as the poem of *Scilla's
Metamorphofis* is more properly named, was, however,
a work in which its author owed little to his predeceffors, and had nothing to fear from his contemporaries. It is no fmall merit in Lodge that in this
work he was the inventor, or the introducer into
Englifh literature, of a clafs of poem which has thriven
amongft us, and which counts Shakefpeare, Keats,
and even Wordfworth (in *Laodamia*) among its direct
cultivators. This was the minor epic in which a
claffical fubject is treated in a romantic manner.
Lodge fuftains his theme through nearly 150 ftanzas,
and if his narrative manner leaves much to be defired,
his ftyle is fluent and coloured, and his fancy is well
fupported. But the great intereft of this poem, and
one which has never fully received the attention it
deferves, is the influence which it had upon the mind
of Shakefpeare. It is not too much to fay that *Venus
and Adonis* is a direct imitation of *Glaucus and Scilla*—
an imitation, indeed, which vaftly outfhines its original,
but none the lefs was diftinctly compofed in emulation
of the older poem. The ftanza in which the two
poems are written is the fame, and the relation
between the volumes of 1589 and 1593 becomes
quite ftartling when we realize that thefe verfes occur
in the earlier poem:—

" He that hath feen the fweet Arcadian boy
  Wiping the purple from his forced wound,

His pretty tears betokening his annoy,
His fighs, his cries, his falling on the ground,
    The echoes ringing from the rocks his fall,
    The trees with tears reporting of his thrall;

" And Venus ftarting at her love-mate's cry,
Forcing her birds to hafte her chariot on,
And full of grief at laft with piteous eye,
Seen where all pale with death he lay alone,
    Whofe beauty quailed, as wont the lilies droop,
    When wafteful winter winds do make them ftoop.

" Her dainty hand addreffed to daw her dear,
Her rofeal lip allied to his pale cheek,
Her fighes, and then her looks and heavy cheer,
Her bitter threats, and then her paffions meek;
    How on his fenfelefs corpfe fhe lay a-crying,
    As if the boy were then but new a-dying."

This is very clofe to the earlieft manner of Shakefpeare; and, if we turn from *Glaucus and Scilla* to
Venus and Adonis, we fhall be ftruck by the refemblance in many points. There can be no doubt
that the young Shakefpeare borrowed from LODGE
his tone, the mincing fweetnefs of his verfification,
and the " precious" ufe of fuch words as " lily,"
" purple," " cryftal," and " primrofe." None of the
predeceffors of the greateft of our poets had fo direct
an influence upon his early ftyle as LODGE, and this
muft certainly be accounted not the leaft of the
claims of the latter to our attention.

The remaining poems in the volume of 1589 are
worthy of careful examination. A poem " In commendation of a Solitary Life" is a very delicate and

refined compofition, and one which might be taken
as a typical example of the poetry of reflection in
the age of Elizabeth. "A Beauty's Lullaby," on
the other hand, is confeffedly a work of the author's
youth, and returns to the unwieldy verfification and
confufed volubility of a preceding generation, in
which rhetoric had taken the place of fancy. " Sundry fweet Sonnets," with which the collection clofes,
contain a variety of interefting lyrical experiments;
the little madrigal, beginning "A very Phœnix, in
her radiant eyes," and the fong of which this is a
verfe—

> " The birds upon the trees
>   Do fing with pleafant voices,
> And chant in their degrees
>   Their loves and lucky choices,
> When I, whilft they are finging,
> With fighs mine arms am wringing,"

fhould be omitted from no anthology of Elizabethan
verfe; the fonnets are moft of them written in that
fpurious form of fixteen lines invented by Watfon in
his *Hekatompathia*, but in a fingle inftance LODGE
gives us here a fonnet of fourteen lines. He founds
it, evidently, upon French ufage, for it is in alexan-
drines. The proper Elizabethan fonnet had not yet
been prefented to the public, though Sidney's had
doubtlefs been widely circulated in manufcript.

The progrefs of poetical tafte was fo rapid in the
ninth decade of the fixteenth century that we may
trace it almoft year by year. It feems to me impoffible that fo very intelligent and fenfitive a poet

as Lodge could have written thefe "Sundry fweet Sonnets" after Sidney's death in 1586. He might very well publifh them later, indeed; and yet I feel much inclined to think that *Scilla's Metamorphofis* was but reprinted in 1589. Of its author's adventures and manner of life between 1584 and 1590 we know only this, that he was engaged in at leaft one freebooting expedition to Spanifh waters. In the very interefting preface to *Rofalynde* he tells us that he accompanied Captain Clarke in an attack upon the Azores and the Canaries. His expreffions are fo eloquent, and breathe fo exactly the grandiofe fpirit of the age of Elizabeth that we may quote them with advantage. "Having," he fays to his friend Lord Hunfdon, "with Capt. Clarke made a voyage to the Iflands of Terceras and the Canaries, to beguile the time with labour, I writ this book, rough, as hatched in the ftorms of the ocean, and feathered in the furges of many perilous feas." No account of this particular expedition has been preferved, and we may believe that it did not materially differ from many others of which a record has been kept by Purchas or Hakluyt.

The romance of *Rofalynde: Euphues' Golden Legacy,* which appeared in 1590, is the next, and by far the moft important of Lodge's longer productions. "Room," fays the author, "for a foldier and a failor, that gives you the fruits of his labours that he wrought in the ocean, when every line was wet with a furge, and every humorous paffion counterchecked with a ftorm." It is very pleafant to imagine the

C

17

young poet, in the fame picturefque drefs in which his fellow-foldiers fought the Spanifh Armada, ftretched on the deck of his fhip while fhe failed under a tropical fky, and fetting the amorous paffions of the Foreft of Arden to the monotonous mufic of the ocean. But for us the great intereft of this, the beft of LODGE'S works, confifts in the fact that Shakefpeare borrowed from it the plot of one of the moft exquifite of his comedies, *As You Like It*. With the exceptions of Rofalynde herfelf, of Phœbe, and of Adam, the trufty fervant, Shakefpeare has altered all the names which LODGE gives to his perfons. Sir John of Bordeaux (Sir Rowland de Bois) has two fons, Saladyne (Oliver) and Rofader (Orlando); the younger of thefe departs from his brother's houfe in dudgeon, and arrives at the court of Torrifmond, King of France (Frederick), who has banifhed his brother Gerifmond (the Duke), the rightful monarch, to be an outlaw in the foreft of Arden. At the ufurper's court Rofader meets the wreftler Norman (Charles), and challenges him to try a fall in the prefence of Rofalynde and her friend Aliena [1] (Celia), the falfe king's daughter. All then follows as in *As You Like It*, except that there were in LODGE'S ftory no equivalents to Jacques, Touchftone, and Audrey. We put LODGE at a great difadvantage when we compare his crude invention with Shake-fpeare's magical infight and perfect vifion; it is more fair to compare the *Rofalynde* as a ftory with the

---

[1] It will be remembered that Celia adopts this name in the foreft.

tales of LODGE's immediate contemporaries. In it, and in the *Menaphon* of Greene, which was probably written about the fame time, though publifhed in 1589, we find the two cotyledons between which fprang up the fhoot which has fpread into the mighty tree of Englifh fiction. In thefe languid and cumbrous ftories it may be difficult to trace any promife of the fubtlety of *Far from the Madding Crowd*, or of the vivid realifm of *A Modern Inftance*, but the procefs of evolution which has led from Greene and LODGE to Mr. Hardy and Mr. Howells has been confiftent and direct. Already in thefe Euphuiftic romances we trace in embryo certain qualities which have always been characteriftic of Anglo-Saxon fiction, a vigorous ideal of conduct, a love of ftrength and adventure, an almoft Quixotic reverence for womanhood. Before their time anything like a coherent tale in profe had been unknown in Englifh; chronicle-hiftory had been attempted with occafional fuccefs, but not purely imaginative invention. If we compare the *Rofalynde* of LODGE with the *Menaphon*, which is Greene's mafterpiece, we are firft ftruck with the ftrong fimilarity between the methods of the two friends. They had acted and reacted on each other, until it would be difficult, without much reflection, to be fure whether one rich dreamy page were the work of Greene or of LODGE. The verfes would always help us to difcriminate, and by and by we fhould perceive that in the conduct of his ftory LODGE is more fkilful and more bufinefs-like than Greene, who becomes entangled in his own garlands and arabefques. The *Rofalynde* is really very pleafant reading for its own fake, and as the author appears to have invented the plot, we may give him credit for having conceived a feries of romantic fituations which Shakefpeare himfelf was content to accept. The life in the foreft of Arden is charmingly defcribed. Shakefpeare gives us a fheep-cote, fenced about with olive-trees, but in LODGE the banifhed king is found feafting with the outlaws under a grove of lemons, and Rofader, while he refts from hunting lions with a boar-fpear, infcribes his fonnets on the foft bark of a fig-tree. Thefe anachronifms cannot difturb thofe who enter into the fpirit of either romance. The light which is blown down the deep glades of Arden, and falls lovingly on the groups in their paftoral mafquerade, is that which never fhone on fea or land, but which has coloured the romantic vifion of dreamers fince the world began. And it is very curious that the generation which faw the whole of Europe plunged into civil and international wars, when the roar of cannon became a common found in the ears of Chriftendom, and when the whole religious and focial polity of man was undergoing noify revolution, fhould turn with fpecial fondnefs to the contemplation of Arcadias and Eldorados, out of fpace, out of time; and that, on the very eve of the Armada, LODGE fhould have failed under the battlements of Terceira with his brain full of Rofader's melancholy amoret in praife of beauteous Rofalynde's perfeftion.

The verfe in the *Rofalynde* demands particular

notice. It is as far fuperior to the profe in excellence as LODGE himfelf was to Goffon or Gabriel Harvey. Such a ftanza as

> " With orient pearl, with ruby red,
> With marble white, with fapphire blue,
> Her body every way is fed,
> Yet foft in touch and fweet in view;
> Nature herfelf her fhape admires,
> The Gods are wounded in her fight,
> And Love forfakes his heavenly fires,
> And at her eyes his brand doth light,"

and the pieces beginning " Firft fhall the heavens want ftarry light," " Love in my bofom like a bee," and " Turn I my looks unto the fkies," are of the firft order of excellence. Nothing fo fluent, fo opulent, fo melodious had up to that time been known in Englifh lyrical verfe, for we muft never forget that when thefe exquifite poems were given to the public, the *Faery Queen* itfelf was not yet circulated. In thefe love-fongs a note of paffion, a foaring and fhouting mufic of the lark at heaven's gate, was heard for the firft time above the fcholaftic voices of fuch artificial poets as Watfon, and for a moment, to an obfervant eye, LODGE might have feemed, next after Spenfer, the foremoft living poet of the Englifh race. Only, however, for a moment, fince the vafter luminary of Shakefpeare was on the horizon, attended and preceded by Hefper and Phofphor, Marlowe, with the pride of his youth, and Sidney, with his pofthumous glory. And then the

full morning broke, and LODGE in his fweet colours
of the funrife was fet afide, and forgotten in a blaze
of daylight.

Something of this muft have been dimly felt by
Greene and LODGE. They did not confefs that they
were fuperfeded, and from LODGE at leaft we have
no word of petulance at the fuccefs of younger men.
But from this date there is lefs effort made to breaft
the accomplifhment of the age, and we find in both
poets a recurrence to the eftablifhed forms of their
art. Greene, indeed, during the brief remainder of
his life, abandoned paftoral romance in favour of thofe
treatifes of " coney-catching " of which LODGE had
fet him the example in his *Alarum againft Ufurers.*
That the friendfhip between thefe eminent men had
become clofe we have many evidences. LODGE, who
muft have been reading Ronfard or Baïf, addreffed
an octett in French to Greene in 1589, as an introduction to the *Spanifh Mafquerado* of the latter poet,
in which he addreffes him as " mon Greene," and
" mon doux ami." The fuccefs of *Rofalynde* in
1590 was inftant, and this romance continued to be
printed for nearly a century. LODGE was encouraged
to take up literature as a profeffion, and his publi-
cations during the next five years were very numerous.
On the 2nd of May, 1591, he iffued " from my
chamber," prefumably in London, a piece of hack-
work, the *Life of Robin the Devil,* a pfeudo-hiftorical
account of the vices, adventures and penitent end of
Robert le Diable, firft, or as LODGE inaccurately
ftates, fecond Duke of Normandy, whofe brief career

clofed on the 2nd of July, 1035, and whofe eccentric vigour of character had collected a whole train of myths about his memory. This pamphlet was evidently a profeffional piece of work, but it is very far from being one of Lodge's lefs fuccefsful pieces. The poems which he fcattered through its pages difplay, it is true, much lefs originality and brilliance than thofe in *Rofalynde*, but the ftory, fuch as it is, is well told, and there are profe paffages, fuch as the voluptuous defcription of the Bower of Editha, which are equal to the beft which Lodge has left us. It is perhaps not unworthy of remark that it is in this book that we firft detect that fympathy with the Catholic creed, and with Roman forms of penitence and ritual, which became more and more marked in Lodge's writings, and which have led to the fhrewd conjecture that he was already fecretly a member of the Roman communion.

At the clofe of *Rofalynde* Lodge promifed that, if the public encouraged his labours, he would next prepare his *Sailor's Calendar*. This work, which, if it ever appeared, has been hopeleffly loft, was probably an account of the author's expedition to the Azores with Capt. Clarke, and would doubtlefs have been rich in fuch autobiographical touches as we can ill be content to mifs. In October, 1764, there was fold from the library of Mr. John Hutton, of St. Paul's Churchyard, a black-letter volume by Lodge, entitled *A Spider's Web*, which has not turned up fince. Several of his exifting works remain in unique exemplars, and there are, therefore, it is poffible, other lacunæ in our lift of his productions. The next book which comes under our notice is one of the rareft of all, and its entire difappearance would denude its author of little of his glory. Before, however, we confider the *Catharos*, which was apparently publifhed late in 1591, and during its author's abfence from England, we muft deal with the circumftances which led him abroad. Thomas Cavendifh was a young fquire of Suffolk, who, upon attaining his majority, had fitted out a fhip, and had gone with Sir Richard Grenville on a privateering expedition to the Weft Indies. His courage was extraordinary, his judgment above that of a boy of twenty-one, and his power over men almoft magical. In July of the following year he fet out, at his own coft, on an enterprife which greatly impreffed the imagination of the age, the circumnavigation of the globe, and this he accomplifhed in September, 1588. He ravaged the coafts of many peaceful and favage nations, and returned to England with filken fails and every oftentation of wealth. So brilliant had been his fuccefs that he was encouraged, although his conftitution had fuffered in his adventures, to undertake a ftill more important piratical enterprife. On the 26th of Auguft, 1591, "three tall fhips and two barks," with Thomas Cavendifh at their head, fet fail from Plymouth, bound for the coaft of China and the Philippine iflands. Cavendifh failed on board the "Leycefter," and among the company of gentlemen who manned the fecond fhip, the "Defire," a galleon of 140 tons, in which Cavendifh had made his previous voyage, was THOMAS LODGE, the poet, who was now about thirty-four years of age. There may have been in him a hereditary love of this fpecies of adventure, for his father, the fober mayor of London city, had in the poet's infancy taken part in a peculiarly infamous expedition of the kind, the voyage of Robert Baker to Guinea, in 1562, with the " Minion" and the " Primrofe." It was in the courfe of this expedition, and of that which followed it in 1563, that the traffic in negro flaves was fet in motion.

It was neceffary for Cavendifh to avoid thofe particular portions of the globe which he had ravaged in his voyage of circumnavigation, and we hear of his landing firft on the coaft of Brazil, which he had formerly avoided. He ordered an attack on the town of Santos, while the people were at mafs; the furprife was accomplifhed, but no ufe was made of the fuccefs, and the failure of Cavendifh's judgment was foon made apparent. From the 15th of December, to the 22nd of January 1592 the little fleet remained at Santos doing nothing; the captain of the " Roebuck," the third galleon, was told off in command of thofe who preferred to fpend this time on fhore, and LODGE was among the latter. The Englifhmen took up their abode in the College of the Jefuits, and LODGE occupied himfelf, as he tells us, among the books in the library of the Fathers. He had by this time, perhaps on one of his previous expeditions, made himfelf mafter of the Spanifh language. Something which he met with in a book at Santos fuggefted to

D

him the idea which he proceeded to weave into a new romance. Meanwhile the Englifh fleet were driven from their pofition by want of food, and proceeded down the coaft of Brazil to the Straits of Magellan. " Here," fays LODGE, " I had rather will to get my dinner, than to win fame;" and, indeed, a fpirit of diffenfion and mutiny began to render life on board the Englifh fhips almoft unbearable. Cavendifh, who could bear his men through unruffled fuccefs, but who was too young and too inexperienced for calmnefs in misfortune, feems to have loft his head altogether. The cold was extreme, the fhips were feparated by violent ftorms, and at laft Cavendifh left the " Leycefter" and came on board the " Defire," where LODGE was, bitterly denouncing his own men, and refufing to fail with them any longer. The officers of the " Defire" held parley accordingly with thofe of the " Leycefter " and Cavendifh was perfuaded to go back to the latter. LODGE feems to have fhared the common diflike of Cavendifh, for in 1596 he fpeaks of him as one " whofe memory, if I repent not, I lament not." In the midft, however, of thefe fufferings and difturbances, while they lay ftorm-bound among the icy cliffs of Patagonia, LODGE occupied himfelf by writing his Arcadian romance of the *Margarite of America*, which he printed four years later. In the preface to that book he fays:—" Touching the place where I wrote this, it was in thofe Straits chriftened by Magellan; in which place to the fouthward many wondrous Ifles, many ftrange fifhes, many monftrous Patagoñes, withdrew my fenfes: briefly, many bitter

and extreme frofts at midfummer continually clothe
and clad the difcomfortable mountains; fo that there
was great wonder in the place wherein I writ this,
fo likewife might it be marvelled, that in fuch fcanty
fare, fuch caufes of fear, fo mighty difcouragements,
and fo many croffes, I fhould deferve to eternize
anything." The weary months fpent to no purpofe
within the Antarctic Circle muft have fretted the
fpirits of all the companions of Cavendifh. At laft
it feems to have become plain to them that autumn
was coming on, and that they would not get through
to the Pacific at all. The "Defire" fet off alone on her
return voyage, and LODGE, if he was ftill on board
of her, landed, after difappointment, fuffering, and
almoft ftarvation, on the coaft of Ireland, on the
11th of June, 1593. The crew of the fhip had been
reduced to fixteen, and of thefe only five were in
tolerable health. Cavendifh himfelf died of a broken
heart, at the age of twenty-nine, before he completed
what Purchas calls "that difmal and fated voyage, in
which he confummated his earthly peregrinations."

This voyage appears to have cured LODGE of all his
youthful vivacity, although his wandering fpirit foon
broke out again. During his abfence of twenty-two
months great changes had occurred. Three of thofe
poets with whofe names his had been moft clofely
united had died during that interval; thefe were
Watfon, Greene, and Marlowe. But he found that
his memory had been fupported during his abfence,
in one cafe, certainly, by a friend whom he fhould
never fee again. In 1591, immediately after his

departure, had been publifhed his *Catharos*, or, as
the fub-title names it, *A Nettle for Nice Nofes*.
This has become one of the rareft, and muft always
have been one of the moft infignificant of his pro-
duions. Three friends, Diogenes, Philoplutos, and
Cofmofophos, whofe names bewray their didactic purpofe, carry on a dreary dialogue on the fubject of the
feven deadly fins as they are practifed in Athens, or
rather London. Diogenes is a cynic moralift, who
claims that his own life is χαθαρὸς, *pure*, and who bitterly
reflects on the conduct of his fellow-citizens. The
Nettle for Nice Nofes has no literary merit; it is an
early example of the rabid and pedantic profe fatire
of the Elizabethan age, a ftyle of cheap literature
which pandered to the refpectable lower middle clafs,
and foftered its prejudices. Here and there we find
a touch of LODGE's eloquent Euphuifm, but as a
whole this is among the tameft of his books. In-
finitely better and more characteriftic is the romance
of *Euphues' Shadow*, which appeared the following
year, and the editing of which was one of the laft
performances on earth of Robert Greene. LODGE,
as appears from the preface, wrote from America to
Greene, begging him to fee this book through the
prefs and to felect a patron. The title of the romance
directly recalls the famous work of Lyly, and it is in
Euphues' Shadow that LODGE comes neareft to his
great precurfor. Thofe far-fetched references to the
claffics, thofe applications to man's eftate of a fabulous
zoology and botany, thofe involved and fonorous
fentences, each a very microcofm in itfelf, all thefe

features of Lyly's extraordinary ftyle are reproduced by Lodge with the moſt ſtartling precifion. We have the beaſt Varius, with his rich ſkin but rank fleſh, the bird Struchio, the populous and pompous city of Pafan, the horn of the ferpent Ceraſtes, the virtues of the herb Abrotamum, almoſt before we have fairly ſtarted in the ſtory; and the manner of Lyly is caught with fingular art and precifion. Probably this was done on purpofe, for it is certain that after a few pages the author becomes weary of this antithetical apparatus and panoply of examples, and finks to the rich, eafy ſtyle that was native to him. The lyrics, which are more fparfely than ufual fcattered over the pages of this romance, are not in Lodge's brighteſt vein, and no one of them would be felected as among his moſt characteriſtic pieces.

It is probable that both of Lodge's furviving plays were firſt acted during his abfence from England. We know that this was the cafe with *A Looking Glaſs for London and England*, in which Greene had been his collaborator. This drama was per-formed by Lord Strange's fervants on the 8th and 27th of March, 1592, and again on the 19th of April and the 7th of June of the fame year. A paffage of Greene's poſthumous *Groat's Worth of Wit* has been raſhly confidered to refer unqueſtionably to Lodge. After exhorting Marlowe, Greene proceeds: "With thee I join young Juvenal, that biting fatiriſt, that laſtly with me together writ a comedy." It is per-haps not much to the point that the *Looking Glaſs* is not a comedy at all, but a tragedy; but it is almoſt certain that when Juvenal is mentioned Nafh is always meant. Nafh had made himfelf many enemies by his pafquils, and was widely known, which LODGE was not, as a "biting fatirift." It is poffible that Nafh may have affifted Greene in writing his *George a Greene*, or in compofing fome other comedy which no longer exifts. At all events, our defire to clutch at every fhred of biographical allufion muft not blind us to the fact that by Juvenal Greene can hardly have intended LODGE, or any one but Nafh. In a tract printed in 1867, Dr. C. M. Ingleby carefully fifted and collated all the evidence for the popular affumption that LODGE was himfelf a player, and he fhowed it to reft upon abfolutely no bafis at all. That fomebody called Lodge failed to pay his tailor's bill, and left Henflowe refponfible for the debt, is one of those tantalifing little facts which may mean everything or nothing, and upon which it is exceedingly dangerous to dogmatife. LODGE had certainly very little dramatic faculty, and there is no evidence to fhow that at any period of his life he tried to eke out this talent by actual ftage experience. Of his two plays, the *Looking Glafs for England and London* is by far the more interefting. It is very primitive in form; the ferious part of the plot deals with the arrogance and licence of Rafni, King of Affyria. Neither in manner nor in metrical peculiarity are thefe defcriptions of the pride of Niniveh like anything elfe to be found in the works of Greene or LODGE. Whichever of them wrote the opening fcenes of the *Looking Glafs* was frefh from witneffing the performance of Marlowe's *Tamburlaine the Great,* and was anxious to outdo the young mafter himfelf in the " fwelling bombaft of bragging blank verfe." It is probably Lodge to whom we owe the rant of thefe " drumming decafyllabons," which occafionally foften to a richnefs which reminds us of the lyrics in *Rofalynde.* This is the language in which the King of Cicilia thinks fit to defcribe King Rafni:—

" If lovely fhape, feature by nature's fkill
    Paffing in beauty fair Endymion's,
    That Luna wrapped within her fnowy breafts,
    Or that fweet boy that wrought bright Venus bane,
    Transformed into a purple hyacinth,
    If beauty nonpareil in excellence
    May make a king match with the Gods in gree,
    Rafni is God on earth, and none but he."

Unfortunately, although the authors of the *Looking Glafs* borrowed from Marlowe fomething of his boifterous mufic and his high key of paffion, they poffeffed none of his founder dramatic qualities. The piece is a ftrange old-fafhioned farrago of bombaft and fatire; when Rafni and the Ninivites are not mouthing, low comic perfonages in the ftreets of London are talking Elizabethan flang. A certain Ofias ferves as chorus, and fhifts the clumfy fcenes. Jonas is thrown ftraight out of the mouth of the whale on to the ftage, and the vengeance of heaven falls on Niniveh with a grotefque attempt at realifm. Yet poor as is the *Looking Glafs,* it is a better play than Lodge's fole unaffifted effort at dramatic compofition, *The Wounds of Civil War,* firft printed in 1594.

31

The dull and tame fcenes of this hiftorical play, in which there is hardly an attempt at action, and where there is even a melancholy abfence of rant, hardly allow themfelves to be read. At one point LODGE remembers who he is, and Marius, in exile on the Numidian mountains, recites with great fatisfaction a fonnet and a long madrigal, like thofe carved on the trees of Arden by Rofader and Montanus. It may be faid that there is no female character in *The Wounds of Civil War*, for though Cornelia and Fulvia crofs the ftage, and then at the clofe recrofs it, they have no further bufinefs to perform. The play contains its fole hiftorical intereft in the fact that it was the precurfor of thofe tragedies of Roman hiftory which form fo fplendid a part of the repertory of Shakefpeare and Ben Jonfon.

During 1593, the year of his return from South America, LODGE's pen was particularly active. It is probable that he refumed his legal connection, for, on the title-page of his *Life and Death of William Longbeard*, he once more ftyles himfelf " of Lincoln's Inn." This tract is a pfeudo-hiftorical romance of the fame kind as LODGE's previous *Robert the Devil*, but more haftily put together, and eked out with a variety of fhort ftories about famous pirates, and the melancholy fates of learned men. The tale which gives its name to the volume is adorned by a variety of odes and fonnets, which are pretty in themfelves, but prepofteroufly out of place in fuch a profaic narrative of crime and its reward. LODGE was better occupied during the fame year by contributing lyrics to the mifcellany called *The Phœnix Neſt*, which was printed by John Jackſon, and nominally edited by a certain R.S. In the induction to his next publication, *Phillis*, LODGE feems to claim for himfelf the refponfibility of the *Phœnix Neſt*, in which we find no lefs than thirteen of his pieces which occur nowhere elfe. *Phillis* itſelf, however, is a far more important publication than either of thefe. It is, in fact, from a critical point of view, the beſt of all LODGE's works, *Roſalynde* excepted. Among the cycles of Elizabethan fonnets it takes an early place, being preceded by Sidney's *Stella*, Daniel's *Delia*, and Conftable's *Diana*, and accompanied by Barnaby Barnes' *Parthenope*, and Watfon's poſthumous *Tears of Fancy*. LODGE's fonnets are particularly rich in fingle lines, fuch as :—

"The falling fountains from the mountains falling,"

and in ſhort paffages of extraordinary felicity, fuch as :—

"The rumour runs that here in Ifis fwim
    Such ſtately fwans, fo confident in dying,
That when they feel themfelves near Lethe's brim
    They fing their fatal dirge when death is nighing;
And I, like thefe, that feel my wounds are mortal,
    Contented die for her whom I adore,
And in my joyful hymns do ſtill exhort all
    To die for fuch a faint, or love no more."

But it is rare to find a fonnet which preferves this level of excellence throughout. That beginning

"How languifheth the primrofe of Love's garden,"

has found its way into the anthologies, and

"I wrote in Myrrha's bark, and as I wrote,"

E

33

with its beautiful pine-wood fcenery, is almoft as worthy of popularity. The ufe of the double rhyme gives a unique fweetnefs to many of Lodge's fonnets, and in almoft all of them, even where the conftruction is moft lax and the fenfe moft obfcure, the diction is particularly rich. The volume contains, befides fonnets, fome of Lodge's beft fongs and lyrics, in particular " Love guides the rofes of thy lips," " My Phillis hath the morning fun," and " My matchlefs miftrefs, whofe delicious eyes," each of which might be quoted as a type of the exotic poetry of the age. The whole book was dedicated to Lady Shrewfbury. It clofes with a long, dreary, and exceffively obfcure elegiac poem called " The Complaint of Elftred," which may have given Shakefpeare a faint fuggeftion of the form of his *Lover's Complaint*, and which tells thofe hiftories of Locrine and Sabrina, which were dramatifed two years after with the affumption of Shakefpeare's name, and in a fubfequent generation occupied the attention of Milton.

When Jofeph Hall brought out his *Virgidemiarum* in 1597, and boafted with youthful braggadocio—

> " follow me who lift
> And be the fecond Englifh fatirift,"

he forgot or neglected to remind his readers that Lodge had, in 1595, publifhed in his *Fig for Momus* four or five fatires which led the way for future effays in this vein fo diftinctly that to overlook them was an act of bad faith or of bad hiftory. This was another cafe in which Lodge fet a fafhion which has been followed by every Englifh writer of the fame kind. The fatire in heroic couplets has paffed from LODGE through Hall, Donne, Dryden, Pope, Churchill, Crabbe, and Byron, to fuch rare later efforts as have been effayed, without any change of outward form, and LODGE deferves the credit of his difcovery. His fatires feem to have attracted no notice in his own age, for he was never encouraged to print that "whole centon of them," which, he says, were in his poffeffion. The *Fig for Momus*, which was fent out to the world on the 6th of May, 1595, was in feveral ways a tentative volume. LODGE proved himfelf an innovator again by publifhing in it, for the firft time in Englifh, epiftles in verfe to private perfons, founded in form upon thofe of Horace. Of thefe epiftles feveral addrefs private perfons in terms of friendfhip. One to Michael Drayton, to whom an eclogue in the fame volume is infcribed under the pfeudonym of Rowland, fhows the exiftence of an intimate affection between LODGE and the young author of *Idea*, and is an early teftimony to the dignified efteem with which Drayton was regarded by his contemporaries. An eclogue in the *Fig for Momus* is dedicated to Samuel Daniel, an Oxford man who had gone up to Magdalen after LODGE's time, and who had lately made himfelf noticeable for a very pure and intelligent vein of reflective poetry. Daniel and Drayton were men of the beft clafs, gentlemen who held themfelves aloof from the vulgar ftruggle of the wits, and it is fignificant that they, and no longer the rough fort of profeffional pamphleteers, fhould appear as LODGE's

friends and affociates. He was now approaching the
age of forty; the new canons of literary tafte which
he had been among the firft to inftitute, were now
being adopted by authors of far greater power and
frefhness than he. Shakefpeare was in motion; the
riotous crew of the dramatifts were lifting up their
voices, and LODGE breathed along his oaten flute
with lefs confidence, and betrayed a certain growing
agitation year by year. The *Fig for Momus* marks
his lateft appearance as a poet, fince the fonnets of the
Margarite of America certainly, and thofe publifhed
in *England's Helicon* probably, were the work of
feveral years prior to their publication. LODGE's
fatires, eclogues, and epiftles are very monotonous
in ftyle, and do not command attention by their
vigour or concifion. The thought is rarely bright
enough, or the expreffion nervous enough to demand
definite praife. The beft that can be faid of them
is that they are lucid and Horatian, efcaping the
faults of thofe fucceeding fatirifts who thought themfelves tame unlefs they took Perfius, or even, perhaps,
Lycophron, as the model of their obfcurity.

In 1596 LODGE's activity as an original writer
culminated, and practically clofed. We poffefs no lefs
than four diftinct volumes publifhed by him in that
year. On the 15th of April he gave to the world
his profe difquifition of *The Devil Conjured.* It is
a tedious foliloquy on virtue, put into the mouth of a
" virtuous and folitary Hermit called Anthony," and
bears a fort of whimfical refemblance in its conception,
though certainly none in its execution, to the *Ten-*

tation de St. Antoine of Guſtave Flaubert. The
author himſelf thought highly of this performance,
and even went ſo far as to contemptuouſly deſcribe
his former poems and romances as mere corncockles,
while this was the real wheat of his brain. The
preface, indeed, is a palinode; there can be little doubt
that he had now taken religion, and that his early
amorous writings, though always innocent enough,
ſeemed to him to call for penitence. It appears from
the dedication to Sir John Forteſcue, that LODGE
was now ſuffering from miſreports, and it is probable
that he was already ſuſpected of being a Catholic.
This element in his nature is ſtill more apparent,
though yet not openly avowed, in *Wit's Miſery and the
World's Madneſs*, another proſe diſquiſition, of a
pſeudo-philoſophical kind, which he iſſued from his
houſe at Low Leyton, on 5th of November of the
ſame year, 1596. The LODGE family had always
been aſſociated, more or leſs vaguely, with this village,
which lies in the Hundred of Becontree, in Eſſex,
about ſix miles to the north-eaſt of London. The
meſſuage or farm of Malmaynes, in the ſame hundred,
was originally given by Lady Lodge in her will to
her ſon THOMAS, but the gift is ſet aſide in a codicil,
and certain lands on the borders of Suffolk and Eſſex,
at or near Nayland, are bequeathed to the poet
inſtead. Sir Thomas Lodge's houſe, however, had
been at or near Low Leyton, and it may be conjec-
tured that by ſome means or other his ſecond ſon
had come into poſſeſſion of it. By this time, it would
ſeem, LODGE's firſt wife was dead, and he had married

Mrs. Jane Albridge (or Aldred), a widow lady, a Catholic, whofe firft hufband had been a dependent of Lodge's early patron, Sir Francis Walfingham, and who had herfelf been ufeful to the Catholics at Rome and other places in the days of their darkeft perfe- cution. The future Mrs. Lodge has retained a minute niche in hiftory as a cat's-paw in the hands of the detractors of the Earl of Arundel during his imprifonment in the Tower in 1586. Bearing thefe circumftances in mind, it is by no means extraordi- nary that a leaning towards Catholic pfychology of the more obvious kind, fuch as we find it expreffed in the *Devil Conjured* and in *Wits' Mifery and the World's Madnefs*, fhould have taken the form of direct Romanifm in the "*Profopopeia,* or Tears of the Holy, Bleffed, and Sanctified Mary, the Mother of God." It has been doubted, I cannot conceive upon what grounds, that this little treatife, although figned with the familiar letters T. L., is actually by our THOMAS LODGE. It is true that in two copies thefe initials have been reverfed by the printer, but, in my opinion, the ftyle of the text is fufficient to demonftrate that this is one of LODGE's genuine tracts, and the open profeffion of Catholic doctrine is no more than what we have been gradually prepared for by the whole tenor of the poet's career. If there is any caufe for aftonifhment, it is that LODGE fhould have ventured to come forward under fo thin a difguife, at a time when it was ftill dangerous to avow diffent from the Church of England.

In the midft of this bufy year, 1596, and in fpite

of all his denunciation of his early amatory writings,
LODGE bethought him of the romance which he had
compofed in the Straits of Magellan in the winter
of 1592, and he publifhed it on the 4th of May under
the title of *A Margarite of America.* This is one
of the prettieft of his ftories. It has abfolutely
nothing to do with America, fave the accident of its
compofition there; it is a tragical narrative of the
loves of Arfadachas, fon and heir to the Emperor of
Cufco, and Margarita, whofe father was King of
Mufcovy, and who dwelt in a fortrefs "fituate by a
gracious and filver-floating river, environed with curious planted trees to minifter fhade and fweet-fmell-
ing flowers." LODGE has expended his richeft fancy
on this work; the heroine's father cannot be murdered
in his bed, but that this article of furniture is defcribed
as of black ebony, fet about with rubies and carbuncles; the lady herfelf, fummoned to her fate,
paufes that fhe may decently array herfelf in a graff-
green robe, embroidered with daifies; and if a poli-
tical meeting is to be held by the nobles of Cufco, it
has to be arranged in "a fair arbour, covered with
rofes and honeyfuckles, paved with camomile, pinks,
and violets, and guarded with two pretty cryftal
fountains on every fide." The paffages of verfe,
fonnets, and canfonets, are of the fame fweet and
mellifluous order, and recall the interludes of the
Rofalynde. It does not feem to have been obferved
that the elaborate piece beginning—

"With Ganymede now joins the fhining fun,"
is an example, the earlieft in Englifh literature, of a

feftina formed on the exact plan of that form of verfe, as invented by Arnaut Daniel and employed by Dante. An examination of the length of the lines and of the arrangement of the tornada, fhows that LODGE was following an Italian, and not a Provençal model. The latter, indeed, he could fcarcely be expected to meet with. When we except the *Rofa-lynde* and the *Phillis*, *A ·Margarite of America* is perhaps the work of LODGE's which will beft reward the ordinary reader.

LODGE now retired from the profeffion of poetry, and adopted that of medicine. According to Anthony à Wood, he took his degree of Doctor of Phyfic at Avignon. This muft have been at leaft as early as 1600, for in that year certain paffages from his known poems, were quoted in *England's Parnaffus* with the attribution " Doctor LODGE." He alfo contributed original poems to *England's Helicon*, a mifcellany of the fame year. As a phyfician, he rapidly attained a great reputation, and was ranked among the leading Englifhmen in the profeffion. On the 25th of October 1602, " THOMAS LODGE, Doctor of Phyfic, of the Univerfity of Avenion," was incorporated in the Univerfity of Oxford. In the fame year he produced a verfion of the works of Jofephus, which was fo popular, that between 1602 and 1670 it paffed through no fewer than feven editions. In 1603, LODGE appeared for the laft time before the public as an original author, with a *Treatife of the Plague*, dedicated to the Lord Mayor and Corporation of London, and applicable to the epidemic at that moment raging in the City.   Contemporary allufions to him are not rare in the occafional literature of the early part of the feventeenth century.   In the firft act of that curious play *The Return from Parnaffus*, which, though not printed until 1606, was acted in 1602, LODGE is thus referred to as a phyfician and as a Euphuift:—

> " For Lodge and Watfon, men of fome defert,
>   Yet fubject to a critic's marginal;
> Lodge for his oar in ev'ry paper boat,
> He that turns over Galen ev'ry day,
> To fit and fimper 'Euphues Legacy.'"

In a MS. " Poetical Common Place Book of a Cambridge Student," which was perhaps begun in 1611, there is a coarfe fatirical piece againft "London Phyficians," in which LODGE is thus mentioned :—

> " And old Doctor LODGE,
>   That leaues of to doge,
>   Will you neuer leaue?"

This not very intelligible apoftrophe poffibly points to the fact that in fpite of his reputation—and in his *Troia Britanica*, in 1609, Heywood had given him a place among the fix moft famous Englifh doctors —LODGE was occafionally put to great ftraits for a livelihood.   In the meantime we may be allowed to print for the firft time a letter which exifts among the Domeftic State Papers, and which reveals fomething of the intrigues in which LODGE and his Catholic wife were unqueftionably engaged :—

" S^r, haveinge mett wth fo convenient a meffenger I cannot but congratulate yor departure hence to liue in fuch con-

F

tentment as their I heare you doe. wch as I wifh more and
more to increafe fo doubt I not but that you will alwayes
be mindefull of ye well wiffhinge frendes you have left behinde
yo^u. In my laft lettre to you, I requefted that Mrs Lodge
might haue continued heare at leafte for fome fix or feaven
monethes but fithence that tyme havinge bin at the
Mofcovia houfe and not findinge that her ftay heare might
doe me the good I expe&ed and that I hould it no
reafonable requeft fo longe to difjoyne man and wief I leave
the orderinge of y^t bufines to yor owne further confideracōn.
Wiffhinge that Mr Griffin for that my felfe fhall be often
abfent from hence wer fully authorized by a lettre of Attorney
from you, to haue the managinge of that bufines from tyme
to tyme. And that further you will write yor lettres as
occacōn fhall be offered to the M^r of the company and yor
lettres of particular dire&ion to Mr Griffin or others to fuch
effe& as I fhall from tyme to tyme require it. The
fhippinge wch went forth two yeare fithence is not yet all
returned & theirfore no accoumpt paft as yet of that
viage, yet it is proffered that the fiftye pounde may goe in
adventure this yeare againe wch argueth that the principall
remayneth whole, but yet cannot be gotten out and theirfore
I hould it beft againe to adventure it, and fo Mrs Lodge in
yor abfence hath undertaken to doe. And fome bodye muft
from tyme to tyme be heare to let the company what they
will adventure or els the ftocke for y^t yeare lieth deade.
Notw^thftandinge all the difficultyes this age feemeth for
this p^rfent to inviron us wth all, y^t we fhall ftill be hable to
drawe breath in England and I hope ere it be longe to fee
you willinge and defirous to looke homewarde, for though
much hath bin attempted againft us in parliament yet,
hitherto nothinge is done harder then of oulde, nor as I hope
will be. I pray you S^r advertize me howe I might place
Robin their, and what the charge would be to kepe him at
his booke or what you thinke of it, if I could gett him placed

wth Sr Willm Standley, and lett me heare fometymes from you I pray yo^w we lye ftill at o^r oulde lodginge. And thus wth my hartye commendacōns & my wiues to you wth yor fervants dutye I ende London this ixth of March 1605.

"Yo^r lovinge frende

"W. JENISON."

"To the worfhipfull his louinge frende
"Mr Thomas Lodge, Doctor in Phificke."

Our next glimpfe of the poet-phyfician fhows him to us once more fetting out upon his travels. A memorandum in the Privy Council Regifters, dated January 10, 1616, mentions "A paffe for THO. LODGE, Doctor of Phyfic, and Henry Sewell, gent., to travel into the Arch-Duke's Country, to recover fuch debts as are due unto them there, taking with them two fervants, and to return agayne in five moneths." It has been fuggefted that the real object of his journey was to avoid procefs on the part of Alleyn, who arrefted LODGE immediately upon his return. LODGE feems to have left England again as foon as this trouble was over and to have remained abroad, probably practifing in the Low Countries until 1619. In his treatife called *The Poor Man's Talent*, firft printed in 1881, he defcribes a remedy "which," he fays, "I have often tried in the Royal Hofpital at Mecklin upon foldiers that grew lame by cold."

Of LODGE's remaining years few memorials are in exiftence. That he was in eafy circumftances may be gathered from the fact that in 1612 he raifed a monument in the Church of Rollefton, Notts, to the memory of his younger brother, Nicholas Lodge, lord of that manor, in whofe will a legacy of two gold bracelets is made to the wife of the poet. In 1614 LODGE publifhed a tranflation of the works of Seneca, and a copy of this book is in exiftence, given by LODGE to Thomas Dekker in the year of publication. About 1623 he compiled *The Poor Man's Talent*, a medical text-book for the ufe of his wife's old patronefs, Anne, Countefs of Arundel. In this work LODGE ufes expreffions which could only proceed from the mouth of a Catholic, and fuch a phrafe as "I will fet down a remedy which St. Dominic revealed to a poor devout woman," leave us no room to doubt that by this time, at all events, he had definitely joined that communion to which he had all his life been leaning.

LODGE became a very prominent practitioner during the laft years of his life. His private houfe was ftill at Low Leyton, but he faw his London patients originally in Warwick Lane, afterwards in Lambert Hill, and finally, fhortly before his death, in Old Fifh Street. He died, it is faid, of the plague, in 1625, being then in his fixty-feventh or fixty-eighth year, and on the 12th of October of that year adminiftration of his effects was granted to his widow, Jane Lodge, who muft herfelf have been an elderly woman at the time, her name having come forward in connection with the Arundel family juft forty years before.

THOMAS LODGE was a ftrange compound of ftrength and weaknefs, of imitation and originality. His intelligence and activity gave him a prominence in

the literature of the time which his mind was hardly
vigorous enough to fuftain. He would have, as his
fatirift fays, "his oar in every paper boat," and
could not conceive the poffibility of failing in any
departmcnt of literature. As a fact, however, he is
a fignal failure in drama, in fatire, and in philofophy,
and his unfuccefsful efforts in thefe directions occupy
a large fection of his entire works. His almoft
fervile attitude towards the bold affectations of Lyly
would make us at one moment deny LODGE all true
originality, if we were not immediately confronted
by the fact that he was himfelf a pioneer in half a
dozen fields of poetical invention. The introducer
into Englifh of the romantic epic, of the heroic fatire,
and of the heroic epiftle, cannot be overlooked in
any hiftorical fummary of our literature. But LODGE's
real excellence is as a lyrical poet, and in the richnefs of his fancy as a profe romancer. His profe
ftyle, judged by fevere modern canons, or even compared with the poetical ftyle of his own age, is not
lefs intolerable than that of moft of his contemporaries.
Englifh profe, as an inftrument for the clear expreffion of unaffected thought, had hardly begun to
exift. LODGE's beft romances are as lucidly and
gracefully written as was at that time poffible. They
never can, however, take again a living place in
literature; but this honour muft not be denied to
the beft of their author's fongs and fonnets. In
that glowing age no one could exprefs the jubilant
extravagance of love with a fuller note, with a more
luxurious mufic, with more affluent and redundant

imagery. His intellectual languor prevents the complete, or rather the continuous expreffion of this golden ecftacy, and we are often left to wonder that a lyrift who˙ was fo thrilling a moment ago can now be fo infipid. But in a few of his beft fongs he fuftains his flight till the mufic is perfect, and in thefe he reaches the topmoft level of fuccefs. The author of " Like to the clear in higheft fphere," was as genuine a poet as ever breathed, and whether in thefe moments of great infpiration, or in his hours of langour and extravagance, LODGE is always the very type and exemplar of a man of letters in the irregular and romantic age of Elizabeth.

EDMUND W. GOSSE.

NOTE.

To the courtefy of the Rev. Charles J. Robinfon we owe the communication of this entry, from the Minutes of the Court of the Merchant Taylors' Company, held 23rd March, 157$\frac{9}{1}$:—

"Item the forefaide M^r· and Wardens have admitted THOMAS LODGE, fil', Thome L. militis, Edmond Greenock, fil...... G......, Thomas Morgan, fil...... M......, William Widnell, fil, William W., mercator fciffor, Robert Smythe, fil, Robert S. Jarrett Keyne, fil, John K., fifhmonger, Samuel Lane, fil, John L., vintner, are admitted of the number of thofe l. fchollars that are limited to be taughte within o^r schole."

[The reference is to fifty scholars who were to pay 2s. 6d. a quarter.]

BIBLIOGRAPHICAL INDEX.

———————◆———————

I. An Epitaph of the Lady Anne Lodge.

Nothing is known of this Epitaph except what is to be found in the following entry from the " Stationers' Regifters" (Mr. ARBER'S *Tranfcript*, vol. ii., p. 363):—

"23. December [1579]

" Edward white.—Lycenced vnto him vnder the handes of the wardens *An epitaphe of the lady ANNE LODGE* by T LODGE
iiij^d"

II. [A Reply to Stephen Goffon's Schoole of Abufe in Defence of Poetry Muſick and Stage Plays by Thomas Lodge.   1580?] fm. 8vo, 24 leaves.

Black letter. Has neither title nor imprint. Two per-fect copies known: one in the library of Mr. S. Chriftie-Miller at Britwell, and the other in the Bodleian Library, Oxford. It was reprinted by the *Shakefpeare Society* in 1853.

III. AN Alarum againft Vfurers. *Containing tryed experiences* againft worldly abufes. WHEREIN GENTLE-MEN may finde good counfells to confirme them, and pleafant Hiftories to delight them: and euery thing fo interlaced with varietie: as the curious may be fa*tisfied*
A

*with rareneſſe, and the curteous with plea*ſure. Heere-
unto are annexed the deleɛ̄table hiſtorie of *Forbonius*
and *Priſceria:* with the lamentable Complaint of Truth
ouer *England.* Written by *Thomas Lodge,* of *Lincolnes Inne,* Gentleman. *O Vita! miſero longa, fælici
breuis.* ¶ Imprinted at London by T. Eſte, for Sampſon Clarke, and are to be ſold at his ſhop by Guyld
Hall.   1584, 4to, 46 leaves.

Black letter. Two perfeɛ̄t copies known: one in Mr. S.
Chriſtie-Miller's Library, and the other in the Bodleian
Library. It is thus entered in the "Stationers' Regiſters"
(Mr. ARBER'S *Tranſcript,* vol. ii., p. 428):—

" 4to novembris [1583]

"Sampſon Clarke.—Licenced vnto him vnder th[e h]andes of
the Biſshop of LONDON and maſter Newbery, *Tryed experiences of worldelie abuſes* by THOMAS LODGE . . vj^d/ "

This traɛ̄t was reprinted by the *Shakeſpeare Society* in 1853.

IV. SCILLAES Metamorphoſis: *Enterlaced* with the vnfortunate loue of *Glaucus. VVhereunto is annexed the
deleɛ̄table diſcourſe* of the diſcontented *Satyre*: with
ſundrie other moſt abſolute Poems and Sonnets. *Contayning the detestable tyrannie of Di*ſdaine, and Comicall
triumph of Conſtancie: Verie fit for young Courtiers
to peruſe, and coy Dames to remember. By *Thomas
Lodge* of Lincolnes Inne, Gentleman. *O vita! miſero
longa, fælici breuis.* Imprinted at London by *Richard
Jhones,* and are to be ſold at his ſhop neere Holburne
bridge, at the ſigne of the Roſe and Crowne.
                                         1589, 4to, 24 leaves.

Black letter. Only one perfect copy known, that in the Dyce Collection, South Kenfington Mufeum, London. The Bodleian copy is imperfect. This tract was re-iffued in 1610, a copy of which edition was in the library of the late Mr. Frederic Ouvry, V.P.S.A., London. It was originally entered in the "Stationers' Regifters" as follows (Mr. ARBER'S *Tranfcript*, vol. ii., p. 530):—

> "22 Septembris [1589]
> "Ric. Jones.—Entred for his copie *The hiftory of GLAUCUS, and*
> T. LODGE   *SYLLA*: vnder the hand of mafter HARTWELL
> and mafter Cawood . . . . vj ᵈ"

Mr. Collier, defcribing the re-iffue of 1610, fays:—

"This edition, with the title-page of 1610, is even more rare than the original impreffion; but the fact is that in 1610 all that was done was to give the work a new fore-front, leaving the text exactly as it ftood in 1589, when it firft came out. It was not reprinted, for in all other refpects the impreffions are identical— the fame errors, the fame faulty letters, and the fame peculiarities of type. It is pretty clear that the copies dated 1589 did not fell, and that they fubfequently came into the hands of a bookfeller, who merely had a new title-page thrown off, and did not choofe even to put his own name at the bottom of it. Confidering the variety and excellence of the contents, and recollecting that 'By Thomas Lodge of Lincolnes Inne, Gentleman,' was placed upon the original title-page, as well as fubfcribed to the dedication, we cannot but wonder that it did not meet with a fale fufficient to exhauft the impreffion of 1589. Lodge never mentioned it in any of his many fubfequent and popular works, nor was it ever noticed by his contemporaries; and we feel convinced that fome peculiarity attended its publication in the firft inftance, and its re-appearance in 1610, which we are unable to explain."

After quoting the title-page of the edition of 1589, Mr. Collier continues:—

" Richard Jones, the Stationer, feems to have been a rare hand at an attractive defcriptive title-page, and we are perfuaded that Lodge had nothing to do with the infertion of fuch words as 'delectable difcourfe' and 'moft abfolute poems and fonnets.' One point, however, feems probable—that the 'puff' did not anfwer its pur-pofe, and that, at the end of more than twenty years, fo many copies remained on hand as to make a re-iffue of them advifable. We look in vain through the eight and forty pages for fome expla-nation of this circumftance, unlefs it be to be found in the dedi-cation to ' Mafter Rafe Crane, and the reft of his moft entire well willers, the Gentlemen of the Innes of Court and Chauncerie,' where Lodge fpeaks ambiguoufly of the mode in which his manu-fcript had efcaped from his hands to the prefs: there he calls what the title-page announces as '*abfolute Poems*,' ' imperfit poems,' and refers to ' the bafe neceffity of an extravagant mate,' as having caufed them to be made public by ' a needie pirate.' This is not faying much for Jones, the publifher, and we know from Nicholas Breton that he was not a very fair-dealing trades-man."—(*Bibliographical Account*, 1865, vol. i., pp. 464-5.)

V. Rofalynde. Euphues golden legacie: found after his death *in his Cell at Si*lexedra. *Bequeathed to Philautus fonnes* nourfed vp with their *father in* England. Fetched from the Canaries. *By T. L. Gent.* LONDON, Imprinted by *Thomas Orwin* for *T. G.* and *John Busbie.* 1590, 4to, 70 leaves.

Black letter. Only one copy of the edition of 1590 is known to exift, and is in the library of Mr. S. Chriftie-Miller, Britwell. It is, however, defective of Sheet R: this laft has been fupplied in the reprint from the fecond edition of 1592, and is diſtinguiſhed by being encloſed within ſquare brackets. Probably on account of the uſe made of it by Shakeſpeare, it went through at leaſt ten editions between 1590 and 1642. It was originally entered in the "Stationers' Regiſters" as follows (Mr. ARBER'S *Tranſcript*, vol. ii., p. 564):—

"6 Oƈtobris [1590]
"Nicholas Lynge.—Entred for their copie vnder th[e h]andes
John Buſbye./ of Doƈtor STALLARD and the wardens
E[*u*]*PHUES golden legacye found after his
Deathe at his Cell at Selexidra* . . vj^d/"

VI. THE Famous, true and hiſtoricall life of *Robert* ſecond Duke *of* Normandy, *ſurnamed for* his monſtrous birth and behauiour, *Robin* the Diuell. *VVherein is contained his diſſolute life in his youth,* his deuout reconcilement and vertues in his age: Interlaced with many ſtraunge and miraculous aduentures. Wherein are both cauſes of profite, and manie conceits of pleaſure. By *T. L. G.* Imprinted at London for *N. L.* and *Iohn Buſbie,* and are to be ſold at the Weſt dore of Paules.
                    1591, 4to, 45 leaves.

Black letter. The only perfeƈt copy known is in the library of Mr. S. Chriſtie-Miller, Britwell. Mr. Collier thus deſcribes it:—

"The dedication is to the 'true Mœcenas of learning M. Thomas Smith,' and it is dated 'from my chamber, 2 Maij, 1591:' in it Lodge apologiſes for his 'rude and homely written hiſtory,' and promiſes to inſcribe to Smith hereafter ſomething which ſhall better merit his patronage. His addreſs, 'to the courteous Reader,' contains a ſpecimen of his 'homely' writing, when Lodge tells him that he has derived his materials from 'the old and ancient antiquaries,' and that he has publifhed 'as much as he had read, and not fo much as they had written.' Therefore, he did not profefs to be fully and completely informed upon the fubject, and his narrative, which is in profe, contains proofs of various deficiencies, befides intereft. It is the dulleft and dryeft of Lodge's productions, and we might almoft fancy that it was from an inferior pen. . . . The work is divided into feparate chapters, and the effort of the author to extend his matter to a faleable-fized volume is obvious. A MS. note in Heber's copy ftated that in Rawlinfon's Catalogue an edition of 1599 is mentioned: if fo, we apprehend that it was merely a mifprint, and that 'Robin the Devil' was printed only once, and that in 1591. It bears ftrong evidence of poverty of pocket, which occafioned poverty of invention. Lodge's 'Rofalynd' of 1590 had procured him a certain degree of popularity, and in 1591 he might be anxious to avail himfelf of it, and therefore brought out two new works, both of inferior merit, 'Catharos' and 'Robin the Devil.'"—(*Bibliographical Account*, 1865, vol. i., p. 471.)

VII. CATHAROS. Diogenes in his *Singularitie*. Wherein is comprehended his merrie *baighting fit for all mens benefits: Christened by him*, A Nettle for Nice Nofes. By *T. L.* of Lincolns Inne, Gent: 1591. AT LONDON, Printed by *VVilliam Hoskins* & *Iohn Danter, for* Iohn Busbie. 4to, 33 leaves.

Black letter. Four copies known: one in the Britifh Mufeum; another in the Bodleian; a third in Bridgewater-houfe; and the fourth in the library of the late Mr. Frederic Ouvry, V.P.S.A., London. This work is thus defcribed by Mr. Collier:—

" This work is a profe fatire upon the vices of perfons of all ranks, and it is delivered by Diogenes from his tub in the prefence of two perfons, called Philoplutos and Cofmofophos, who vifit him principally to obferve him 'in his fingularity.' All that he fays of Athens is applicable to London; and the thought was not a happy one, fince it makes Diogenes guilty of very abfurd anachronifms: befides citing Cicero and Virgil, he quotes freely from the New Teftament, refers to the proceedings of the Council of Nice, and even introduces three ftanzas fromAriofto, which Diogenes thus excufes himfelf from rendering:—' I had rather fome other fhould take the paynes to tranflate thefe verfes into our mother tongue, than my felfe; for now a dayes the world fwarmeth with fuch a number of privie Ariftarchi, that thinke no meate can be good that is not fod in their owne broath, nor proverbe well applyed that hath not paft their pen.' This of courfe refers to the critical fpirit that prevailed in England at the latter end of the reign of Elizabeth: Sir John Harington publifhed his verfion of the ' Orlando Furiofo ' in 1591. Lodge's ' Catharos ' reminds us, in fome important refpects, of Sir T. Elyot's 'Pafquil the Plain.' " —(*Bibliographical Account*, 1865, vol. i., p. 470.)

VIII. *EVPHVES SHADOW,* THE Battaile of the Sences. Wherein youthfull folly is fet downe in his right figure, and vaine fancies are prooued *to produce many offences.* Hereunto is annexed the Deafe mans Dialogue, contayning Philamis Athanatos: *fit for all fortes to perufe, and the better forte to* practife. By T. L. *Gent.* LONDON Printed by Abell Ieffes, for Iohn Busbie, and are to be fould at his fhop in Paules Churchyard, neere to the Weft doore of Paules. 1592, 4to, 52 leaves.

Black letter. Three copies known: one in the Peterborough Cathedral Library; another in the Britifh Mufeum; and the third in the Capell Collection, Trinity College, Cambridge. It is thus entered in the " Stationers' Regifters " (Mr. ARBER'S *Tranfcript*, vol. ii., p. 604):—

"xvij° ffebruarij [1592]
"Nicholas Lynge.—Entred for their copie vnder th[e h]andes
John Bufbye./ of mafter HARTWELL and mafter Watkins/
  EUPHUES Shadowe./ with *the Deathe mans*
  Dialogue annexed . . . . . . vj^d"

The work is thus defcribed by Mr. Collier:—

" In his dedication to Vifcount Fitzwaters, Greene tells his patron
that Lodge had left this tract behind him for publication; and fuch
may have been the fact; but he at the fame time informs the
' Gentlemen Readers' that he had already ' put forth fo many of
his own labours' that they might be weary of his name: this ftatement tends to confirm the notion that he reforted to the expedient
of palming ' Euphues Shadow' upon Lodge, who was abfent, and
could not contradict him; and who, if he had been then actually
refident in England, would not have had much reafon to complain
that fo popular an author as Robert Greene had paid him the com-
pliment. Until fome further evidence is produced, . . . it
muft remain undecided whether the tract be by one or by the
other. Greene was determined that his inftrumentality in the
matter, whatever his fhare may have been, fhould not be imputed
to any other perfon, and therefore fubfcribed the dedication with
the addition of the county from which he was known to have
come—' Rob. Greene *Norfolcienfis.*' In the year of the appearance
of the tract under confideration, Greene faid of himfelf, ' I neede
not make long difcourfe of my parentes, who for their gravitie and
honeft life is well knowne and efteemed amongft their neighbors,
namely in the Cittie of Norwich, where I was bred and borne.'
. . . He profeffed to Lord Fitzwaters that Lodge, ' in his laft
letters,' had enjoined him to print ' Euphues Shadow;' but it is
more than doubtful whether Lodge did write, or could have
written, to Greene in the interval fince his failing with Cavendifh,
and the whole affair reads more like a pretext than a reality.
However, in our day it is a matter of little confequence, and

certain it is that there is nothing in the production itfelf that fhould have made Lodge very anxious to own it. On the other hand, if the publication were a failure, Greene by this expedient had avoided all refponfibility; and the more pofitive he reprefented Lodge in his directions to have ' Euphues Shadow' printed, the more Greene fhifted any weight from his own fhoulders.

" After the addrefs ' To the Gentlemen Readers,' the ftory, fuch as it is, commences, but the few and common-place incidents are not worth detailing; and the language, we feel affured, was the language of Greene, with precifely his thoughts, his images, and his modes of expreffion. The fort of epiftle from ' Philautus to his fonnes living at the Court,' with which the piece commences, is exactly like Greene's compofition, and it ferves to introduce certainly one of the dulleft performances of the period: as if Greene, having written it, was unwilling to avow it, while his neceffities drove him to the fale of it, not under his own name, but under that of a poet with whom he was known to have been acquainted."—(*Biblio. Account,* vol. i., p. 264.)

IX. THE Life and Death of william Long beard, the moft famous and witty Englifh Traitor, borne in the Citty of London. Accompanied with manye other *moft pleafant and prettie hiftories, By T.* L. of Lincolns Inne, Gent. *Et nugæ feria ducunt.* Printed at London by Rychard Yardley and Peter *Short, dwelling on Bread-ftreat hill, at the* Signe of the Starre.

1593, 4to, 36 leaves.

Black letter. Two copies only are known to exift: one in the Bodleian Library, and the other was in the poffeffion of the late Mr. Frederic Ouvry, V.P.S.A., London. Thefe two copies differ from each other very materially. The one in the Bodleian wants the Latin legend in the title-page, as well as the leaf containing the dedication to Sir William Web,

B

and the addrefs "To the Gentlemen Readers:" Mr. Ouvry's copy has all that is wanting in the former, and is confequently *unique*. On comparing the title-pages it was found that they were almoft but not quite identical in type and fpacing; and Mr. Collier fuggefts that Mr. Ouvry's copy was the later of the two, and that Lodge added the Latin motto as a kind of apology for the flightnefs of the work. "The want of the fecond leaf in the Bodleian copy is a capital defect: the addrefs 'To the Gentlemen Readers' is the moft characteriftic feature of the book, as protefting againft the Euphuiftic jargon which was then in fafhion." Mr. Collier thus defcribes the work:—

"Here again we apprehend that Lodge was infpired more by poverty than by poetry: ftill, it is a confiderable improvement upon the work laft reviewed ["The famous true and hiftoricall life of Robert fecond Duke of Normandy."] . . . . There was an interval of two years between it and 'Robin the Devil,' and Lodge does not appear to have been then preffed quite fo feverely by his neceffities: neverthelefs, there are in it many marks of hafte, want of materials, and a determination to make the moft of fuch as he could obtain. The account of 'William Longbeard' was mainly derived from the Chroniclers, and in Stow's *Annales* they are found under the date of A.D. 1196. . . . . Lodge did not fcruple to mix fiction with facts, in order to render his work acceptable, and various poems are interfperfed, moft of which are fuppofed to be addreffed by Longbeard to 'his faire lemman Maudeline.' Some of thefe appear to be original, fome are avowedly imitated from the French, and others are acknowledged tranflations from the Italian, but without the names of the authors. The original poems are not very original, and the imitations are fometimes far from happy. . . . . 'The Life and Death of William Longbeard' fills nearly thirty-six pages; and then follow the 'manye other moft pleafant and prettie hiftories' announced on the title-page, beginning with an account of 'famous pirats who in times paft were Lordes of the fea:' thefe are Dionides, Stilcon, Cleonides, Chipanda, Millia, and Alcomonius among the ancients, and Francis Enterolles and Monaldo Guecca among the moderns; but Bargulus, 'the ftrong Illyrian pirate' of Shakefpeare (2 Henry VI., ac. iv., fc. 1) is not mentioned, either by that name, or *Abradas*, or *Apradas*, as it is given in the old play of 'the Contention,' 1594, in R. Greene's 'Menaphon,' 1587, and his 'Penelope's Web,' printed about 1588.

" Lodge's wifh here was to increafe the bulk of his traft, and as the materials already employed were fcanty, he added other matters, fuch as 'the hiftorie of Partaritus, King of Lombardie'—'the wonderfull dreame of Afpatia'—'a wonderfull revenge of Megollo'—'the memorable deeds of Valafca'—'an excellent example of continence in Frauncis Sforza'—'of many learned men, ancient and moderne, who violently and infortunatelie ended their daies'—'how King Roderigo loft his kingdome'—'of manie famous men, whoe, leaving the government of the Commonweale, gave themfelves over to private life'—'a moft fubtile difpute amongft Ambaffadors'—and finally, 'the ftrange Lawes of Tyrfus the Tyrant,' which rather baldly ends the publication."—(*Biblio. Account*, vol. i., p. 472.)

" The Life and Death of William Longbeard " was included by Mr. Collier as one of his *Green Series* of Reprints (1864-66).

X. *PHILLIS*: Honoured with Paftorall Sonnets, Elegies, and amo*rous delights*. VVhere-vnto is annexed, the tragicall complaynt of *Elstred*. *Iam Phœbus difiungit equos, iam Cinthia iungit*. At London, Printed for Iohn Busbie, and are to be fold at his fhoppe, at the Weft-doore *of Paules*.   1593, 4to, 42 leaves.

Roman letter. Three perfeft copies known: one in the poffeffion of Mr. S. Chriftie-Miller, Britwell; another in the

Drummond Collection, Edinburgh Univerſity Library; while a third was in the poſſeſſion of the late Rev. Thomas Corſer, Stand Rectory, Mancheſter. An imperfect copy is in the Capell Collection, Trinity College, Cambridge. Of the Britwell copy, Mr. David Laing thus writes (Introduction to Lodge's " Defence of Poetry," &c., *Shakeſpeare Society*, 1853, p. lxx):—

" The Britwell copy, formerly Mr. Heber's, has a curious variation in a duplicate leaf, B 1, or ' The Induction.' In the third verſe, the lines, as firſt printed—

> ' And thou, the Aſcrean Poet of our time,
> Vnder whoſe ſtile conceit was neuer matched,
> The Genius of my muſe,' &c.--

were changed as follows:—

> ' And thou, the true Octauia of our time,
> Vnder whoſe worth, beauty was neuer matched;
> The Genius of my Muſe,' &c.

In like manner, the laſt lines of the fourth verſe—

> ' Yet theſe, I hope, vnder your kinde aſpect,
> (Thow flower of knight-hood) ſhall eſcape neglect '—

were thus altered—

> ' Yet theſe, (I hope) vnder your kind aſpect,
> (Moſt worthy Lady) ſhall eſcape neglect.'

This evidently ſuggeſts that the poems, before publication, were intended to have been dedicated to ſome perſon of diſtinction, referred to in the ſeventh verſe—

> ' Under a great Mecenas I have paſt you;'

and that a proſe dedication, as well as this leaf of induction, may have been cancelled, and replaced with that to Lady Shrewſbury."

12

Mr. Collier thus defcribes the book:—

"Although this work has been mentioned by nearly all bibliographers and biographers, not one of them has produced a fpecimen from it, nor offered any fuch criticifm as would enable readers to form a judgment of its merits. It is by Thomas Lodge, and is in fome refpects an imitation of Daniel's 'Delia,' which had come out in the year before, and was twice printed in 1592. Lodge's work had not the fame degree of popularity, for it was never reprinted, although, in confequence of its excellence, quotations were made from it in poetical mifcellanies of the time. . . . . Lodge's chief merit is as a lyric poet: his heroics are generally heavy and dull, but many of his fonnets, eclogues and elegies are written with playfulnefs, grace, and vigour. . . . . 'The Complaint of Elftred' was evidently introduced by Lodge at the end of his 'Phillis,' 1593, becaufe Daniel had introduced 'The Complaint of Rofamond' at the end of his 'Delia,' 1592. Elftred narrates the ftory of Locrine, which came out in a dramatic form in 1594, was printed in 1595, and has been falfely imputed to Shakefpeare, when, in fact, it belongs to Charles Tylney, the brother of the Mafter of the Revels. The cataftrophe of Lodge's poem is the drowning of Elftred and her daughter Sabrina by the jealous Guendolin, but it is in every refpect inferior to Daniel's 'Rofamond,' and in a different form of ftanza—fix lines inftead of feven. . . . . His [Lodge's] 'Elftred' we confider an undoubted failure."—(*Bibliographical Account*, 1865, vol. i., p. 467.)

XI. A Spiders Webbe. 1594.

This piece is not now known to be in exiftence. It is thus entered in the "Stationers' Regifters" (Mr. ARBER'S *Tranfcript*, vol. ii., p. 652):—

"7° die Iunij./ [1594]

"Nicholas Linge./.—Entred for his Copie vnder th[e h]ande of Mafter Cawood a booke entituled *a fpiders webbe* . vj^d"

In the fale of the library of " Mr. John Hutton, late of St. Paul's Church-yard, London," in 1764, a copy of this work, bound up in one volume with feveral others by Lodge, was fold for the fum of fix fhillings (fee Mr. David Laing's Introduction *ut fupra*, p. lxxvi.).

XII. THE VVOVNDS of Ciuill VVar. Liuely fet forth in the true Tragedies of *Marius and Scilla*. As it hath beene publiquely plaide in London, by the Right Honourable the Lord high Admirall his Seruants. VVritten by *Thomas Lodge* Gent. *O Vita! mifere longa, fælici breuis*. LONDON, Printed by Iohn Danter, and are to be fold at the figne of the Sunne in Paules Church-yarde. 1594, 4to, 39 leaves.

Roman letter. Several copies of this play are in exiftence, viz., in the Bodleian Library; Britifh Mufeum (2 copies); Mr. S. Chriftie-Miller, Britwell; Mr. Frederic Ouvry, V.P.S.A., London; and in the Dyce Collection, South Kenfington Mufeum. It is thus entered in the " Stationers' Regifters" (Mr. ARBER'S *Tranfcript*, vol. ii., p. 650):—

"xxiiij^{to} Die maij [1594]
John Danter./—Entred for his Copie vnder th[e h]and of Mafter Cawood a booke intituled *the woundes of Civill warre liuely fett forthe in the true Tragedies of MARIUS and SCILLA* . . . . vj^d C."

It was reprinted in Dodfley's Collection of *Old Plays*, 1825, vol. viii.; and again in the fourth edition of the fame collection in 1876, vol. vii.

Mr. Collier remarks in his Notes to the reprint of the Play in 1825:—

" In courfe of the incidents of this hiftorical Tragedy, Lodge
has very much followed the lives of Marius and Sylla, as given by
Plutarch: he was a fcholar, and it was not neceffary therefore for
him to refort to Sir Thomas North's tranflation from the French,
of which Shakefpeare availed himfelf, and of which there were
many editions fubfequent to its firft appearance in 1579. It is
pretty evident, however, from a comparifon of a few paffages
quoted in the notes in the progrefs of the play, that Lodge did
employ this popular work, although he has varied fome of the
events, and efpecially the death of Sylla. It is not, perhaps,
poffible now to fettle the point when this Tragedy was firft reprefented on the ftage, but it was moft likely fome time before its
publication in 1594. We know that Lodge had written in defence
of the ftage before 1582, and it is not unlikely that he did fo becaufe he had already written for it. . . . . The verfification
of *The Wounds of Civill War*, certainly affords evidence that it
was penned even before Marlowe had improved the meafure of
dramatic blank verfe, which Shakefpeare perfected: it is heavy,
monotonous, and without the paufes fubfequently introduced; if
therefore Lodge produced it after Marlowe's *Edward II.* was
brought out, he did not at leaft profit by the example. All the
unities are fet at defiance."

XIII. A fig for Momus: *Containing* Pleafant varietie, in-
    cluded in Satyres, *Eclogues, and Epiftles, by T. L. of
    Lincolnes Inne Gent.* Che pecora fi fa, il lupo felo
    mangia. AT LONDON Printed for Clement Knight,
    and are to bee folde at his fhop at the little North-
    doore of Paules Church.   1595, 4to, 35 leaves.

Roman letter. Two copies are known to be in exiftence:
one in the Bodleian Library, and the other in the poffeffion
of Mr. S. Chriftie-Miller, Britwell. It is thus entered in

the " Stationers' Regifters " (Mr. ARBER'S *Tranfcript*, vol. ii., p. 295):—

"Secundo die Aprilis [1595]
" CLEMENT   Entred for his copie vnder the wardens handes a
KNIGHT   booke intituled/ *A figge for MOMUS*/   .   .   vj^d "

After referring to the Auchinleck reprint, publifhed in 1817, of this tract, Mr. Collier goes on to fay:—

" The original is, perhaps, the moft common of Lodge's many productions; but the Satires, Eclogues, and Epiftles contain many interefting temporary allufions, and one piece is efpecially addreffed to Spenfer and another to Drayton, both by their poetical names of Colin and Rowland. This work, as we have elfewhere remarked [*Biblio. Account*, vol. i., p. 357], gives Lodge priority to Hall as an Englifh fatirift."—(*Bibliographical Account*, 1865, vol. i., p. 476.)

XIV. THE DIVEL coniured. LONDON Printed by Adam Iflip for William Mats, dwelling in Fleetftreet at the fign of the Hand and Plough. *Anno* 1596.

4to, 45 leaves.

Black letter. Four copies known to exift: one in the Britifh Mufeum; another in the Bodleian; a third in the poffeffion of Mr. S. Chriftie-Miller, Britwell; and the fourth in the poffeffion of Mr. Alexander Young, Glafgow.

XV. *A Margarite of America. By T. Lodge.* Printed for *Iohn Busbie*, and are to be *fold in S. Dunstons churchyard in* Fleet-ftreet, at the little fhop *next Cliffords Inne.*   1596, 4to, 47 leaves.

Black letter. Three copies known: two in the Britifh Mufeum, and one in the Bodleian.

Prosopopeia

THE
TEARES

OF THE HOLY,

BLESSED, AND SANC-
tified *Marie*, the Mother
of GOD.

LVKE 2:

And moreouer, the swoord shall pearce thy
soule, that the thoughts of many hearts
may be opened.

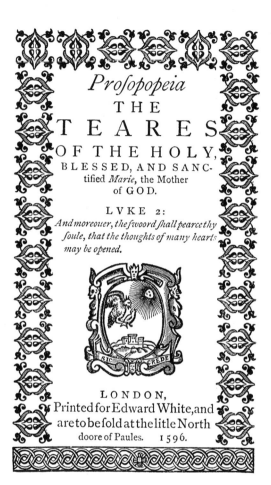

LONDON,
Printed for Edward White, and
are to be sold at the litle North
doore of Paules. 1596.

XVI. *Profopopeia* CONTAINING THE TEARES OF THE
holy, bleffed, and fanctified MARIE, the Mother of
GOD. *Lvke* 2. *And moreouer, the fwoord fhall pearce
thy foule, that the thoughts of many hearts may be opened.*
LONDON. *Printed for E. White.* 1596, 8vo, 63 leaves.

Roman letter. Three copies known: one in the Archi-
epifcopal Library, Lambeth; another in the Drummond
Collection, Edinburgh Univerfity; and a third in the
Bodleian Library. The copy from which the prefent reprint has been made is the Lambeth one; and befides the
remarkable difference in the initials attached to the dedication to the Counteffes of Derby and Cumberland, the title-
page differs from the other two copies. A typographical
facfimile of the Drummond and Bodleian title-page is
given on the preceding page for the fake of comparifon.

This tract was firft afcribed to Lodge by Mr. Collier in
a communication to the "Shakefpeare Society" (*Shakes.
Soc. Papers*, vol. ii., p. 156); and, again, in his *Bibliographical Account*, 1865 (vol. i., p. 476). The following
extract is taken from the latter work:—

"The initials of the author, T. L., are appended to the dedication, and we have little doubt that they belong to Thomas
Lodge. It is ftated that there exifts one other exemplar of this
production, and that the initials are there reverfed: this may be
fo, though we apprehend it is a miftake; but authors who were
frequently before the public did it fometimes, for the fake of
variety, or concealment.

"The fact no doubt is, that Lodge from this date, 1596, completely altered the character of his productions: he wrote no more
upon light, trivial or profane fubjects, fuch as his fatires, novels or
plays, but devoted himfelf to fcience as a Phyfician, and he bade
farewell to his loofer compofitions in the work before us. There-

fore it is that he tells the Reader, in a prefixed Epiftle, 'Some, I know, will condemn me, and that juftly, for a Galba (who begat foul children by night, and made fayre pictures by daie); to whom I anfwere, that I paint fair things in the light of my meditation, who begot the foule forepaffed progenie of my thoughts in the night of mine error.'

"Surely nothing can be plainer; and we are to recollect that Nafh, the friend and companion of Lodge, had purfued the very fame courfe, and in his 'Chrift's Tears over Jerufalem,' publifhed in 1593 and again in 1594, had taken leave of his earlier efforts, though he was afterwards compelled to return to them. We are therefore well fatisfied, that T. L., fubfcribed to the dedication of 'Profopopeia' to the Countefs of Derby, were intended for the initials of Thomas Lodge, and that to him, and to him only, the work belongs.

"Excepting that it is the production of a diftinguifhed play-poet, there is little in it to attract attention: it is not written with much eloquence or freedom, and the beft fentences have a con-ftraint about them, without leaving the impreffion of fincere piety and remorfe. . . . .

"We cannot conclude without quoting the only allufion in the volume to his contemporaries—viz., to Robert Southwell and Nicholas Breton: he fays, 'For other have wept (as Peter his apoftafie, Marie her loffe and miffe of Chrift) their teares wrought from them either for repent or love. But thefe teares of Marie the bleffed are not onely ratified by a motherlie compaffion, a working charitie, and unftayned love, but a manifeft prophefie.'

"The only reafonable objection we feel to affigning 'Profo-popeia' to Lodge is that it really is not good enough for him; but when Nafh wrote his 'Chrifts Teares,' he alfo fell below the level of his natural genius. He fhowed in his renewed attack upon Harvey in his 'Have with you,' &c., 1596, the true fuperiority of his powers; but Lodge, having in 1596 once relinquifhed his pofition as a poet, never feems to have wifhed to recover it. Nafh was driven to it by Gabriel Harvey's refufal of the amends offered."

On the foregoing conclufion of Mr. Collier's, Mr. David Laing makes the following obfervations (Introduction to "The Defence of Poetry, Mufic and Stage-Plays," &c., *Shakes. Soc.*, 1853, p. xlv.):—

" Befides thefe tracts of 1596, Mr. Collier has affigned to Lodge another printed in the fame year, confidering it to be a Palinode, or recantation by the author of his previous writings, as ' the foule forepaffed progenie of my thoughts, in the night of mine error,' and to have been fuggefted by, and written in imitation of Nafh's ' Chrift's Teares over Jerufalem.' It bears this title : ' Profopopeia, containing the Teares of the holy, bleffed, and fanctified Marie, the Mother of God,' and is dedicated ' To the Right noble, the Mother Counteffe, Counteffe of Darby, and the vertuous and devout Counteffe of Cumberland.' I have not included it in the lift of Lodge's works, being perfuaded that it ought to be afcribed to fome other author. Except in the dedication, there is no re- femblance to Lodge's ftyle; and, if he could have written thefe words—' Now at laft, after I have wounded the world with too much furfeit of vanitie, I maye bee by the true Helizeus, cleanfed from the leprofie of my lewd lines, and beeing wafhed in the Jordan of grace, imploy my labour to the comfort of the faithfull '—it would at leaft have fhown little of a repentant fpirit, to have pro- duced within a few months his ' Difcovery of the Devils Incarnate of this Age.' But befides this, if the copy defcribed by Mr. Collier has the initials T. L., others, both to the Dedication and the Addrefs to the Reader, have (and poffibly more correctly) L. T. If one conjecture, therefore, may be allowed to take the place of another, it may be fuggefted, that this tract fhould rather be attri- buted to Laurence Twyne, gentleman, one of a literary family, who, in 1576, ' gathered into Englifh ' ' The Patterne of painefull Adventures,' or the Hiftory of Apollonius, Prince of Tyre, from which Shakefpeare derived many of the incidents in his ' Pericles.' Anthony Wood fays, of John Twyne, who died in 1581, that his eldeft fon ' was Lawrence Twyne, who was fellow of All Souls

College, and Bachelor of the Civil Law, an ingenious poet of his time, as feveral copies of verfes fet before books, written in commendation of their refpective authors, do fufficiently atteft. He was a married man, lived at Hardacre, in Kent, and left iffue behind him, at his death, feveral children.'"

Mr. Collier again in "Additions, Notes, and Corrections" to his *Biblio. Account* (vol. i., p. xxiii.), makes the following remarks on Mr. Laing's ftatement:—

"Mr. D. Laing of Edinburgh, an excellent judge, and a very learned literary antiquary, has given it as his opinion that L. T. (as the letters feem placed in a copy he had feen, but which we have not) are the initials of Laurence Twyne, the tranflator of the novel of 'Apollonius of Tyre,' on which 'Pericles' is founded. Mr. Laing, however, fails to fhow in what way the repentant fpirit difplayed in 'Profopopeia' was called for in the cafe of Twyne, whereas, in the cafe of Lodge, it is obvious, after the life he had led up to 1596. When we fay that L. T., inftead of T. L., is a miftake, we mean, of courfe, that it was an error on the part of the old printer."

It might be fuggefted here, in fupport of Mr. Collier's very probable afcription, that "Profopopeia" is a work very likely to have come from the pen of a Roman Catholic, and there is now the beft ground for holding that Lodge was of that communion.

XVII. VVITS MISERIE, and the VVorlds Madneffe: *Difcouering the Deuils Incarnat of this Age.* LONDON, Printed by *Adam Iflip*, and are to be fold by *Cuthbert Burby*, at his fhop by the Roiall-Exchange.
1596, 4to, 59 leaves.

Black letter. Three copies known: two in the Bodleian Library, and one in the poffeffion of Mr. S. Chriftie-Miller,

Britwell. " One of thefe copies," fays Mr. Laing, " exhibits a curious typographical miftake in the firft line of the title, having WILS MISERIE, in place of WITS MISERIE."

XVIII. A LOOKING Glaffe, for London and Englande. Made by Thomas Lodge Gentleman, and *Robert Greene. In Artibus Magister.* LONDON Printed by Thomas Creede, and are to be folde by William Barley, at his fhop in Gratious ftreete.

1598, 4to, 35 leaves.

Black letter. Only one copy of the firft edition of 1594 is known to exift, and is in the poffeffion of his Grace the Duke of Devonfhire. His Grace was kind enough to fay that but for the accidental mifplacement of the volume he would have been glad to lend it for reproduction. In thefe circumftances, the fecond edition of 1598 was reforted to. Several copies are known to exift, two of which are in the Bodleian Library. It was entered in the "Stationers' Regifters" as follows (Mr. ARBER'S *Tranfcript,* vol. ii., p. 645):—

" 5 Marcij [1594]

"Thomas Creede.—Entred for his copie vnder the wardens, handes / a booke intituled *the lookinge glasse for London/* by THOMAS LODG[E] and ROBERT GREENE gent . . vj^d "

It has been reprinted by the Rev. Mr. Dyce in his various editions of the Dramatic Works of Robert Greene.

XIX. THE FAMOVS AND MEMORABLE WORKES OF IOSEPHVS, A MAN OF MVCH HONOVR AND LEARNING AMONG THE IEWES. Faithfully tranflated out of the

Latin, and French, by *Tho. Lodge* Doctor in Phyficke. Bernardus Epiftola ad Suggerium. *Tunc retentia incundius bona clarefcunt, cum fuerint malis comparata prioribus.* Printed at the charges of *G. Bifhop, S. Waterfon, P. Short,* and *Tho. Adams.* 1602, folio.

Roman letter. The Dedications, &c., by Lodge will be found printed in the Mifcellaneous Pieces: the tranflation itfelf has not been reproduced. It was feveral times reprinted during the feventeenth century.

XX. A TREATISE of the Plague: Containing the nature, fignes, and accidents of the fame, with the certaine and abfolute cure of the Feuers, Botches and Carbuncles that raigne in thefe times: And aboue all things moft fingular Experiments and preferuatiues in the fame, gathered by the obferuation of diuers worthy Trauailers, and felected out of the writings of the beft learned Phifitians in this age. *By Thomas Lodge, Doctor in Phificke.* LONDON Printed for Edward White and N. L. 1603, 4to, 43 leaves.

Roman letter. Several copies known: one in the Britifh Mufeum, &c.

XXI. THE WORKES *both Morrall and Natural of* LVCIVS ANNÆVS SENECA. *Tranflated by T. Lodge D: of Phis:* London Printed by William Stansby. Folio.

Such is the title on the centre of an emblematical page reprefenting *Morientis Effigies, Ingr. by W. Hole,* followed

by a printed title-page: "THE WORKES OF LVCIUS AN-
NÆVS SENECA, Both Morrall and Naturall. CONTAINING,

1. *His Bookes of Benefites.*
2. *His Epiſtles.*
3. *His Booke of Prouidence.*
4. *Three Bookes of Anger.*
5. *Two Bookes of Clemencie.*
6. *His Booke of a Bleſſed Life.*
7. *His Booke of the Tranquilitie of the minde.*
8. *His Booke of the Conſtancie of a Wiſeman.*
9. *His Booke of the Shortneſſe of Life.*
10. *Two Bookes of Conſolation to* MARTIA.
11. *Three Bookes of Conſolation to* HELVIA.
12. *His Booke of Conſolation to* POLIBIVS.
13. *His ſeuen Bookes of Naturall Queſtions.*

Tranſlated by THO. LODGE, *D. in Phyſicke.* LONDON
Printed by *William Stansby.* 1614." The title-page to
"The Epiſtles" on page 161 gives the date as 1613, thus:
"*LONDON* Printed by *William Stansby.* 1613."

"At an interval of ſix years," ſays Mr. Laing, "this
tranſlation was republiſhed, with an emblematical engraved
title-page—' R. E., [Elſtrack] ſc.'—the deſign is quite diſtinct
from the former, and in the centre, 'THE WORKES OF
LVCIVS ANNÆVS SENECA Newly Inlarged and Corrected
by Thomas Lodge D.M.P. LONDON *Printed by Willi:
Stansby.* [Colophon.] LONDON, Printed by WILLIAM
STANSBY, dwelling in Thames-ſtreete, by *Pauls*-vvharfe
next to Sᵗ. *Peters* Church. 1620."

XXII. A LEARNED SUMMARY Upon the famous *POEME
of William of Saluste Lorde of Bartas. Wherin are
diſcovered all the excellent ſecretts in Metaphyſicall,
Phyſicall, Morall, and Historicall knowledge. Fitt for*

the learned to refreſh theire memories, and for younger
ſtudents to abreviat and further theire ſtudies: Wherin
nature is diſcovered, art diſcloſed, and hiſtory layd open.
Tranſlated out of French, by T.L.D.M.P. LONDON
Printed for Iohn Griſmand And are to be ſould at his
ſhoppe in Paules alley at the ſigne of the Gunne. Anno
1621.

Roman letter. The Dedication, &c., by Lodge will be
found reprinted with the Miſcellaneous Pieces.

The exiſtence of this tranſlation—unknown to the late
Mr. David Laing—was diſcovered from the following entry
ın the "Stationers' Regiſters" (Mr. ARBER'S *Tranſcript,*
vol. iv., p. 42):—

"8°. Nouembris. 1620

" John Griſman Entred for his copie vnder the handes of
maſter TAUERNOR, and maſter Lownes warden, A booke
called *A Comentary vpon* DU BARTAS, tranſlated out of
Ffrench by Doĉtor. LODGE . . . . vjᵈ"

Copies of this firſt edition are in the Britiſh Muſeum,
Bodleian Library, &c. It was reprinted in 1637, by
another publiſher, viz., Andrew Crooke. A copy of this
edition is in the London Library.

XXIII. THE POORE MANS TALENTT.

[1623?] 43 leaves.

Now printed from manuſcript for the firſt time. It is
principally in the handwriting of Lodge: ſeventeen leaves
at the beginning appear to have been written in another
hand, with correĉtions here and there by the author. It

was purchafed by Mr. J. Payne Collier at the fale of the books of the Duke of Norfolk, who died December 16th, 1815.

The Lady Anne Countefs of Arundel, to whom "The Poore Mans Talentt" was dedicated—a facfimile of the dedicatory epiftle in the author's autograph will be found inferted in the prefent publication—was fifter and coheir of Thomas Lord Dacres, and was born on March 31ft, 1557. She was married at an early age to Philip Earl of Arundel, who died in the Tower on October 19th, 1595. In 1857 the late Duke of Norfolk publifhed from a manufcript in his poffeffion a contemporary biography of herfelf and her hufband, entitled "The Lives of Philip Howard Earl of Arundel, and of Anne Dacres his wife," written by one who lived with her clofe upon fourteen years. After the death of her hufband, her time was divided between her devotions and acts of charity. From feveral paffages in this biography fhe appears to have had confiderable fkill in the healing art. For example:—"Another kind of almes befides all thefe fhe practif'd very much, confifting in medicines, falves, plafters, and other remedies to all kind of people who either wanting will, or means to go to Doctors and Chirurgeons, came to her for the cureing of their wounds and diftempers. And her charity herein was fo famous, that not only neighbors, but feveral out of other fhires, twenty, forty, and more miles diftant, did refort unto her to that end, and fcarce a day paffed iu which many did not come, fometimes more than threefcore have been counted in one day and to every one that came befides advice and medicines if the matter did require it, fhe ufually gave fome almes in money if they were poor, as many were." This trait in her character accounts, no doubt, for the appearance of the "Poore Mans Talentt." Indeed, Lodge in the twelfth chapter remarks—" And God he knowes I reveale them as my laft Teftamentt of Love towards yor Ho^r and the poores helth which you tender." The Countefs of Arundel died on April 19th, 1630, having furvived her hufband nearly thirty-five years. Her fon Thomas Earl of Arundel, "diftinguifhed himfelf in the reign of Charles the Firft as a collector of antiquities and works of art."

XXIV. MISCELLANEOUS PIECES. 24 leaves.

A REPLY

TO

STEPHEN GOSSON'S

SCHOOLE OF ABUSE

IN DEFENCE OF

POETRY MUSICK AND STAGE PLAYS

BY

THOMAS LODGE

1580?

Rotogenes can know *Apelles* by his line though he fe him not, and wife men can confider by the Penn the aucthoritie of the writer thoughe they know him not. the Rubie is difcerned by his pale rednes, and who hath not hard that the Lyon is knowne by hys clawes. though *Æfopes* craftie crowe be neuer fo deftlye decked, yet is his double dealing efely defiphered: & though men neuer fo perfectly pollifh there wrytings with others fentences, yet the fimple truth wil difcouer the fhadow of ther follies: and beftowing euery fether in the bodye of the right M. tourne out the naked diffembler into his owen cote, as a fpectacle of follye to all thofe which can rightlye Iudge what imperfections be. There came to my hands lately a litle (woulde God a wittye) pamphelet, baring a fayre face as though it were the fcoole of a bufe but being by me aduifedly wayed I fynd it the oftfcome of imperfections, the writer fuller of wordes then iudgement, the matter certaiuely as ridiculus as ferius. afuredly his mother witte wrought this wonder, the child to difprayfe his father the dogg to byte his mayfter for

A.   his

his dainty morcell. but I fe (with *Seneca*) y^t
the wrong is to be fuffered, fince he difpray-
feth, who by coftome. hath left to fpeake
well. bot I meane to be fhort: and teach the
Maifter what he knoweth not, partly that
he may fe his owne follie, and partly that I
may difcharge my promife, both binde me.
therefore I would wifh the good fcholmay-
fter to ouer looke his abufes againe with
me, fo fhall he fee an ocean of inormities
which begin in his firft prinfiple in the difprayfe of poetry. And firft let me familiarly
confider with this find faulte what the learned haue alwayes efteemed of poetrie. *Seneca* thoughe a ftoike would haue a poeticall
fonne, and amongft the auncienteft *Homer*
was no les accompted then *Humanus deus.*
what made *Alexander* I pray you efteme of
him fo much? why allotted he for his works
fo curious a cloffet? was ther no fitter vnder
prop for his pillow thē a fimple pamphelet?
in all *Darius* cofers was there no Iewell fo
coftly? forfoth my thinks thefe two (the one
the father of Philofophers, the other the
cheftaine of chiualrie) were both deceiued
if all were as a *Goffon* would wifh them, yf
poets paynt naughte but palterie toyes in
vearfe, their ftudies tended to folifhneffe,
and

and in all their indeuors they did naught els
but *agendo nihil agere*. Lord howe *Virgils*
poore gnatt pricketh him, and how *Ouids*
fley byteth him, he can beare no bourde, he
hath rayfed vp a new fect of ferius ftoikes,
that can abide naught but their owen fhadowe, and alow nothing worthye, but what
they conceaue. Did you neuer reade (my o-
uer wittie frend) that vnder the perfons of
beaftes many abufes were diffiphered? haue
you not reafon to waye? that whatfoeuer e-
ther *Virgil* did write of his gnatt, or *Ouid* of
his fley: was all couertly to declare abufe?
but you are (*homo literatus*) a man of the
letter little fauoring of learning, your giddy
brain made you leaue your thrift, and your
abufes in London fome part of your honeftie. You fay that Poets are fubtil, if fo, you
haue learned that poynt of them, you can
well glofe on a trifleling text. but you haue
dronke perhaps of *Lethe*, your gramer learning is out of your head, you forget your
Accidence, you remēber not, that vnder the
perfon of *Æneas* in *Virgil* the practice of a
dilligent captaine is difcribed vnder yᵉ fhadow of byrds, beaftes and trees, the follies
of the world were difiphered, you know not,
that the creation is fignified in the Image
A. 2.   of

of *Prometheus*, the fall of pryde in the perſon
of *Narciſſus*, theſe are toyes becauſe they fa
uor of wiſedome which you want. Marke
what *Campanus* ſayth, *Mira fabularum va-
nitas ſed quæ ſi introſpiciantur videri poſſunt
non vanæ.* The vanitie of tales is wonderful, yet if we aduiſedly looke into them
they wil ſeme & proue wiſe. how wonderful
are the pithie poemes of *Cato?* the curious
comidies of *Plautns?* how brauely diſcoue-
reth *Terence* our imperfectiō in his *Eunuch?*
how neatly diſſiphereth he *Danus?* how plea
ſauntly paynteth he out *Gnatho?* whom if
we ſhould ſeeke in our dayes, I ſnppoſe he
would not be farr from your parſon. But I
ſee you woulde ſeeme to be that which you
are not, and as the prouerb ſayth *Nodum in
Cirpo quærere*: Poetes you ſay vſe coullors
to couer their incouiences, and wittie ſenten-
ces to burniſh theyr bawdery, and you diui-
nite to couer your knauerye. But tell mee
truth *Goſſon* ſpeakeſt thou as thou thinkeſt?
what coelers findeſt thou in a Poete not to
be admitted? are his ſpeaches vnperfect? ſa-
nor they of inſcience. I think if thou haſt a-
ny ſhame thou canſt not but like & approue
thē, are ther gods diſpleſant vnto thee? doth
Saturne in his maieſty moue thee? doth *Iuno*
                                        with

with her riches difpleafe thee? doth *Miner-ua* with her weapon difcomfort thee? doth *Apollo* with his harping harme thee? thou mayft fay nothing les then harme thee be-caufe they are not, and I thinke fo to be-caufe thou knoweft them not. For wot thou that in the perfon of *Saturne* our decaying yeares are fignified, in the picture of angry *Iuno* our affections are diffiphered, in yᵉ per fon of *Minerua* is our vnderftāding fignifi-ed, both in refpect of warre, as policie. when they faine that *Pallas* was begotten of the braine of *Iupiter* their meaning is none o-ther, but that al wifedome (as the learned fay) is from aboue, and commeth from the father of Lights: in the portrature of *Apollo* all knowledge is denocated. fo that, what fo they wrot, it was to this purpofe, in the way of pleafure to draw men to wifedome: for fe-ing the world in thofe daies was vnperfect, yt was neceffary that they like good Phifi-ons: fhould fo frame their potions, that they might be appliable to the quefie ftomaks of their werifh patients. but our ftudientes by your meanes haue made fhipwrack of theyr labors, our fchoolemaifters haue fo offended that by your iudgement they fhall *fubire pœ nam capitis* for teaching poetry, the vniuer-fitie is litle beholding to you, al their practi-

A. 3.   ces

ces in teaching are friuolus. Witt hath
wrought that in you, that yeares and ftudie
neuer fetled in the heads of our fageft doctors. No meruel though you difprayfe poetrye, when you know not what it meanes.
Erafmus will make that the path waye to
to knowledge which you difprayfe, and no
meane fathers vouchfafe in their ferioufe
queftions of deuinitie, to inferte poeticall
fenfures. I think if we fhal wel ouerloke y^e
Philofophers, we fhal find their iudgemēts
not halfe perfect, Poetes you faye fayle in
their fables, Philofophers in the verye fecrets of Nature. Though *Plato* could wifh
the expulfion of Poetes from his well pub-
liques, which he might doe with reafon, yet
the wifeft had not all that fame opinion, it
had bene better for him to haue fercht more
narowly what the foule was, for his difini-
tion was verye friuolus, when he would
make it naught els but *Substantiam intelec-
tu predictam.* if you fay that Poetes did labour about nothing, tell me (I befech you)
what wonders wroughte thofe your dunce
Doctors in ther reafons *de ente et non ente?*
in theyr definition of no force, and les witt?
how fweate they power foules in makinge
more things then cold be? that I may vfe
                                            your

your owne phrafe, did not they fpende one
candle by feeking another. *Democritus E-
picurus* with ther fcholler *Metrodorus* how
labored they in finding out more worlds thē
one? your *Plato* in midft of his prefifnes
wrought that abfurdite that neuer may be
redd in Poets, to make a yearthly creature
to beare the perfon of the creator, and a cor-
ruptible fubftaunce, an incomprehenfible
God: for determining of the principall caufes of all thinges, a made them naughte els
but an *Idea* whieh if it be conferred wyth
the truth, his fentence. will fauour of Infci-
ence. but I fpeake for Poetes, I anfweare
your abufe, therefore I will difproue, or difprayfe naught, but wifh you with the wife
Plato, to difprayfe that thing you offend not
in. *Seneca* fayth that the ftuddie of Poets, is
to make childrē ready to the vnderftanding
of wifedom, and yᵗ our auncients did teache
artes Eleutherias. i. liberales, becaufe the inft
ruɛted childrē by the inftrumēt of knowledg
in time became *houines liberi. i. Philofophye.*
it may be that in reding of poetry, it happe
ned to you as it is with the Oyfter for fhe
in her fwimming receiueth no ayre, and you
in your reeding leffe inftruɛtion. it is reported that the fhepe of *Enboia* want ther gale,
and

and one the contrarye fide that the beaftes
of *Naxus* haue *distentum* fel. Men hope that
fcollers fhould haue witt brought vpp in the
Vniuerfite, but your fweet felfe with the
cattell of *Enboia*, fince you left your College
haue loft your learning. you difprayfe *Max*
iminns Tirius pollicey, and that thinge that
that he wrott to manifeft learned Poets me
ning, you atribute to follye. O holy hedded
man, why may not *Iuno* refemble the ayre?
why not *Alexander* valour? why not
Vliſſes pollice? will you haue all for yon
owne tothe? muft men write that you maye
know theyr meaning? as though your wytt
were to wreft all things? Alas fimple *Irus*,
begg at knowledge gate awhile, thou hafte
not wonne the maftery of learning. weane
thy felfe to wifedome, and vfe thy tallant in
zeale not for enuie, abufe not thy knowledge
in difprayfing that which is pereles: I fhold
blufh from a player, to become an enuioufe
preacher, if thou hadft zeale to preach, if for
Sions fake thou coldft not holde thy tougue,
thy true dealing were prayfe worthy, thy re-
uolting woulde counfell me to reuerence
thee. pittie weare it, that poetrye fhould be
difplaced, full little could we want *Buchan-*
nans workes, and *Boetius* comfortes may
not

not be baniſhed. what made *Eraſmus* labor
in *Euripides* tragedies? did he indeuour by
painting them out of Greeke iuto Latine
to manifeſt ſinne vnto vs? or to confirme vs
in goodnes? Labor (I pray thee) in Pam-
phelets more prayſe worthy, thou haſte not
ſaued a Senator, therefore not worthye a
Lawrell wreth, thou haſt not (in diſprouing
poetry) reproued an abuſe, and therfore not
worthy commendation. *Seneca* ſayth that
*Magna vitæ pars elabitur male agentibus,
maxima nihill agentibus, tota alind agentibus*, the moſt of our life (ſayd he) is ſpent e-
ther in doing euill, or nothing, or that wee
ſhould not, and I would wiſh you weare ex-
empted from this ſenſure, geue eare but a
little more what may be ſaid for poetrie, for
I muſt be briefe, you haue made ſo greate
matter that I may not ſtay on one thing to
long, leſt I leaue an other vntouched. And
firſt whereas you ſay, yᵗ *Tullie* in his yeres
of more iudgement deſpiſed Poetes, harke
(I pray you) what he worketh for them in
his oratiō *pro Archia poeta* (but before you
heare him leaſt you fayle in the incounter,
I would wyſh you to to followe the aduiſe
of the daſterdlye *Ichneumon* of *Ægipt*, who
when ſhee beholdeth the *Aſpis* her enemye
to

to drawe nighe, calleth her fellowes together, bifmering her felfe with claye, againft
the byting and ftroke of the ferpent, arme
your felfe, cal your witts together: want not
your wepons, left your inperfect iudgement
be rewardede with Midas eares. you had
neede play the night burd now, for you day
Owl hath mifconned his parte, and for to
who now a dayes he cryes foole you: which
hath brought fuch a fort of wondering birds
about your eares, as I feare me will chat-
ter you out of your Iuey bufh. the worlde
fhames to fee you, or els you are afrayde to
fhew your felfe. you thought poetrye fhould
want a patron (I think) when you fyrfte
publifhed this inuectiue, but yet you fynd al
to many euē *preter expectationē*, yea though
it can fpeake for it felf, yet her patron *Tullie* now fhall tell her tale, *Hæc studia* (fayth
he) *adolefcentiam alunt, Senectutem oblec-
tant, fecnndas, res ornant, aduerfis perfugium
ac Solatium prebent, delectant domi, non im-
pediunt foris, pernoctant nobifcum, peregri-
antur rusticantur.* then will you difprayfe y^t
which all men commend? you looke only vp
on ye refufe of ye abufe, nether refpecting the
importance of ye matter nor the weighe of y^e
wryter. *Solon* can fayne himfelfe madde, to
further

further the *Athenians*. *Chaucer* in pleafant
vain can rebuke fin vncontrold, & though he
be lauifh in the letter, his fence is ferious.
who in Rome lamēted not *Rofcius* death? &
cāft thou fuck no plefure out of thy *M. Clau
dians* writings? hark, what *Cellarius* a lear:
ned father attributeth to it. *acuit memoriam*
(faith he) it profiteth yᵉ memory. yea & *Tully*
atributeth it for prais to *Archias* yᵗ vpon any
theame he cold verfify extēpory. who liketh
not of the promptnes of *Ouid?* who not vn-
worthely cold boft of himfelf thus *Quicquid
conabar dicere verfus erat.* who then doothe
not wonder at poetry? who thinketh not yᵗ it
procedeth frō aboue? what made yᵉ *Chians* &
Colophonians fal to fuch controuerfy? Why
feke yᵉ *Smirnians*, to recouer frō yᵉ *Salamini
ans* the prais of *Homer*? al wold hane him to
be of ther city, I hope not for harme, but becaufe of his knoledge. *Themiftocles* defireth
to be acquainted wᵗ thofe wᶜ could beft difci-
pher his praifes. euen *Marius* himfelfe, tho
neuer fo cruel, accōpted of *Plotinus* poems.
what made *Aphricanus* efteme *Ennius?* why
did *Alexander* giue prais to *Achilles* but for
yᵉ prayfes which he found writtē of hym by
Homer? Why eftemed *Pompie* fo muche
of *Theophanes Mitiletus* or *Brutus* fo
greatlye the wrytinges of *Accius? Fuluius*
was

was fo great a fauorer of poetry, that after
the Aetolian warres, he attributed to the
Mufes thofe fpoiles that belonged to *Mars*.
in all the Romaine conqueft, hardeft thou
euer of a flayne Poete? nay rather the Em-
perours honored them, beautified them with
benefites, & decked their fanctuaries which
facrifice. *Pindarus* colledg is not fit for fpoil
of *Alexander* ouercome, nether feareth poetry ye perfecutors fword. what made Auftin
fo much affectate ye heauenly fury? not folly,
for if I muft needes fpeake, *illud non aufim
affirmare*, his zeale was, in fetting vp of the
houfe of God, not in affectate eloquence, he
wrot not, he accompted not. he honnored
not, fo much that (famous poetry) whyche
we prayfe, without caufe, for if it be true
that *Horace* reporteth in his booke *de arte
poetica*, all the anfweares of the Oracles
weare in verfe. among the precife Iewes,
you fhall find Poetes, and for more maieftie
Sibilla will prophefie in verfe. *Hiroaldus*
can witnes with me, that *Dauid* was a poet,
and that his vayne was in imitating (as S.
Ierom witneffeth) *Horace, Flaccus,* & *Pinda
rus,* fomtimes his verfe runneth in an *Iam
bus* foote, anone he hath recourfe to a *Saphi
er* vaine, and *aliquando, femipede ingreditur.*
                                        afk

afk *Iofephus*, and he wil tel you that Efay,
Iob and Salomon, voutfafed poetical practifes, for (if *Origen* and he fault) not theyre
verfe was *Hexameter, and pentameter*. Enquire of *Caffiodorus*, he will fay that all the
beginning of Poetrye proceeded from the
Scripture. *Panlinus* tho the byfhop of *No-
lanum* yet voutfafe the name of a Poet, and
Ambrofe tho he be a patriarke in *mediolanū*
loueth verfifing *Beda* fhameth not yᵉ fcience
that fhameleffe *Goffon* mifliketh. reade ouer
Lactantius, his proofe is by poetry. & Paul
voutfafeth to ouerlooke *Epimenides* let the
Apoftle preach at Athens he difdaineth not
of Aratus authorite. it is a pretye fentence
yet not fo prety as pithy. *Poeta na fcitur orator fit* as who fhould fay, Poetrye commeth
from aboue from a heauenly feate of a glorious God vnto an excellent creature man,
an orator is but made by exercife. for if wee
examine well what befell *Ennius* amonge
the Romans, and *Hefiodus* auong his con-
trimen the Gretians, howe they came by
theyr knowledge whence they receued their
heauenly furye, the firft will tell vs that fle-
ping vpon the Mount of *Parnaffus* he drea-
med that he received the foule of *Homer* into him, after the which he became a Poete,
the

the next will aſſure you that it commeth not
by labor, nether that night watchings bringeth it, but yᵗ we muſt haue it thence whence
he fetched it wᶜ was (he ſaith) frō a wel of yᵉ
Muſes wᶜ *Cabelimus* calleth *Porū*, a draught
whereof drewe him to his perfeċtion, ſo of a
ſhephard he becam an eloquēt poet. wel thē
you ſee yᵗ it commeth not bp exerciſe of play
making, nether inſertiō of gawds, but from
nature, and from aboue: and I hope yᵗ *Aristotle* hath ſufficiently taught you: that *Natura nihil fecit frustra.* *Perſeus* was made
a poete *diuino furore percitus.* and whereas
the poets were ſayde to call for the Muſes
helpe ther mening was no other as *Iodocus
Badius* reporteth, but to call for heauenly in
ſpiration from aboue to direċt theyr ende-
deuors. nether were it good for you to ſette
light by the name of a poet ſince yᵉ oftſpring
from whence he cōmeth is ſo heauenly. *Sibil
la* in hir anſwers to *Æneas* againſt hir will
as the poet telleth vs was poſſeſſed wᵗ thys
fury, ye wey conſideratly but of the writing
of poets, & you ſhal ſe that whē ther matter
is moſt heauenly, their ſtile is moſt loftye. a
ſtrange token of the wonderfull efficacy of
the ſame. I would make a long diſcourſe vn
to you of *Platoes* 4. furies but I leue them
it

it pitieth me to bring a rodd of your owne
making to beate you wythal. But mithinks
while you heare thys I fee you fwallowe
down your owne fpittle for reuenge, where
(God wot) my wryting fauoreth not of enuye. in this cafe I coulde wyfhe you fare
farre otherwyfe from your foe yf you pleafe
I wyll become your frende and fee what a
potion or receypt I can frame fytt for your
diet. and herein I will proue my felfe a prac
tifer, before I purdge you, you fhall take a
preparatiue to dif burden your heauy hedde
of thofe grofe follis you haue conceued: but
the receipt is bitter, therefore I would wyfh
you firft to cafteu your mouth with the Su-
ger of perfeueràce: for ther is a cold collop yᵗ
muft downe your throate yet fuche a one as
fhall chaūge your complection quit. I wyll
haue you therfore to taft firft of yᵗ cold riuer
Phricus, in *Thratia* which as *Ariftotle* reporteth changeth blacke into white, or of
Scamandar, which maketh gray yalow yᵗ
is of an enuious mā a wel minded perfon, re
prehending of zeale yᵗ wherin he hath finned
by folly, & fo being prepard, thy purgation
wyll worke more eafy, thy vnderftandinge
wyll be more perfit, thou fhalt blufh at thy
abufe, and reclaime thy felfe by force of
argument

argument ſo will thou proue of clene recouered patient, and I a perfecte practiſer in
framing ſo good a potion. this broughte to
paſſe I with the wil ſeeke out ſome abuſe
in poetry, which I wil ſeeke for to diſproue
by reaſon firſt pronounced by no ſmal birde
euen *Ariſtotle* himſelf *Poetæ* (ſayth he) *mul-
ta mentiuntur* and to further his opinion ſeuer *Cato* putteth in his cencure.

Admiranda canunt ſed non credenda poetæ.
theſe were ſore blemiſhes if obiected rightly and heare you may ſay the ſtreme runues
a wronge, but if it be ſo by you leue I wyll
bring him ſhortly in his right chanel. My
anſwere ſhall not be my owne, but a learned
father ſhall tell my tale, if you wil know his
name men call him *Lactantius:* who iu hys
booke *de diuinis inſtitutionibus* reeſoneth
thus. I ſuppoſe (ſayth he) Poets are full of
credit, and yet it is requeſite for thoſe that
wil vnderſtand them to be admoniſhed, that
among them, not onely the name but the
matter beareth a ſhow of that it is not: for if
ſayth he we examine the Scriptures litter
allye nothing will ſeeme more falls, and if
we way Poetes wordes and not ther meaning, our learning in them wilbe very mene
you ſee nowe that your *Catoes* iudgement
as

of no force and that all your obiections you
make agaynſt poetrye be of no valor yet leſt
you ſhould be altogether diſcoraged I wyll
helpe pou forwarde a little more, it pities
me to conſider the weaknes of your cauſe I
wyll therfore make your ſtrongeſt reaſon,
more ſtroug and after I haue builded it vp
deſtroy it agayn. Poets you confeſſe are e-
loquent but you reproue them in their wan-
tonneſſe, they write of no wiſedom, you may
ſay their tales are friuolus, they prophane
holy thinges, they ſeeke nothing to the perfection of our ſoules. theyr practiſe is in o-
ther things, of leſſe force: to this obiection I
anſwer no otherwiſe then Horace doeth in
his booke *de arte poetica* where he wryteth
thus.

Silueſtres homines ſacer interpreſque deorum
Sedibus, et victu ſœdo deterruit orpheus.
Dictus ob hoc lenire Tigres rabidoſque leones.
Dictus et Amphion Thebanæ condit vrbis
Saxa mouere ſono, teſtudius et prece blanda
Ducere quo vellet fuit hoc ſapientia quondam.
Publica priuatis ſecernere ſacra prophanis.
Concubitu prohibere vago, dare Iura maritis,
Opida moliri leges, niſcidere ligno.

The holy ſpokeſman of the Gods
With heauely Orpheus hight:
Did driue the ſauage men from wods.

B   And

18

And made them liue aright.
And therefore is fayd the Tygers fierce,
And Lyons full of myght
To ouercome: *Amphion*, he
Was fayd of Theabs the founder,
Who by his force of Lute dyd caufe,
The ftones to part a fonder.
And by his fpeach them did dere{ct}.
Where he would haue them ftaye:
This wifedome this was it of olde
All ftrife for to allay.
To giue to euery man his owne,
To make the Gods be knowne
To driue each lecher from the bed,
That neuer was his owne.
To teach the law of mariage,
The way to build a towne,
For to engraue thefe lawes in woods
This was thefe mens renowne.
I cannot leaue *Tirtheus* pollicy vntouched,
who by force of his pen could incite men to
the defence of theyr countrye. if you require
of yᵉ Oracle of *Apollo* what fucceffe you fhal
haue: *refpondet bellicofo numine* lo now you
fee your obie{ct}ions my anfwers, you behold
or may perceiue manifeftlye, that Poetes
were the firft rayfors of cities, prefcribers of
good lawes, mayntayners of religion, diftur
bors

bors of the wicked, aduancers of the wel dif-
pofed, inuētors of laws, & laftly the very fot
paths to knowledg. & vnderftādiᵍ ye if we
fhold beleue Herome he wᵢl make *Platos* ex
iles honeft mē, & his peftiferous poets good
preachers: for he accounteth *Orpheus Muf-
cus*, & *Linus*, *Christians*, therefore *Virgil* (in
his 6. boke of *Æneiados* wher he lernedly de
fcribeth yᵉ iourny of *Æneas* to *Elifum*) affer-
teneth vs, yᵗ among them yᵗ were ther for the
zeale they beare toward there country, ther
wer found *Quinque pij vates et Phœbo digna
loquti* but I muft anfwer al obiectiōs, I muft
fil euery nooke. I muft arme my felf now, for
here is the greateft bob I can gather out of
your booke forfoth *Ouids* abufes, in defcry-
bing whereof you labour very vehementlye
termīg him letcher, & in his perfon difpraife
all poems, but fhall on mans follye deftroye
a vniuerlfal cōmodity? what gift what perfit
knowledg hath ther bin, emong yᵉ profeffors
of wᶜ ther hath not bin a bad, on the Angels
haue finned in heauē, *Adā* & *Eue* in earthly pa
radife, emōg yᵉ holy apoftles vngratious Iu
das. I refon not yᵗ al poets are holy but I af
firme yᵗ poetry is a heauēly gift, a perfit gift
then wᶜ I know not greater plefure. & furely
if I may fpeak my mind I thīk we fhal find
B. 2.   but

but few poets if it were exactly wayd what
they oughte to be your *Mufcouian* ftraungers, your *Scithian* monfters wonderful by
one *Eurus* brought vpon one ftage in fhips
made of Sheepefkins, wyll not proue you a
poet nether your life alow you to bee of that
learning if you had wifely wayed yᵉ abufe of
poetry if you had reprehended yᵉ foolifh fantafies of our poets *nomine non re* which they
bring forth on ftage, my felf would haue liked
of you & allowed your labor. but I perceiue
nowe yᵗ all red colloured ftones are not Rubies, nether is euery one *Alexandar* yᵗ hath
a ftare in his cheke, al lame men are not *V-*
ulcans, nor hooke nofed men. *Ciceroes* nether
each profeffer a poet, I abhore thofe poets
that fauor of ribaldry, I will with the zealous admit the expullcion of fnche enormities poetry is difpraifed not for the folly that
is in it, bnt for the abufe whiche manye ill
Wryters couller by it. Beleeue mee the
mageftrats may take aduife, (as I knowe
wifely can) to roote out thofe odde rymes
which runnes in euery rafcales mouth. Sa-
uoring of rybaldry, thofe foolifhe ballets,
that are admitted, Make poets good and
godly practifes to be refufed. I like not of a
wicked *Nero* that wyll expell *Lucan*, yet admit

mit I of a zealous gouernour that wil feke
to take away the abufe of poetry. I like not
of an angrye *Augustus* which wyll banifhe
Ouid for enuy, I loue a wife Senator, which
in wifedome wyll correct him and with aduife burne his follyes: vnhappy were we yf
like poore *Scaurus* we fhoulde find *Tiberius*
that wyll put vs to death for a tragedy making but moft bleffed were we, if we might
find a iudge that feuerely would amende the
abufes of Tragedies, but I leaue the refor-
mation thereof to more wyfer than my felfe,
And retourne to Goffon whom I wyfhe to
be fully perfwaded in this caufe, and therefore I will tell hym a prety ftory, which *Iu-
stin* wryteth in the prayfe of poetrye. The
Lacedemonians when they had lofte many
men in diuers incountryes with theyr ene-
myes foughte to the Oracles of Apollo re-
quiring how they myght recouer theyr lof-
fes, it was anfwered that they mighte ouercome if fo be that they could get an *Atheni-
an* gouernor, whereupon they fent Orators
vnto the *Athenians* humbly requefting them
that they woulde appoynt them out one of
theyr beft captaynes: the *Athenians* owinge
them old malice, fent them in fteede of a *fol-
dado vechio* a fcholar of the Mufes. in fteede
of

of a worthy warrior a poore poet, for a couragious *Themistocles* a filly *Tirthetus*, a
man of great eloquence and finguler wytte,
yet was he but a lame lymde captaine more
fit for the coche then the field, the *Lacedemonians* trufting the Oracle, receued the cham
pion, and fearing the gouernment of a ftranger, made him ther Citizen. which once don
and he obteining the Dukdome, he affended
the theater, and ther very learnedly, wyfh-
ing them to forget theyr folly, and to thinke
on victory they being acuate by his eloquēce
waging battail won the fielde. Lo now you
fee that the framing of common welthes, &
defence therof, proceedeth from poets, how
dare you therfore open your mouth againft
them? how can you difprayfe the preferuer
of a countrye? you compare *Homer to Me-
thecus*, cookes to Poetes, you fhame your
felfe in your vnreuerent fimilituds, you may
fee your follyes *verbum fapienti fat.* where
as *Homar* was an ancient poet, yow difalow
him, and accompte of thofe of leffer iudgement. *Strabo* calleth poetry, *primam fapi-
entiam. Cicero* in his firfte of hys Tufcu-
lans attributeth yᵉ inuencion of philofophy,
to poets. God keepe vs from a Plato that
fhould expel fuch men. pittie were it that the
memo-

memory of thefe valiant victours fhould be
hidden, which haue dyed in the behalfe of
ther countryes: miferable were our ftate yf
we wanted thofe worthy volumes of poetry
could the learned beare the loffe of *Homer?*
or our younglings the wrytings of the *Man-
tuan?* or you your volumes of hiftoryes? beleue me yf you had wanted your Myfteries
of nature, & your ftately ftoryes, your booke
would haue fcarce bene ledde wyth matter.
if therefore you will deale in things of wifdome, correct the abufe, honor the fcience, re
newe your fchoole, crye out ouer Hieru-
falem wyth the prophet, the woe that he pro
nounced, wifh the teacher to reforme hys
lyfe, that his weake fcholler may proue the
wyfer, cry out againft vnfaciable defyre in
rich men, tel the houfe of Iacob theyr iniqui
ties, lament with the Apoftle the want of
laborers in the Lords vineyards, cry out on
thofe dume doggs that will not barke, wyll
the mightye that they ouermayfter not the
poore, and put downe the beggers prowde
heart by thy perfwafions. Thunder oute
wyth the Prophete *Micha* the mefage
of the L O R D, and wyth hym defyre
the Iudges to heare thee, the Prynces
of Iacob to hearken to thee, and thofe of
B. 4.   the

the houfe of Ifraell to vnderftande then tell
them that they abhorre iudgement, and preuent equitie, that they iudge for rewardes,
and that theyr priefts teach for hyre, and the
prophets thereof prophefie for money, and
yet that they faye the Lorde is wyth them,
and that no euil can befall them, breath out
the fweete promifes to the good, the curffes
to the badde, tell them that a peeace mufte
needes haue a warre, and that God can
rayfe vp another Zenacharib, fhew thē that
Salamons kingdome was but for a feafon and that aduerfitie cometh ere we efpye
it. thefe be the fonges of Sion, thefe be thofe
rebukes which you oughte to add to abufes
recouer the body, for it is fore, the appedices
thereof will eafely be reformed, if that wear
at a ftaye, but other matter call me and I
muft not ftaye vpon this onely, there is an
eafier tafk in hand for me, and that which if
I may fpeak my confcience, fitteth my vain
beft, your fecond abufe Goffon, your fecond
abufe your difprayfes of Mufik, which you
vnaduifedly terme pyping: that is it wyll
moft byte you, what fo is a ouerftay of life,
is difplefant to your perfon, mufik may not
ftand in your prefence, whereas all the lear
ned Philofophers haue alwayes had it in
                                    reuerence,

reuerence. *Homar* commendeth it highly, referring to the prayſes of the Gods whiche Goſſon accompleth foliſhneſſe, looke vppon the harmonie of the Heauens? hange they not by Muſike? doe not the *Spheares* moue? the *primus* motor gouerne. be not they *inferiora corpora* affeĉted *quadam ſumpathia* and agreement? howe can we meaſure the debilitie of the patient but by the diſordered motion of the pulſe? is not man worſe accompted of when he is moſt out of tune? is there any thinge that more affeĉteth the fence? doth there any pleaſure more acuat our vnderſtanding. can the wonders y^t hath wroughte and which you your ſelfe confeſſe no more moue you? it fitteth well nowe that the learned haue ſayd, *muſica requirit generoſum animū* which ſince it is far from you, no maruel though you fauor not that profeſſion. it is reported of the *Camelion* that ſhee can chaunge her ſelfe vnto all coollors ſaue whyte, and you can accompte of all thinges ſaue ſuch as haue honeſty. *Plutarch* your good Mayſter may bare me witnes, that the ende whereto Muſick was, will prooue it prayes worthy, O Lorde howe maketh it a man to remember heauenly things. to wōder at the works of the creator, *Eloquence* can

can ftay the fouldiars fworde from flayinge
an Orator, and fhall not mufike be magni-
fied which not onely faueth the bodye but is
a comfort to the foule? Dauid reioyfeth fingeth and prayfeth the Lorde by the Harpe,
the Simbale is not remoued from his fanc
tuary, the Aungels fyng *gloria in excelfis.*
Surely the imagination in this prefent inftant, calleth me to a deepe confideration of
my God. looke for wonders where mufike
worketh, and wher harmonie is ther folow-
eth increcible delectation. the bowels of the
earth yeld. where the inftrument foundeth
and *Pluto* cannot keepe *Proferpina* if *Orphe
us* recorde. The Seas fhall not fwallowe
Arion whilft he fingeth, nether fhall hee perifh while he harpeth, a doleful tuner yf a di-
ing mufition can moue a Monfter of yᵉ fea.
to mourne. a Dolphin refpectet a heauenlye recorde. call your felfe home therefore
and reclayme thys follye, it is to foule to
bee admitted, you may not mayntaiue it. I
hadd well hoped you woulde in all thefe
thynges haue wifelye admytted the thyng,
and difalowe naughte but the abufe, but
I fee your mynde in your wrytinge was
to penn fomewaht you knowe not what,
                                    and

and to confyrme it I wot not howe, fo that
your felfe hath hatched vs an Egge yet fo
that it hath bleft vs wyth a monfterus chic-
kin, both wythoute hedde, and alfo tayle,
lyke the Father, full of imperfection and
leffe zeale. well marke yet a lyttle more,
beare with me though I be bytter, my loue
is neuer the leffe for that I haue learned of
Tullye, that *Nulla remedia tam faciunt
dolorem quam quæ funt falutaria,* the fharper medycine the better it cures, the more
you fee your follye, the fooner may you a-
mende it. Are not the ftraines in Mufike
to tickle and delyght the eare? are not our
warl:ke inftruments to moue men to valor?
You confeffe they mooue vs, but yet they
delight not our eares, I pray you whence
grew that poynt of Phylofophy? it is more
then euer my Mayfter taught mee, that a
thynge of founde fhoulde not delyghte the
eare. belyke yee fuppofe that men are monfters, withoute eares, or elfe I thynke you
wyll faye they heare with theire heeles,
it may bee fo, for indeede when wee are
are delighted with Mufike, it maketh our
heart to fcypp for ioye, and it maye bee
perhaps by affending from the heele to the
hygher partes, it may moue vs, good
policie

policy in footh, this was of your owne coy-
ning your mother neuer taught it you, but
I wyll not deale by reafon of philofophye
wyth you for that confound your fences, but
I can afure you this one thinge, that this
principle will make the wifer to miflike
your inuention, it had bene a fitter ieft for
your howlet in your playe, then an ornamēt
in your booke. but fince you wrote of abufes
we may licence you to lye a little, fo yᵉ abufe
will be more manifeft. lord with how goodly a cote haue you clothed your conceiptes,
you abound in ftoryes but impertinent, they
bewray your reeding but not your wifedom
would God they had bin well aplyed. But
now I muft play the mufitian right noleffe
buggs now come in place but pauions and
mefures, dumps & fancies & here growes a
great queftion, what mufick *Homer* vfed in
curing yᵉ difeafed gretians, it was no dump
you fay, & fo think I, for yᵗ is not apliable to
fick men, for it fauoreth Malancholie. I am
fure, it was no mefure, for in thofe days they
were not fuch good dāfers for foth thē what
was it? if you require me. if you name me the
inftrumēt, I wyl tel you what was yᵉ mufik.
mean while a gods name let vs both dout, yᵗ
it is no part of our faluation to know what it
was

was nor how it went? when I fpeak wyth
Homer next you fhall knowe his anfwere.

But you can not be content to erre but you
muft maintain it to. *Pithagoras* you fay a-
lowes not that mufik is decerned by eares,
but hee wifheth vs to affend vnto the fky &
marke that harmony. furely thys is but one
doctors opinion (yet I diflike not of it) bnt
to fpeake my confcience my thinkes mufike
beft pleafeth me when I heare it, for otherwife the catter walling of Cats, were it not
for harmonie: fhould more delight mine eies
then the tunable voyces of men. but thefe
things are not the chiefeft poynts you fhote
at, thers fomewhat els fticketh in your fto-
mak God graunt it hurt you not, from the
daunce you runn to the pype, from 7. to 3.
which if I fhoulde add I beleeue I coulde
wreft out halfe a fcore incoueniences more
out of your booke. our pleafant confortes do
difcomfort you much, and becaufe you ly ke
not thereof, they arr difcomendable, I haue
heard it is good to take fure fotinge when
we trauel vnknowen countryes, for when
we wade aboue our fhoe latchet *Appelles*
wyll reprehende vs for coblers, if you had
bene a father in mufick and coulde haue decerned of tunes I would perhaps haue likt

your

your opinion fumwhat where now I abhor
it, if you wear a profeffor of that practife I
would quickly perfwade you, that the ad-
ding of ftrings to our inftrument make the
found more hermonious, and that the mixture of Mufike maketh a better concent. but
to preach to vnfkillfull is to perfwad yᵉ brut
beaftes, I wyl not ftand long in thys point
although the dignitye thereof require a volume, but howe learned men haue efteemed
this heauenly gift, if you pleafe to read you
fhall fee. *Socrates* in hys old age will not difdain to learn yᵉ fcience of Mufik amōg child
ren, he can abide their correctiōs to, fo much
accoūted he that, wᵗ you contemn, fo profitable thought he yᵗ, wᵗ you miflik. *Solon* wil e-
fteme fo much of yᵉ knowledg of finging, yᵗ he
wil foner forget to dye thē to fing. *Pithagoras* liks it fo wel yᵗ he wil place it in *Greace.*
aud *Aristoxenus* will faye yᵗ the foule is mufik. *Plato* (in his booke *de legibus*) will af-
firme that it can not be handled without all
fciences, the *Lacedemonians* & *Cretenfis* wer
fturred to warre by Anapeftus foote, and
Timotheus with the fame incenfed kinge
Alexander to batel, ye yf *Boetyus* fitten not,
on *Tauromitanus* (by this *Phrigian* found)
haftened to burn a houfe wher a ftrūpet was
hidden. fo litle abideth this heauēly harmony
                                        our

our humane filthines, y^t it worketh wonders
as you may perceue moft manifeftly by the
hiftory of *Agamemnon* who going to ye Troian war, left at home a mufitian y^t playde the
Dorian tune, who w^t the foote *Spondeus* preferued his wife *Clitemnestra* in chaftity & ho
nefty, wherfore fhe cold not bee deflowred
by *Ægistus*, before he had wickedly flain the
mufitian. fo y^t as the magnetes draweth Ior
ne, & the Theamides (w^c groweth in *Ægipt*)
driueth it away: fo mufik calleth to it felfe al
honeft plefures, & difpelleth frō it all vaine
mifdemanors. y^t matter is fo plētiful that I
cannot find wher to end, as for beginnings
they be infiuite, but thefe fhall fuffice. I like
not to long circūftances wher les doe ferue.
only I wifh you to accoupt wel of this heauēly concent, w^c is ful of perfettiō, proceding
frō aboue, drawing his original frō the motion of ye ftars, frō the agrement of the planets, frō the whifteling winds & frō al thofe
celeftial circles, where is ether perfit agree-
mēt or any *Sumphonia*. but as I like mufik
fo admit I not of thos that depraue the fame
your pipers are as odius to mee as your
felfe, nether alowe I your harpinge merye
beggers: although I knewe you my felfe a
profeffed play maker, & a paltry actor. fince
which ye windmil of your wit hath bin tornd

fo

fo long wyth the wynde of folly, that I fear
me we fhall fee the dogg returne to his vo-
mit, and the clenfed fow to her myre, and the
reformed fcholemayfter to hys old teaching
of follye. beware it be not fo, let not yonr
booke be a blemifh to your own profeffion.
Correct not mufik therfore whē it is praies
worthy, leaft your worthleffe mifliking bewray your madnes. way the abufe and that
is matter fufficient to ferue a magiftrates
animaduerfion   heere may you aduife
well, and if you haue any ftale rethorik florifh vpon thys text, the abufe is, when that
is a pplyed to wantonneffe, which was
created to fhewe Gods worthineffe. When
yᵉ fhamefull reforts of fhameles curtezanes
in finful fonnets, fhall prophane vertue
thefe are no light finnes, thefe make many
goodmen lament, this caufeth parents hate
there right borne children, if this were refor
med by your policie I fhould efteme of you
as you wyfh. I feare me it fareth far other
wyfe, *latet anguis in herba*, vnder your fare
fhow of confcience take heede you cloake
not your abufe, it were pittie the learned
fhould be ouerfeene in your fimpleneffe, I
feare me you will be politick wyth *Macha-
uel* not zealous as a prophet, Well I will
                                    not

not ſtay long vpon the abuſe, for that I ſee it is to manifeſt, the remembraunce thereof is diſcommendable among the godly, and I my ſelf am very loth to bring it in memory. to the wiſe aduiſed reader theſe mai ſuffice, to flee the *Crocodel* before hee commeth, left we be bitten, and to auoyde the abuſe of muſik, ſince we ſe it, left our miſery be more When we fall into folly. *Ictus piſcator ſa-pit*, you heare open confeſſion, theſe abuſes are diſclaimed by our Goſſon, he is ſory that hee hath ſo leudlye liued, & ſpent the oyle of his perfection in vnſauery Lampes. he hath *Argus* eyes to watch him now, I wold wiſh him beware of his Iſlington, and ſuch lyke reſorts, if now he retourne from his repen-ted lyfe to his old folly, Lord how foule wil be his fall. men know more then they ſpeak if they be wiſe, I feare me ſome will bluſhe that readeth this, if he be bitten, wold God Goſſon at that inſtant might haue a watch-man. but I ſee it were needeleſſe, perhaps he hath *Os durum*, and then what auayleth their preſence. Well, I leaue this poynt til I know further of your mynde, mean while I muſt talke a little wyth you about yᵉ thyrd abuſe, for the cater coſens of pypers, theyr names (as you terme them) be players, & I

       C.   think

thinke as you doe, for your experience is fuf
ficient to enforme me. but here I muſt loke
about me, *quacunque te tigeris vlcus est*, here
is a taſk that requireth a long treatis, and
what my opinion is of players ye now ſhall
plainly perceue. I muſt now ſerch my wits,
I ſee this ſhall paſſe throughe many ſeuere
ſenſors handling, I muſt aduiſe me what I
write, and write that I would wyſh.   I way
wel the ſerioufnes of the cauſe, and regarde
verymuch the Iudges of my endeuor, whom
if I could I would perſwade, that I woulde
not nouriſh abuſe, nether mayntaine that
which ſhould be an vniuerſall diſcomoditye.
I hope they wil not iudge before they read,
nether condemne without occaſion   The wiſeſt wil alwais carry to eares, in yᵗ they are
to diſerne two indifferent cauſes.   I meane
not to hold you in ſuſpēc, (ſeuere Iudges) if
you gredely expeɛt my verdit brefely this it
is.

Demostines thoughte not that *Phillip*
ſhoulde ouercome when he reproued hym,
nether feared *Cicero Anthonies* force, when
in the Senate hee rebuked hym.   To the ignorant ech thinge that is vnknowne ſemes
vnprofitable, but a wiſe man can foreſee and
prayſe by proofe. *Pythagoras* could ſpy oute
in

in womens eyes two kind of teares, the one
of grefe the other of difceit: & thofe of iudge
ment can from the fame flower fuck honey
with the bee, from whence the Spyder (I
mean the ignorant) take their poifon. men yᵗ
haue knowledge what comedies & tragedis
be, wil comend thē, but it is fufferable in the
folifh to reproue that they know not, becauf
ther mouthes wil hardly be ftopped. Firfte
therfore if it be not tedious to Goffon to har
ken to the lerned, the reder fhal perceiue the
antiquity of playmaking, the inuentors of
comedies, and therewithall the vfe & como-
ditye of thē. So that in yᵉ end I hope my labor fhall be liked, and the learned wil foner
conceue his folly. For tragedies & comedies
Donate the gramarian fayth, they wer inuen
ted by lerned fathers of the old time to no o-
ther purpofe, but to yeelde prayfe vnto God
for a happy harueft, or plentifull yeere. and
that thys is trewe the name of Tragedye
doeth importe, for if you confider whence
it came, you fhall perceiue (as *Iodocus
Badius* reporteth) that it drewe his original
of *Tragos, Hircus,* & *Ode, Cantus,* (fo called)
for that the actors thereof had in rewarde
for theyr labour, a Gotes fkynne fylled
wyth wyne. You fee then that the fyrfte

C. 2. matter

36

matter of Tragedies was to giue thankes
and prayſes to GOD, and a gratefull
prayer of the countrymen for a happye
harueſt. and this I hope was not diſcommendable. I knowe you will iudge is far-
theſt from abuſe. but to wade farther, thys
fourme of inuention being found out, as the
dayes wherein it was vſed did decay, and
the world grew to more perfeƈtion, ſo yᵗ witt
of the younger ſorte became more riper, for
they leauing this fourme, inuented an other,
in the which they altered the nature but not
yᵉ name: for for ſonnets in prayſe of yᵉ gods,
they did ſet forth the ſower fortune of many
exiles, the miſerable fal of haples princes,
The reuinous decay of many coutryes, yet
not content with this, they preſented the
liues of *Satyers*, So that they might wiſelye
vnder the abuſe of that name, diſcouer the fol
lies of many theyr foliſh fellow citeſens. and
thoſe monſters were then, as our paraſites
are now adayes: ſuche, as with pleaſure reprehended abuſe. as for commedies becauſe
they bear a more pleſanter vain, I wil leaue
the other to ſpeake of them. *Tully* defines
them thus. *Comedia* (ſaith he) is *Imitatio
vitæ, ſpeculum conſuetudinis, & imago veri-
tatis*, and it is ſayde to be termed of *Comai*,
(emongſt

(emongfte the Greekes) whiche fignifieth
Pagos, & *Ode*, *Cantus*: for that they were ex-
crcifcd in the ficldc. they had they beginning
wyth tragedies, but their matter was more
pleffaunt, for they were fuche as did repre-
hend, yet *quodam lepore.* Thefe firft very rud-
ly were inuented by *Sufarion Bullus*, & *Mag
nes*, to auncient poets, yet fo, that they were
meruelous profitable to the reclamynge of
abufe: whereupon *Eupolis* with *Cartinus*, &
Aristophanes, began to write, and with ther
eloquenter vaine and perfeꞔtion of ftil, dyd
more feuerely fpeak agaynft the abufes thē
they: which *Horace* himfelfe witneffeth. For
fayth he ther was no abufe but thefe men reprehended it. a thefe was loth to be feene one
there fpeꞔtacle. a coward was neuer prefent
at theyr affemblies. a backbiter abhord that
company. and I my felfe could not hane bla
med your (Goffon) for exempting your felfe
from this theater, of troth I fhoulde haue
lykt your pollicy. Thefe therefore, thefe wer
they that kept men in awe, thefe reftrayned
the vnbridled cominaltie, whervpon *Horace*
wifely fayeth.

   Oderunt peccare boni, virtutis amore.
   Oderunt peccare mali, formidine penæ.
          The

The good did hate al ſinne for vertues loue
The bad for feare of ſhame did ſin remoue.

Yea would God our realme could light vppon a *Lucillius*, then ſhould the wicked bee
poynted out from the good, a harlot woulde
ſeeke no harbor at ſtage plais, leſt ſhe ſhold
here her owne name growe in queſtion: and
the diſcourſe of her honeſty cauſe her to bee
hated of the godly. as for you I am ſure of
this one thing, he would paint you in your
players ornamēts, for they beſt becam you.
But as theſe ſharpe correĉtions were diſa-
nulde in Rome when they grewe to more
licenciouſnes: So I fear me if we ſhold prac
tiſe it in our dayes, the ſame intertainmente
would followe. But in ill reformed Rome
what comedies now? a poets wit can cor-
reĉt, yet not offend. *Philemon* will mitigate
the correĉtions of ſinne, by reprouing them
couertly in ſhadowes. *Menandar* dare not
offend yᵉ Senate openly, yet wants he not a
paraſite to touch them priuely. *Terence* wyl
not report the abuſe of harlots vnder there
proper ſtile, but he can finely girde thē vnder
the perſon of *Thais*. hee dare not openly tell
the Rich of theyr couetouſneſſe and ſeuerity
towards their children, but he can controle
them

them vnder the perfon of *Durus Demeas*. he
muft not fhew the abufe of noble yong gen-
tilmen vnder theyr owne title, but he wyll
warne them in the perfon of *Pamphilus*. wil
you learne to know a parafite? Looke vpon
his *Dauus*. wyl you feke the abufe of courtly
flatterers? behold *Gnato*. and if we had fome
Satericall Poetes nowe a dayes to penn
our commedies, that might be admitted of
zeale, to difcypher the abufes of the worlde
in the perfon of notorious offenders. I know
we fhould wifely ryd our affemblyes of many of your brotherhod. but becaufe you may
haue a full fcope to reprehende, I will ryp
vp a rablemēt of playmakers, whofe wrigh-
tinges I would wifhe you ouerlooke, and
feeke out theyr abufes. can you miflike of
Cecillius? or difpife *Plinius?* or amend *Ne-*
uius? or find fault with *Licinius?* where in offended *Actilius?* I am fure you can not but
wonder at *Terrence?* wil it pleafe you to like
of *Turpelius?* or alow of *Trabea?* you mufte
needs make much of *Ennius* for ouerloke al
thes, & you fhal find ther volums ful of wit if
you examin thē: fo yᵗ if you had no other maf
ters, you might deferue to be a doctor, wher
now you are but a folifhe fcholemaifter. but
I wyll deale wyth you verye freendlye,

C. 4.

I wil refolue eueri doubt that you find, thofe
inftrumentes which you miflike in playes
grow of auncient cuftome, for when *Roffius*
was an Aᴄᷲtor, be fure that as with his tears
he moued affeᴄᷲtions, fo the Mufitian in the
Theater before the entrance, did mornefully
record it in melody (as *Seruius* reporteth.)
Theaᴄᷲtors in Rome had alfo gay clothing &
euery mās aparel was apliable to his part
& perfon.   The old men in white, yᵉ rich men
in purple, the parafite difguifedly, the yong
men in gorgeous coulours, ther wanted no
deuife nor good iudgemēt of yᵉ comedy, whēc
I fuppofe our players, both drew ther plaies & fourme of garments. as for the appoin
ted dayes wherin comedies wer fhowen, I
reede that the Romaynes appoynted them
on the feftiual dayes, in fuch reputation
were they had at that time.   Alfo *Iodocus
Badius* will affertain you that the aᴄᷲtors for
fhewing pleafure receued fome profite. but
let me apply thofe dayes to ours, their actors to our players, their autors to ours.
furely we want not a *Roffius*, nether ar ther
great fcarfity of *Terrences* profeffiō, but yet
our men dare not nowe a dayes prefume fo
much, as the old Poets might. and therfore
they apply ther writing to the peoples vain
where

wheras, if in the beginning they had ruled,
we fhould now adaies haue found fmal fpec
tacles of folly. but (of truth) I muft confes
with *Aristotle*, that men are greatly delighted with imitation, and that ic were good to
bring thofe things on ftage, that were altogether tending to vertue: all this I admit, &
hartely wyfh, but you fay vnleffe the thinge
be taken away the vice wili contiuue, nay I
fay if the ftyle were changed the practife
would profit. and fure I thinke our theaters
fit, that *Ennius* feeing our wāton *Glicerium*
may rebuke her, if our poetes will nowe become feuere, and for prophaue things write
of vertue: you I hope fhoulde fee a reformed
ftate in thofe thinges, which I feare me yf
they were not, the idle hedded commones
would worke more mifchiefe. I wifh as zea
loufly as the beft that all abufe of playinge
weare abolifhed, but for the thing, the antiquitie caufeth me to allow it, fo it be vfed as
it fhould be. I cannot allow the prophaning
of the Sabaoth, I praife your reprehenfion
in that, you did well in difcommending the
abufe, and furely I wyfh that that folly wer
difclaymed, it is not to be admitted, it maks
thofe finne, whiche perhaps if it were not,
would haue binne prefent at a good fermon.

it

it is in the Magiſtrate to take away that or
der, and appoynt it otherwyſe. but ſure it
were pittie to aboliſh yᵗ which hath ſo great
vertue in it. becauſe it is abuſed. The Germanes when the vſe of preaching was forbidden them, what helpe had they I pray
you? forſoth the learned were fayne couertly
in comodies to declare abuſes, and by playing to incite the people to vertues, whē they
might heare no preaching. Thoſe were lamentable dayes you will ſay, and ſo thinke
I, but was not this I pray you a good help
in reforming the decaying Goſpel? you ſee
then how comedies (my ſeuere iudges) are
requeſit both for ther antiquity, and for ther
commoditye. for the dignity of the wrigh-
ters, and the pleaſure of the hearers. But
after your diſcrediting of playmaking, you
ſalue vppon the ſore ſomewhat, and among
many wiſe workes there be ſome that fitte
your vaine: the practiſe of paraſites is one,
which I meruel it likes you ſo well ſince it
bites you ſo ſore. but ſure in that I like your
iudgement, and for the reſt to, I approue
your wit, but for the pigg of your own ſow,
(as you terme it) aſſuredly I muſt diſcom-
mend your verdit, tell me Goſſon was all
your owne you wrote there: did you borow
nothing

nothing of your neyghbours? out of what
booke patched you out *Ciceros* oration?
whence fet you *Catulins* inucctiue. Thys is
one thing, *alienam olet lucernâ non tuam.* fo
that your helper may wifely reply vpon you
with *Virgil.*

 Hos ego verficulos feci tulit alter honores.

I made thefe verfes other bear the name.
beleue me I fhould preferr Wilfons. fhorte
and fweete if I were iudge, a peece furely
worthy prayfe, the practife of a good fcholler, would the wifer would ouerlooke that,
they may perhaps cull fome wifedome, out
of a players toye. Well, as it is wifedome
to commend where the caufe requireth, fo it
is a poynt of folly to praife without deferte.
you diflike players very much, theyr dealings be not for your commodity, whom if
I myghte aduife they fhould learne thys of
Iuuenal.

 Viuendum est recte,
cum propter plurima, tum his
 Præcipue caufis: vt linguas manci piorum
Contēnas. Nā lingua mali pars peffima ferui.

We ought to leade our liues aright,

         For

For many caufes moue.
Efpecially for this fame caufe,
Wifedome doth vs behone.
That we may fet at nough thofe blames,
which feruants to vs lay,
For why the tongue of euel flaue,
Is worft as wifemen euer fay.

Methinks I heare fome of them verifiing
thefe verfes vpon you, if it be fo that I hear
them, I wil concele it, as for the ftatute of
apparrell and the abufes therof, I fee it manifeftly broken. and if I fhould feeke for example, you cannot but offend my eyes. For
if you examine the ftatuts exactly, a fimple
cote fhould be fitted to your backe. we fhold
bereue you of your brauerye, and examine
your aūceftry, & by profeffion in refpect of ye
ftatute, we fhould find you catercofens with
a, (but hufh) you know my meaning, I muft
for pitie fauor your credit in that you weare
once a fcholler. you runne farther to Car-
ders, dicers, fencers, bowlers, daunfers, &
tomblers. whofe abufes I wold rebuke with
you, had not your felf moued other matters.
but to eche I fay thus, for dicing I wyfhe
thofe that know it not to leaue to learn it, &
let the fall of others make them wifer.   Yf
they

they had an *Alexander* to gouern they fhold
be punifhed, and I could wifh them not to a
bufe the lenitie of their prince. *Cicero* for a
great blemifh reputeth that which our gen-
tilmen vfe for brauery, but *fufficit ista leui-
ter attigiffe*, a word againft fencers, & fo an-
end. whom I wifh to beware with *Demonax*
left admitting theyr fencing delightes, they
deftroy (with the *Athenians*) the alters of
peace, by rayfing quarrellous caufes, they
worke vprores: but you and I reproue thē
in abvfe, yet I (for my part) cannot but allow the practife fo it be well vfed. as for the
filling of onr gracious princes cofers with
peace, as it pertaineth not to me, becaufe I
am none of her receiuors, fo men think vnleffe it hath bine lately you haue not bene of
her maiefties counfel. But now here as you
begin folifhly, fo furely you end vnlernedly.
prefer you warre before peace? the fword be
fore the Goune? the rule of a Tyrant, before yᵉ happy days of our gracious Queen?
you know the philofophers are againft you,
yet dare you ftand in handy grips wyth *Cicero*: you know that force is but an inftrumēt
when counfell fayleth, and if wifedome win
not, farwel warre. Afke *Alphonfus* what
counfellors he lyketh of? hee will fay his
bookes?

46

bookes. and hath not I pray you pollicy alwais ouermaftered force? who fubdued *Hanibal* in his great royalty? he yᵗ durft knock
at Rome gates to haue thē opened is nowe
become a pray to a fylly fenator. *Appius
Claudius et fenex et cœcus* a father full of
wifedome can releue the ftate of decaying
Rome. and was it force that fubdued *Mari
us?* or armes that difcouered *Catulins* con-
fpiracies? was it rafh reuendg in punifhing
Cethegus? or want of witt in the difcouerye
of treafon? *Cato* can correct himfelfe for tra-
ueling by Sea, when the land profereth paf
fage, or to be fole hardy in ouer mutch hazard. *Aristotle* accompteth counfell holye, &
Socrates can terme it the key of certentye.
what fhal we count of war but wrath, of bat
tel but haftines, and if I did rule (with *Augustus Cæfar*) I woulde refufe thefe coun-
felers. what made yᵉ oracle I praye you accompt of *Calchas* fo much? was it not for
his wifedome? who doth not like of the go-
uerner that had rather meete with *Vnum
Nestorem* then *decem Aiaces?* you cannot
tame a Lyon but in tyme, neither a Tigres
in few dayes. Counfell in *Regulus* will preferring the liberty of his country before his
lyfe, not remit the deliuery of *Carthaginian*
captiues

captiues, *Hanibal* fhall flefh himfelfe on an olde mans carkas, whofe wifedome preferued his citye. *Adrian* with letters can gouerne hys legions, and rule peafablye his prouinces by policye. afke *Siluius Italicus* what peace is and he will fay?

Pax optima rerum quas homini nouiſſe.
datum est, pax vna triumphis
Innumeris potior, pax custodire ſalutem.
Et ciues æquare potens.

No better thing to man did nature
Euer giue then peace,
Then which to know no greater ioy,
Can come to our encreafe.
To fofter peace is ftay of health,
And keepes the land in eafe.

Take coufell of *Ouid* what fayth he?
Candida pax homines, trux decet atra feras.
To men doth heauenly peace pertaine,
And currifh anger fitteth brutifh vaine?

Well as I wifh it to haue continuance, fo I praye God wyth the Prophet it be not a bufed. and becaufe I think my felfe to haue fufficiently anfwered that I fuppofed, I
conclude

conclude wyth this. God preferue our peac-
able princes, & confound her enemies. God
enlarge her wifedom, that like *Saba* fhe may
feeke after a *Salomon:* God confounde the i-
maginations of her enemies, and perfit his
graces in her, that the daies of her rule may
be continued in the bonds of peace, that the
houfe of the chofen Ifralites may be mayn-
teyned in happineffe: laftly I frendly
bid Goffon farwell, wyfhinge
him to temper his penn
with more difcre-
tion.

FINIS.

A N
Alarum againſt Vſurers.

Containing tryed experien-
𝖈𝖊𝖘 𝖆𝖌𝖆𝖎𝖓𝖘𝖙 𝖜𝖔𝖗𝖑𝖉𝖑𝖞
abuſes.

WHEREIN GENTLEMEN

may finde good counſells to confirme them,
and pleaſant Hiſtories to delight them:
and euery thing ſo interlaced with
varietie: as the curious may be ſa-
tisfied with rareneſſe, and the
curteous with plea-
fure.

𝕳𝕰𝕰𝕽𝕰𝖀𝕻𝕿𝕺 𝕬𝕽𝕰 𝕬𝕻-
𝖓𝖊𝖝𝖊𝖉 𝖙𝖍𝖊 𝖉𝖊𝖑𝖊𝖈𝖙𝖆𝖇𝖑𝖊 𝖍𝖎𝖘𝖙𝖔𝖗𝖎𝖊 𝖔𝖋 Forbonius 𝖆𝖓𝖉 Priſceria: 𝖜𝖎𝖙𝖍 𝖙𝖍𝖊 𝖑𝖆𝖒𝖊𝖓-
table Complaint of Truth o-
uer *England*. Written by *Tho-*
mas Lodge, of *Lincolnes*
Inne, Gentleman.

O Vita! miſero longa, fœlici breuis.

❡ Imprinted at London by
T. Eſte, for Sampſon Clarke, and are
to be ſold at his ſhop by Guyld Hall.
1 5 8 4.

¶ *To The Right worſhipfull, Sir* Philip Sidne *Knight, indued with all*
perfeƈtions of learning, and titles of Nobilitie:
Thomas Lodge Gen. wiſheth continuance of
honour, and the benefits of happie
Studie.

T is not (noble Gentleman) the titles of
Honour that allureth me, nor the nobilitie
of your Parents that induceth me, but the
admiration of your vertues that perſwa-
deth me, to publiſh my pore trauailes vnder your vndoubted proteƈtion. Whom I
moſt humbly intreate, not onely in ſo iuſt a cauſe to pro-
teƈt me, but alſo in theſe Primordia of my ſtudies, after
the accuſtomed prudence of the Philoſophers, to confirme with fauourable acceptaunce, and continuaunce as
the equitie of the cauſe requireth. I haue ſet downe in
theſe fewe lines in my opinion (Right Worſhipfull) the
image of a licentious Vſurer, and the colluſions of diue-
liſh incrochers, and heerevnto was I led by two reaſons:
Firſt, that the offender ſeeing his owne counterfaite in
this Mirrour, might amend it, and thoſe who are like
by ouerlauiſh profuſeneſſe, to become meate for their
mouths, might be warned by this caueat to ſhunne the
Scorpion ere ſhe deuoureth.

A. ij.   May

3

The Epiſtle Dedicatorie.

May it pleaſe your Worſhippe, to fauour my
trauailes, and to accept my good will: who incouraged
by the ſucceſſe of this my firſtlings will heereafter in
moſt humble ſigne of humanitie continue the purpoſe I haue begunne, commending the cauſe
and my ſeruice to your good liking: who
no doubt compaſſed with incompe-
rable vertues, will commend
when you ſee occaſion, &
not condemne with-
out a cauſe.

Your VVorships in all
dutie to commaund,
Thomas Lodge.

¶ *To The Right worſhipfull, my cur-*
teous friends, the Gentlemen of the Innes of Court,
Thomas Lodge of Lincolnes Inne Gentle-
man, wiſheth proſperous ſucceſſe in
their ſtudies, and happie euent in
their trauailes.

Vrteous Gentlemen, let it not ſéeme
ſtraunge vnto you, that hee which hath
long time ſlept in ſilence, now beginneth publikely to ſalute you, ſince no
doubt, my reaſons that induce me here-
vnto be ſuch, as both you may allowe
of them, ſince they be well meant, and account of them
ſince they tend to your profit. I haue publiſhed héere of
ſet purpoſe a tried experience of worldly abuſes, deſcri-
bing héerein not onely thoſe monſters which were baniſhed *Athens*, I meane Vſurers, but alſo ſuch deuouring caterpillers, who not onely haue fatted their fingers with many rich forfaitures, but alſo ſpread their
venim among ſome priuate Gentlemen of your profeſſion, which conſidered, I thought good in opening the
wound: to preuent an vlcer, and by counſelling before
eſcape, forewarn before the miſchiefe. Led then by theſe
perſwaſions, I doubt not, but as I haue alwayes found
you fauourable, ſo now you will not ceaſe to be friendly, both in protecting of this iuſt cauſe, from vniuſt ſlander, and my perſon from that reproch, which, about two
yeares ſince, an iniurious cauiller obiected againſt me:
You that knowe me Gentlemen, can teſtifie that neyther my life hath bene ſo lewd, as yᵗ my companie was
odious, nor my behauiour ſo light, as that it ſhuld paſſe
the limits of modeſtie: this notwithſtanding a licenti-

A. ii. ous

5

ous *Hipponax*, neither regarding the aſperitie of the
lawes touching ſlaunderous Libellers, nor the offſpring
from whence I came, which is not contemptible, attem-
ted, not only in publike & reprochfull terms to condemn
me in his writings, but alſo ſo to ſlander me, as neither
iuſtice ſhuld wink at ſo hainous an offēce, nor I pretermit a commodious reply. About thrée yeres ago one *Stephen Goſſon* publiſhed a booke, intituled, *The ſchoole of
Abuſe*, in which hauing eſcaped in many & ſundry cōclu-
ſions, I as the occaſion thē fitted me, ſhapt him ſuch an
anſwere as beſéemed his diſcourſe, which by reaſon of the
ſlendernes of yᵉ ſubieȼt (becauſe it was in defēce of plaies
& play makers) yᵉ godly & reuerent yᵗ had to deale in the
cauſe, miſliking it, forbad yᵉ publiſhing, notwithſtanding
he comming by a priuate vnperfeȼt-coppye, about two
yeres ſince, made a reply, diuiding it into fiue ſeȼtiōs, &
in his Epiſtle dedicatory, to yᵉ right honorable, ſir *Fran-
ces Walſingham*, he impugneth me with theſe reproches,
yᵗ I am become a vagarāt perſon, viſited by yᵉ heuy hand
of God, lighter then libertie, & looſer thē vanitie. At ſuch
time as I firſt came to yᵉ ſight héerof (iudge you gentlemen how hardly I could diſgeſt it) I bethought my ſelfe
to frame an anſwere, but conſidering yᵗ the labour was
but loſt, I gaue way to my miſfortune, contenting my
ſelfe to wait yᵗ opportunitie wherein I might, not according to the impertinacie of the iniurye, but as equitye
might countenance mée, caſt a raine ouer the vntamed
curtailes chaps, & wiping out the ſuſpition of this ſlander from the remēbrance of thoſe yᵗ knew me, not counſell this iniurious *Aſinius* to become more conformable
in his reportes: and now Gentlemen hauing occaſion
to paſſe my trauailes in publike, I thought it not amiſſe
ſomewhat to touch the ſlaunder, & prouing it to be moſt
wicked & diſcommendable, leaue the reſt to the diſcretion of thoſe in authoritie, who if the Gentleman had not
plaid bo péep thus long, would haue taught him to haue
counted his cards a little better: and now *Stephen Goſſon*

6

The Epiſtle.

ſon let me but familiarly reaſon with thée thus. Thinkeſt thou yᵗ in handling a good cauſe it is requiſite to induce a falſ propoſitiō, although thou wilt ſay it is a part
of Rethorike to argue *A Perſona*, yet is it a practiſe of
ſmall honeſtie to conclude without occaſion: if thy cauſe
wer good, I doubt not but in ſo large & ample a diſcourſe
as thou hadſt to handle, thou mighteſt had left the honor
of a gentleman inuiolate. But thy baſe degrée, ſubiect to
ſeruile attempts, meaſureth all things according to ca-
uelling capacitie, thinking becauſe nature hath beſtow-
ed vpō thée a plauſible diſcourſe, thou maiſt in thy ſwéet
termes preſent the ſowreſt & falſeſt reports yᵘ canſt imagine: but it may be, yᵗ as it fortuned to yᵉ noble man of *I-
taly*, it now fareth wᵗ me, who as *Petarch* reported, giuē
greatly to yᵉ intertainmēt of ſtrangers, & pleaſure of the
chaſe, reſpected not the braue & gorgious garments of a
courtier, but delighted in ſuch clothing as ſéemed yᵉ place
where he ſoiourned, this noble gentleman returning on
a time frō his game, found all his houſe furniſhed with
ſtrangers, on whō beſtowing his accuſtomed welcome,
he bent himſelf to yᵉ ouerſéeing of his domeſtical prepa-
ratiō, & cōming to yᵉ ſtable among the horſ kéepers of his
new come gueſts, & reprehending one of thē for faulting
in his office, yᵉ felow impatient of reproofe, & meaſuring
yᵉ gentleman by his plaine coat, ſtroke him on the face, &
turned him out of yᵉ ſtable, but afterward attending on
his maſter, & perceiuing him whom he had ſtroken to be
yᵉ Lord of yᵉ houſe,he humbly craued pardō: yᵉ gentleman
as patient as pleſant, not only forgaue him yᵗ eſcape, but
pretely anſwered thus, I blame not thée good fellow for
thy outrage, but this companion, pointing to his coate,
which hath made thée miſtake my perſon. So at this inſtant eſtéeme I M. *Goſſon* hath dealt with me, who not
meſuring me by my birth, but by yᵉ ſubiect I hādled like
Will Summer ſtriking him yᵗ ſtood next him, hath vp-
braided me in perſon, whē he had no quarrell, but to my
cauſe, & therein pleaded his owne indiſcretiō, & loded me
with

7

The Epiſtle.

with intollerable iniurie. But if with *Zoylus* hée might kiſſe the gibet, or with *Patacion* hop headleſſe, the world ſhoulde bée ridde of an iniurious ſlaunderer, and that tongue laboured in ſuppoſitions, might be nailed vp as *Tullies* was for his *Philipicall* declamations. But good *Stephen*, in like ſorte will I deale with thée, as *Phillip* of *Macedon* with *Nicanor*, who not reſpeẛting the maieſtie of the king, but giuing himſelfe ouer to the petulancie of his tongue vainly inueighed againſt him, whom notwithſtanding *Philip* ſo cunningly handeled, that not onely he ceaſed the rumor of his report, but alſo made him as lauiſh in commending, as once he was profuſe in diſcommending: his attempt was thus performed, he ſéeing *Nicanor* ſorely preſſed with pouerty, reléeued him to his content. Wherevpon altering his coppie, and breaking out into ſingular commendation of *Philip*, the king concluded thus: Loe, curteſie can make of bad good, and of *Nicanor* an enimie, *Nicanor* a friend. Whoſe aẛtions my reprouer, I will now fit to thée, who hauing ſlaundered me without cauſe, I will no otherwiſe reuenge it, but by this meanes, that now in publike I confeſſe thou haſt a good pen, and if thou kéepe thy Methode in diſcourſe, and leaue thy ſlandering without cauſe, there is no doubt but thou ſhalt bée commended for thy coppie, and praiſed for thy ſtile. And thus deſiring thee to meaſure thy reportes with iuſtice, and you good Gentlemen to anſwere in my behalfe if you heare me reproched. I leaue you to your pleaſures, and for my ſelfe I will ſtudie your profit.

Your louing friend,
Thomas Lodge.

BARNABE RICH
Gentleman Souldier, in
praife of the Author.

IF that which warnes the young beware of vice,
  And fchooles the olde to fhunne vnlawfull gaine,
If pleafant ftile and method may fuffice,
  I thinke thy trauaile merits thanks for paine,
  My fimple doome is thus in tearmes as plaine:
That both the fubieƈt and thy ftile is good,
Thou needs not feare the fcoffes of Momus brood.

If thus it be, good Lodge continue ftill,
  Thou needft not feare Goofe fonne or Ganders hiffe,
Whofe rude reportes paft from a flaundrous quill,
  Will be determind but in reading this,
  Of whom the wifer fort will thinke amis,
To flaunder him whofe birth and life is fuch,
As falfe report his fame can neuer tuch.

¶ IOHN IONES *GEN-*
tleman, in praife of the
AVTHOR.

THough not my praife, yet let my wifh preuaile,
  Who fo thou be that lift to read this booke,
I neuer yet by flatterie did affaile,
  To count that good that moft did pleafe my looke.
                              ¶.   But

9

But alwaies wifht my friends fuch ftile to vfe,
  As wife might like, though foolifh would refufe.

In opening vice my friend who fpends his time,
  May count by priuate good no profit loft,
What errors fcape in young and luftie prime,
  Experience (badge of truth) may quickly coft.
Who fets the marke, that makes men fhunne the fand,
  Deferues good words, his proofes for profit ftand.

For common good to croffe a few mens vaines,
    Who like to Midas would that all were golde,
I count not miffe, fince there vnlawfull gaines
    Makes fome men fink, whom birth might well vphold.
I know the fore, the fcarre is feene to plaine,
    A bleffed ftate where no fuch wils doo raine.

In briefe, I praife this booke for pretie ftile.
  For pithie matter, Gentle be thou iudge,
O would my wifh fome fancies might beguile,
    Then faire reuenewes fhould not fit a fnudge.
A world to fee how Affes daunce in golde,
  By wanton wils, when Gentles ftarue for colde.

Whofe errors if it pleafe fucceeding age,
  To fee with fighs, and fhun with fad aduice,
Let him beholde this booke, within whofe page,
  Experience leaues her chiefeft proofes of price.
And thanke the youth that fuffered all thefe toiles,
  To warne thee fhun that rocke which many fpoiles.

FINIS.

GEntlemen, fince the preffe cannot paffe without efcape, and fome things are fo miftaken, as without
correction they will be very grofe. May it pleafe you
when you read to correct, efpecially, fuch principall errours as thefe that followe.

Folio. 30. b. Line. 4. For woed, Read wonne.
Folio. eod. Line. 8. For colde, Read cloudes.
Folio. eod. Line. 15. For fhowde, Read fhoard.
Folio. eod. Line. 30. For concluding. Read concluded.
Foli. 31. a. Lin. 34. For prefents a fecrets méete, Read
wth féemly fecret gréete.

For the reft I referre them to your difcretion, who
can diftnguifh coulours, and either better, or
fit words to your fantafies.

Your friend:
Thomas Lodge.

AN ALARVM
againſt Vſurers.

O maruell though the wiſe man accompted all things vnder the ſun vain,
ſince the chéefeſt creatures be mortall:
and no wonder though the world runne
at randon, ſince iniquitie in theſe later
dayes hath the vpper hand. The altera-
tion of ſtates if they be lookt into, and the ouerthrow of
houſes, if they be but eaſely laid in open viewe, what
eye would not ſhed teares to ſée things ſo tranſitorie?
and what wiſedome woulde not indeauour to diſſolue
the inconuenience?

There is a ſtate within this our Common wealth,
which though it neceſſarily ſtand as a piller of defence
in this royall Realme, yet ſuch are the abuſes that
are growen in it, that not onely the name is become o-
dious by ſomes errour, but alſo if the thing be not narrowly lookt into, the whole lande by that meanes will
grow into great inconuenience: I meane the ſtate of
Merchants, who though to publyke commoditie they
bring in ſtore of wealth from forrein Nations, yet ſuch
are their domeſticall praćtiſes, that not only they inrich
themſelues mightelye by others misfortunes, but alſo
eate our Engliſh Gentrie out of houſe and home. The
generall facultie in it ſelfe, is both auncient and law-
dable, the profeſſours honeſt and vertuous, their aćtions
full of daunger, and therefore worthy gaine, and ſo ne-

B.   ceſſary,

ceffarye this forte of men be, as no well gouerned ftate may be without them.

But as among a trée of fruite there bée fome withered fallings, and as among wholefome hearbes there growes fome bitter *Colloquintida*; fo it cannot be, but among fuch a number of Marchaunts, there fhoulde bée fome, that degenerate from the true name and nature of Marchaunts. Of thefe men I write, and of none other, my inuectiue is priuate, I will not write generall: and were it not I refpected the publyque commoditie more then my priuate prayfe, this matter fhoulde haue flepte in hugger mugger. Of thefe vngracious men I write, who hauing nothing of themfelues, yet greedelye grafpe all things into their owne handes.

Thefe be they that finde out collufions for Statutes, and compaffe lande with commoditie, thefe bée the boulfterers of vngracious pettie Brokers: and by thefe men (the more is the pittie) the prifons are replenifhed with young Gentlemen: Thefe bée they, that make the Father carefull, the mother forrowfull, the Sonne defperate: Thefe bée they that make crooked ftraight, and ftraight crooked, that can clofe with a young youth, while they coufen him, and féede his humoures, till they frée him of his Farmes. In briefe, fuch they bée, that glofe moft fayre then, when they imagine the worft, and vnleffe they bée quicklye knowen, they eafelye will make bare fome of the beft of our young Heires that are not yet ftayed: whome zealouflye I befeech to ouer-looke this my writing: for what is fette downe héere, eyther as an eye witneffe I will auowe, or informed euen by thofe Gentlemen, who haue fwallowed the Gudgen, and haue bene intangeled in the hooke, I haue approouedlye fette downe.

Such

14

Such bée thoſe forte of men, that their beginning
is of naught, ſette vp by the deuotion of ſome honeſt
Marchauntes, of whome taking vp their refuſe commoditie, they imploye it to this vngodly and vnhoneſt
purpoſe.

They finde out (according to theyr owne vayne)
ſome olde ſoaking vndermininig Solicitour, whom
they both furniſh with money and expence, to ſette
him foorth, and gette him more creditte: This good
fellowe muſt haunte Ordinaryes, canuaſſe vp and
downe Powles, and as the Catte watcheth the praye
of the Mouſe, ſo dilygentlye intendes hée to the com-
paſſing of ſome young Nouice, whome by Fortune
eyther hée findeth in melancholyke paſſions at the
Ordinarye, or at pennileſſe deuotion in Powles, or
perhappes is brought acquaynted with him by ſome
of his owne brotherhoode. Him he handeleth in theſe
or ſuch lyke tearmes, both noting place and circum-
ſtaunce.

GEntleman, why bée you ſo melancholye? Howe
falleth it out, that you are not more lyghtſome?
Your young yeares mée thinkes ſhoulde loathe ſuch
ſollome aſpeĉtes, I maye not anye waye imagine a
cauſe why you ſhoulde bee penſiue: you haue good
Parentes, you want no friendes, and more, you
haue lyuelyhoodes, which confidered, trulye you
committe méere follye to bée ſo meruaylouſlye ſadde
and wonderfullye ſorrowfull, where you haue no occaſion.

If you want money, you haue creditte, (a gift
which who ſo euer inioyeth nowe a dayes, hée is
able to compaſſe anye thing: and for that I ſée ſo
good a nature in you, (if proferred ſeruice ſtinke
not) I will verye willynglye (if ſo bée you will open

B. ij.   your

your eftate to me) further you in what I may, and perhaps you fhall finde your felfe fortunate, in falling into my companie.

The young Gentleman, vnacquainted with
fuch like difcourfes, counting all golde that glyfters,
and him a faithfull frend that hath a flattering tongue,
opens all his minde to this fubtill vnderminer, who fo
wringeth him at laft, that there is no fecrete corner in
the poore Gentlemans heart, but he knoweth it: after
that, framing his behauiour to the nature of the youth,
if he be fad, fober: if youthly, riotous: if lafciuious,
wanton: he laboureth fo much, that at laft the birde is
caught in the pit-fall, and perceiuing the vaine of the
youth, he promifeth him fome reliefe by his meanes:
the Gentleman thinking he hath God almightie by the
héele, holdes the Diuell by the toe, and by this meanes,
is brought to vtter wracke and ruine. The Broker
furnifhed of his purpofe, hauing learned the Gentlemans name, lodging, want, & welth: & finding all things
correfpondent to his purpofe, hies him to his fetter vp,
who reioyceth greatly at his good happe, and rewards
this wicked feducer with a péece of gold. To be briefe,
at firft iffue on the Gentlemans bonde, this broking
knaue receiues fortie or fiftie poundes of courfe commoditie, making him beléeue, that by other meanes monie
maye not be had, and fwearing to him, that there will
be great loffe, and that he could wifh the Gentleman
would rather refufe then take. But the youth not eftée-
ming the loffe, fo hée fupplye his lacke, fets him forwarde, and giues the willing Iade the fpurre, who finding all things meate in the mouth, makes fale of this
Marchaundize to fome one of his greateft fraternitie,
and if it be fortie, the youth hath a good peniworth if in
ready money he receiue twentie pound, and yet the money repayable at thrée moneths ende. The Broker in
this matter, getteth double fée of the Gentleman,
treble

treble gaine in the ſale of the commoditie, and more, a thouſand thankes of this diuelliſh Vſurer.   Truly Gentlemen, it is wonderfull to conceiue, (yet are there ſome of you can tell if I lie) how this Sicophant that helpt our youth to get, now learneth him to ſpend: What faith he? my young maſter, what make you with this olde Satten doublet? it is ſoilde, it is vnfit for a Gentlemans wearing, apparell your ſelfe as you ſhoulde bée, and ere fewe dayes paſſe, I will acquaint you with as braue a dame a friend of mine, as euer you knew. Oh how ſwéete a face hath ſhe, and thus dilating it with rethoricall praiſes, to make the Gentleman more paſſionate, it falleth out that the mand Fawlcon ſtoops to lure, and all things are fullfilled according to his Brokers direction.   Promiſes are kept on both partes, and my youth is brought acquainted with Miſtres Minxe: this harlot is an old beaten dogge, and a maintainer of the brothell houſe brotherhoode, a ſtale for young nouiſes, and a limme of Sathan himſelfe, whoſe behauiours and ieſtures are ſuch, as the world cannot imagine better, if the Gentleman wéepe, ſhe wil waile: if he ſorrow, ſhe will ſigh: if he be merrie, ſhe will not be modeſt.   To conclude, her leſſon is ſo taught her, as ſhe can recken without booke: Lorde what riotouſneſſe paſſeth in apparell, what lauiſhneſſe in banketting, what looſeneſſe in liuing, and in verie ſhort ſpace, our youth which was fligge, is nowe at leake, his purſe is emptie, and his miſtres begins to lowre, which he perceiuing, & earneſtly bent to continue his credit with his Curtiſan, comes to his vngratious Broker, whom with faire tearmes he deſireth, and with humble ſuites more earneſtlye beſéecheth to further his credite in what hée may.   Who ſéeing which way the Hare windeth, begins to blame him of his liberalitie, and yet only is the cauſe of his ſpending, and after a few priuie nippes, bearing ſhew of good meaning, but yet indéed his way is to trie

B. iij.   conclu-

conclufions, hée hafteth to the principall his good mafter
Merchant, whom he findeth altogether prompt & redy at
a becke, to fend abroad his refufe commoditye for crackt
angels: which conclufiō is betwéene thē both may eafily
be imagined, but yᵉ end is this, yᵉ Broker returns to my
folitarie youth, & recountes vnto him, firft to make him
feareful, how many places he hath ben at, when he hath
not vifited one, how many he hath defired, yet how few
are redie to plefure, at laft he breketh out, & telleth him
yᵉ whole, affuring him yᵗ he is to think wel of his mafter
fcrape-penie yᵉ vfurer, who is willing in hope of his wel
dooing to let him haue once more of his incōmodious cōmodity, vpon refonable affurāce. To be briefe, yᵉ bargain
is quickly beaten out, yᵉ broker laieth yᵉ loffe, yᵉ gentlemā
eftéemeth not fo his néed be ferued, yᵉ Merchaunt laughs
at his folly in his fléeue, & to conclude, yᵉ bonds are deliuered, yᵉ curfed cōmoditie receiued, & at this fecond mart,
how fpéeds our yoncker think you? perhaps of 50. pounds
in ware, he receiueth 30. pounds in ready money, & yet yᵉ
money repayable at thrée months end. O incredible &
iniurious dealings, O more then Iudaicall coufonage,
truely Gntlemen this that I write is true, I my felfe
knowe the paymafter, naie more, I my felfe know certainly, that by name I can recken among you fome, that
haue ben bitten, who left good portiōs by their parents,
& faire landes by their aunceftors, are defolate now, not
hauing friends to reléeue them, or money to affray their
charges. A miferable and wretched ftate is this, full of
inconuenience, when fuch eie fores are not féene in a cō-
mon weale, when fuch abufes are winked at, when fuch
defolation is not perceiued, & wonderfull it is, yᵗ among
fo many godly lawes, made for yᵉ adminiftration of iuftice, ther be none found out: for thefe couetous malefac-
tors, purchafed arms now, poffeffe yᵉ place of ancient pro-
genitors, & men made rich by yoūg youths miffpēdings,
doe feaft in yᵉ halls of our riotous young fpend thrifts.

It

againſt vſurers. 4

It will be anſwered, it is yᵉ gentlemens owne folly, & I
graunt it, yet of their folly who ſhould beare the blame?
truely the bier, who hauing experience to couſin, might
haue alſo conſcience to forbeare thē: nay among yᵉ rabble-
mēt of ſuch as we find to haue ſalue in their youth, how
many experienced men find we at yeares of diſcretion?
who hauing only yᵉ name of gentrie left thē to promote
them to honor, & finding no reléefe any way, are inforced
either in forren coūtries to end their liues miſerably or
deſperatly, ſome more vngratious, are a pray for yᵉ gal-
lous, chooſing rather to die with infamie, then to liue to
beg in miſerie. But to leaue this to his place, & to returne frō whence we haue digreſſed. Our gentlemā hauing got new ſupplie, is pricked on to new ſinne, & the
miniſter of yᵉ diuel feruing at his elbow, perſwades him
to new change, for varietie faith he, is meruelouſly to be
admitted of, eſpecially in ſuch cauſes: & withall bringes
him to a new gameſter, a wittie worldling, who more
cunningly can handle him thē yᵉ firſt, & hath more ſhifts
of deſcant for his plain ſong, (but this by yᵉ way is to be
noted, yᵗ the broker hath his part of yᵉ gaines with yᵉ curtiſan, & ſhe coſins for them both,) this miniō ſo traineth
our ſeduced youth in folly, as not only himſelfe is at her
cōmand, but alſo his ſubſtance remaineth to her vſe, this
high priſed cōmoditie is imploied to yᵉ curtiſans brauery, & ſhe which makes him brutiſh in behauior, doth em-
ty his repleniſhed purſe: thus yᵉ eie of reſon is cloſed vp
by ſenſualitie, & the gifts of nature are diminiſhed, by yᵉ
diſordinate vſage of beſtly venery. Supplies are ſought
for euery way, by his wicked broker, to bring him to ruine, & to work his vtter confuſiō. Thus, thus, alas, yᵉ father before his eies, & in his elder yeres, beholdeth as in
a mirror, yᵉ deſolation of his owne houſe, and hearing
of the profuſeneſſe of his vngratious ſonne, calleth him
home, rebuketh him of his error, and requeſteth account
of his money miſſpended: Hée (taught and inſtructed
ſuffici-

fufficiently to coulour his follie by his vngodly miftres, and curfed mifleader) at his returne to his father,
maketh fhewe of all honeftie, fo that the olde man lead
by naturall affection, is almoft perfwaded that ye truth
is vntruth: yet remembring the priuie conueiaunce of
his youthly yeares, & déeming thē incident to his young
fonne, he difcourfeth with him thus.

O my fonne, if thou kneweft thy Fathers care, and
wouldeft aunfwere it with thy well dooing, I might
haue hope of the continuaunce of my progeny, & thou be
a ioy to my aged yeres. But I feare me the eyes of thy
reafon are blinded, fo y^t neither thy fathers teares maye
perfwade thée, nor thine owne follies laide open before
thine eyes, reduce thée, but that my name fhall ceafe in
thée, and other couetous vnderminers fhall inioye the
fruites of my long labours. How tenderly good boye in
thy mothers lyfe waft thou cherifhed? How déerely beloued? How well inftructed? Did I euer entice thée to
vice? Nay rather enforced I thée not to loue vertue?
And whence commeth it that all thefe good inftructi-
ons are fwallowed vp by one fea of thy follie? In the
Vniuerfities thy wit was praifed, for that it was preg-
nant, thy preferment great, for that thou deferuedft it,
fo that before God I did imagine, that my honour fhuld
haue beginning in thée alone, and be continued by thy
offspring, but béeing by mée brought to the Innes of
Court, a place of abode for our Englifh Gentrie, and the
onely nurferie of true lerning, I finde thy nature quite
altered, and where thou firft fhuldeft haue learnt law,
thou art become lawleffe: Thy modeft attire is become
immodeft brauerie, thy fhamefaft féemelynes, to fhameleffe impudencie: thy defire of lerning, to loitering loue:
and from a fworne fouldier of the Mufes, thou art become a mafter in the vniuerfitie of loue, & where thou
knoweft not anie waie to get, yet feareft thou not out-
ragioufly to fpend. Report, nay true report, hath made
me

me priuie to many of thy eſcapes, which as a Father
though I couer, yet as a good father, tenderly I will rebuke. Thy portion by yeare from me, is ſtanding fortie
pounds, which of it ſelfe is ſufficient both to maintaine
you honeſtly and cleanly: beſides this, you are growne
in Arrerages within this two yeares no leſſe then 100.
pound, which if thou wilt looke into, is ſufficiēt for thrée
whole yeres to maintaine an honeſt familie. Now how
haſt thou ſpent this, forſooth in apparell, and that is the
apteſt excuſe: and lauiſhneſſe in that, is as diſcommendable as in anie other, if in apparell thou paſſe thy
boundes, what make men of thée? A pródigall proude
foole, and as many faſhions as they fée in thée, ſo manie
frumpes will they affoord thée, counting thée to carrye
more bombaſt about thy belly, then wit in thy head.
Naye my ſonne, muſe not vppon the worlde, for that
will but flatter thée, but weigh the iudgement of God,
and let that terrefie thée, and let not that which is the
cauſe of pride, nuſſell thée vp as an inſtrument of
Gods wrathfull indignation. What account reapes a
young man by braue attire? Of the wiſe he is counted
riotous, of the flatterer, a man eaſily to be ſeduced, and
where one will afford thée praiſe, a thouſand will call
thée proud, the greteſt reward of thy brauerie is this, ſée
yonder goes a gallant Gentleman: and count you this
praiſe worth ten ſcore pounds? Truely ſonne, it is better to be accounted wittie, then wealthy, and righteous,
then rich, praiſe laſteth for a moment that is grounded
on ſhewes, and fame remaineth after death, that procée-
deth of good ſubſtaunce: chooſe whether thou wilt bée infamous with *Eroſtratus,* or renowmed with *Ariſtides,*
by one thou ſhalt beare the name of a Sacriledge, by
the other, the title of Iuſt, the firſt maye flatter thée
with ſimilitude, the laſt will honour thée indéede, and
more, when thou art dead. Sonne, ſonne, giue eare to
thy Fathers inſtruĉtions, and grounde them in thy

C.   heart,

heart, fo fhalt thou bée bleffed among the elders, and be
an eye fore vnto thy enimies. A fecond griefe, nay more,
a corafiue to my heart (young man) is this, you are both
prodigall in apparell, and in life, and vngratious and
vngodly curtifans, (as I vnderftand) are become the mi-
ftreffes of your mafterfhip: & thinkeft thou this report
could come to thy Fathers eare, and not grieue him?
Sonne, I had rather thou fhouldeft bée accounted foolifh then amorous, for the one may be borne withall, the
other is moft odious. Incontinencie (you͠g man) is yͤ root
of all inconuenience, it dulleth the memorie, decayeth
the bodie, and perifheth the bones, it makethftedfaft fickle, beautifull deformed, and vertuous vicious: it im-
payreth mans credit, it detraƈteth from his honour, and
fhortneth his daies, a harlots houfe is the gate of hell,
into the which whofoeuer entereth, his vertues doe become vices, his agilitie is growne to flouthfulneffe, and
from the child of grace, he is made the bondflaue of perdition. The wifeft by lewde loue are made foolifh, the
mightieft by luft are become effeminate, the ftouteft
Monarkes to miferable mecockes. I wot well (my child)
that chaft loue is neceffarie, but I know (my fonne) that
lecherie is horrible. A harlots wanton eie is the lure of
the diuell, her faire fpéeches, the fnares of fin, & the more
thou delighteft in her companie, yͤ more hepeft thou the
wrath of God againft thy felfe: Let *Lais* looke neuer
fo demurely, yet *Lais* is *Lais*, meafure not thy liking by
lookes, for there be fome holy diuells: to bée briefe, the
end is this, he is beft at eafe that leaft meddeleth with
anie of them. *Demofthenes* will not buie repentaunce
fo déere, as with high fummes to purchafe tranfitorie
pleafures, and I had rather thou fhouldeft learne of a
Philofopher, then bée inftruƈted by thy owne fancie,
marke this axiome, there is no vertue which is odious
after it is attained to, but the pleafures of loue are then
moft loathfome, when they are determined: and therefore

fore no vertues: and to conclude, not to be ſought after. It is idleneſſe my ſonne, that ſeduceth thée, for the
minde that is well occupyed, neuer ſinneth. When thou
enterpriſeſt anie thinges, meaſure thine owne fortune
by other mens ſucceſſe: as thou conſidereſt of theyr
ends, ſo imagine of thine owne. Thinke with thy ſelfe
the wiſeſt haue fallen by loue, as *Salomon*, the richeſt,
as *Anthonie*, the proudeſt, as *Cleopatra*, the ſtrongeſt,
as *Sampſon*, and by how many degrées they did excéede
thée, by ſo many circumſtaunces preuent thy ruine. It
is inough for ſillie Birdes to be lead by the call of the
Fowler, and for men it is moſt conuenient to flye ap-
paraunt goods, & ſticke to that which is indéede. Though
thine eie perſwade thée the woman is beautifull, yet let
thy experience teach thée, ſhée is a Curtiſan, and wilt
thou eſtéeme of painted Sepulchres, when thou knoweſt certaine and determined ſubſtaunces? Doe we buie
ought for the faireneſſe or goodneſſe? Spangled Hobbie horſes are for children, but men muſt reſpeéte
things which be of value indéede. I imploie my money
vppon thée, not to the vſe thou ſhouldeſt be lewde, but
for that I woulde haue thée learned. It gréeueth mée
to heare reportes of thy companie kéeping, for where
thou offendeſt in the two formoſt, thou art altogether
nuſled in this, and truelye I can not but meruayle
at thée, that béeing borne reaſonable, to make eleétion,
thou art ſo vntoward in picking out thy choice: Agrée
light and darkeneſſe? Or the *Icknewmon* with the
Aſpis? Doeth the Wéeſell loue the Cockatrice? Or
gentle borne, ſuch as bee vngratious? No my Sonne,
broking bugges are not companions for continent
Courtyers: for who ſo eyther accompanyeth them, is
eyther accounted a ſpende thrifte, or one that is Sir
Iohn Lacke lande, eyther of their fraternitie, or elſe a
verie foole.

C. ij.   Finde

Finde me out anie one of them, that in thy aduerfitie
will helpe thée, or in thy mifdemeanor aduife thée. Nay,
fuch they are, as will rather binde thée prentice with
Sathan, then exhort thée to efchew finne. They bée the
Caterpillers of a Common weale, the fting of the Ad-
der, nay, the priuie foes of all Gentrie, and fuch they be,
that if they get, they care not how vngodly, and if they
coufen, they care not how commonly: So that thrée vices haue nowe taken hold of thée, firft prodigalitie, the
enimie to continencie, next lafciuioufneffe, the enimie
of fobrietie, and thirdly ill company, the decayers of thy
honeftie. The meanes to auoyde thefe euills are manifeft but they muft be followed: it is not fufficient to
knowe a fault, but it is wifedome to amend it: Humble
thy heart (my fonne) to the higheft, and the more thou
confidereft of him, the leffe wilt thou care for this flefh:
For what is the body better by the gay rayment? truly
no more then ye foule is by fuperfluous zeale, for as the
one is foolifh, fo is the other franticke. Leaue luft, leaft
it lofe thée, vfe chaft delights for they will comfort thée,
it is better driuing a toye out of memorie by reading a
good leffon, then by idleneffe to commit an errour, which
is fawced with repentaunce. Of néedleffe euills make
no accompt, ye leffe you accompany ye worft, the more wil
you be fought to by the beft. Eafie is it to fay well, but
the vertue is to doo well: O my déere childe, as thy frend
I exhort thée, and as thy louing father I command thée,
to confider of the tender care I haue of thée, and to imploy all thy indeuours now to my comfort: if thou haft
runne away, call thy felfe home, and waye within thy
heart the reward both of vertue, and the difcredite by
vice, fo the honour of the one will incite thée, the infamy
of the other will deterre thée. For thofe debts that haue
ouerpaft thée, in hope of amendement I will fée them
fatiffied, and if héereafter thou fall into the lyke lurch, I
promife thée this, that as now I deale with thée as a father

ther, ſo then will I accompt of thée as a reprobate. Thou
féeſt fire and water before thée, chuſe to thy liking: in
dooing well, I will reioyce in thée, in dealing otherwiſe,
I will nothing accompt of thée.

The father with teares hauing ended this his exhor-
tarie, is aunſwered in humble ſort of his diſſembling
ſonne, thus.

Whatſoeuer (good father) hath paſſed, is irreuocable,
but what is to come may be conſidered of: it is naturall in me to fall, and vertuous to recouer my ſelfe. I
confeſſe good ſir, I am guiltie of errour, and haue faulted highlye, yet not ſo greatlye as you intimate: the
world now a dayes is rather bent to aggrauate then to
couer eſcapes. Wherefore, as the firſt ſtep to amendement is repentance, ſo (deare father) I am ſorrie for that
is paſt, and moſt earneſtly requeſt you to continue your
fauour, and no doubt but your ſonne ſhall behaue himſelfe héerafter to your comfort.

The father delighted with his ſonnes diſcréete and
humble aunſwere, conceiueth hope of amendment, and
returneth him to the Innes of the Court againe, and
ſetting him on free foote, exhorteth him to follow vertue,
and intentiuely to long after learning. But he, whoſe
heart was pliable to receiue all impreſſions, no ſooner is
out of the view of his fathers houſe, but began to forget his olde promiſes, and renewes the remembrance of
his miſtreſſe, deuiſing by the way how to delight her,
and what ſutes to prouide that may ſatiffie her. To bée
briefe, being returned to *London*, and quit of his fathers
feruants, (yᵉ newes of his arriuall being blazed abroad)
his Broker in poſt haſt comes and ſalutes him, his miſtreſſe by tokens and ſwéete letters gréetes him, hée
maketh his marchant ioyfull in the receipt of the money, and miſtreſſe Minxe merrie for the returne of her
young copeſmate.

To be briefe, in poſt haſt he poſteth to her chamber,

C. iij.　　　where

where Lord what friendly gréetings paffe, what amorous regardes, how fhe blameth him of his delaye, and
with fained teares watereth his youthly face, howe fhée
fweares that fhe is conftant, and yet a curtifan: howe
fhe vowes fhe is continent, and yet common: truly it
were a matter to make a Comedie on, to fée both their
actions, and to note their difcourfes: their needes not
many or long fermons on this, mafter Brokers help in
fhort fpace is fought for: for the money my youths father gaue him, hath bought his miftreffe a fute of the
new fafhion. The Broker readie at a becke, without
delay furnifheth him with money: it is lamentable to
report euery loffe, and fith in another place I meane to
fet them downe, I will not motion them héere. In fhort
fpace, our Marchant beginneth to looke after more affuraunce, and where to fore he was content with obligation, he now hunteth after ftatutes. (This kind of bond
Gentlemen is well knowen among you, the vfurers by
this time haue built mannor houfes vpon fome of your
lyuelihoods: and you haue loft that for little, which
will not be recouered with much.) The force whereof
our youth confidering not, fo he haue foyfon of money:
the world to be fhort, at the laft falleth out thus, both
land, mony, & all poffibilities, either by father or friends,
are incroched vpon, by this gentle mafter Scrape-peny,
fo that now our youth finding neither furetie nor fimi-
litude, by his flattering vfurer is laid vp clofe for efcaping. Let him write to his hufwife Miftreffe Minxe,
fhe difdaineth him: let him intreate the Broker he re-
fufeth him, let him make fute to the vfurer, he faith hée
fhall not coufen him: thus (this Gentleman that neyther by his fathers counfell woulde refufe, nor by his
owne experience be perfwaded, to auoyde the eminent
daunger that hanged ouer his head, is brought to confufion, and thofe friends that fawned on him before in
profperitie, now frowne at him in his aduerfitie, thofe
that

that depended with flattering words in time of wealth on his finding, now altogether diſdaine him that cannot finde himſelfe. Loe Gentlemen what it is to winke at good counſell, and to preferre young attempts before old experience: ſée héere the fruites of contempt, and lette theſe leſſons ſerue you to looke into: had this Gentleman regarded aduice, had he conſidered of his eſtate, himſelfe had bene at libertie, his friends in quiet. But (alas the while) our heires now a dayes haue running heads, which makes their parents abounde in teares: ſome are led with nouelties in forreine Nations, ſome with prodigalitie in their owne Countrey: ſome with pride, the firſt fruites of all impietie: ſome by loue, the ladie of looſeneſſe. If one hunteth after vertue, how many hundreds doo dayly practiſe vice? Let the experience of this young Nouice (my youthly countrey men) make you warie, and ſée but into this one parcell of his lyfe, and giue your iudgement of his misfortune: his wit was ſufficient to conceiue vertue, yet knowing (with *Medea*) the beſt, he headlong runne to the worſt. Natures giftes are to be vſed by direction: he had learning, but hée applied it ill: he hadde knowledge, but hée blinded it with ſelfe opinion. All graces whatſoeuer, all ornaments what ſo they be, either giuen vs by our fore-parent, or grafted in vs by experience, are in themſelues as nothing: vnleſſe they be ordered by the power of the moſt higheſt. What care conceiue you, may be comperable to this young Gentlemans fathers ſorrow? who ſéeth his houſe pluckte ouer his head: his ſonne impriſoned to his greate diſcredite, and the vſurer the onely gainer, and yet the moſt vileſt perſon.

Nowe, what becommeth of our youth thinke you? his Father refuſeth him, diſpoſſeſſing the ryghte heyre of what hée maye, and poore hee is lefte deſolate and afflicted in priſon. And in theſe dayes how many are infected with this deſperate diſeaſe, Gentlemen
iudge

iudge you, I my felfe with teares haue heard fome priuie complaints, and lamented my friends miffortunes,
falne fo fodainly. My good friends y^t are héerafter to enter into this world, looke on this glaffe: it wil fhew you
no counterfait, but the true image of a rebellious fonne,
and the rewarde of contempt of parents, account your
felues happie to learne by others experience, and not to
be pertakers of the actuall forrowe: Obey your parents, for they loue you, truft not to ftraungers, for they
will vpbraide you of their benefite, it is better to haue
the ftripes of a friend, then the kiffes of a flatterer. *Plato* would haue young men to looke in the glaffe, for two
caufes, the one, that if they founde themfelues beauty-
full in vifage, and of exquifite ftature, they might inde-
uor to make the vertues of their minde, anfwerable to
the liniaments of the bodie: the other, that if they found
themfelues of deformed fhape, they fhould féeke to beau-
tifie the fame by the inward perfections of the minde, &
for two caufes my good friends, woulde I wifh you to
confider of this mans fall, and read his miffortune: the
one, that not being yet nipped, you may preuent: the o-
ther, that being but yet a little galled, you would holde
backe.

Eft virtus placidis abftinuiffe bonis.

As the Loadftone draweth yron, fo let good counfail
conquere your affections, as the *Theamides* of *Aegyp*
driueth awaie yron, fo let the feare of God difpell al
worldly plefures: If a fimple man fall to decay, it may
be borne withall, if a man of wifdome grow in arre
rages, may we not blame his follie? It is better to bé
enuied then pittyed, for thou art pittied alwaies in mif
fortune, but enuied at time of thy profperitie. To bé
briefe (Gentlemen) ouerlooke this aduifedly, & you fhal
finde many things worthy the noting, and no few mat
ters written for your cōmoditie. This miferable young
man, ouerwhelmed thus on euerie fide with manifold
                                                        and

and ſundry cares, beholding his moſt vnfortunate ſtate, in wofull termes in the priſon houſe breketh into theſe complaints.

Alas vnhappic wretch that I am, that hauing a good father that did cheriſh me, a tried mother that tenderly nouriſhed me, many friends to accompanie me, faire re-uenewes to inrich me: haue heaped ſorrowe on my owne head by my Fathers diſpleaſure, refuſed of my friends for my miſdemeanour, & diſpoſſeſſed of my land by my prodigalitie. O inceſtuous luſt that entereſt the hart, & conſumeſt the bones, why followed I thée? & O vngodly pleaſure why didſt thou flatter me? O wicked and vngracious man that haſt vndone me, and woe be vnto thée (vile wretch) that in my miſerie doeſt thus leaue me. What ſhall become of me poore wretch? faine now would I begge that bread, which vainlye I haue ſpent: now too too late doo I ſée, that fainedneſſe is no faith, and he that truſts to this world, cleaues to a bro-ken ſtaffe. Alas, how ſhould I attaine to libertie? or by what meanes may I eſcape my confuſion? My Father hath accepted of another ſonne, and all by reaſon of my lewdneſſe: O that I had reſpected his vnfained teares, O that I had accepted his good aduice, O that I had re-iected my flattering friends. But I ſée no hope is lefte me, my creditour is too cruell, yet hath he couſoned me: and faine would I be his bond ſlaue, woulde he releaſe me: but ſince no hope is lefte me of recouerie of my E-ſtate, I referre my cauſe to God, who as he will remit my offence, ſo will he redreſſe my miſerie and griefe.

Whileſt in theſe or ſuch like tearmes, the poore young man bewayles his heauie happe, ſodainly enters his couſoning creditour, and in outwarde ſhew bewai-lyng his misfortune, yet in very truth the onely ori-ginall cauſe of his deſtruction, comforteth him in theſe or ſuch like termes.

Gentleman, the exigent and extremitie that you are

        D.   now

now at, though it be most tedious vnto you, it is most
lamentable in my opinion. Thefe young yéeres to tafte
of forrowe fo foone, is ftraunge, confidering all circum-
ftaunces: but fince the caufe procéedes of your owne
lewd miffpending, mine be the loffe in part, but the gre-
ter muft your affliction be. I hoping of your well dooing, neither denied your pleafure nor profite, yet in liew
and recompence of all, I finde iuft nothing: a few fubfcribed papers I haue, and fome money I haue recey-
ued, but nothing to my principall, and yet notwithftanding fo fauourable wil I be vnto you, as if you procure
me any one furetie I will releafe you. To léefe my money I were loath, and to kéepe you héere it were more
loathfome. I wold doo all for the beft, not hindering my
felfe, fo you would ftraine your felfe to fatiffie me fomewhat.

The Gentleman knowing in himfelfe his vnability,
beginneth in truth to open his ftate, protefting, that neither of himfelfe, nor by any one at the prefent he is to
doo any thing, no not fo much as if he releafed him to
pay his charges, fuch is his miferie, in that all his frends
had giuen him ouer, wherevpon moft humbly he befée-
cheth him, to way his caufe, promifing any feruice what
fo euer may be: if fo be it wil pleafe him to fet him frée.
Mas vfurer fmelling out the difpofition of the youth,
beginnes to bring him to his bowe after this fort.

The world at thefe dayes is fuch (my friende) as
there is fmall refpect had of thofe which haue nought,
and great honour attributed vnto them, that will moft
néerly looke to themfelues: which I perceiuing, haue giuen my felfe (as naturally men are inclined to féeke
after glory) to the hoording vp of riches, to the end that
my pofteritie might be raifed vp, and my fathers name
(which as yet is of no accompt) might by my meanes
become worfhipfull. To perfourmaunce of this, trulye

I

I haue neither ben idle nor euill occupied: my thoughts haue wholly bene ſet of gettings, and who ſo nowe a dayes hath not the like meaning, his purpoſe will grow to ſmall effect. And though of my ſelfe, I doo what I may, yet (as it is neceſſary) I muſt haue miniſters, wher by that which I looke for may be brought to my hands: otherwiſe, my ſtocke might lye without vſaunce to my vtter vndooing. Wherevpon, if thou wilt followe my direction and be ruled by my counſell, I will releaſe thée of priſon, and ſet thée at libertie: reſtore thée to thy wonted credite, and countenaunce thée with my coyne, ſo that in ſhorte ſpace thou maiſt haue money in thy purſſe, and other neceſſaries to ſet thée vp againe. Thou ſéeſt that now thou art miſerable, but I will make thée fortunate: thou now art almoſt foodleſſe, by me thou ſhalt be ſatiffied with the beſt: thy friends now diſdain thée, the day ſhall come that they ſhall ſéeke to thée: now art thou without apparell, through me thou ſhalte bée coſtlye attired: naye, what pleaſure ſoeuer thou ſhalt either imagine for thy preferment, or wiſh for to doo thée good, thou ſhalt both finde me ready to performe it, and friendly to continue it.

The Gentleman ſurpriſed with this ſodaine ioye, and vnacquainted good ſpeaches (not dreading that the Serpent laye hidden in the graſſe) moſt willinglye aſ-ſented, promiſing to the aduenture of his lyfe, (ſo his creditour woulde be his wordes maſter,) to doo his in-deauour to perfourme his will, as hée ought to doo. The Vſurer ſéeing the minde of his priſoner, preciſe-lye bent to doo his commaunde, openeth his heart vnto him thus.

Gentleman, for that I haue an opinion of your honeſtye, and truſte in your ſecrecye: I will open vnto you my minde, and according as I finde your aunſwere, I will ſhape your deliueraunce. Such time

as you were at libertie, you know you had acquaintaunce with manye Gentlemen, and they not of the
meaneft: who at fometimes as well as your felfe were
deftitute of filuer: fuch as thofe be you muft finde out
for me, I will delyuer you prefentlye: apparayle you
in print, giue you money in your purffe, and at fuche
an Ordinarye fhall you lye, where the greateft reforte
is: your behauiour and vfage towardes all men muft
be verye honeft, efpeciallye in all caufes looke into the
natures of men. If you fpie out any one Gentleman
penfiue, enter into difcourfe with him, if you maye
perceiue, that either by parentage or poffeffion, hée is
worthie credite, laye holde on him, feede him with money if he want, and (as though it procéeded of your own
good nature) profer him to be bound for him: if he accept your offer, come to me, I will furnifh him: nowe
you may deuide the commoditie or the money betwéen
you, and out of your part (confidering me after the big-
neffe of the fumme) take the reft for your owne fée:
which if you looke into, in a yeare will growe vnto no
fmall fumme. This is the Load-ftone muft lead you:
and by all meanes you muft fafhion your felfe to féede
humours: this is an honeft meanes to lyue by, this is
a way to libertie, by this you may pleafure your felfe
and to conclude in dooing this, you maye mightelye in
fhort fpace inrich me. When you haue found out one fit
to your vaine, remember this leffon, that what fo euer
vauntage you get of him, either for me, or for your felf
care not how little paper and inke he can fhewe of
yours, kéepe ftill your owne ftake cléere. In thefe matters you muft be verie circumfpect, for there be now a
daies fuch vnderminers ftart vp, that fcarce a man can
imagine his owne profit but they preach it a broad, and
laye it open. Thus doo you fée whereto you muft
truft: howe faye you nowe, will you be content to doo
this·

The

32

The young man aunſwereth, Good ſir, there is nothing that you haue ſayde that by mée ſhall anie wayes
be forgotten, I am readie and willing to put in practiſe
what you haue taught, and no doubt you ſhall finde me
ſo diligent, y^t your ſelfe ſhal ſay, you were happie in putting me in truſt. In briefe the concluſion is this, the v-
ſurer glad of this new Gentleman broker, diſchargeth
him, ſets him a floate: now who ſo braue as our late priſoner, or who ſo frolicke? The olde ſorrowes are forgotten, and new inuentions to couſin, poſſeſſe the recep-
tacle of his reaſon. His olde acquaintaunce flocke about
him, ſome reioycing at his recouered libertie, ſome wō-
dering at his ſodaine brauerie, yet fewe ſuſpecting his
pretended and hidden knauerie. Of them ſome he ſalu-
teth humblye, ſome ordinarilye, he was not ſo well inſtructed, but it is as well performed. Now who but our
Gentleman is a companion for the beſt, and a couſiner
of the moſt, he ſtaies not long before he be prouided of a
praie, whom he ſo ordereth, as himſelfe is pertaker of y^e
halfe, though the other be paymaſter of the whole, and
as thoſe that are in the heate and extremitie of an ague,
deſire drink to ſatiſfie their drought: ſo this young gentleman that is brought into bondes by one couſining
ſpend thrift, hauing once entered foote in the high waie
of prodigalitie, continueth headlong his courſe to his
owne confuſion. But by the way it is to be noted, that
this Gentleman which is brought into the laps by our
late priſoner, hath his poſſeſſion & portion alotted him, ſo
that our vſurer & his mate worke vpon ſure groundes.
Two or thrée Obligations and commodities receiued,
our vſurer grows to new deuiſes, and ſets his ſchollers
to practiſe them, ſaith he, I muſt now haue you learne,
to bring in this your friend to paie your debtes, and by
this meanes you ſhall bring it about, you ſhall when
next time he ſhall demaund your helpe, tell him that of
me there will be had no money before your olde bondes

D. iij. be

be canceled, fo that vnleffe he deale with me, by fome
meanes to acquit that, it is vnpoffible to attaine vnto
anie farther fupplie. You may alleadge vnto him howe
in fuch like extremities you haue ftucke, and will fticke
vnto him, and defire him in fo eafie a requeft he wil not
leaue you deftitute, by this meanes fhall you be rid of
your olde debts, and be as frée from inconuenience as e-
uer you wer. No fooner hath our feducer learnt this leffon, but forth he trudgeth to find out this young mafter,
if poffible may be, if fo be he as yet be ftored, he doth either make him fpend it or lend it, & vpō his new requeft
of fupply, openeth vnto him all the circumftance which
before he had learned, & fo cunningly handleth him, that
the Gentleman defirous of money is eafilye content.
Wherevpon the matter is handeled thus betwixt the
Merchaunt and this Gentleman broker to preuent inconuenience, if the brokers bond be an hundreth pounds,
the Merchant will lend fiftie more, and maketh yᵉ young
man to feale an abfolute bond as his owne debt, fo that
the defperate debte of the decayer coufoned, by his
meanes is brought to be the true debt of this filly Gentleman. Naie when they haue fatted both their fingers,
they leaue not thus, but from money fhoote at land, for
if the Gentleman haue 500. pound in ftocke payable at
24. or 25. yeares, they will fo worke as all that fhall
be their proper goods, which they will recouer out of the
executors hands, either by attachment or otherwife, and
befides that, fo cunningly will they deale, that although
they haue fufficient affuraunce in hand alreadie, yet wil
they not leaue till they get an other more fure ftring to
their bowe, therby to compaffe the poore Gentlemans
lands. At his want they will deale thus. This Gentleman and the broker muft bée inuited by the Merchant,
when amongft other table talke, M. Scrape-penie féeles
my youth if his monie be gone, & offring fpéeches of wil-
lingnes to prouide him alwaies at his néed, fets on by a
becke

beck his coufoning mate, to procure yᵉ gentlemā to craue more mony, which he doth, yᵉ merchant cunningly coulering his craft, anſwereth him thus. Gentlemā you ſée I am far out already, & vpon your ſingle bond I haue diſburſt a round ſum of money, no leſſe then 500. poundes, which in a poore mans purſe as I am, is no ſmall quantitie, neuertheles if you wil affoord me farther affurāce, I wil not ſtick in redie mony once more to lend you 30. pounds. The gentleman neuer tofore vſed to receiue redy mony at yᵉ firſt hāds, begins to yéeld him harty thāks & humbly to pray him to demand & he will performe, for faith he, conſidering your honeſt dealing, I cannot think you may imagine any reſonable aſſurance which I wil not feale to. Why thē quoth yᵉ merchant, yᵉ matter ſtandeth thus, if ſo be you will feale me an eſtatute for my mony, no ſooner ſhal you haue done it, but you ſhal haue yᵉ mony, all your bonds in, & a defefance to, this yᵗ I offer is reaſonable, & to morrow if you will I will doe it. Agréed quoth yᵉ Gentleman, & ſo takes his leaue, the next morrowe according to promiſe, the Gentleman fealeth the aſſurance, acknowledging an eſtatute, before ſome one Iuſtice of the bench, and comming to his Merchants houſe for his money, is delaied for that daie of, & in fine, his abſolute anſwere is this, that without a furetie he promiſed him none: he takes witneſſe of his friend (as he tearmeth him) a pretty péece of witneſſe, when he ſéeth no remedie, he demaundeth his bondes, & he witholdeth thē, he craues his deceafance, & cannot haue it. Thus is yᵉ poore Gentlemā brought into a notable miſchiefe, firſt in being coufoncd of his mony, next deluded by his eſtatute wᵗout defeafance (for if yᵉ defeafāce be not deliuered yᵉ fame time or daie, yᵉ ſtatute is, it is nothing auailable) thirdly by his bonds detaining, which may be recouered againſt him, & continue in full force, and the vſurer that playes all this rie, will yet be counted an honeſt and well dealing man. But flatter them who ſo liſt for me,

I

I rather wifh their foules health, then their good coun-
tenances, though I knowe they will ftorme at me for o-
pening their fecrets, yet truth fhall countenaunce mée
fince I féeke my countries cōmoditie. Héere you fee two
houfes deftroied manifeftly, yᵉ one of them, from a Gentleman made a craftie coufoner, the other of them from a
landed man, a filly poore wretch. And wonderfull it is
to fée, confidering the afperitie of the Penall ftatutes fet
downe by her Maieftie, and her honourables Péeres in
the Parliament. How pretie collufions thefe cunning
merchants can find to infringe them. One priuate practife they haue in deliuerie of yᵉ commoditie, to make the
condition of the Obligation thus. The condition, &c. is
this, that if the within bound, *T. C.* his heires, executors
or affignes, doe well and truely pay or caufe to be paide
to yᵉ aboue named *M. S.* the fum of 40. pounds of lawful
mony of *England*, at his own dwelling houfe, fcituated
& being in Colman ftréet, which he yᵉ fayd *T. C.* ftandeth
indebted vnto him for, if fo be that he the fayd *M. S.* or *S.*
his wife be in life, yᵗ then. Otherwife, &c. Now in this cō-
ditiō, yᵉ cafual mart bringeth it out of cōpaffe of ftatute,
thus by collufions M. Scrape-penie gathers vp his money. Others worke by ftatute and recognifaunce, making their debter to difcharge in their bookes of account the receit of fo much money, where indéede they
had nothing but dead commoditie. Other worke by
liues, as if fuch a one liue thus long, you fhall giue mée
during his or her life 10. pounds a yeare, for 30. pounds,
and be bound to the performaunce of that by ftatute. O-
ther fome deale in this forte, they will picke out among
the refufe commoditie fome pretie quantitie of ware,
which they will deliuer out with fome money, this fum
may be 40. pound, of which he will haue you receiue
10. pound readie money, and 30. pounds in commoditie,
and all this for a yeare: your bonde muft be recognifaunce, now what thinke you by all computation your
commo-

commoditie will ariſe vnto, truely I my ſelfe knew
him that receiued the like, and may boldly auouch this,
that of that thirtie pounds commoditie, there coulde by
no broker be more made then foure nobles: the commoditie was Lute ſtringes, and was not this thinke you
more then abhominable vſurie? Naie common loſſes, &
yᵉ reaſonableſt is, for 36. pound for thrée months, accounted a good penie worth, if there be made in redie mony,
20. pounds, naye paſſing good if they make 25. poundes,
I haue knowen of fortie, but ſixtéene pound, and tenne
ſhillings. Theſe be general payments, and receits, incident to the moſt part of the young Gentlemen that I
knewe deale that wayes: and truely I my ſelfe knowe
within my time, no few number of Gentlemen, which
are vtterly vndone by this meanes, and vnleſſe this e-
uill be preuented, and Gentlemen take not more héede,
more will followe after. But if the puniſhment of theſe
men were *In diſcretione Iudicis*, notwithſtanding the
lawe were couloured with all by them, yet the conſcience of the iudge woulde cut ſuch ill members off. In
former ages theſe things being knowen, were lookt vnto, and now when moſt puniſhment is menaced, vſurie
is moſt practiſed. Well may we now ſée that the craftie haue as many cautiles, as the diſcréet cautions. If
we had as ſeuere lawes in *England*, as once in *Athens
Solon* ſet downe, wée ſhoulde then caſt a rayne ouer
the head ſtrong vnrulyneſſe of theſe Caterpillers: there
it was not lawfull, the Father béeing liuing, that a-
nye money ſhoulde bée lent vnto the ſonne: who béeing vnder his Fathers gouernement, was not to bée
ordered according to his owne lyking: and there who-
ſoeuer did tranſgreſſe this lawe, it was ordayned that
hée might haue no recouerye, nor bée reléeued anye
waye by iuſtice, for that it was doubted, that the ſonne
hauing no wayes to aunſwere that hée did owe, ſhould
eyther be inforced by practiſing coniurations in the Ci-

E. tie,

tie, or exercifing priuye thefte in his Fathers houfe, to ridde and difcharge himfelfe of the burthen of his debte.

The *Aegyptians* and *Athenians* féeing the errour of couetous vfurie to take footing in their prouinces, by approued iudgement concluded, that by no inftrument, plea, execution, or other meanes in lawe, a bodie might bée detained: the originall béeing for corrupt gaines.

The *Romanes*, who not onelye inuented, but imitated thofe Lawes which confounded errour, by decrée of Senate, (with the *Athenians*,) in the very fame tearmes as they, didde fette downe, that no money fhould bée lent to young heyres vppon intereft, neyther allowing the detinue pleadable, nor the vfurie aunfwerable, hauing a priuate eye into the vnmeafurable and gréedie intents of thofe couetous carles, who compaffe the Fathers landes before the Sonne come to it.

In the Lawe of the twelue Tables, orders in this caufe were prefcribed, and directions fet downe by the Tribunes: among whome, a man of rare vertue, *Lucius Genutius* inftituted and made a law, where in he enacted, that no vfurie, nor vfurers fhoulde bée allowed.

Lucius Lucullus féeing this errour alreadye creapt thorough all *Afia*, and (lyke a wife gouernour) wylling to preuent, not onelye made a Law to auoyde all occafion of vnlawfull gaines, but alfo appoynted punifhmentes to thofe that were fubiect to the errour.

Tiberius Cæfar as curious as the reft for common good, didde with as greate circumfpection as might bée, take awaye the caufe, and difplace the effecte of this mifchiefe; not fuffering that to take
heade

heade in his gouernement, that was the capytall
enimie of a well ordered State: *Claudius Cæſar*
not yéelding to his Aunceſtours in honourable actions, renewed theſe Lawes: *Veſpatian* continued
them: and *Marcus Antonius Pius*, with *Alexander Seuerus* eſtabliſhed them with publike inſtru-
mentes: who to the fore-paſſed erroures by farther
inſight ioyned this, That by this vnlawfull getting, manye of the beſt and moſt auncient houſes
in all *Italy*, were brought to vtter ruyne, and confuſion.

The *Indians* diſdayning ſuch ſeruile attemptes, not
onely miſlikte of lending, but alſo forbad borrowing,
neither is it lawfull for an *Indian* to proffer, nor agrée-
able for one of the Nation to ſnffer iniuryes: diſdayning among them both the vſe of oblygations, and the
abuſe of pawning.

Hatefull was this errour in *Licurgus* Common
weale of *Sparta*, whereas not onely the name was o-
dious, but alſo the thing it ſelfe was aſperlye puniſhed.

Agis King of the ſame Citie, ſéeing the practiſes of
the couetous to work ſo wōderfully as they ſeemed, not
onely puniſhed the attempters of vnlawfull profite,
but alſo in the open market place, hée burnt all the
bondes and Oblygations of the rich Bankers in the
Citie.

In *Thebes* it was by ſtatute forbidden, that anye
man ſhould be put in office, that within tenne yeares
before the election had practiſed any vnlawfull chaffe-
ring.

The *Germanes* in theyr taxations of antiquitie:
whereas they bounde the Théefe to reſtore double
the thing he ſtole, they ordeyned that the vſurer ſhuld
make recompence foure folde for his iniurie. And in

E. ij.

bor-

borrowing the felicitie of all thefe Countries, wée are not fo happie, as to abridge thofe errours that they moft miflykt off: But héere perhappes fome curyous maintainer of vnneceffarie members will conclude, that the ftate cannot anie wayes bée hindered by anie thefe actions, inferring that the diffolution of one familie, is the fetting vp of another: which in as many vertues maye match, and with as greate value imploie it felfe in the ftate, as the other that is decayed.

Héerevnto I fhape this aunfwere, that if it bée true, that the nobilitie of the Father worketh in the childe, I cannot fée howe thefe vpftartes maye anie waies employe themfelues in honourable Actions, when as neither their aunceftours euer knewe more then their Beads, or their Fathers other then vnlawfull gaines: and howe canne it bée that where the minde onely worketh in feruile fubiects, it fhould anie waies be eleuated to attempt honourable exploits? But be it thefe forte of men are neceffarie both in thẽfelues, & for their Countrie, which cannot be concluded, in that they be broken members: yet muft they conclude by the (touchftone of truth) the Scriptures, that their neceffarineffe in this world, makes them vnneceffary for God: by whofe prefidents if they fhould leuell their lawes, I am afraid the graft wold be fo ftiffe in the bending, that it would be rather thought more neceffarie for the fewell, then worthy the correction. In the moft happieft man yᵗ euer was, whether philofopher or otherwife, I find this, yᵗ one onely blemifh in his actions hath made them ben noted for an error: now if thefe men fhuld in their enterprifes be gazde into, I feare me yᵗ as in the black Iet is féene no white: in the deadlye poifon is founde no preferuatiue: in the fprouting iuie, no fruite: on the vnneceffarie thiftle no grapes: fo in thefe men the mifchiefe

chiefe woulde be ſo manifeſt, that the ſhew of vertue would be extinguiſhed. So that I can neceſſarily conclude this, that both theſe ſorte of men are vnneſſarye for thcmſelues, vnméete for their countrey, vnfit for a family, yea conuenient for nothing, but to preſent the painter with the true image of couetouſnes. For themſelues how can they be profitable, in deſtroying theyr ſoules, and martering their bodies? in conſuming themſelues with thought, in deuiſing of newe attemptes to delude. If they compare but their hearts ſorrow, with their exceſſe gain, they ſhall finde this moſt certain, that the encombrances of the minde are ſo peyſant, that they doo by oddes weigh downe their commoditie in the ballaunce. What is it to get good, and to looſe happineſſe? to enioye much riches, and little reſt? to haue manye Lordſhips, and much hart-breake? Alas, what are the goods of fortune, that they ſhould entice? or the pleſures of the fleſh, that they ſhould allure? If our ſtately pallaices were to continue permanent, if our worldly riches were to make our after yeares renowmed, if euery thouſand of our ducates, were to benefit vs but with a hundred good precepts: I wold beare with couetouſnes with the beſt, & practiſe it with the moſt: but ſince we ſée that much hording cannot be without ſinne, much getting without griefe, much profite without paine, much increaſe of goods, without decreaſe of vertues, I cannot but conclude with the philoſophers, that the hoording vp of riches maketh many impreſſions of vices. And that thoſe that are no wayes profitable for themſelues, are not worthy the names of citizens in a ſtate: whereas, when all things ſhould be limitted by vertue, how can vſury be winkt at, when it is no way legitimate. Our lawes in this ſtate, although they ſuffer a commoditie, yet confirme not they taking: concluding héerein, a meruaylous pollicye: to thoſe haue in ſight, which is,

that leauing it euident, that where neither Lawe of
God can limit them, nor difpofing of right fuffer them,
nor preuention of errours withdrawe them from punifhing this error, and not letting it flip they as willyng
to pul away by péece-meals, not to confound altogether:
like wife Surgions eate out the dead flefh, by fundrye
plaifters, and no fodaine corofiue, thereby wifely warning the wife to pull back by curtefie, and the indurate
by beholding their forberance, to feare the fcourge when
it fhal come.

Yet fome will héere adde and inferre, (though
vnneceffarily,) that thofe whom I héere fo afperlye re-
prehend, are as religious as the beft, haunt the Church
with the moft, at their buriall be as bountifull as the
godlieft, and therefore it may not be thought, that féeing
fo many goods, they fhould follow the bad. To whom I
aunfwere, If they heare correction of fin by often haun-
ting of fermons, yet continue their wickedneffe, when
they know what it worketh: their actions are wicked,
their liues diffolute, their endes defperate. For theyr
bountie at their burialls, that is but their laft action, &
their beft attempt: but if we looke into the confiderati-
ons of their benificence, I doubt not but we fhall finde
whereas their fhooe wringeth them. If they are liberall
to leaue them a memorie when they are gone, alas they
ftriue againft the ftreame: for this it will fall out, perhaps they fhal haue a few poore womēs praiers for their
blacke gownes, but a thoufande decayed Gentlemens
curfes for their high exactions. If they be bounteous in
hope to recompence y^t which is paft, alas it is as much,
as to caft water to ftop a gappe, or gather brambles to
builde mannor houfes. If wée but lookt into in this their
penie doale, we fhall finde a kinde of impulfion in all
thinges: Truely, truely, I feare mée, if Mas vfurer
knewe

knewe he fhoulde liue, hée had rather haue a fayre pawne for his foure nobles, then a thoufand prayers of a poore woman: and the forfaiture of a Leafe for his xx. poundes, then the funerall Epitaph of the vniuerfities for his laft willes liberalitie. Since theretore impulfion forceth them to be bounteous, not frée will liberall, we muft accompt of them thus that they are both vnworthie praife, being vnwilling to be bountifull, and little to bée eftéemed of, though their pretence bée neuer fo perfeét. What praife deferueth he that will proffer medicines to a whole bodie? or the fpur to a willing horfe? or the raine to an vnwildie colt? or honor to a peruerfe man: fhall we conclude, becaufe yᵉ vfurer is rich, he is righteous? Becaufe wealthie? Wife: becaufe ful of golde, therefore godly? I feare me it wil fall out, that fome of our fcrape penies, are as worthie to be deliuered to perdition, as *Sauanacola* of *Rome,* of whom *Marulus* maketh mētion) who not fatiffied with exceffiue gain in his life time, at his death became a praie to diuells: It gréeueth me to confider of yᵉ vnhappie ftate of fome, who like fine cloth are deuoured with thefe moths, like white cambricke are ftained with thisyron mould: like filly birds, are deceiued with the call of this Fowler. O vnhappy ftate, ftaind with fo vnprofitable members, whofe féete tread the wayes of errours, mindes imagine mifchiefe, heartes are indurate, confounding the fatherleffe, oppreffing the widow, making all poore, and themfelues onely rich.

A lamentable cafe it is, to fée howe true fimplicitie, the maintainer of peace, is almoft altogether exiled out our common weale: and that worldlye wit doeth wade fo farre, as heauenlye wife are brought into admiration of their mifchiefe. In other notable Gouernementes and common weales, this one vice hath hadde a fall, and héere where it
fhould

fhould be moft detefted, it is moft vfed. Great hath bene
our wifdomes in repreffion of côfpiracies, great our policies in maintaining of peace, circumfpeĉt our preuēti-
ons to efchew mutinies: and yet the long time we haue
laboured in this, yet dayly more and more it groweth
to head: and whereas the other vices haue bene exterminated by good looking to, this (though altogether loa-
thed) is moft lookt after. And in this cafe I muft appeale
to you (right Honorable) whofe wifedome is continually imployed, to the maintenaunce of our ftate: & craue
you caft your eye afide, and but looke into the worlde a
lyttle, lette your Herauldes Bookes be fpied into, confider the ftate that hath bene, and now is: and I feare
me there will fome teares fall, and more care be conceiued. Alas I know it well, that many auncient coates
will be found there vncountenaunced, and it is to bée
found out, that fome flêepe on their beddes of downe,
in thofe mannor houfes, which were builded for the
ftaye of fome of our beft noble feigniors. Nay, is it not
true, that more are eaten out with vfury, then anye o-
ther abufe whatfoeuer? And although Commiffions are
gracioufly graunted from her Maieftie, as a moft mer-
cifull Prince, and from your Honors, as moft fage, fatherly, and prudent tenderers of gentry, grown into pouertie: yet fuch is the contempt of fome men, as they
neither meafure commaund, nor haue refpeĉt to confcience. The reuerend Fathers and eyes of Religion in
this Common weale, how exclaime they on this vice,
and pronounce the wrathfull threates of the Almightie
againft thefe vngracious gatherers? yet how flenderly
they regard them, their manifeft & notorious mifchiefes
beare record. So that it is to be feared, that when neither
honourable command may controll them, nor diuine admonition reclaime them, they are growen into a reprobate fenfe, and hane forfaken the Law of the Lord, and
hunted after the whore, and are dronken with the ly-
cour

cour of her abhominations.

Principijs obſta ſero medicina paratur,
Cum mala per longas inualuere moras.

Noble Lords, may it pleaſe you yet a little more to giue me leaue, that as I haue manifeſted the miſchelfe, ſo (to my ſlender conceit) I may imagine a ſalue. The Nobilitie, Gentrie, and other heires whatſoeuer, either by reaſon of their Fathers tenour are wardes vnto her Maieſtie, or elſe by the tender prouiſion of their Parents, they are lefte to the diſcretion of their kinſſolke. For thoſe that by her Maieſties prerogatiue, by ye death of their Fathers, fall into her protection: the moſt part of them are begged by Gentlemen, and committed to their tuition: among whome, as there be ſome prouident and carefull to conſider of the childes commoditie, ſo (I feare me) other ſome are ſelfe minded, and gréedie of their owne gaine: which if ſo be it fall out, I feare me the childe that is vnder this gouernment will happely miſcarrie, for if maintenance come from the protector ſlenderly, the nature of the youth béeing noble, will couet after ſupplie, and ſo through the couetouſnes of the one, growes the confuſion of the other, and by this meanes growes ye Gentleman into ye Merchants booke in arrerages, when his warden furniſheth him not according his degrée and calling: but it may be, that there bée purpoſes imagined by the gouernour, and practiſed by the Merchaunt, ſo that the one will not bée pertaker of the ſhame, yet will he not ſticke to beare part of the gaine. But to let further matters wittingly ouerſlip, for that I finde it good to winke at ſomewhat: returne we to the other ſortes of heires, lefte to the tuition of friendes: among whome there growe lyke inconueniences, as in the former: for nowe a dayes kinſfolkes are as couetous as others, and as craftye as the beſt, whoſe priuate conueyaunces the young heires knowe, and ſeuerallye when they be ſought into, will

F. open.

open. But for the ordering of all thefe thinges, and
the recouering of this ftate, it were conuenient that
the Warden of the Wardes vnder her Maiefties protection, fhould at the receit of the Gentleman, be bound
according to the value, to the honourable, that
haue authoritie in that cafe, for the vfage of the Gentleman, and that certaine ftipend might be fet downe an-
nuallye for his prouifion, rather with the moft then
leaft, fo that then it will fall out, that hauing fufficient
of his owne, he will not depend on the fupplie of an
other. The like annimaduertion if it bée had in refpect
of the other, and the care of taking the bonds, and prefixing the portion fet downe by the direction of certaine
Iuftices of peace in euerie fhéere, we fhoulde haue leffe
complaints to trouble your honours, and merchauntes
fhould want young minifters to ridde them of their refufe cōmoditie. I haue glaunced into a matter (my good
Lord) which if wifdome confideratly looke into, there
will growe an exquifite platforme. Thefe caufes right
honourable are neceffarie, and needfull to be noted, and
fuch they be, that no doubt they will be as beneficiall to
the ftate, as anie other whatfoeuer: For by this meanes
your honours fhall be praifed, the wardens wel thought
of, the Gentlemen kept in good ftate, and the Merchant
abridgde of his craftie dealings. I haue heard this caufe
lamented of among the moft part of that profeffion, who
loth their title fhould be attributed to fo outragious
dealers. If they will defire the name, let them vfe the
nature, & let not all the whole order bée blemifhed, by
a few difordered dealers blame: but to leaue this to your
honourable and graue confideration, and to returne to
your curteous Gentlemen, to whome this matter moft
pertaineth, & for whofe onely caufe this pain is taken: I
moft earneftly befées you looke into your owne ftates,
& confider with your felues, the mifery & mifchiefe that
groweth by thefe follies: confider yᵉ end of all thefe practifes,

tiſes which the vſurers doe put in vre, forſooth it is to
make you beggers, where now your ſupplies be plentifull, & to emptie your purſes, where now they are repleniſhed: conſider of their mercy, either it is impriſonment,
or elſe libertie with more ſhame: weygh of their ends
agréeing to theyr life: it was a pretie and wittie ſaying
which was written,

Auaro quid mali optes ni vt viuat diu.

Wiſh a couetous man no more miſchiefe, then that
he may liue long. For he dieth daily in care, and con-
ſumeth in thought: refraine prodigalitie, ſo ſhall you
haue no néed of thē: bée continent, ſo ſhall you be ſought
to of them: leaue them to their owne luſts, they are not
of yᵉ Lord: let your garments be comely, & not coſtly: for
a comly continent man is more eſtéemed of, then a coſtly ſpende thrifte accompted of. It is the vertues of
your mindes, the perfeꞔtions of your vnderſtandinge,
your intelleꞔtuall contemplacions, that makes you accounted of among the wiſe, and beloued among the
learned: In your profeſſions be ſtudious, for yᵗ brings
profit: an houre well ſpent, is better then a dayes pleaſure: eſchew thoſe things that may decay your memory, & in euery good aꞔtion cōtinue to the end: truſt not to
apparant goodes, beléeue not creduloudly yᵉ faire ſpoken,
be as prouident to eſchew trouble, as the enuious is
prudent to procure your diſcomfort: looke on nothing
that may altar you from a man, thinke on nothing that
may miſlead you, if you promiſe, performe it, but in promiſing vſe diſcreation: theſe be the fruites of expery-
ence, learnt by ſome in ſorrowe, and lette them bee
praꞔtiſed by you in ſecuritie. Let not the gariſh ſhew of
a preſent pleaſure, the ſillie ſhadowe of an earthlye
delyght, a tranſitorie ſimilitude of a momentanye
glorye, make you followe that which wyll coſte
you manye ſighes and ſundrye ſorrowes (when
you looke into your ſtate, and ſee howe you are

F. ij.   compaſ-

compaffed of friendes, fmilde vpon by fortune, beautified by nature, pefe&ted by art, when you perceiue care
hath not yet forrowed your forhead: labour euen then
to continue friendes, to make peace with fortune, to
mainetaine nature, to ftudye arte, and béeing fréed
as yet from trouble, fence your a&tions fo ftrong, as they
may neuer become troublefome. *Aurelius* in his Court
féeing certaine Philofophers vfing vnféemely ieftures,
wagging their heads, toying with theyr garments, and
ftamping with their féete, gathering by their exteriour
behauiour, how vnapt their a&tions were in refpe&t of
their precepts, expulfed them the court, as vnméete to be
preferred to honours. Although not *Marcus Aurelius*,
but wife *Saba* now gouerning, think you that gracious
Elizabeth cannot as well finde out a vain head vnder a
wauing feather, a diffolute minde vnder a codpéece dub-
let, a wanton thought vnder a ftraunge habite, as the
Emperour vnder a lyght iefture? Yes truely (Gentlemen): no doubt but that eie y^t winketh at moft things,
féeth many, and that wonderfull capacitie that compre-
hendeth fo much difcipline, cannot ouerflip the miflyke
of mafking brauerie. If one errour were as much banifhed *England*, as it was *Rome*, neither fhould idleneffe offer the couetous opportunitie, neither the idle
be coufened by the couetous. It is idleneffe that maketh amorous, it is idleneffe that maketh fafcionatiue,
it is idleneffe that bréedes exceffe, it is idleneffe that
deftroyeth all humane happineffe, the eye fixed on
heauenlye contemplations, gazeth not on earthlye
beautie, the thought occupyed on remembrance of moral
preceptes, neuer vouchfafe the mifdéemings of the fantafie: ye bodie fubdued by affidious trauaile, is neuer altered by the motions of the flefh: the hope grounded on
immortality, hath not reference to an houres pleafures.
So that man is neuer altered in himfelf, enimie of himfelfe, procurer of his parents troubles: but euen then
chief-

chiefly, whē idlenes is predominant, follypreferred, & faſhions to féed, fantaſies allowed of. The meanes then to
auoyd the Vſurers booke, is to be continent: the way to
be continent, is not to be idle: the reward of not béeing
idle, is the daily increaſe of more knowledge: and the
increaſe of more knowledge maketh a man happie. The
ſting of the Aſpe confoundeth in ſlumbers, the venome
of idleneſſe, waiteth careleſſe opportunities: truly gentlemen, the firſt ſtep to auoyd expence, is to grow in contempt of brauerie, which if our noble younge youthes
wold practiſe for a while, it wold ſo fall out, yᵗ not onely
vaine fantaſies ſhould ceaſe, fonde faſhions finde no fa-
uourers, and the vſurer hauing his odde refuſe commodities dead id his hand, would either affoorde better pe-
niworths, or féeke for forreine traffique. But to leaue
you Gentlemen to your good counſailes, and returne to
you good maſter vſurers, whoſe eares glowe at the re-
hearſall of theſe enormities, I muſt pray you giue mée
leaue to make vp a concluſion, and to finiſh theſe fewe
lines with an admonition for your cauſe, and though
the corrections I vſe be bitter, account of them the better, for why they be more cordiall. A gréedie deſire of
gayne, is the diſeaſe that infecteth you, ſome termes it
thriftineſſe, ſome néerneſſe, but in plaine tearmes, it is
vſurie: and that is nought els but a gréedie deſire of o-
ther mens goods, and this by the commandement is forbidden to be followed, and therefore irreligious are they
that vſe it. The man that coueteth gold, conceiueth not
goodneſſe, his appetite is of the earth, and thoſe that are
earthly minded, fauour not the things that are of God.
What though you cloath your ſelues in ſimplicitie of
Doues, and your inwarde habite be worſe then the vo-
cacite of Wolues, he that made you knoweth you, and
he whom you offend can (and will) puniſh you: you wil
ſay you were naturally borne, (as *Tully* witneſſeth) to
take care for your ſelues, and to prouide *Victum* & ve-
F. iij.   *ſtitum,*

ſtitum, meate and clothing: and I graunt it, but where find you, either Ethnike, prophane, or ſacred ſentence, to confirme your extreame hoording vp of golde, yea then moſt earneſtly, when you are moſt rich? The labourſome Ant gathereth not in exceſſe, but ſufficient prouiſion for the Winter, yet without reaſon: and you which are reaſonably borne, hoorde vp more, then orderly (at firſt ſight) you well knowe howe to imploy. You long after *Nabals* vineyard with *Ieſabel*, but the dogs ſhall deuour you in the gate: you heape houſe vpon houſe, land vpon land, *Quaſi numquam ſit periturum ſæculum*, as though this world would laſt euer, but ſodainly ſhal the wrath and curſe of the Lord fall vpon you, and (without ſpéedie repentaunce) he will conſume you in a moment. O turne ſpéedely vnto the Lord, and put not off from daie to daie, leaſt his wrath be hot againſt you, and he make you pertakers of the plagues of *Chore* and *Abiram*. Remember your olde eſcapes that haue paſt you, conſider of their falls that are decayed by you, and your ſelues if you haue anie contrition, and compunction of heart, wil lament the generall misfortune with me. Did you ariſe of nothing? Were you calde from baſe degrée to high eſtate? From poore ſeruants wer you made rich maſters? Why, your goods make anſwere, ſaying, you haue more then you can well ſpend, and I déeme the greater your talent is, the more you haue to anſwere for: but weigh in your ſelues, howe this greate maſſe of money grew vnto you: you muſt count that this Farme came to your handes by the forfayture of ſuch a Leaſe: this money became yours, by the vertue of ſuch an Obligation: you haue ſcrapte vp this ready coyne, by making *Centum pro cento*: nay, you haue vndone theſe manye poore Gentlemen, onely by inriching your ſelfe. Too true it is, (alas) (and wiſedome priuately bewaileth it, to looke into your crueltie, and Gentlemens folly) that

ma-

many houfes are decayed by yonr meanes, and that
you are Lords of that, which fhould be the portion of
more profitable fubiects: whofe miferie driueth them to
trie conclufions in all places: and both to forfake their
Countrey, I pray God not to alter their confcience.
Nay in thefe extremities that they are driuen into,
which of you either reléeueth them? or comforteth them
in their forrowes? fo farre are you (you worldlings) frō
leffening their miferies, as that (*Perillus* like) you inuent new tortures, to driue them from your doores, calling them vacabonds, and bride well birdes: who in
very truth were your beft Mafters and fetters vp, but
your felues with *Perillus* fhall taft of the engines you
haue prouided for others, and the Lorde fhall pittie the
fatherleffe, and comfort the afflicted, when that dread-
full daye fhall come, in which the heauens fhall be opened, and the Sonne of man fhall come to iudgement:
how will the cafe then ftand with you? fhall your welth
then acquite you? No, no, the Iudge is not partiall, he
is iuft in all his dooings, and true in all his fayings.
In that day the horrour of your confcience fhall condemne you, Sathan whom you haue ferued fhall accufe
you, the poore afflicted members of Chrift fhall beare
witneffe agaynft you, fo that in this horror and confufion, you fhall defire the mountaines to fall vpon you,
and the hils to couer you from the fearfull indignation
of the Lord of hoftes, and the dredfull condemnation of
the Lambe Iefus. When it fhalbe found out, that you
wer rich, yet reléeued none: that you were of wealth, yet
comforted none: that you rather replenifhed the prifons,
then releafed the prifoner: that your life be found fawced with crueltie, and no one action fauoring of mercie:
the Lord fhal place you among the goates, & pronounce
his *Ve* againft you, he fhall thunder out this fentence,
Goe you curfed into euerlafting fire, prepared for the
diuell

diuell and his angeles. This is the reward of wickedneffe, this is the punifhment of crueltie: looke vpon this
therefore (you worldly minded men,) and confider of
thefe fayings: harden not your hearts, but be you con-
uerted, reléeue the poore, be harbourfome, reftore to the
owner that you haue wrefted from him, and turne,
turne, turne vnto the Lord (I beféech you) leaft you perifh in your owne abhominations: and to conclude, accompt of me as your wel wifher, who for publike commoditie haue opened your inconueniences, and for brotherly amitie, counfailed you to call your felues home:
and I beféech you as fpéedely reclaime you from your
errors, as I doo brotherly admonifh you of your efcapes.
How happie were I that hauing leffe caufe, might haue
leffe matter to write on? And hapleffe are you, if not
won with thefe warnings, you giue more occafion to be
written on: now ftay you where you are, & alter your
natures, and where you were accuftomed to doo ill, now
acquaint your felues to follow goodnes, and then it will
thus fal out, that I which exclaimed vpon you for your
vices, will then honour you for your vertues: & where
in common affemblies your name growes odious in
publike audience, you maye be praifed for your good
life. The Lord fend our Gentlemen more wit,
our vfurers more confcience, and vngodli-
neffe a fall: fo Nobilitie fhall not decay, but the finner fhal be reclai-
med, and wickednes con-
founded.

FINIS.

¶THE DELECTABLE

Hiſtorie of Forbonius and
Priſceria.

IN *Memphis* (the chiefeſt citie of *Aegypt*) a place moſt renowmed by reaſon of the opulencie of the princes that haue gouerned that Monarchie: at ſuch time as *Siſimithres* was head Prieſt of the ſame, & *Hidaſpes* gouernour of the Prouince, a noble Gentleman called *Forbonius* (highly accounted of for his vnreprouable proweſſe, and among the beſt ſort allowed of for his vnſpekable vertues) made his abode, whoſe tender yeares not yet ſubieɛt. to the experience of more riper iudgement (as the winding Iuie about the ſtately Oke) entangled it ſelfe with many amorous obieɛts, now allowing this choice, now approuing yᵗ perſon, ſtraight admitting a third. But the fates hauing regiſtred his laſt opiniō in euerlaſting & permanent deſtinie, made his manifolde aſpeɛtes (as yet not ſtayed) to light vpon one ſeemely impreſſion, and to allow of but one onely paragon: yet ſo ſealed they his opinion, as (if it be true that the gods euer were laſciuious) I thinke the chiefeſt commaunder of the Heauens might vouchſafe of ſuch dalliance, and be onely amorous in this, that knowing heauenly perfeɛtions to be reſident in earthly ſubſtance, he would either borrow fire of *Venus* to make the creature pliable, or carrie fire into the heauens from whēce *Promotheus* firſt did ſteale lightning. Fauorable

G.   was

was the climate, that allowing vniuerſally to all the creatures it compaſſed onely, blackneſſe, vouchſafed *Priſceria* (*Forbonius* miſtres) ſuchſwéet fauor, who borne of noble parents within the citie, (as of *Solduuius*, vizeroie of that Prouince adioyning to the citie, and *Valduuia*, daughter and heire of *Theagines* of *Greece*, the cōpartener of ſorrowe with *Caricleala*, the ſtraunge borne childe of the *Aegyptian* king:) not onely match al titles of honour with exquiſiteneſſe of proportion, but alſo ſo coupled the perfections of the minde, with the proportion of the bodie, as rather nature might diſdaine her induſtrye, not art repent her of the dowrie ſhe had granted her: this ſwéet fixed Comet coaſted *Forbonius* affectiōs, who like the careful Marriner, hauing (amidſt the froſtie night) ſought for his Loade ſtarre, and at breake of morning (his eies almoſt dazled with looking) found it out: ſo our noble young Gentleman, hauing paſt ouer many perſonages wᵗ a ſlight ouer looke, at laſt finding out his miſtres alotted him by fate, yéelded willinglye vnto importunitie of the Deſtinies, and wonne altogether to bée ſubiect, béeing captiued with fancie, hée applyed himſelfe wholye to the accompliſhment of his deſires, and the attainment of his miſtreſſe fauour: and for that the Goddeſſe of loue is plyable to all benignitie, as not ſuffering a true ſeruitour to bée long vnrewarded: it ſo fortuned, that ſhe proſperouſly furthered our noble *Aegyptian* in his purpoſe, preferring him by opportunitie to the ſight of his deſired pleaſures: for the propinquitie of their abode was ſuch, as that *Priſcerias* chamber windowe, had a proſpect into *Forbonius* garden, by which meanes, the Gentleman in his meditations might beholde his miſtres, and *Priſceria* (béeing by the equitie of the deſtinies prefigurated to ſtraunge miſſortune) might haue occaſion to looke, and féeing, might loue: but as this conueniencie was fauourable one waie, ſo was the frowarde diſpoſition of the

the parents, vntoward on the other parte for *Solduuius*,
whether lead thereto by appointment, or driuen to the
exigent, by fome former mallice borne by the progeni-
tors of *Forbonius*: had neither a lyking to the youth, nor
a longing to haue his daughter marryed: eyther lead
by couetoufneffe, for that he woulde not ftreffe his coffers, or by enuie, for that he contemned *Forbonius*: yet
what is concludąd fecretly amidft the heauens, cannot
be circumuented with mans circumfpeétion: for *Forbonius* as one which depended onely on the fauour of
Prifceria, though fortune had bereft him of occafion to in-
ioy, yet would not he be feuered from the benefite to beholde her whom he loued: who warmed with the fame
fire, in increafing his flame, kindled her owne fancie, &
being as willing as the other to procure remedie to her
paffion, with manye chaunge of coulours, and fundrye
fwéete afpeéts, opened that to her feruant, which he wifhed for in his miftres: who (with like forrowes requiting euerie circumftance) as one willing and borne to
attempt: at fuch time as *Prifceria* folitarily folaced her
felfe at her windowe: in mournefull melodye (making
his Lute tunable to the ftraine of his voice) he recorded
this Sonet.

THE Turtle pleafed with his fhe compeare,
    With fweet afpeéts, and many a turning lure,
Defcribes the zeale in tearmes fhould well appeare,
    If nature were fo gratious to affure
The filly bird with fpeech as well as I:
Who ftopt of fpeech by turnes my woes defcrie.

And though perhaps my tearmes by diftance be,
    Seaioynd from thee: I wis my mournfull mone,
Doth pearce thine eares, and Eccho tells for me,
    In fowre reports: would fhe and I were one.
                    G. ii.   For

For whom I liue, and whom I onely loue,
Whofe fweet afpects my dying fancies moue.

And if the aire by yeelding calme confent.
    Make fweet Prifceria priuie to my fuite,
Vouchfafe deere fweet, that beautie may relent,
    And graunt him grace, whom diftance maketh mute:
So either hope fhall make me climbe the skie,
Or rude repulfe enforce my fancies flie.

    Prifceria not altogether priuie to the report, yet con-
cluding all purpofes to hir owne fantafie, conceyuing
by his manifolde fighes, afpectes, and motions, where-
vnto he applyed his actions, with a folempne fighe, as
wifhing him prefent, and a féemely bent, as requiting
his curtefie, betooke hir felfe to hir pillowe, where comparing euerye accident together, both of the zeale fhée
bare to *Forbonius*, and of the profer he proffered to her,
fhe brake out into thefe fpéeches.
    Alaffe (vnhappie *Prifceria*) what vntoward deftinie
hath befallen thée? That in thy flowring yeares and
prime of beautie, thou art become a thrall to vncertaine
pleafure, neyther knowing from whence the errour
firft fprong, nor by what Treacles it may at laft bée
expelled. If it bée that nature enuying my perfections hath allotted mée this purgatorie, that hauing
at frée becke all the benefites of Fortune, yet I
fhould with inwarde bondes bée inchained with the
holdefaft of fancie. Alaffe that in prefixing the torment, fhée hath not proffered a remedye, or in beftowing an vlcer, hath not vouchfafed a corrafiue. Howe
ftraungely am I martyred, fillye maide that I am?
That by one onelye looke haue conceyued fuch an impreffion, as neyther arte can alter with medicine, nor
time eate out with continuaunce.
    Woe is mée that I loue, yet fortunate am I
                            that

that I hate not, for by the one, I am depriued of lybertie: by the other, I fhall onerpaffe the forrow by fureneffe. Yet are thy thoughts more fauorable to thée *Prifceria*, then the fucceffe in thy loue will be fortunate. Thou louelt *Forbonius*, and why? for his vertue: yet thy father hateth him vpon olde grudges, with whom when rancour preuayleth, what may be more lookt for, then contempt and denyall? But *Forbonius* féeketh *Prifcerias* fauor, not *Solduuius* friendfhip: but *Prifceria* cannot enioy *Forbonius*, without *Solduuius* fauor. But *Forbonius* will by happie marriage conclude all mallice, but thy father hauing an enuious mind, will haue a fufpitious eare. Alas why imagine I wonders in my fancy, hoping that thofe deftenies (which inthralled my affeftion) wil fubieft my fathers refolutions: fince neither reafon alloweth me any probablitie to worke vpon, neither hath *Forbonius* any motion as I fée to compaffe ought: well, to the fatiffaftion of my friend, and to the contentment of my forrowing hart: my freend fhall know my zeale, and I will continue my affeftion, which being begun with fo wonderfull caufes, muft néedes finifh with a miraculous effeft.

With thefe conclufions fhe fell a fléepe, leauing me, to returne to *Forbonius*, who being tormented with the fame furie, and troubled with equall fancie, féeing his light to be eclipfed, I meane his Miftreffe vanifhed, began heauely to complaine himfelfe in thefe or fuch lyke termes.

Alas you deftinies, whofe courfes are ineuitable: how fortuneth it, that in beftowing cafualities in mās life, you prefcribe not meanes to preuent miffortunes? and onelye beginning to fefter the heart, prefixe no prefidents, whereby the humours may be expelled. If all things are to be referred vnto an ende, what may I wel imagine of my eftate? who intercepted by all occafions, muft either finifh my miffortunes miferably, or defpe-

G. iij.

rate-

rately. O loue, iuſtly maiſt thou be counted licentious, whereas thou neither preſcribeſt limites to thy ſelfe, to inthrall: nor meanes to thy ſubiects to attain libertie. But why exclaime I on him, that hath bleſt me with a benefit? as though the fate that made *Forbonius* happie in louing, cannot eſtabliſh his ſucceſſe, as that it ſhall not be meaſured by miſfortune. I glorie in the benefit of my martirdome, ſince a certain inward hope aſſureth me, that diuine beautie cannot be ſequeſted from iuſt pittie, nor a tried ſeruice in loue, requited with a diſ-dainfull hate. But fooliſh man that I am, howe maye it be, that in ſéeking beautie, I labour not to attaine it? & deſiring to enioy a benefit, I attempt not to make triall of my Miſtreſſe bountie? Why, by laſt nights becke ſhe vouchſafed ſome ſhew of acceptaunce: and that may as well be of reproofe as lyking. (O *Forbonius,*) it is a ſil-ly hope that is conceiued by ſignes, either attempt fur-ther, or perſwade thy ſelfe of no fauour. Her father (ſil-ly wretch) enuieth thée, and thinkeſt thou to compaſſe his daughter? alas, faint hope is this when as thoſe that ſhould build vp, doo deſtroy: when ſuch as ſhoulde per-ſwade, doo diſſwade: when as he that dooth commaund moſt earneſtly, dooth forbid. But loue hath no reſpect of conſanguinitie, but hauing onely relation to him which he fauoureth, delighteth onely in the poſſeſſion of his choyce, yet is not *Forbonius,* ſure ſhe loueth: well, I ſée he that will be fortunate, muſt hazard, and that man that will be gracious in his Miſtreſſe eye, muſt by out-ward attempts and vnaccuſtomed purpoſes, ſéeke to con-firme his happineſſe.

Wherevpon (vpon ſundry concluſions) he inferred thus, that the next day, by certaine rare attemptes, hée would either finiſh that he had ſo long ſought for, or pe-riſh in the perfourmance of his enterpriſe: and the day ſeruing to attempt that which he imagined by night, he bethought himſelfe of the *Gymnoſophiſts* of yᵉ coun-trey,

trey, among whom remembring one of fingular experience, and notable lerning, he reforted vnto him, opening
firft, how he was inthralled by fancie, how precluded by
all occafions, efpecially by the fathers difdaine, next, how
fome opportunitie ferued him, laftly how the agony tormented him, defiring the Philofopher, whofe wifedome
coulde fée into all caufes, to fearch out the fatall Exigent of his loue. *Appollonius* (for fo the *Gymnofophift*
was called) hauing calculated the Gentlemans natiui-
tie, and féeing fome planets retrogate: couering the afperitie of the deftenies, with the hidden fecrecie of an
Artift, difcourfed thus.

O *Forbonius*, if as *Socrates* did his golde, thou drown
thy affeétions, it would follow that with him thou fhuldeft enioy frée libertie of thy felfe, and not fuffer thy af-
feéts to rule thy reafon. Art thou bewitched by *Circes*?
of a humane fhape haft thou gotten a beaftly forme? of
a man borne to reafonable aétions, wilt thou now fwallow an vnreafonable miffortune? If many cares be the
decayers of the minde, if many forrowes the confumers
of the body, better were it by day to ftudie the lyberall
Sciences, then at fuch time as we fhoulde imploye our
felues to honourable attempts, to become vnhonourably
licentious. Alas *Forbonius* confidering what a louer is,
what a louer fuffereth, what a louer féeketh, I finde the
perfon idle minded, I finde his patience an infupporta-
ble forrow, I finde himfelfe not himfelfe, in y^t he is vnreafonable. The daily aétions of a louer are difcommen-
dable, the night exclamations fo odious, as that they in
this cōuert nature, who fhadowing ye world with dark-
nes, limitting each creature his reft, yet they euen in y^t
time labor in out-cries, in which they fhuld take conuenient reft. My good friend, ye greteft wifdome is to meafure euery attēpt w^t his cafualties, & if ought happen y^t
may féeme impoffible, to caft off the rayne, and fuffer
it to paffe in that forme it was concluded in.

                                                    Thou

Thou loueſt (*Forbonius,*) better wer it thou didſt loath: for by loathing thou canſt but be compted vnnaturall, but by louing thou mayſt fortune to be vnfortunate. If all thinges be ordered by the higher powers, it is vayne you muſt conclude to infringe what is concluded on, if the deſtenies haue appoynted; that *Forbonius* ſhall not be happie in inioying *Priſceria, Forbonius* is not reaſoning in ſuing for *Priſceria.* Vnhappie *Paris* in *Helen,* though fortunate in inioying her beautie: but when loue begins with a fading benefit, it endeth with an euerlaſting ſorrow. The concluſion of a wiſe man muſt be, to yéelde to the neceſſitie of Fate, and to continue contented with that which cannot be altered by ſucceſſion. Tell me by the immortall Gods, my good friend I beſéech thée, what happines conceiueſt thou poſſible to follow, either in enioying thy Lady, or finiſhing thy loue? Alas, the greateſt ſwéete is a continuall ſower, and after many vnfortunate repulſes, a ſodain miſfortune makes an ende of many a yeeres courting. I ſpeake all this to this ende (my *Forbonius,*) becauſe I would preuent that by counſell in thée, which otherwiſe (if thou follow thine owne lure) will be a confuſion to thy ſelfe. Thou comeſt to me for counſell to compaſſe loue, and I would confirme thée, that thou ſhouldeſt auoyd the occaſions of following loue. Thou wouldeſt by my meanes ſtrayne arte to ſubdue nature, yet I labour both to direct by arte, and to ſuppreſſe by nature. Truly (my good friend) looking but to the hidden ſecretes of nature, I finde thée ſubiect to manye miſfortunes, and no way to be remedied but by one only vertue. Thou ſhalt (after long toyles) compaſſe that thou hopeſt for, yet when thy greateſt pleſures begin to take the originall: euen then ſhall they finde their exigent. Since therfore the reuolutions of the heuens conclude, that by onely continent forbearaunce, thou ſhalt be diſburdened of many miſfortunes, I beſéech thée lette this tranſi-

tranfitorie pleafure be accompted off as it is, and finifh
vp thy loue with my counfell: fo fhalt thou be fortunate
in preuenting deftenie, and continue in happines, wher
too much loue may make thee vnluckie.

Forbonius lead by the inconftant opinion of his young
yeares, not waying the graue and fatherly councell of
Appollonius, aunfwered him thus.

O Father, when the wound is giuen, it is ill coun-
fayling how to auoyd the ftripe, and when the heart is
captiuated, there can be but fmall recouery by counfell;
how wer it poffible for me to reftrain that in my felfe,
which the Gods could not limit in their Deities? Eafie it is for the whole Phifition to counfell the fick patient, but when yᵉ extremitie wringeth exceffiuely, none
bideth the martirdome but the afflicted. O *Appollonius* my minde meafureth not the iniquitie of fate, neyther doo I féeke limits for that, which by no direction can
be exterminated from out my heart. So that good father
rather refpect my prefent fute, then my future difcom-
moditie, and by your counfell make ende to my forrowes: whereby it will thus come to paffe, that enioying the pleafure I long wifh for, I may more boldlye
beare the affault of froward fortune when it commeth.
If it be onely death, that my enemie Fate threteneth
me with, let me enioye this benefit, as for Fortune, I
will be friende to her enemie, the which is the graue,
and acquaynting my foule but with the onely *Idea* of
my Miftreffe, thinke my felfe as happie, as they that
haue walkt by *Elifian* fieldes, a long fpace to their content.

Appollonius willing to doo him good, yet forrie hée
could not preuaile with his counfaile, at length began
thus.

Since my *Forbonius* thou wilt be ruled by no coun-
fayle, thou muft be pertaker of thine owne forrowe. As
for thy requeft, I will fo fatiffie thée, as not onely thou
fhalt

ſhalt at thy pleaſure conceiue thy Miſtreſſe minde, but alſo open vnto her the ſecrettes of thy heart, by which meanes thou ſhalt héerein haue accompliſhment of thy wiſh, though in ſo dooing thou ſhewe but lyttle wiſe-dome. Wherevpon, reſorting to his ſtuddie, he brought foorth a mirrour of notable operation, a praſticke in proſpeſtiue, which deliuering to *Forbonius*, he commended it thus.

O my friend, I deliuer thée that héere to féede thy humour, which was compoſed to comprehend Arte. In this myrrour thou maiſt after thou haſt written thy minde: taking the Sunne beame, ſend the refleſtion to thy miſtreſſe eye, wherby ſhe may as legeably read thy letters, as if they were in her handes, and by thy inſtruſtions made priuie to the ſecrets of thy glaſſe, retourne thine aunſwere in that very forme in which thou ſendeſt.

For the reſt, I leaue it to your diſcretions, and good fortune, wiſhing all things to fall out as proſperouſlye in your loue, as you would, and as I wiſh.

Our noble youth (*In amours*) hauing furniſhed himſelfe of that he ſought for, repayred vnto his ſtudie, where deuiſing in what tearmes he might follicite his Miſtres, at laſt he cyphered out his ſorrowes in this ſe-quell.

*T*Hat fancie that hath made me thrall to thy beau-tie (ſwéete *Priſceria*) commendeth my ſubmiſſion to thy good grace: beféeching thee to be as fauourable in miniſtring a remedie, as thy beautie was readie to procure my thraldome. I make no refiſt in this my louing torment, but onely yéeld my ſelf ſubieſt to yᵉ impreſſion. Maye it therefore pleaſe thée (ſwéete *Priſceria*) to be as beneficial in this, as the Gods are in their bounty, who for euery faithfull interatie, returne a gratefull ſatiſ-faſtion. And heerein maiſt thou ſée my faith to be ſted-faſt

faſt, ſince Arte it ſelfe ſerueth opportunities, and mini-
ſtreth me both a meanes to open my hidden ſorrowes,
and thée a meſſenger to bewray thy ſilent ſecrets. I beféech thée (by the ſwéete ſtatues that are builded for the
Goddeſſe that is honoured in *Paphos,*) to be as iuſt in
returning fauour, as I am forwarde in bewraying my
fancie: ſo ſhalt thou haue the poſſeſſion of him, that is
by deſtinies appoynted thy aſſured beadſ-man, and I
enioy thoſe pleſures, in which I may be only fortunate.
Till then I muſt write my ſelf as I am, The moſt vnhappieſt louer that liueth.

Forbonius.

This cyphered out in faire charećters, and diſpoſed in
ſuch termes as his fancie then prefixed him, he tooke his
way into his garden, waiting ſome neceſſarye opportunitie, to put his purpoſed attempts in praćtiſe, and to
bewray his woes to *Priſceria:* who woūded with the remembraunce of *Forbonius* perfećtions, and féeing no
waye but his preſence a meane to expell ſorrowe, betooke her ſelfe to her accuſtomed proſpećte, and with
longing lookes ſhe leuelled at his loue, which was alre-
die ſtroken with her beautie.
The Gentleman fitted by theſe conuenient occaſions beganne his Philoſophicall demonſtration, and
taking his aſpećte as neceſſarilye as hée might, hée
preſented *Priſceria* with his penſiue ſubmiſſion: who
confirmed by ſo conuenient opportunitie, betaking
her ſelfe with all ſpéede poſſible to her ſtudie, and by
a becke charging him with no leſſe diſpatch to giue at-
tendaunce: ſhe gaue annſwere to his amorous intreaties with this gracious affabilitie.

H. ij.   The

THe Climate *Forbonius* where vnder I was borne, (beléeue me) either hath prefigured me the deſtenie to be inamoured by thée, or thée the ſubieƈt that ſhoulde befot me: and truly héerein the working of the Gods are ſecret, who imploy ſuch thoughts in me, as now by thy letters I finde wrought in thée, making a vnitie in both thoſe hearts, who by reaſon of parents enuies, are like to finde fatall concluſions. And whereas by ne-ceſſitie of fate I finde my ſelfe wholly captiuated to thy pleaſures, I doubt not but that God whome wée ho-nour for his brightneſſe, and who by his lightening mi-niſtreth to our miſfortunes, will be fauourable in our procéedings. For me, if thy conſtancie be ſuch as my true zeale is, I beſéech thée by the ſame Godddeſſe to ſuccour me, by whome I found my ſelfe firſt inthralled and made ſubieƈt to thée: meane while I will write as thy ſelfe, and reſt as I am. The moſt vnhappieſt louer that lyueth.

Priſceria.

Theſe concluſions being miniſtered with the ſame aſpeƈtes they were profered, the two poore couple had no other meanes to noate the effeƈte of their priuate ioyes, but onely by ſilent ſmiles, gracious regardes, and trickelyng teares, and ſuch lyke amorous aƈtions, each one wiſhing the other, either happie in poſſeſſing their delyght, or fortunate, if by death they were reléeued of their ſorrowe: and being intercepted by the cloſure of the euening, they betooke themſelues both of them to their reſtleſſe pillowes, concluding vpon many pur-poſes, how to finiſh their languiſhing and tormenting martirdome.

Forbo--

Forbonius as one born to attempt, concluded with himfelfe, confidering how fauourably all occafions fawned
vpon him) to attempt yͤ ftealing awaie of *Prifceria*: who
poore foule in carefull dreames imagining of her dayes
fancies, was foreftaled of all fauour by the vnhappie
approch of her father, who furnifhed with all worldlye
policies to preuent what he miflyked, and compaffe that
he fufpeĉted: perceiuing by his daughters folome af-
peĉts, fome fecret forrow yͭ troubled her, hauing remembred that axiome of the Philofophers, that dreames
are the prefigurations of dayes forrowe, watched his
time fo néerely, that euen at that verie inftant he entered the chamber of his daughter, when drowned in her
fwéet delightfull dreames, fhe begā at his entrie to cry
out thus. O fortunate *Forbonius!* which her father mar-
king verie precifely, and concluding wherevpon the figh
tooke his holde faft, awaking his daughter on a fodaine,
verie cunningly compaffed her thus.

O my *Prifceria*, let it not feeme ftraunge vnto thée,
to beholde thine aged Fathers vnaccuftomable acceffe,
fince he is now perplexed with vnacquainted feares. A-
laffe my daughter, thy father féeing thée beautifull, is
not careleffe of thy comfort, neither can he that laboured to bring thée to lyght, fuffer thée to paffe thy dayes
in loathfome miflyke. At this inftaunt when I entered
thy chamber, in thy dreame (as me féemed) thy foule betokening (as it fhuld féeme) fome daies forow or plefure,
exclaimed thus: O fortunate *Forbonius*, thou knoweft
how hatefull the perfon thou diddeft name is to thy father, who if he be fortunate in thy dowrie, I loue him:
I fhal eftéeme him vnfortunate in the fauour thou wilt
affure him: who béeing a collop of my flefh, wilt not allowe of that, which is loathfome to thy father: O *Prifceria Solduuius* féeth, and thy fecrete dreames bewraie
that the fortunacie of *Forbonius*, is eyther vnfortunate
for thy felfe, or not allowable by thy Fathers opinion.

Thy chaunge of conſtitution, thy hidden ſorrowe, my ſwéet child made me ſuſpitious, but now the verie true meſſenger of thy minde confirming me, I muſt without circumſtance conclude, that *Priſceria* loueth her fathers enimie, that *Priſceria* deſireth *Forbonius* fauour, and deteſteth her fathers choice, which if it be ſo, O my daughter, I feare me thy loue will not be ſo fauourable, as my diſdaine bitter, wherefore if thou art intangled, ſince thou knoweſt my opinion, forbeare, or if no wiſedome will conclude thée within limites, my diſpleaſure ſhall exclude thée from out all benefit of my fauour. Chooſe now *Priſceria*, whether with calme perſwaſions thou wilt yéeld to my bent, or by vnaccuſtomed diſpleaſure bée pertaker of thy Fathers wrath.

Vpon theſe concluſions, *Priſceria* all abaſhed, ſhaking of the drowſineſſe of her dreaming, made aunſwere to *Solduuius* in theſe tearmes.

Theſe ſtraunge ſuppoſitions, my good Father, argue the ſlender opinion of your ſelf, who by the vncertaineſt ſigns y^t may be, confirme your opinion as you pleaſe. In my dreames you ſaid I called *Forbonius* fortunate, and may it not bée, that as my tongue vttered y^t it thought not, your minde immagineth that which is not? counting euerye lyght ſhadowe a ſubſtaunce, and euery little ſimilitude of truth, an vndoubted demonſtration. Did I call thine enimie fortunate? Truely Father I feare me I might iuſtly conclude it, for he poore Gentleman little dreameth on diſpleaſures, when at ſuch time as reſt ſhould occupie your ſences, you moſt trauaile in your rancour: by certaine tokens as you ſaie, you conclude, that I am affectionate, and by this ſilly concluſion of a dreame, you inferre an vndoubted trueth, that I am enamoured with *Forbonius*, and if perhaps the neceſſitie of the fates be ſuch, *Priſceria* ſhall finde her ſelfe happie in louing *Forbonius*, by thoſe meanes her

her Father may ceafe rancour, and take reft, and his
daughter fatiffied with that fhe féeketh for, be no farther
troubled with dreaming fantafies.

Solduuius perceyuing by thefe fpéeches the certain-
tie of his daughters affeétion, as one altogether enraged, calling vp his wife, and raifing his feruaunts, left
the fillye maide all amafed at his fodaine departure,
whereas the olde man exclaiming vppon the difobedi-
ence of his daughter, and thundering out many reuen-
ges againft poore *Prifceria*, caufed his horfes to be fadde-
led, and perforce (contrarie to her expeétation) made her
bée conuayed to *Farnufium*, a mannor houfe of his
owne, a place for the folytarineffe more fit for a *Ty-
mon*, then conuenient for a beautifull Ladie, the onely companie there being fhepheards, who vpon the *Vaft*
mountaines recorded the praife of the Countrie fauourer *Pan*, and the rurall amitie betwéene them, and their
Countrie laffes. Thus from ftately Court, from the regards of her fwéet friend, from the plefures that follow
the Citie, her companions were rurall maidens, her re-
tinue frolicke fhepheardes: whofe flight capacitie not
yéelding anie comfort to allaie the Gentlewomans for-
rowings, made her (to her more hart griefe) continue her
penfiueneffe, and fup vp her conceiued forrow in filence.
But to repeat the moane on the other fide that amorous
Forbonius made, when by certain report he had notice of
his miftres departure, were wonderfull, who béeing in
himfelfe altogether confounded, not knowing where
to finde her out which was the onely miftres of his fantafie, Lord with how many fighes breathed he forth his
forrowe, and compaffed on euerie fide with difpairing
ioyes, in the verie fame garden where tofore hee repea-
ted his pleafures, hée in thefe waylefull tearmes re-
counted his miferies.

Alas vnfortunate *Aegyptian*, whofe faithful affeétiōs
are fo immutable, as thy naturall colour is vnftainable.
How

How iniurious are the deſtinies? that graunting thée life, they dayly haſten thy deſtruction, that vouchſafing thée pleſure, they ſuffer it not to be permanent: that admitting thée the benefit of beauties good grace, they depriue thée of the poſſeſſion and bleſſing of that thou deſireſt. Alaſſe what ſhall befall mée? when the glorie of my eyes are dimmed? when the pleaſures of my heart are determined? whē ſhe whom I loue néereſt, is farther off frō my preſēce? whē yᵉ iniurious repulſes of yᵉ father, makes euery attempt of *Forbonius* vnfortunate. Wo is me, what way may I imagin to make an end of my miſerie? Should I with diſpairing raſhneſſe finiſh vp the *Cataſtrophe* of my troubles? Should I béeing bereft of her by whom I liue, diſpoſſeſſe my ſelfe of that ſhe moſt doth like? Should I in making my ſelfe onelye fortunate by yᵉ alaie of my ſorrows, leaue *Priſceria* to her daily mournings, both to lament my deceaſure, & her froward deſtinie? no *Forbonius*, it is but vaine quiet that is to her diſcontentment, who béeing equally inthralled wᵗ thy ſelfe, will as willingly be pertaker of thy torment as thy ſelf. But why waile I thus in feminine ſorow, when my happineſſe is to be accompliſhed by manly attempt? *Solduuius* rigour hath cauſed *Priſcerias* abſence, yet cannot the fathers diſpleaſure determine the daughters loue, ſhe liueth to thy wiſh *Forbonius*, ſhe loueth to thy weale *Forbonius*, ſhe wilbe cōſtant til death *Forbonius*, why ſhouldeſt thou then leaue her vnſought for, *Forbonius?* Attempt vain man, to ſeke out thine aſſured, let not the diſtance of place diſanull thy good hap? *Solduuius* baniſhment is concluded within the limites of *Aegypt*, and ſince it is ſo, either *Forbonius* will attaine her he deſireth, or reuenge the vniuſt rigour of an iniurious Father.

Vpon this reſolution, as a man quite diſpoſſeſſed of himſelfe, he haſted to *Apollonius*, recounting vnto him how all things had fortuned, beſéeching him (not without

without foifon of teares) to féeke out by art where *Prifceria* was conuerfant, and to direct him by counfell, who
altogether was confounded with difpaire. *Apollonius*
by exteriour fignes conceiuing the interiour heartes-
griefe, and féeing the poore young Gentleman martyred
fo miraculoufly, comparing times and reuolutions, attained to the knowledge of her abroad, and concluding
in himfelfe to comfort him, which almoſt difpaired, hée
fpake thus to *Forbonius.*

My good friend, whence groweth it, that neyther the
nobilitie of thy aunceſtors? nor thy forepaſſed attempts?
neither the benefit of thy miſtres fauour can confirme
thée, but that thou wilt be carefull for that which thou
haſt alreadie almoſt compaſſed. Pluck vp your heart my
fwéete *Forbonius*, for thy *Prifceria* is not farre from thée.
Farnufium a mannor houfe of her Fathers, feated Eaſt
out of this Citie, whereas fhe is fo circumfpectly lookt
into, that by anie meanes, vnleſſe by fecret and conuenient pollicie, thou canſt come to the accomplifhment of
thy defire. Thou muſt therefore attyred altogether
like a fhepheard, depart this citie, and by fome conuenient meanes procure the kéeping of fome one Farmers
fhéepe, which is refident among thofe mountaines, by
whofe meanes thou fhalt fall in acquaintance with the
garden of thy miſtres, called *Sotto,* and hauing conuenient occafion to fatiffie thy affection, poffeffe thy felfe of yᵗ
thou haſt long defired.

Forbonius concluding his replie with hartie thanks,
fodainly departed, & remembring himfelfe of one *Cor-
bo,* a tenaunt of his, which had his mantion houfe verie
conueniently, feated hard by the mannor houfe of *Soldu-
nius,* he haſtely fhaped his iourney vnto him, & making
him priuie to yᵗ he defired, & fwearing him to be conſtant
& continue fecret, he betooke himfelfe to yᵉ kéeping of his
tenants fhéepe, & not forgetting to driue his flocke néere
vnto the lawnd wheras *Solduuius* feruants grafed their

I.   fhéepe,

fheepe, he fo demeaned himfelfe, that not onely he attay-
ned the fauor of *Sotto* which he fought for, but alfo for
his curteous affabilitie was accoūted of amōg yᵉ whole
troup of heards men for yᵉ beft finger, & yᵉ tunableft Mufition. His Aeglogs were fo deleɛtable, & the deliuery of
them fo delicate. Whervpon by good fortune it fo fel out,
yᵗ *Forbonius* vnder the coulourable name of *Arualio*,
was defired by *Sotto*, to refort vnto yᵉ mānor houfe, who
informed him of all yᵗ hapned, telling him of the careful
demeanour of his forowing young miftres, who pleafed
with nothing but with folitarie muficke, pined her felfe
awaie wᵗ melancholy, & not without caufe, (faid he,) for
my old mafter hath forbiddē me yᵉ admitting of any one
to her prefence, not fuffering her to paffe the limits of
my warie eie: nor allowing her to walke wᵗout yᵉ caftel
walles for her recreation. For my fake therfore chaunt
her fome melodie, & refort with me to a conuenieet arbour within our garden, whereas fhée walking for her
recreation, may perhaps take fome delight in thy forow-
full mournings, in yᵗ they moft fit her fantafie. *Forbonius* as willing to wend, as he defirous to perfwade, accompanied *Sotto* to *Farnufium*, wher hauing a place appointed him to apply his Aeglogs, and the Goddeffe before him whom he fhould deuine vpon, hée vnder thefe
fecrets defcribed his paffions.

A Midft thefe Mountaines on a time did dwell,
A louely fhepheard who did beare the bell.
For fwéete reports and many louing layes:
Whom while he fed his flocke in defart wayes,
A netheards daughter deckt with louely white,
Behelde and loude the laffe *Corinna* hight.
Him fought fhe oft with many a fwéete regard,
With fundrie tokens fhe her futes preferd,
Her care to kéepe his féeding flocke from ftray,
Whilft careleffe he amidft the lawnes did play.

Her

Her fwéete regards fhe fpent vpon his face,
Her Countrie cates fhe fent to gaine his grace,
Her garlands gaie to decke his temples faire,
Her doubled fighs beftowd on gliding aire,
Her pleafant kiffe where fhe might fteale a touch,
Corinnas zeales to *Corulus* was fuch.
He wanton fhepheard glorying in her fute,
Thefe fignes of zeale to folly did impute:
Not waying of her many louing fightes,
Her watrie eyes, her fecret moane by nights:
Her careleffe comfort in her fruitfull ewes,
Her monefull Aeglogs full of carefull fhewes,
But fcorning that, (which might that Godhead moue,
Who in a fhepheards forme, for *Ioues* behoue,
Did charme the watchman of the heifer faire,
For whofe behoofe the thunder left the aire.)
He left the place where fhe did loue to bide,
And draue his flocke another way befide.
Whofe dire difdaine (the God that kindles loue,
And makes impreffions ftraungly from aboue
Mifliking) ftrake with fancie at that ftower,
The filly fhepheard wounded by his power.
Now fought for that which he tofore did fhun,
And now the heat of fancie firft begun,
To ftraine a yéelding in his reftleffe minde:
Such are the wounds that paffe from fancie blinde,
That *Corulus* will now *Corinna* woe,
Though earft he loathd and fcorned fo to dooe.
Now fhe that fought with many a fwéete afpeét,
Is fude to now by him that did negleét.
Now bountifull is fwéete *Corinnas* grace,
Now like the Sunne in welkin fhines her face,
Her eyes like *Gemini* attend on *Ioue,*
Her ftately front was figured from aboue,
Her daintie nofe of Iuorie faire and fhéene,
Bepurfurate with ruddie rofes béene.

I. ij.   Her

Her cherie lips doth daunt the morning hiew,
From whence a breath ſo pleaſant did inſew,
As that which laide faire *Pſiches* in the vayle,
Whome *Cupide* woode and woed to his auayle.
Within the compaſſe of which hollowe ſwéete,
Thoſe orient ranks of ſiluer pearles doe méete,
Prefixing lyke perfection to the eie,
As ſiluer colde amidſt the ſummers ſkie:
For whence ſuch wordes in wiſdome couched be,
As Gods from thence fetch their Philoſophie:
Her dimpled chin of Alablaſter white,
Her ſtately necke where nature did acquite
Her ſelfe ſo well, as that at ſodaine ſight,
She wiſht the worke were ſpent vpon her ſelfe,
Her cunning thus was ſhowde vpon the ſhelfe:
For in this pile was fancie painted faire,
In either hand an aſure pipe ſhe bare:
By one repeating many a ſwéete conſent,
By other comfort to the heart ſhe ſent.
From which a ſeemely paſſage there doth ſhow,
To ſtrangers pleaſures that are plaſt alow,
Like to the forrowe *Phaeton* did leue,
Amidſt the welkin when he did receiue,
His Fathers charge, and ſet the world on fire:
In this faire path oft paced ſwéete deſire,
At euerie turne beholding with delight,
That Marble mount that did affect the ſight.
Of virgins waxe the ſwéet impreſſion was,
The cunning compaſſe thereof did ſurpaſſe,
For art concluding all perfections there,
Wrote this report, All graces bideth here.
Which *Cupide* ſpying built his manſion ſo,
As ſcorning thoſe ſwéete graces to beſtoe
On mortall man, with bowe ibent doth waite,
Leaſt *Ioue* ſhould ſteale impreſſions by deceit.

And

And wondring at the crifped coment faire,
In thought concludes it méeter for the aire
Then mortall mould: next which the ftately thies,
Like two faire compaft marble pillers rife,
Whofe white dooth ftaine the daintie driuen fnow:
Next which the knées with luftie bent below
Conioynd with nerues and cords of Amber fwéete,
This ftately pyles with gladfome honour gréete,
Such ftately knées as when they bend a lite,
All knées doo bend and boow with ftrange delyght.
Her calues with ftranger compaffe doo fuccéed,
In which the afures ftreames a wonder bréede,
Both art and nature therein laboured haue,
To paint perfeftion in her coulours braue,
Next which, the pretie ground worke of the pile,
Doth fhew it felfe and wonder doth beguile,
The ioyntes whereof combind of Amber fwéete,
With corall cords, yéeld bent to féemely féete.
From which, whofe lift to lift his gafing eye,
Shall greater caufe of wonder foone efpie.
When on the backe he bends his wauering looke,
In which the worke and tafke *Diana* tooke,
When with *Arachne* for the prife fhe ftraue,
Both art and nature there excelled haue.
Where from *Pigmalions* image féemely white,
Where clofe conueiaunce paffing *Gordians* plight,
Where louely *Neftar* drinke for all the Gods,
Where euerie grace is ftained there by ods.
Will not content with gafing looke for more,
And fpie thofe armes that ftand his fight before,
Which for their mould the *Aegyptian* wonders paffe,
Which for their beautie ftaine the Chriftall glaffe,
Which in their motion maifter natures fwéete,
Where blufhing ftreames prefent a fecrets meete,
Will now amazde, conclude at laft of this,
That in the hands all grace concluded is.

I. iii. Where

Where Nature limits euer fatall time,
Where Fortune figures pleaſure in her prime,
Whence ſpred thoſe fingers tipt with Iuorie,
Whoſe touch *Meduſas* turne may well ſupplie,
Where to conclude as now the ſhepheard déemes
All grace, all beautie, all perfeᶜtions ſéemes.
Thus *Corulus* with many ſecret thoughts,
Diuines on her whom erſt he ſet at naughts:
And forſt by ſcorch of inward ſhrowded fire,
He ſéekes for her his fancie did require.
Who fraught with woes in ſecret ſhrowdes renude,
Her ſilent griefe vnſure of that inſude.
Her *Corulus* with warie ſearch at laſt
At ſodaine found: and as a man agaſt
At that he ſaw, drew backe with feare, and than
Remembring of his woes his ſute began:
O ſwéete *Corinna* bleſſed be the ſoyle
That yéelds thée reſt amidſt thy dayly toyle,
And happie ground whereon thou ſateſt ſo:
Bleſt be thy flocke, which in theſe lawnes doo go,
And happie I, but hauing leaue to looke:
Which ſaid, with feare he pawſ d, and bloud forſooke
His palie face, till ſhe that wrought the fire,
Reſtorde the red, and kindled ſwéete deſire.
And with a baſhfull looke beholding him,
Which many months her pleaſant foe had bin:
She caſt her armes about his drooping necke,
And with her daintie fingers dawde him vp.
And kiſſing of his palie coloured face,
(Like as the Gods) by touch did ſoone diſplace
The ſowre, that alterd the poore ſhepheards ſwéete,
When thus ſhe gan her *Corulus* to gréete:
O louely ſhepheard happie be the hower,
In which (I know not by what ſecret power)

The

74

The Gods haue fent thée hether to thy frend, }
Alas what griefe fhould *Corulus* offend? }
Whom faireft Nimph might well a liking lend. }
Thy grafing Ewes with vdders full of milke,
With fruitfull fléece and wooll as fofte as filke,
Take glory in the fatneffe of this foyle
And praife theyr Maftres care and bufie toyle:
And now accufe thée of thy drooping mone,
Tis but enough for me to wayle alone
For why *Corinna* onely hapleffe is.
Poore *Corulus* at laft reuiude by this,
Gan fighing filence now to interrupt
And banifh feare which did his hope corrupt.
And thus he faid: O Nimph of beauties traine,
The onely caufe and eafer of my paine:
Tis not the want of any worldly ioy,
Nor fruitleffe bréed of Lambes procures my noy,
Ne figh I thus for any fuch mifhap:
For thefe vaine goods I lull in fortunes lap.
But other gréefes and greater caufe of care,
As now *Corinna* my tormenters are.
Thy beautie Goddeffe is the onely good,
Thy beautie makes mine eyes to ftreame a flood,
Thy beautie breakes my woonted pleafant fléepe,
Thy beautie caufeth *Corulus* to wéepe:
For other ioyes they now but fhadowes be,
No ioye but fwéete *Corinnas* loue for me.
Whereon I now beféech thée, by that white
Which ftaines the lilly, and affects my fight,
By thofe faire locks whereas the graces reft,
By thofe fwéete eyes whereas all pleafures neft:
Doo yéelde me loue, or leaue me for to die.
Corinna ftudious for to yéeld reply,
With many teares bedewd the fhepheards face,
And thus at laft fhe fpake: *O happie place,*

The

The which the Gods appoynted for my good.
What bleſſed Nimph within this ſacred wood
Hath pleaded poore *Corinius* lawfull cauſe?
Or be they dreames that now my fancie drawes?
O *Corulus* ne readſt thou ſue to me,
Nor ſpend the teares for to accepted be,
Since long ere this I would haue bent to bow,
If modeſt feare could well haue taught me how.
In happie bonds of *Himen* I am thine:
No plead thou grace to her that dooth incline.
Thus with a kiſſe ſhe ſealed vp the déed:
When as the ſhepheard glad of happie ſpéed
Embracing her he had deſired long,
Gan call for grace to her he ſo did wrong.
Confirmed thus with mutuall glad conſent,
They finiſht vp the marriage that they ment.
Great was the day, and euery field compéere
Delighted in the pleaſure of his déere.
Poore I alone in ſad lamenting layes,
Depriued of the pleaſure of my dayes,
In carefull tunes in briefe concluding thus:
O happie times and planets gracious.
When in a mirrour beautie did behold
The hidden woes, my muſe could wel vnfold:
And with a liking looke ſhape ſome replie.
But woe is me, ſince fathers crueltie
In changed formes hath altred termes of ſute,
And altering place hath made my Goddeſſe mute.
Who honouring *Pan*, may hap the perſon ſée,
Whom habit ſtrange perſwades it ſhould be me.

*T*His delectable Aeglogue finiſhed by the amorous
Forbonius gaue occaſions to *Priſceria* to ſatiſfie
the thoughts that then troubled her fantaſie. For confounded in her ſelfe, not knowing what to conclude of
that

that the fhepheard *Arualio* had reported, yet welnigh
perfwades that the reporter was he fhe liked off, with a
féemely grace, not minding to incurre the lighteft fufpition, turning toward *Forbonius*, whofe hand was on
his half-penie, fhée fayd thus.

Gentle fhepheard, that Nimph thou loueft fhuld alter from womanhood, that confidering thy true zeale, &
exquifite proportions, would not requite thy loyaltie,
with the benefit of her loue. Truly Madame (aunfwered the imagined *Arualio*, and I thinke my felfe gracious in this, that for her whom I loue I am enioyned
this torment, wherevpon turning himfelfe a fide, and
drying vp the teares which fhould bewray his fancie, he
was at laft knowen by *Prifceria*, who altogether amazed at the prefence of *Forbonius*, forgetting welnie the
infortunacie fhe was intangled in, caft her armes about
his necke, yet colouring with a féemly difdain to fhadow her opinion, and blindfold fubtill *Sotto*, fhée fayde
thus. Truly fhepheard, if I may preuaile with thy miftres, thou fhalt not be vnrewarded for this curtefie: &
Madame (faid *Forbonius*) might I counfell your Ladi-
fhip, you fhould not forrow for that maye be compaffed
at your pleafure.

This faid, *Sotto* taking *Arualio* by the hand, tooke
his leaue of his young Miftreffe thus: My young Ladie, I as ftudious of your pleafure as may be, haue
brought you this young fhepheard to laugh at, & if his
mufick like you, you fhall haue euery day at the leaft a
lay or two. And héerin fhalt thou doo me no fmall pleafure faid *Prifceria*? & fo with a féemly regard fhaping a
loth departure, yᵉ two fhepherds reforted to their flocks,
Arualio altogether amazed at his miftres beautie, and
Sotto very iocond he had fitted his young Ladies fancie
fo well: wherupon yᵉ old fhepheard, turning to our folitarie & diftreffed *Arualio*, faid thus, What maks thée
thus follom my youthly compéere? ceafe to gréeue thy

K. felfe

ſelfe about thoſe thinges that may be compaſſed, if thou
loue, time ſhal eate out that which Treacle cannot, and
thou ſhalt either be fortunate in poſſeſſing hir thou deſireſt, or in ouerpaſſing thy paſſions with good gouernment, leaue loue to thoſe that like her. *Arualio* not to
ſéeke of curteous humanitie, gaue him this aunſwere.
O *Sotto*, it is not the loue that gréeueth me, but the
meanes to compaſſe loue: I labour not to attain loue,
but to poſſeſſe the profits of my long ſeruice in loue: as
for time, it may worke wonders in them that are re-
pulſed: but when *Cupid* is gracious, and occaſions vnfortunate, thinke you yᵗ this is not a bitter ſowre? Yea,
but anſwered *Sotto*, & if it be ſo *Arualio* plucke vp thy
ſprights, and doubt thou not, but if thou prooue dily-
gent in pleaſing my young miſtreſſe, I meane not to
be idle, if I may know whom thou likeſt of. As for that
doubt not, ſaid our diſguiſed *Forbonius*, for ſince I know
by thy onely meanes my loue is to be compaſſed, I wil
not ſtick in ſo ſlight a pleaſure to profit, when as by thy
meanes I may onely ſuccour my ſelfe. In ſuch lyke
termes paſſing ouer their weriſome walke: At laſt they
betooke themſelues each of them to the folding of their
ſhéep, for it was welnie night, and the Sunne was ſtée-
ped in the Ocean: wherupon *Arualio* the ſhepheard, be-
comming now *Forbonius* indéede, haſted him home vnto his Tenaunts houſe, making him both priuie of his
happie fortune, and concluding with himſelfe howe to
performe that he wiſhed for, and for that long trauayle
requireth ſome quiet, he betooke himſelfe to reſt: where
recompencing al his nights wakings, with a quiet ſléep:
At dawne of day he returned in his counterfeit habite
vnto the field, and vnfolding his flocke, he draue them
into thoſe paſtures, that wer adioyning to *Sottos* walk:
who no ſooner ſpied *Arualio*, but ſaluting him very cur-
teouſly, he earneſtly intreated him, (ſetting all excuſes
apart)

apart) to go to *Farnufium,* and in the beſt ſort that hée might to ſolace the vnfortunate *Prifceria,* who onely wayting that occaſion, commending his flocke to the ouer-ſight of the old man, & accompanied with *Saracca* the daughter of the old *Sotto,* he was preſented to his deſired, within the caſtle, who by the abſence of *Sotto,* finding all occaſions to ſerue her turne, hauing ſent fillye *Sarraca* about ſome fléeueleſſe arrant, ſhe taking the occaſion profered, ſaid thus to *Forbonius:* Bleſt be that ſwéete conceipt of thine (O my friend) which to the vnfortunate rigour of my father, hath adapted ſo conuenient an end.   Now maiſt thou with as great pleaſures enioye thy deſired, as with déepe perplexities thou haſt ſorrowed in her abſence.   Now neither diſtaunce can ſeuer vs from imbracing, nor the watchfull eye of my fether, intercept thée of thy wiſh.   Sée héere thy *Prifceria,* who though the Fates worke neuer ſo contrarie, will liue to *Forbonius,* and onely loue *Forbonius.*

This ſaid, with many kiſſes comforting him which was almoſt ouercome with pleaſaunt imaginations, ſhe was returned this aunſwere by her moſt aſſured fauourer.

O *Prifceria,* if ouerpreſſed with manye ſuſpitious thoughts, if made pertaker of the infernall tortures in *Phlegeton,* if ſubiect to the puniſhment of the Daughters of *Danaus,* or affixed to the torture that martereth *Titius,* I ſhould be confirmed by this onely benefit in opinion, and made conſtant in all miſfortunes, yea, euen to ouercome the inſupportable trauailes of the fiſters, and be enabled with conſtancie to ſubdue all torments what ſo euer, by remembraunce onely of one gratious regard.   It is neither thy fathers rancor ſwéet *Prifceria,* nor diſtance of place, nor any one occaſiõ what ſoeuer, can either ſequeſter me of my hope, nor thée of the poſſeſſion of thy wiſhed: caſt off therefore all doubt

K. ij.   of

of after dole, & aſſure your ſelf, that as this pleſure hath
his originall this preſent inſtant, ſo by my meanes ere
long it ſhalbe continued for euerlaſting memory. Paſſing the time in ſuch like pleaſures, and miniſtering a
remedie vnto each others torments, I cannot tell, whether by the iniquitie of deſtenie, or otherwiſe: *Solduuius* learning out *Forbonius* departure, and ſuſpitious of
his forward attempts, at that very inſtant arriued at
Farnuſium, when the two amorous couple, little doubting his ſodaine approch, were coaſted with this ſower,
in midſt of all their ſwéete, that the enemie of their pleſures euen then entred the Caſtle, when as it ſéemed
the fates had prefixed them that conueniencie & opportunitie to allaye their long ſorrowing. The brute of
whoſe aduent brought to the eares of *Priſceria*, Lorde
how ſhe was confounded in her ſelf, how diſmaid was
Forbonius at that inſtant, how at yᵗ very time were they
both aſtonied, when moſt circumſpeÄtion ſhould be had:
ſo that ſcarce they had then dried vp their teares, when
as *Solduuius* entring the chamber, quicklye diſcouered
the whole counterfaite (for iealous eyes inflamed with
rancour pretermit nothing) wherevpon the olde man
at firſt, nothing at all deluded by the ſtraunge habite,
ſpying out their procéedings, laying violent hands on
Forbonius cauſed him forcibly to be conueyed to the
ſtrongeſt tower in the Caſtle, and tourning himſelfe
to *Priſceria*, he began thus.

O thou wicked and vngracious mayd, degenerating
from the Nobilitie of thy aunceſtours, and led by vn-
ſéemly affeÄtions, not direÄted by the likings of thy tender parents, in what tearmes ſhuld I accuſe thée? or bewray my ſorrowes? Woe is me, that am inforced to be
an eie witneſſe of mine owne ſorow, & to behold yᵗ with
mine eyes, that I hate in my heart: Is this the reward
of bréeding children? Is this the benefite that is reapt
by iſſue? Are theſe the pleaſures that befall Parentes?

O

O *Solduuius,* happie hadft thou bene, if either *Prifceria* had béene vnborne, or thou vnmarried, by the one thou fhouldeft haue efcaped this prefent miferie, by the other preuented the vntoward forrow that now confoundeth thée. Is thy loue to be fixed there where I hate? or fhuldeft thou be amorous of him who is odious to thy Father? O vile wretch borne among the *Hircan* Tygres, which refpecting not thy Fathers felicitie, ouerburtheneft his olde yeares with vnlooked for calamitie: but if euer iuft Gods pittied a lawfull complaint, I doubt not but they that minifter iuftice to all men, wil wreak the iniuries thou haft done to me.

Thus fayd, he fate down altogether confounded with melancholie. When as *Prifceria* finding occafion to fpeake for her felfe, began thus.

Who féeketh O father, to preuent the deftinies, laboreth in vaine, and who indeauoureth to alter nature, as he ftriueth againft the ftreame, fo muft he perifh in his owne ouerwéening: the Gods haue concluded our loue, and will you being a creature féeke to infringe it? Alaffe my father, why fhould my pleafure be your difcomfort? or that by which I liue, proue that which moft you hate? Doe not you héerein breake nature? who laie violent hands on your owne flefh, and féeke to alter that by rigor, that was ordained by diuine inftinct? O lette your rancor ouerflip (my good father) and if euer humble fute preuailed with an honourable minde, ceafe to hate him whom I loue: and couple vs both together, whom the Gods hauing ioyned in an affured league of friendfhip, it cannot be but iniuftice to alter their procéedings.

Solduuius not able to digeft the furie of his paffion, nor willing to weigh of the fubmiffiue requeft of his daughter, interrupted her thus: And is it not fufficient or thée (vaine wench as thou art) to paffe the limites of nature? but to continue thy error too? Thinkeft thou to

K. iij.   compaffe

compaſſe me with teares, who without ſighes cannot call to memorie thy eſcape? no *Priſceria*, both thou ſhalt ſée, and that varlet ſhall knowe, that my diſpleaſure will not be finiſhed but w^t bloud, nor my anger ſatiffied, till I haue confounded him, who hath diſcomforted me. Whervpon flinging out of the chamber in a great rage, and faſtening both boltes and lockes, he with his traine reſorted to the impriſonned poore ſhepheard, his capitall enimie *Forbonius*, whom after he had taunted with theſe vniuſt tearmes, he procéeded further to this vniuſt reuenge: Thou curſed and abhominable caitiſe, is it not ſufficient by the iniuries of thy Father *Clunamos*, to moue my patience, but that thou in perſon muſt violate my daughter? Thinkeſt thou that the Gods deteſt not theſe iniuryes? when as with wicked attemptes thou bewitcheſt the daughter, and maſſacreſt the Father? naie nether in iuſtice will they pretermit the offence, nor will nature ſuffer me to beare with thine errour: prepare thy ſelfe therefore to make him recompēce with thy bloud, whom thou haſt troubled with thy attempt.

Forbonius confounded with ſorrowe, and amazed at this auſtere iudgement, yet remembring the nobilitie that was alwayes accounted in him, aunſwered him thus.

Although enraged rancour hath made thée paſſe the limits of honour, (O *Solduuius*) yet paſſe not ſo farre in thy reſolutions, as to ſtaine the dignitie of thy perſon, with the martyrdome of a guitleſſe Gentleman. If I did hate thy daughter, that lyttle enuye that grewe by my Fathers diſpleaſure, might by reaſon grow to déepe and rooted mallice, but when I loue *Priſceria*, why ſhoulde I bée contempned of *Solduuius*? It ſhould ſéeme that loue was not accompted lothſome among the gods, when as prefixing a puniſhment to all eſcapes, they preſcribe an honour to this: chiefly concluding it to be

a

a vertue: wherevppon thou muſt conclude, that eyther thou contemneſt the decrées of the Gods, or meaſureſt all thinges by thine owne mallice. Thou threatneſt me with death (vaine man) and I weigh not the diſſolution of my bodie: for this I aſſure thée, as long as I may liue, I will honour *Prifceria*, and béeing dead, my ghoſt ſhall perſecute thée with reuenge, and proſecute my affections towarde my beſt beloued. So *Prifceria* lyue, *Forbonius* careth not to dye, the onely memorie of whome ſhall make mée conſtaunt in miſfortunes, and willing to withſtande the brunt of thy crueltie: wherevpon my concluſiō is, that if *Solduuius* for faithful aſſurance wil become a friendlye allower of *Forbonius*, he which by reaſon of the mallice of his Father had once cauſe to hate him, will now honour him, and that ſtrife which ſeparated two ſo noble families, ſhal now be finiſhed in our happy marryage: if this like not, procéede as thou pleaſeſt. In granting mée fauour, thou ſhalt finde honour, in bereauing mée of lyfe, thou ſhalt finiſh all my miſfortunes.

The diſcourſe of *Forbonius* thus ended, *Solduuius* began thus, after yᵗ he had ſomewhat digeſted his cholar: Although *Forbonius* the iniuryes thou haſt offered me, together with former diſpleaſures, be ſufficient to continue my reſolution, yet weyghing with my ſelfe that it is vaine to alter that which is prefixed by deſtinye, wonne by reaſon which directeth all men, and by the tender loue I beare my Daughter, which ſhoulde preuayle with a Father: I yéelde thée thy loue to inioye in chaſt wedlocke, and wheres thou lookedſt I ſhoulde bée thy tormentour, loe I am nowe contented to be thy vnlooked for Father. Wherevppon taking *Forbonius* by the hande, and conueying him to *Prifcerias* chamber, hée confirmed the Gentleman in his former purpoſe, and his daughter of his aſſured fauour,

vſing

vſing theſe kind of tearmes to diſcouer his intention: My daughter, that father that euen now hainouſly miſlikt of thy louer, now gloryeth in thy lyking, & he which whilome hated *Forbonius*, now vouchſafeth him his ſon in lawe: wherevpon comfort your ſelues with mutuall ſolace, & to morrow we will to the Citie to finiſh vp yᵉ ceremonies. The two louers compaſſed with incredible pleaſures, & not able to ſuppreſſe the affeꞔions that poſſeſſed thē, but by breaking out into ſpéech: they both humbled thēſelues to aged *Solduuius*, returning him by yᵉ mouth of *Forbonius* theſe thanks. O noble gentleman, it may not be erpreſſed by tongue, what I imagine in heart, who by your meanes, of the moſt vnfortunateſt man that liueth, am become the only happie man of the world: notwithſtanding this in lew of all fauour I wil returne you, that both by that meanes all priuate quarrells ſhall ceaſe betwéene our two families, and you regiſtred in our *Aegyptian* Records, for the onely peacemaker of *Memphis*. In theſe ſwéete ſpeaches ouer paſſing the daie & night, the next morrow the whole traine poſted to *Memphis*, whereas by the high Prieſt of the Sun they were ſolempnly eſpowſed, and after many ſorowes were recompenſed with nuptiall pleaſure. Now Ladies and Gentlewomen, I muſt leaue this to your conſideration, whether the louers for their conſtancie are more to be commended, or the olde man for his patience more to be wondered at: I leaue you to fit that concluſion, till you haue read what is written, promiſing you that if my rude diſcourſe haue wrought you anye pleaſure, I will both labor héerafter to ſerue all occaſions, and ſo fixe my ſtudies as they ſhall not farre differ from your fantaſies: and thus crauing you to winke at an errour, and commend as the cauſe requireth, I take my leaue: willing to be made priuie if I haue anye wayes trauayled to your contentment.

FINIS.

TRVTHS COM-
plaint ouer England.

MY mournfull Mufe *Melpomine* drawe néere,
    Thou faddeft Ladie of the fifters thrée,
And let her plaints in paper now appéere:
    Whofe teares lyke Occean billowes féeme to bée:
And fhould I note the plaintiffes name to thée?
Men call her *Truth*, once had in great requeft,
But banifht now of late for crafts beheft.

Amidft the reft that fet their pen to booke,
    She pickt me out to tell this wofull tale,
A fimple Poet, on whofe workes to looke,
    The fineft heads would thinke it verie ftale:
    Yet though vnworthie, to my friends auaile
I take the toile, and praie my Mufes aide:
To blazon out the tale of *Truth* difmaide.

Such time as *Phœbus* from the couloured fkie,
    Did headlong driue his horfes t'ord the Weft,
To fuffer horned *Luna* for to prie,
    Amidft the dufkie darke, new raifde from reft,
    As I in fragrant fields with woes oppreft:
Gan walke to driue out melancholy griefe,
Which in my heart at that time had the chéefe.

It was my hap faft by a riuers fide,
    To heare a rufull voice lamenting thus,
You iulling ftreames, euen as your waues diuide:
    So breakes my heart with paffions perillous,
    Which faine I would vnto the world difcuffe,
Were anie héere for to recount my moane,
Whofe wofull heart for inward griefe doth grone.
            L.   Which

Which fayd, fhe caft her dewed eyes afkance,
    And fpying me, gan rowfe her heauie head,
And praide me pen her fad and heauie chance,
    And fhe recounted it that prefent fted,
    I did agrée, and graunting *Truth* me fed
With thefe reportes, which I fet downe in vearfe,
Which gréeues my Mufe for forrowes to rehearfe.

Whilome (déere friend) it was my chaunce to dwell,
    Within an Iland compaft with the waue,
A fafe defence a forren foe to quell.
    Once *Albion* cald, next *Britaine Brutus* gaue,
    Now *England* hight, a plot of beautie braue,
Which onely foyle, fhould féeme the feate to bée,
Of Paradife, if it from finne were frée.

Within this place, within this facred plot,
    I firft did frame, my firft contented bower,
There found I peace and plentie for to float,
    There iuftice rulde, and fhinde in euerie ftowre,
    There was I lou'de and fought too euerie howre,
Their Prince content with plainneffe loued Truth,
And pride by abftinence was kept from youth.

Then flew not fafhions euerie daie from *Fraunce*,
    Then fought not Nobles nouells from a farre,
Then land was kept, not hazarded by chaunce,
    Then quiet minde preferud the foile from iarre,
    Cloth kept out colde, the poore reléeued were.
This was the ftate, this was the luckie ftowre,
While *Truth* in *England* kept her ftately bowre.

Iuftice did neuer looke with partiall eyes,
    Demofthenes was neuer dum for golde,

The

The Princes eares were ope to pesants cries,
  And false suspect was charely kept in holde,
  Religion flourisht, liuings were not solde
For lucre then, but giuen by desart,
And each receiu'd, & preacht with zealous hart.

Then learning was the Loadstone of the land,
  Then husbandman was frée from shiftes of lawe,
Then faithfull promise stoode in stéed of band,
  The Drones from busie Bée no *Mel* could drawe,
  Then loue, not feare, did kéepe the state in awe:
Then, then did flourish that renowmed time,
When earth and ashes thrusted not to clime.

For as the horse well mand abides the bit,
  And learnes his stop by raine in riders hand,
Where mountaine colt that was not sadled yet,
  Runnes headlong on amidst the fallowed land,
  Whose fierce resist scarce bends with anie band:
So men reclaimde by vertue, tread aright,
Where led by follies, mischiefes on them light.

Vse masters all, vse nurtereth mortall wayes,
  Vse, vse of good, continues happie state,
Vse, vse of mée, made *England* then haue praise,
  But since abuse hath banisht me of late.
  Alasse the while, there runnes another rate,
Which while by sad insight I looke into,
I sée the want of those that haue to doe.

And yet I sée not *Sodome*: some are good,
  Whose inward bowels dayly melt in mone,
To sée how *Britane* now is raging wood,
  Hard hearted, flintie minded, all in one,
  Bent to abuse, and leauing me alone.

L. ij.

Alone-

Alonely lead with careleffe fhew of peace,
Whereas fecure regard doth finne increafe.

Some, fome there be whom zeale hath fwallowed vp,
    Firft, bleffed Prince, of whom I finde reléefe,
Some noble péeres that taft errors cup,
    Some godly Prelates in the Church are chéefe,
    Some Lawiers lead by zeale, lament my greefe.
Some Merchants follow God, not fwallow golde,
Some countrie Swains loue truth you may be bolde.

Yet as great ftore of Darnell marres the féed,
    Which elfe would fpring within a fertile field:
And as the fruitfull bud is choakt by wéede:
    Which otherwife a gladfome grape would yéeld,
    So fometimes wicked men doe ouerwéeld,
And kéepe in couert thofe who would direct,
The common ftate, which error doth infect.

Yet *Truth* muft neuer alter from his name,
    Good Prince fayd I, ye good: what of her felfe?
And that is good, for Princes that doe frame.
    Themfelues to priuate good, doo fubiects good,
    Yet that's not that fame goodneffe I would name:
Good Prince, good people, that's the good I craue,
Of Princes goods, that goodneffe would I haue.

For as the great commaunder of the tides,
    God *Neptune* can allay the fwelling feas,
And make the billowes mount on either fides:
    When wandering kéeles his cholar would difpleafe:
    So Princes may ftirre vp and foone appeafe,
The commons heart to doe: and to deftroy
That which is good, or this, which threates anoy.

                                For

For common ſtate can neuer ſway amiſſe
  When Princes liues doo leuell all a right,
Be it for Prince that *England* happie is,
  Yet hapleſſe *England* if the fortune light:
That with the Prince, the ſubiects ſéeke not right,
Vnhappie ſtate, vnluckie times they bée,
When Princes liues and ſubiects diſagrée.

I know not I whence come theſe wayward woes,
  Whoſe ſodaine ſhowes portend this ſodain change,
Yet dooth miſ doubt ſuch ſodaine feares diſcloſe,
  As *Truth* this preſent doubts the ſequell ſtrange:
When ſtable head, lets ſtaileſſe members range,
I feare me: as the buildings truſt to ſand,
So euery blaſt will ſtroy with turne of hand,

When as in Court by proud contempt I ſée,
  A faſhion feedes the fancies now a dayes,
When as in Court promotions paſſed be
  By ſelfe opinion: oft the wiſe man ſayes,
The turnes are ſtrange, and fauour ſoone decayes:
And thoſe whom fortune windeth now a floate,
By change of fauour, ſoone may change their coate.

When as election dooth but paſſe by fence,
  Then muſt I déeme the world is fed by ſhowes:
When gariſh beautie cauſeth vaine expence,
  It ſéemes the man ſhould ſée, but little knowes,
Repentaunce is the fruite by louing growes:
So when in Court nought but ſuch pleaſures be,
Repentaunce muſt enſue we well may ſée.

But leauing Court, where though the bramble groes,
  Yet zealous care there ſets her ſelfe I fee,
L. iij.   I

Truths complaint

I doo in Court but now complaine of thofe,
  Who practife that that fits not their degrée:
  Whofe vaines by powre full oft corrected be:
But now fuch colours cloake each bad pretence,
That fhowes doo hold the wife in fome fufpence.

But I poore I, though gréeud at courtlike fcapes,
  Lamenting there the lauifh vaine expence,
Haue farther caufe abroad to note efcapes,
  Where craft dooth kéepe true meaning in fufpence:
  And wily worldlings couer their pretence
With holy fhapes, and in a holy coate,
Dooth flattry praife thofe men that fwim a floate:

In Nobles traines, who fées not ftrange mif déemes,
  Where each dooth gape and catch at priuate gaine,
And fléece the Lord, who though he blindfold féemes,
  By oft attempts dooth barre them of their vaines,
  The painfull wretch who toiles with often paines,
He hath faire words, when flattrie fucks the fwéete,
Thus fhowes take place, and *Troth's* trod vnder féete.

In *England* giftes can compaffe each reproofe,
  The bad for gold may foone be counted good,
The wicked gainer for the ftates behoofe,
  The blindeft buzzard to giue heauenly food,
  The fainteft heart in warlikft place hath ftood:
And who giues moft, hath now moft ftore of farmes,
Rackt rents, the Lord with golden fuell warmes.

And Iuftice fore I feare by powre is led,
  The poore may crie, and gladly créepe to croffe,
The rich with wealth, though wealthie now are fed,
  The fimple man now onely beares the loffe,
  The Lawier he the golden crownes doth toffe,

And

And now hath fées at will with cap and knée,
And each man cries, good fir come plead for me.

O fwéete the time, when neither folly might
    Miflead your hopes, nor alter olde decrées.
O happie *Truth* when as with fwéete delight,
    She laboured ftill far confcience not for fees.
O bleffed time, when zeale with bended knées,
Gan bleffe the heauens, that bent their powres diuine,
The Englifh hearts to wifedome to encline.

But now refufd, difdaind, and fet at naught,
    Inforft to féeke for reft in place vnknowne,
I wayle poore wretch, that no redreffe is fought:
    But well I wot, my gréefes are not mine owne,
    Some beare a part and helpe to waile my mone,
But all in vaine: fuch colours now are made,
That thofe would mend the miffe, doo daunce in fhade.

This faid, bewetting all the place with teares,
    And from her eyes expelling flouds of mone,
Her louely lockes befpred about her eares,
    She waude her wings as willing to be gone:
    And after paufe, fhe foard away anone,
And thus fhe faid: You Ilanders adieu,
You banifht me, before I fled from you.
Lenuoy. Beléeue me Countrimen this thing is true.

FINIS.

SCILLAES
Metamorphofis:

Enterlaced
with the vnfortunate loue
of *Glaucus*.

VVhereunto is annexed the delectable difcourfe
of the difcontented *Satyre*: with fundrie other
moft abfolute Poems and Sonnets.

Contayning the detestable tyrannie of Dif-
daine, and Comicall triumph of Conftancie: Verie fit for young Courtiers to
perufe, and coy Dames to
remember.

By *Thomas Lodge* of Lincolnes
Inne, Gentleman.

O vita! mifero longa, fœlici breuis.

Imprinted at London by *Richard Jhones*,
and are to be fold at his fhop neere Holburne
bridge, at the figne of the Rofe and
Crowne. 1589.

TO HIS ESPECIALL
good friend Maſter Rafe Crane,
and the reſt of his moſt entire wellwil-
lers, the Gentlemen of the Innes
of Court and Chauncerie. Tho-
mas Lodge of Lincolnes Inne
Gent. Wiſheth increaſe of
worſhip and continu-
ance in vertue.

VVeete (Maſter *Crane*) I had
not thought at this inſtant to
haue partaked my paſſions
with the print, whoſe diſcontented thoughts ſo long in-
ured to obſcuritie, were diuorſed many
yeares ſince, from vaine glories inordinate
follie: but the baſe neceſſitie of an extraua-
gant melancholie mate, that had no other
vnde of *quod adviĉtum attinet,* but the fore-
ſtalling of other mens inuentions, made my
vnperfit Poems (in ſpite of waſte paper) to
hazard an apprenteſhip in Poules: ſo that,
that which in the firſt peeping foorth was
✶   vvholie

3

wholie predeſtinate to your friendſhip, by an vnderhand marte, is made the mercinarie recreation of euerie ridiculous mate. Our wits now a daies are waxt verie fruitefull, and our Pamphleters more than prodigall; So that the poſtes which ſtoode naked a tedious *non terminus*, doo vaunt their double apparrell as ſoone as euer the Exchequer openeth; and euerie corner is tooke vp with ſome or other penileſſe companion that will imitate any eſtate for a twopennie almes. I could afford you whole ſeruices of abſurdities, that would diſquiet the diſgeſtion of Arte *vſq; ad nauſæam*, were it not that I pittie to particularize ſimple fellowes imperfections, and am altogether loath to aduenture my paines in ſo vngratefull a Prouince. For transformed *Scilla* how euer ſhe hapned now to bee difioyned from diſdainfull *Charybdis*; thinke not, but if they haue good ſhipping they wil meete ere long both in one ſhop; and landed they had at this inſtant, in one and the ſelfe ſame bay, if *Scilla* (the vnfortunater of the two) had not met with a needie pirate by the way. Ariued ſhee

is,

is, though in a contrary coaſt, but ſo wrackt,
and weatherbeaten, through the vnſkilful-
nes of rough writers, that made their poaſt
haſte paſſage by night, as *Glaucus* would
ſcarce know her, if he met her: yet my hope
is Gentlemen, that you wil not ſo much imagine what ſhe is, as what ſhee was; inſomuch
as from the ſhop of the Painter, ſhee is falne
into the hands of the ſtainer. Thus referring
the ſupportăce of my credit, & the inability
of my verſe to your ingenious opinions, I
bid you farewel til the next Tearm; at vvhich
time I hope to entertaine your ſeuerall delights, vvith farre better diſcourſes, and bee
ſuppliant to my good friend Maſter *Crane*, in
ſome or other more acceptable Poem. In the
meane time let my appliable *voluiſſe*, intitle
me to your curteſie: vvhoſe I am during Iife
in all enterchangeable dutie.

Your friend aſſured
Thomas Lodge.

The moſt pithie and pleaſant
Historie of Glaucus and Silla.

Walking alone (all onely full of griefe)
Within a thicket nere to *Iſis* floud,
Weeping my wants, and wailing ſcant reliefe,
Wringing mine armes (as one with ſorrowe wood);
  The piteous ſtreames relenting at my mone
  Withdrew their tides, and ſtaid to heare me grone.
From foorth the channell, with a ſorrowing crie
The Sea-god *Glaucus* (with his hallowed heares
Wet in the teares of his ſad mothers dye)
With piteous lookes before my face appeares;
  For whome the Nimphes a moſſie coate did frame,
  Embroadered with his *Sillas* heauenly name.
And as I ſat vnder a Willow trée,
The louelie honour of faire *Thetis* bower;
Repoſd his head vpon my faintfull knée:
And when my teares had ceaſt their ſtormie ſhower
  He dried my chéekes, and then beſpake him ſo,
  As when he waild I ſtraight forgot my woe.
Infortunate, why wandreth thy content
From forth his ſcope as wearied of it ſelfe;
Thy bookes haue ſchoold thée from this fond repent,
And thou canſt talke by proofe of wauering pelfe:
  Vnto the world ſuch is inconſtancie,
  As ſapp to trée, as apple to the eye.
Marke how the morne in roſeat colour ſhines,
And ſtraight with cloudes the Sunnie traƈt is clad;
Then ſee how pomp through waxe and waine declines,
From high to lowe, from better to the bad:
  Take moiſt from Sea, take colour from his kinde,
  Before the world deuoid of change thou finde.

A 2

With

7

Glaucus and Scilla.

With fecret eye looke on the earth a while,
Regard the changes Nature forceth there;
Behold the heauens, whofe courfe all fence beguile;
Refpect thy felfe, and thou fhalt find it cléere,
    That infantlike thou art become a youth,
    And youth forefpent a wretched age enfu'th.
In fearching then the fchoolemens cunning noates,
Of heauen, of earth, of flowers, of fpringing trees,
Of hearbs, of mettall, and of *Thetis* floates,
Of lawes and nurture kept among the Bées:
    Conclude and knowe times change by courfe of fate,
    Then mourne no more, but moane my haples ftate.
Here gan he paufe and fhake his heauie head,
And fould his armes, and then vnfould them ftraight;
Faine would he fpeake, but tongue was charm'd by dread,
Whil'ft I that fawe what woes did him awaight,
    Comparing his mifhaps and moane with mine,
    Gan fmile for ioy and drie his drooping eyne.
But (loe) a wonder; from the channels glide
A fweet melodious noyfe of muficke rofe,
That made the ftreame to dance a pleafant tide,
The weedes and fallowes néere the bancke that groes
    Gan fing, as when the calmeft windes accorde
    To greete with balmie breath the fleeting forde.
Vpon the filuer bofome of the ftreame
Firft gan faire *Themis* fhake her amber locks,
Whom all the Nimphs that waight on *Neptunes* realme
Attended from the hollowe of the rocks.
    In briefe, while thefe rare parragons affemble,
    The watrie world to touch their teates doo tremble.
Footing it featlie on the graffie ground,
Thefe Damfels circling with their brightfome faires
The loue-ficke God and I, about vs wound
Like ftarres that *Ariadnes* crowne repaires:
    Who once hath feene or pride of morne, or day,
    Would deeme all pompe within their cheekes did play.
                               Nais

Glaucus and Scilla.

Nais faire Nimph with *Bacchus* iuorie touch,
Gan tune a paſſion with ſuch ſweete reports,
And euerie word, noate, ſigh, and pauſe was ſuch,
And euerie Cadence fed with ſuch conſorts,
    As were the *Delian* Harper bent to heare,
    Her ſtatelie ſtraines might tempt his curious eare.
Of loue (God wot) the louelie Nimph complained:
But ſo of loue as forced loue to loue her;
And euen in loue ſuch furious loue remained,
As ſearching out his powrefull ſhaft to proue her,
    He found his quiuer emptied of the beſt,
    And felt the arrowe ſticking in his breaſt.
Vnder a Popler *Themis* did repoſe her,
And from a brier a ſweetfull branch did plucke:
When midſt the brier ere ſhe could ſcarce ſuppoſe her
A Nightingale gan ſing: but woe the lucke;
    The branch ſo néere her breaſt, while ſhe did quicke her
    To turne her head, on ſodaine gan to pricke her.
Whil'ſt ſmiling *Clore* midſt her enuious bluſhes,
Gan blame her feare and pretilie ſaid thus;
Worſe prickes than theſe are found among theſe buſhes,
And yet ſuch prickes are ſcarcelie feard of vs.
    Nay ſoft (ſaid *Chelis*) prickes doo make birds ſing,
    But prickes in Ladies boſomes often ſting.
Thus ieſt they on the Nightingales report,
And on the prickle of the Eglantine
On *Nais* ſong, and all the whole conſort
In publique this ſweete ſentence did aſſigne;
    That while ſome ſmile, ſome ſigh through change of time;
    Some ſmart, ſome ſport amidſt their youthlie prime,
Such wreathes as bound the *Thebans* iuorie brow;
Such gay trickt garlands pleit theſe iollie Dames;
The flowres themſelues when as the Nimphes gan bowe,
Gan vaile their creſtes in honour of their names:
    And ſmilde their ſweete and woed with ſo much glée,
    As if they ſaid, ſweet Nimph come gather mée.

A 3

But

Glaucus and Silla.

But penciue *Glaucus* paffionate with painings,
Amidft their reuell thus began his ruth;
Nimphes, flie thefe Groues late blafted with my plainings,
For cruell *Silla* nill regard my truth:
 And leaue vs two conforted in our gronings,
 To regifter with teares our bitter monings.
The flouds doo faile their courfe to fee our croffe,
The fields forfake their gréene to heare our griefe,
The rockes will wéepe whole fprings to marke our loffe,
The hills relent to ftore our fcant reliefe,
 The aire repines, the penciue birds are heauie,
 The trees to fee vs paind no more are leauie.
Ay me, the Shepheards let their flockes want feeding,
And flockes to fee their palie face are forie,
The Nimphes to fpie the flockes and fhepheards needing
Prepare their teares to heare our tragicke ftorie:
 Whilft we furprifde with griefe cannot difclofe them,
 With fighing wifh the world for to fuppofe them.
He that hath feene the fweete *Arcadian* boy
Wiping the purple from his forced wound,
His pretie teares betokening his annoy,
His fighes, his cries, his falling on the ground,
 The Ecchoes ringing from the rockes his fall.
 The trees with teares reporting of his thrall:
And *Venus* ftarting at her loue-mates crie,
Forcing hir birds to haft her chariot on;
And full of griefe at laft with piteous eie
Seene where all pale with death he lay alone,
 Whofe beautie quaild, as wont the Lillies droop
 When waftfull winter windes doo make them ftoop:
Her daintie hand addreft to dawe her deere,
Her rofeall lip alied to his pale cheeke,
Her fighes, and then her lookes and heauie cheere,
Her bitter threates, and then her paffions meeke;
 How on his fenfeles corpes fhe lay a crying,
 As if the boy were then but new a dying.

             He,

Glaucus and Silla.

He that hath vewd *Angelica* the faire
Beftraught with fancie nere the *Caſpian* fprings:
Renting the treffes of her golden haire,
How on her harpe with pitious notes fhe fings
    Of *Rolands* ruth, ot *Medors* falfe depart,
    Sighing each reft from center of her heart.
How now fhe writes vpon a beechen bow
Her *Medors* name, and bedlam like againe
Calls all the heauen to witnes of his vow,
And ftraight againe begins a mournefull ftraine,
    And how in thought of her true faith forfooken
    He fled her bowres, and how his league was broken.
Aye me who markes her harpe hang vp againe
Vpon the willowes watered with her teares,
And how fhe rues to read her *Rolands* paine,
When but the fhadowe of his name appeares;
    Would make more plainings from his eyes to flee
    Than teares diftill from amber weeping trée.
He that hath knowne the paffionate mifhappes
That nere *Olimpus* faire *Lucina* felt
When as her *Latium* loue her fancie trappes,
How with fufpeét her inward foule dooth melt:
    Or markt the Morne her *Cephalus* complaining,
    May then recount the courfe of all our paining.
But tender Nimphes to you belongs no teene;
Then fauor me in flying from this bower
Whereas but care and thought of croffes been,
Leaue me that loofe my felfe through fancies power,
    Through fancies power which had I leaue to loofe it,
    No fancie then fhould fee me for to choofe it.
When you are fled the Heauen fhall lowre for forrowe,
The day orecaft fhalbe bedtime with fable,
The aire from Sea fuch ftreaming fhowres fhall borrow
As earth to beare the brunt fhall not be able,
    And fhippes fhall fafely faile whereas beforne
    The ploughman watcht the reaping of his corne.

                            Goe

11

Glaucus and Scilla.

Goe you in peace to *Neptunes* watrie found,
No more may *Glaucus* play him with fo prettie;
But fhun refort where folace nill be found,
And plaine my *Scillaes* pride and want of pittie:
 Alas fwéet Nimphs my Godhead's all in vaine,
 For why this breft includes immortall paine.
Scilla hath eyes, but too fwéete eyes hath *Scilla*;
Scilla hath hands, faire hands but coy in touching;
Scilla in wit furpaffeth graue *Sibilla*,
Scilla hath words, but words well ftorde with grutching;
 Scilla a Saint in looke, no Saint in fcorning;
 Looke Saint-like *Scilla*, leaft I die with mourning.
Alas why talke I ſ Sea-god ceafe to mourne her,
For in her nay my ioyes are euer ceafing:
Ceafe life or loue, then fhall I neuer blame her;
But neither loue nor life may finde decreafing.
 A mortall wound is my immortall being,
 Which paffeth thought, or eyes aduifed féeing.
Herewith his faltring tongue by fighs oppreffed.
Forfooke his office, and his bloud reforted
To féede the heart that wholly was diftreffed,
Whilft pale (like *Pallas* flowre) my knée fupported
 His féeble head and arme, fo full of anguifh,
 That they which fawe his forrowes gan to languifh.
Themis the coyeft of this beauteous traine
On hillie toppes the wonderous *Moly* found,
Which dipt in balmie deaw fhe gan to ftraine,
And brought her prefent to recure his wound:
 Clore fhe gathered *Amaranthus* flower,
 And *Nais Aiax* bloffom in that ftowre,
Some chafe his temples with their louelie hands,
Some fprinkle water on his pale wan cheekes,
Some wéepe, fome wake, fome curfe affeƈtions bandes;
To fée fo young, fo faire, become fo weake:
 But not their pitious hearbs, or fprings haue working,
 To eafe that heart where wanton loue is lurking.
          Naithles

Glaucus and Scilla.

Naithles though loath to ſhewe his holy kindnes
On euerie one he ſpent a looke for fauour,
And prayed their pardon vouching *Cupids* blindnes,
(Oh fancies fond that naught but ſorrowes fauour);
   To ſee a louely God leaue Sea Nimphes ſo:
   Who cannot doome vpon his deadly woe ⸫
Themis that knewe, that waters long reſtrained
Breake foorth with greater billowes than the brookes
That ſwetely float through meades with flowres diſtained,
With cheerefull laies did raiſe his heauie lookes;
   And bad him ſpeake and tell what him agreeu'd:
   For griefes diſclof'd (ſaid ſhe) are ſoone releeu'd.
And as ſhe wiſht ſo all the reſt did woe him;
By whoſe inceſſant ſuites at laſt inuited,
He thus diſcouered that which did vndoo him,
And orderlie his hideous harmes recited,
   When firſt which fingers wagge he gan to ſtill them,
   And thus with drierie tearmes of loue did fill them.
Ah Nimphes (quoth he) had I by reaſon learnt
That ſecret art which birdes haue gaind by ſence,
By due foreſight miſfortune to preuent;
Or could my wit controule mine eyes offence:
   You then ſhould ſmile and I ſhould tell ſuch ſtories,
   As woods, and waues ſhould triumph in our glories.
But *Nereus* daughters, Sea-borne Saints attend,
Lake breeding Géeſe when from the Eaſterne clime
They lift vnto the weſterne waters wend
To chooſe their place of reſt by courſe of time,
   Approaching *Taurus* haughtie topped hill
   They charme their cackle by this wondrous ſkill.
The climing mountaine neighbouring ayre welnie,
Hath harbored in his rockes and deſart haunts
Whole airies of Eagles preſt to flie
That gazing on the Sonne their birth right vaunts,
   Which birds of *Ioue* with deadlie fewde purſue
   The wandering Geeſe, when ſo they preſſe in vewe.

B   Theſe

Glaucus and Scilla.

Thefe fearefull flitting troopes by nature tought,
Paffing thefe dangerous places of purfuit:
When all the defart vales they through haue fought,
With pibbles ftop their beakes to make them mute,
  And by this meanes their dangerous deathes preuent
  And gaine their wifhed waters of frequent.
But I fond God (I God complaine thy follie)
Let birds by fenfe exceede my reafon farre:
Whilom than I who was more ftrong and iollie
Who more contemnd affections wanton warre ʕ
  Who leffe than I lou'd luftfull *Cupids* arrowes ʕ
  Who now with curfe & plagues poore *Glaucus* harrowes.
How haue I leapt to heare the *Tritons* play
A harfh retreat vnto the fwelling flouds ʕ
How haue I kept the Dolphins at a bay,
When as I ment to charme their wanton moods?
  How haue the angrie windes growne calme for loue,
  When as thefe fingers did my harpe ftrings moue?
Was any Nimph, you Nimphes was euer any
That tangled not her fingers in my treffe ʕ
Some well I wot and of that fome full many
Wifht or my faire, or their defire were leffe
  Euen *Ariadne* gazing from the fkie
  Became enamorde of poore *Glaucus* eye.
Amidft this pride of youth and beauties treafure
It was my chaunce, you floods can tell my chancing,
Fléeting along *Sicillian* bounds for pleafure,
To fpie a Nimph of fuch a radiant glancing,
  As when I lookt, a beame of fubtill firing
  From eye to heart incenft a deepe defiring.
Ah had the vaile of reafon clad mine eye,
This foe of fréedome had not burnt my heart:
But birds are bleft, and moft accurft am I
Who muft reporte her glories to my fmart,
  The Nimph I fawe and lou'de her, all to cruell
  Scilla, faire *Scilla*, my fond fancies iuell.

              Her

Glaucus and Scilla.

Her haire not truft, but fcatterd on her brow,
Surpaffing *Hiblas* honnie for the view,
Or foftned golden wires; I know not how
Loue with a radiant beautie did purfue
    My too iudiciall eyes, in darting fire
    That kindled ftraight in me my fond defire.
Within thefe fnares firft was my heart intrapped,
Till through thofe golden fhrowdes mine eies did fee
An yuorie fhadowed front, wherein was wrapped
Thofe pretie bowres where Graces couched be:
    Next which her cheekes appeerd like crimfon filk,
    Or ruddie rofe befpred on whiteft milk.
Twixt which the nofe in louely tenor bends,
(Too traitrous pretie for a Louers view:)
Next which her lips like violets commends
By true proportion that which dooth infue;
    Which when they fmile, prefent vnto the eies
    The *Oceans* pride and yuorie paradice.
Her pollifht necke of milke white fnowes doth fhine,
As when the Moone in Winter night beholdes them:
Her breaft of alablafter cleere and fine,
Whereon two rifing apples faire vnfolds them
    Like *Cinthias* face when in her full fhe fhineth,
    And blufhing to her Loue-mates bower declineth.
From whence in length her armes doo fweetly fpred
Like two rare branchie faples in the Spring,
Yeelding fiue louely fprigs from euerie head,
Proportioned alike in euerie thing;
    Which featly fprout in length like fpringborne frends,
    Whofe pretie tops with fiue fweet rofes ends.
But why alas fhould I that Marble hide
That doth adorne the one and other flanke,
From whence a mount of quickned fnow doth glide,
Or els the vale that bounds this milkwhite banke,
    Where *Venus* and her fifters hide the fount,
    Whofe louely Nectar dooth all fweetes furmount.

B 2

Con-

Glaucus and Scilla.

Confounded with defcriptions, I muft leaue them;
Louers muft thinke, and Poets muft report them:
For filly wits may neuer well conceaue them,
Vnleffe a fpeciall grace from heauen confort them.
    Aies me, thefe faires attending *Scilla* won me:
    But now (fweet Nimphes) attẽd what hath vndon me.
The louely breaft where all this beautie refted,
Shrowded within a world of deepe difdaine:
For where I thought my fancie fhould be feafted
With kinde affeſt, alas (vnto my paine)
    When firft I woode the wanton ftraight was flying,
    And gaue repulfe before we talkt of trying.
How oft haue I (too often haue I done fo)
In filent night when euerie eye was fleeping,
Drawne neere her caue, in hope her loue were won fo,
Forcing the neighboring waters through my weeping
    To wake the windes, who did affliſt her dwelling
    Whilft I with teares my paffion was a telling.
When midft the *Cafpian* feas the wanton plaid,
I drew whole wreaths of corrall from the rockes:
And in her lap my heauenly prefents laid:
But fhe vnkind rewarded me with mockes.
    Such are the fruites that fpring from Ladies coying,
    Who fmile at teares, and are intrapt with toying.
Tongue might grow wearie to report my wooings,
And heart might burft to thinke of her deniall:
Nay none be blamde but heauen for all thefe dooings,
That yeeld no helpes inmidft of all my triall.
    Heart, tongue, thought, pen nil ferue me to repent me,
    Difdaine her felfe fhould ftriue for to lament me.
Wretched Loue let me die, end my loue by my death;
Dead alas ftill I liue, flie my life, fade my loue.
Out alas loue abides, ftill I ioy vitall breath:
Death in loue, loue is death, woe is me that doo proue.
    Paine and woe, care & griefe euery day about me houers:
    Thẽ but death what can quel al yᵉ plages of haples louers?
                        Aies

Glaucus and Scilla.

Aies me my moanings are like water drops
That neede an age to pearce her marble heart,
I fow'd true zeale, yet fruiteles were my crops:
I plighted faith, yet falfehoode wrought my fmart:
    I praifd her lookes, her lookes difpifed *Glaucus*,
    Was euer amorous Sea-god fcorned thus ؟
A hundereth fwelling tides my mother fpent
Vpon thefe lockes, and all hir Nimphes were preft,
To pleit them faire when to her bowre I went:
He that hath féene the wandring *Phœbus* creft,
    Toucht with the Chriftall of *Eurotas* fpring,
    The pride of thefe my bufhie locks might fing.
But fhort difcourfe beféemes my bad fucceffe,
Eache office of a louer I performed:
So feruently my paffions did her preffe,
So fwéete my laies, my fpéech fo well reformed,
    That (cruell) when fhe fawe naught would begile me
    With angrie lookes the Nimph did thus exile me.
Packe hence thou fondling to the wefterne Seas,
Within fome calmy riuer fhrowd thy head:
For neuer fhall my faire thy loue appeafe,
Since fancie from this bofome late is fled:
    And if thou loue me fhewe it in departing:
    For why thy prefence dooth procure my fmarting.
This faid with angrie lookes, away fhe hafted
As faft as flie the flouds before the winds:
When I poore foule with wretched forrowes wafted,
Exclaimde on loue, which wit and reafon blinds:
    And banifht from hir bowre with wofull poafting
    I bent my felfe to féeke a forreine coafting.
At laft in wandring through the greater Seas
It was my chance to paffe the noted ftreights:
And wearied fore in féeking after eafe,
Amidft the creekes, and watrie coole receits.
    I fpied from farre by helpe of fonnie beames
    A fruitefull Ile begirt with *Ocean* ftreames.

                Weftward

Glaucus and Scilla.

Weftward I fleeted, and with heedfull eie
Beheld the chalkie cliffes that tempt the aire,
Till at the laft it was my chance to fpie
A pleafant entrance to the flouds repaire;
 Through which I preft, and wondring there beheld
 On either fide a fweete and fruitfull field.
Ifis (the Ladie of that louely ftreame)
Made holiday in view of my refort;
And all the Nimphes of that her watrie realme
Gan trip for ioy, to make me mickle fport:
 But I poore foule with no fuch ioyes contented,
 Forfooke their bowers, and fecretly lamented.
All folitarie rome I heere about,
Now on the fhoare, now in the ftreame I weepe,
Fire burnes within, and gaftly feare without,
No reft, no eafe, no hope of any fleepe:
 Poore banifht God, heere haue I ftill remained,
 Since time my *Scilla* hath my futes difdained.
And heere confort I now with hapleffe men,
Yeelding them comfort, (though my wound be cureleffe)
Songs of remorfe I warble now and then,
Wherein I curfe fond Loue and Fortune dureleffe,
 Wan hope my weale, my truft but bad aduenture,
 Circumference is care, my heart the center.
Whileft thus he fpake, fierce *Ate* charmde his tongue,
His fenfes faild, his armes were folded ftraight,
And now he fighes, and then his heart is ftung;
Againe he fpeakes gainft fancies fond deceit,
 And teares his treffes with his fingers faire,
 And rents his roabs, halfe mad with deepe difpaire.
The piteous Nimphes that viewd his heauie plight,
And heard the fequell of his bad fucceffe,
Did loofe the fprings of their remorfefull fight,
And wept fo fore to fee his fcant redreffe:
 That of their teares there grew a pretie brooke,
 Whofe Chriftall cleares the clowdes of penciue looke.
                Alas

Glaucus and Scilla.

Alas woes me, how oft haue I bewept
So faire, fo yong, fo louely, and fo kinde,
And whilft the God vpon my bofome flept,
Behelde the fcarres of his afflicted minde,
  Imprinted in his yuorie brow by care,
  That fruitleffe fancie left vnto his fhare.
My wandring lines, bewitch not fo my fences:
But gentle Mufe direct their courfe aright,
Delayes in tragicke tales procure offences:
Yeeld me fuch feeling words, that whilft I wright
  My working lines may fill mine eyes with languifh,
  And they to note my mones may melt with anguifh.
The wofull *Glaucus* thus with woes attainted,
The penciue Nimphes agreeud to fee his plight,
The flouds and fields with his laments acquainted,
My felfe amazd to fee this heauie fight;
  On fodaine *Thetis* with her traine approched,
  And grauely thus her amorous fonne reproched.
My fonne (faid fhe) immortall haue I made thee,
Amidft my watrie realmes who may compare
Or match thy might ᚛ Why then fhould care inuade thee,
That art fo yong, fo louely, frefh and faire.
  Alas fond God, it merits great reprouing
  In States of worth, to doate on foolifh louing.
Come wend with me, and midft thy Fathers bowre
Let vs difport and frolicke for a while
In fpite of Loue: although he powte and lowre,
Good exercife will idle lufts beguile:
  Let wanton *Scilla* coy her where fhe will,
  Liue thou my fonne by reafons leuell ftill.
Thus faid the Goddeffe: and although her words
Gaue fignes of counfaile, pompe and maieftie:
Yet natheleffe her piteous eye affoords
Some pretie witneffe to the ftanders by,
  That in her thoughts (for all her outward fhow)
  She mournd to fee her Sonne amated fo.

                                            But

Glaucus and Scilla.

But (welladay) her words haue little force,
The haples louer worne with working woe,
Vpon the ground lay pale as any corfe,
And were not teares which from his eyes did flowe,
  And fighes that witneffe he enioyd his breath,
  They might haue thought him Citizen of death.
Which fpectacle of care made *Thetis* bow,
And call on *Glaucus*, and command her Sonne
To yéelde her right: and hir aduice allow,
But (woe) the man whome fancie had vndone
  Nill marke her rules: nor words, nor wéeping teares
  Can faften counfaile in the louers eares.
The Quéene of Sea, with all hir Nimphes affured
That no perfwafion might reléeue his care:
Knéeling adowne; their faltring tongues enured
To tempt faire *Venus* by their vowed praier:
  The courfe whereof as I could beare in minde
  With forrowing fobbes they vttered in this kinde.
Borne of the Sea, thou *Paphian* Quéene of loue,
Miftris of fwéete confpiring harmonie:
Lady of *Cipris*, for whofe fwéete behoue
The Séepeheards praife the youth of *Theffallie*:
  Daughter of *Ioue* and Sifter to the Sonne,
  Affift poore *Glaucus* late by loue vndone.
So maift thou baine thée in *Th'arcadian* brookes,
And play with *Vulcans* riuall when thou lift,
And calme his iealous anger by thy lookes,
And knit thy temples with a rofeat twift
  If thou thy felfe and thine almightie Sonne,
  Affift poore *Glaucus* late by loue vndone.
May earth ftill praife thée for her kinde increafe:
And beafts adore thée for their fruitfull wombes,
And fowles with noates thy praifes neuer ceafe,
And Bées admire thée for their honnie combes:
  So thou thy felfe and thine almightie Sonne,
  Affift poore *Glaucus* late by loue vndone.

No

Glaucus and Scilla.

No fooner from her reuerent lips were paft
Thofe latter lines, but mounting in the Eaft,
Faire *Venus* in her iuorie coatch did haft,
And toward thofe penciue dames, her courfe addreft;
    Her doues fo plied their wauing wings with flight,
    That ftraight the facred Goddeffe came in fight.
Vpon her head fhe bare that gorgeous Crowne,
Wherein the poore *Amyntas* is a ftarre;
Her louely lockes, her bofome hang adowne
(Thofe netts that firft infnar'd the God of warre:)
    Delicious louely fhine her prettie eies,
    And one her chéekes carnatioon cloudes arife,
The ftately roab fhe ware vpon her back
Was lillie white, wherein with cullored filke;
Her Nimphes had blaz'd the yong *Adonis* wrack,
And *Lædas* rape by Swan as white as milke,
    And on her lap her louely Sonne was plafte,
    Whofe beautie all his mothers pompe defafte.
A wreath of rofes hem'd his Temples in,
His treffe was curlde and cléere as beaten gold;
Haught were his lookes, and louely was his fkin,
Each part as pure as Heauens eternall mold,
    And on his eies a milkewhite wreath was fpred,
    Which longft his backe, with prettie pleits did fhed.
Two daintie wings of partie coulored plumes
Adorne his fhoulders dallying with the winde;
His left hand wéelds a Torch, that euer fumes:
And in his right, his bowe that fancies bind,
    And on his back his Quiuer hangs well ftored
    With fundrie fhaftes, that fundrie hearts haue gored.
The Deities ariu'd in place defired;
Faire *Venus* her to *Thetis* firft befpake,
Princeffe of Sea (quoth fhe) as you required
From *Cefton* which my Sonne, my courfe I take:
    Frollick faire Goddeffe, Nimphs forfake your plaining,
    My Sonne hath power and fauour yet remaining.
              C   With

Glaucus and Scilla.

With that the reuerend powres each other kiſſed,
And *Cupid* ſmil'd vpon the Nimphes for pleaſure:
So naught but *Glaucus* ſolace there was miſſed,
Which to effeɕt the Nimphes withouten meaſure
  Intreate the God, who at the laſt drewe nie
  The place, where *Glaucus* full of care did lie,
And from his bowe a furious dart hee ſent
Into that wound which he had made before:
That like *Achilles* ſworde became the teint
To cure the wound that it had caru'd before:
  And ſodeinly the Sea-god ſtarted vp:
  Reuiude, relieud, and frée from Fancies cup.
No more of loue, no more of hate he ſpoke,
No more he forſt the ſighes from out his breaſt:
His ſodaine ioye his pleaſing ſmiles prouoke,
And all aloft he ſhakes his buſhie creaſt,
  Gréeting the Gods and Goddeſſes beſide,
  And euerie Nimph vpon that happie tide.
Cupid and he together hand in hand
Approach the place of this renowned traine:
Ladies (ſaid he) releaſt from amorous band,
Receiue my priſoner to your grace againe.
  Glaucus gaue thankes, when *Thetis* glad with bliſſe
  Embraſt his neck, and his kind chéekes did kiſſe.
To ſée the Nimphes in flockes about him play,
How *Nais* kempt his head, and waſht his browes:
How *Thetis* checkt him with his welladay,
How *Clore* told him of his amorous vowes,
  How *Venus* praiſd him for his faithfull loue,
  Within my heart a ſodein ioy did moue.
Whilſt in this glée this holy troope delight,
Along the ſtreame a farre faire *Scilla* floated,
And coilie vaunſt hir creaſt in open ſight:
Whoſe beauties all the tides with wonder noated,
  Fore whom *Palemon* and the *Tritons* danced
  Whilſt ſhe hir limmes vpon the tide aduanced.

                 Whoſe

Glaucus and Scilla.

Whofe fwift approach made all the Godheads wonder:
Glaucus gan fmile to fee his louelie foe,
Rage almoft rent poore *Thetis* heart afonder:
Was neuer happie troope confufed fo
    As were thefe deities and daintie dames,
      When they beheld the caufe of *Glaucus* blames.
Venus commends the carriage of her eye,
Nais vpbraides the dimple in her chinne,
Cupid defires to touch the wantons thie,
Clore fhe fweares that euerie eie dooth finne
    That likes a Nimph that fo contemneth loue,
      As no attempts her lawles heart may moue.
Thetis impatient of her wrong fuftained,
With enuious teares her rofeat cheekes afflicted;
And thus of *Scillas* former pride complained;
Cupid (faid fhe) fée her that hath inflicted
    The deadlie wound that harmde my louelie fonne,
      From whome the offpring of my care begonne.
Oh if there dwell within thy breft my boy
Or grace, or pittie, or remorfe (faid fhe)
Now bend thy bowe, abate yon wantons ioy,
And let thefe Nimphes thy rightfull iuftice fee.
    The God foone won, gan fhoote, and cleft her heart
      With fuch a fhaft as caufd her endles fmart.
The tender Nimph attainted vnawares,
Fares like the *Libian* Lioneffe that flies
The Hunters Launce that wounds her in his fnares;
Now gins fhee loue, and ftraight on *Glaucus* cries;
    Whilft on the fhore the goddeffes reioyce,
      And all the Nimphes afflict the ayre with noyfe.
To fhoare fhe flitts, and fwift as *Affrick* wind
Her footing glides vpon the yeelding graffe,
And wounded by affect recure to finde
She fodainely with fighes approcht the place
    Where *Glaucus* fat, and wearie with her harmes
      Gan clafpe the Sea-god in her amorous armes.

Glaucus and Scilla.

Glaucus my loue (quoth fhe) looke on thy louer,
Smile gentle *Glaucus* on the Nimph that likes thée;
But ftarke as ftone fat he, and lift not proue her:
(Ah filly Nimph the felfefame God that ftrikes thée
  With fancies darte, and hath thy fréedome flaine)
  Wounds *Glaucus* with the arrowe of difdaine.
Oh kiffe no more kind Nimph he likes no kindnes,
Loue fléepes in him, to flame within thy breft,
Cléer'd are his eies, where thine are clad with blindnes;
Frée'd be his thoughts, where thine muft tafte vnreft:
  Yet nill fhe leaue, for neuer loue will leaue her,
  But fruiteles hopes and fatall happes deceaue her.
Lord how her lippes doo dwell vpon his chéekes;
And how fhe lookes for babies in his eies:
And how fhe fighes, and fweares fhée loues and léekes,
And how fhe vowes, and he her vowes enuies:
  Truft me the enuious Nimphs in looking on,
  Were forft with teares for to affift her mone.
How oft with blufhes would fhe plead for grace,
How oft with whifperings would fhe tempt his eares:
How oft with Chriftall did fhe wet his face:
How oft fhe wipte them with her Amber heares:
  So oft me thought, I oft in heart defired
  To fée the end whereto difdaine afpired.
Palemon with the *Tritons* roare for griefe,
To fée the Miftris of their ioyes amated:
But *Glaucus* fcornes the Nimph, that waites reliefe:
And more fhe loues the more the Sea-god hated,   (me
  Such change, fuch chance, fuch futes, fuch ftorms beléeue
  Poore filly wretch did hartely agréeue me.
As when the fatall bird of *Augurie*
Séeing a ftormie difmall cloude arife
Within the South, foretells with piteous crie
The wéeping tempeft, that on fudden hies:
  So fhe poore foule, in view of his difdaine
  Began to defcant on her future paine.

              And

Glaucus and Scilla.

And fixing eye vpon the fatall ground,
Whole hoafts of flouds drew deaw from out her eyes;
And when through inward griefe the laffe did found,
The foftned graffe like billowes did arife
    To woe her brefts, and wed her limmes fo daintie,
    Whom wretched loue had made fo weake and faintie,
(Ayes me), me thinks I fée her *Thetis* fingers
Renting her locks as fhe were woe begon her;
And now her lippes vpon his lipping lingers:
Oh lingring paine where loue nill lift to mone her ̧
    Rue me that writes, for why her ruth deferues it:
    Hope needs muft faile, where forrow fcarce preferues it.
To make long tale were tedious to the wofull,
Wofull that read what wofull fhee approoued:
In briefe her heart with déepe difpaire was fo full,
As fince fhe might not win her fwéete beloued.
    With hideous cries like winde borne backe fhe fled
    Vnto the Sea, and toward *Sicillia* fped.
Swéete *Zephirus* vpon that fatall howre
In haples tide midft watrie world was walking;
Whofe milder fighes, alas, had little power
To whifper peace amongft the Godheads talking:
    Who all in one conclude for to purfue,
    The haples Nimph, to fee what would enfue.
Venus her felfe and her faire Sonne gan hie
Within their iuorie Coach drawne forth by doues
After this haples Nimph, their power to trie:
The Nimphes in hope to fée their vowed loues,
    Gan cut the watrie boafom of the tide,
    As in *Cayfter Phœbus* birds doe glide.
Thetis in pompe vpon a *Tritons* back
Did poaft her ftraight attended by her traine;
But *Glaucus* frée from loue by louers wrack,
Séeing me penciue where I did remaine,
    Vpon a *Dolphin* horft me (as he was)
    Thus on the *Ocean* hand in hand we paffe.

        C 3   Our

Glaucus and Scilla.

Our talke midway was nought but ftill of wonder,
Of change, of chaunce, of forrow, and her ending;
I wept for want: he faid, time bringes men vnder,
And fecret want can finde but fmall befrending.
    And as he faid, in that before I tried it,
      I blamde my wit forewarnd, yet neuer fpied it.
What néede I talke the order of my way,
Difcourfe was fteerefman while my barke did faile,
My fhip conceit, and fancie was my bay:
If thefe faile me, then faint my Mufe and faile,
    Haft brought vs where the haples Nimph foiourned,
      Beating the weeping waues that for her mourned.
He that hath féene the Northren blaftes difpoile
The pompe of Prime, and with a whiftling breath
Blaft and difpearfe the beauties of the foile;
May thinke vpon her paines more worfe than death.
    Alas poore Laffe the *Ecchoes* in the rockes
      Of *Sicilie*, her piteous plaining mockes.
Eccho her felfe when *Scilla* cried out *O loue!*
With piteous voice from out her hollow den
Returnd thefe words, thefe words of forrow, (*no loue*)
No loue (quoth fhe) then fie on traiterous men,
    Then fie on hope: then fie on hope (quoth *Eccho*)
      To euerie word the Nimph did anfwere fo.
For euery figh, the Rockes returnes a figh;
For euerie teare, their fountaines yeelds a drop;
Till we at laft the place approached nigh,
And heard the Nimph that fed on forrowes fop
    Make woods, and waues, and rockes, and hills admire
      The wonderous force of her vntam'd defire.
Glaucus (quoth fhe) is faire: whilft *Eccho* fings
Glaucus is faire: but yet he hateth *Scilla*
The wretch reportes: and then her armes fhe wrings
Whilft *Eccho* tells her this, he hateth *Scilla*,
    No hope (quoth fhe): no hope (quoth *Eccho*) then.
    Then fie on men: when fhe faid, fie on men.

Furie

Glaucus and Scilla.

Furie and *Rage*, *Wan-hope*, *Difpaire*, and *Woe*
From *Ditis* den by *Ate* fent, drewe nie:
Furie was red, with rage his eyes did gloe,
Whole flakes of fire from foorth his mouth did flie,
   His hands and armes ibath'd in blood of thofe
   Whome fortune, finne, or fate made Countries foes.
Rage, wan and pale vpon a Tiger fat,
Knawing vpon the bones of mangled men;
Naught can he view, but he repinde thereat:
His lockes were Snakes bred foorth in Stigian den,
   Next whom, *Difpaire* that déepe difdained elf
   Delightleffe liude, ftill ftabbing of her felf.
Woe all in blacke, within her hands did beare
The fatall torches of a Funerall,
Her Chéekes were wet, difpearfed was hir heare,
Her voice was fhrill (yet loathfome therewith all):
   Wan-hope (poore foule) on broken Ancker fitts,
   Wringing his armes as robbed of his witts.
Thefe fiue at once the forrowing Nimph affaile,
And captiue lead her bound into the rocks,
Where howling ftill fhe ftriues for to preuaile,
With no auaile yet ftriues fhe: for hir locks
   Are chang'd with wonder into hideous fands,
   And hard as flint become her fnow-white hands.
The waters howle with fatall tunes about her,
The aire dooth fcoule when as fhe turnes within them,
The winds and waues with puffes and billowes fkout her;
Waues ftorme, aire fcoules, both wind & waues begin them
   To make the place this mournful Nimph doth wéepe in,
   A haples haunt whereas no Nimph may kéepe in.
The Sea-man wandring by that famous Ifle,
Shuns all with feare difpairing *Scillaes* bowre;
Nimphes, Sea-gods, Syrens when they lift to fmile
Forfake the haunt of *Scilla* in that ftowre:
   Ah Nimphes thought I, if euerie coy one felt
   The like miffhappes, their flintie hearts would melt.
                          Thetis

Glaucus and Scilla.

Thetis reioyſt to ſée her foe depreſt,
Glaucus was glad, ſince *Scilla* was enthrald;
The Nimphs gan ſmile, to boaſt their *Glaucus* reſt:
Venus and *Cupid* in their throanes enſtald,
    At *Thetis* beck to *Neptunes* bowre repaire,
    Whereas they feaſt amidſt his pallace faire.

Of pure immortall *Nectar* is their drinke,
And ſwéete *Ambroſia* dainties doo repaſt them,
The *Tritons* ſing, *Palemon* ſmiles to thinke
Vpon the chance, and all the Nimphs doo haſt them
    To trick vp moſſie garlands where they woon,
    For louely *Venus* and her conquering Sonne.

From foorth the fountaines of his mothers ſtore,
Glaucus let flie a daintie Chriſtall baine
That waſht the Nimphs with labour tir'd before:
Cupid hee trips among this louely traine,
    Alonely I apart did write this ſtorie
    With many a ſigh and heart full ſad and ſorie.

Glaucus when all the Goddeſſes tooke reſt,
Mounted vpon a Dolphin full of glée:
Conueide me friendly from this honored feaſt,
And by the way, ſuch Sonnets ſong to me,
    That all the Dolphins neighbouring of his glide
    Daunſt with delight, his reuerend courſe beſide.

At laſt he left me, where at firſt he found me,
Willing me let the world and ladies knowe
Of *Scillas* pride, and then by oath he bound me
To write no more, of that whence ſhame dooth grow:
    Or tie my pen to *Pennie-knaues* delight,
    But liue with fame, and ſo for fame to wright.

Lenuoy.

L Adies he left me, truſt me I miſſay not,
  But ſo he left me, as he wild me tell you:
That Nimphs muſt yeeld, when faithfull louers ſtraie not,
Leaſt through contempt, almightie loue compell you
    With *Scilla* in the rockes to make your biding
    A curſed plague, for womens proud back-ſliding.

FINIS.

Glaucus complaint written
by the said Gent.

THe Billowes that by windes affifting breath
Dooth beate vpon the rocks at laft doo peirce them:
Ah then (thou gentle offpring of my death)
Why faile my plaints when penciue I rehearfe them
To wound thine eares? when as my words excéed them,
And that my fighes in fteade of windes doo leade them.
Along the floods I wander all forlorne,
Nor may the Sea-nimphes fmiles enforce me play:
But if I think, I think vpon thy fcorne,
And if I wifh, I wifh my difmall day,
Oh fruites of loue, oh powrefull courfe of paine!
That one fhould like the thing that hath him flaine.
Looke in my mothers Chriftall face, faire maide,
There read the ftorie of my bitter ftate;
My teares her filuer floatings haue alaid,
Her troubled lookes forefhowe my wretched fate:
If not for me, yet mourne her bitter wéeping,
And pittie him whofe heart is in thy kéeping.
Take pittie *Scilla*, pittie thou thy louer;
For thou art faire, and beautie fhould haue pittie,
Ahlas fhe flies, perfwafions cannot moue her,
She is too wanton, or too foolifh wittie:
Along the floates the fcalie troopes encreafe,
Yet nill fhe loue to maintaine natures peace.
Oh ftepdame *Nature* haft thou fhut thefe faires
Within the rampeir of fo déepe difdaine,
To kill a God with forrowes and difpaires:
Would God thy powre (to leffen all my paine)
Were dead in her; or fancies quenchles fire
Might from my breft with ceafeles courfe retire.

D   But

29

Glaucus complaint.

But all in vaine (fo vaine is loues purfute)
Trie I her eares, and tempt her hardned heart:
Ceafe wretched tongue, twere better ftill be mute,
Than tell a tale of griefe and endles fmart
    To her that grounds her glories on difdaine,
    And takes a pride to viewe my bitter paine.
(Fond that I am) all thefe are faint fuppofes:
Imperious Loue (to fhewe his endles power)
My tender and immortall heart enclofes
Within the center of her louely lowre:
    That all may fée, Loues prifon is her eie,
    And Gods muft ftoope vnto his deitie.
Yet (Loue) allot prefcriptions vnto woe;
Els will the fowre excéed the fwéete by farre:
Or leuell pittie from thy lawles bowe,
That forrowe in exceffe, may caufe a warre
    That may confume, if not confound my life;
    And I may féeme to die amidft the ftrife.
The deafe nill heare: both fhe and Loue together
Haue made a match to aggreuate my griefe:
I fée my hell, there refts no hope in either:
From proud contempt there fpringeth no reliefe,
    What refts there then but fince I may not gaine her,
    In piteous tearmes and teares for to complaine her.

FINIS.

The

The Difcontented Satyre writ-
ten by Thomas Lodge *Gent.*

Vch time as from her Mothers tender lap
  The night arofe, guarded with gentle winds:
  And with her precious dew refrefht the fap
Of bloome and barke (whilft that her mantle blinds
  The vaile of heauen) and euery bird was ftill
  Saue *Philomele*, that did bemoane her ill.
When in the Weft *Orion* lift aloft
His ftarrie creft, and fmil'd vpon the Twins;
And *Cynthia* féemely bright (whofe eie full oft
Had watcht her loue) with radient light begins
  To pierce the vaile of filence with her beames,
  Sporting with wanton cléere on *Ocean* ftreames.
When little winds in beating of their wings,
Did wooe the eies to leaue their wonted wake,
And all was hufht faue *Zephyrus*, that fings
With louely breathings for the Sea-nimphs fake:
  My watchfull griefes perplext my minde fo fore,
  That foorth I walkt my forrowes to deplore.
The doaly feafon that refembled well
My drooping heart, gaue life to my lament:
Each twinckling lamp that in the heauens did dwell
Gan reft his courfe to hearken mine entent:
  Foorth went I ftill deuifing on my feare
  Diftinguifhing each footeftep with a teare.
My working thought deluding of my pace,
At laft did bring me to a defart dale,
(By enuious mountaines robd of *Phœbus* face)
Where growes no hearb to tafte of deaws auaile,
  In midft thereof, vpon a bed of moffe
  A *Satyre* did his reftles bodie toffe.

D 2   Stearne

The discontented Satyre.

Stearne were his lookes, afflicting all the féelds
That were in view; his bushie lockes vndreft
With terror hang, his hauiour horror yéelds,
And with the fight my forrowes were fuppreft;
    So, néere I drewe, when fodenly he roafe,
    And thus in tearmes his purpofe did difclofe.
Blufh daies eternall lampe to fée thy lot,
Since that thy cléere with cloudy darkes is fcard;
Lowre on faire *Cinthia* for I like thée not;
For borrowed beauties, merit no regard:
    Boaft *Difcontent*, naught may depreffe thy powre,
    Since in thy felfe all griefe thou dooft deuoure.
Thou art the God whome I alone adore
Whofe powre includeth difcords all in one,
Confufions are thy foode and fatall ftore,
Thy name is feard where thou art moft vnknowne;
    Thy grace is great, for fortunes laugh and lowre
    Affailes them not, that glorie in thy powre.
The minde through thée diuines on endleffe things,
And formes a Heauen through others fond miflikes;
Time loathes thy haunt, yet lends thée many wings:
Refined wits againft thy bulwarke ftrikes;
    And when their curious thoughts are ouerpaft,
    They fcorne their bookes, and like thy bent at laft.
For who but thou can yéeld them any gaine?
Depriue the world of perfeft *Difcontent*;
All glories end, true honor ftraight is flaine,
And life it felfe in errors courfe is fpent,
    All toile dooth fort but to a forrie end,
    For through miflikes, each learnes for to commend.
What made fierce *Phillips* fonne to manage armes,
To vaile the pride of Perfia by his fword,
But thou my God, that he by others harmes
Might raife his feate: and thereby ftill afford
    A caufe of difcontent to them that loft,
    And hate in him that by their powre was croft.

                                                Le

The discontented Satyre.

Let enuie ceafe, what Prince can make it knowne
How déere he loues his beft eftéemed friends:
For were not fome of purpofe ouerthrowne,
Who may difcerne whereto true fauor tends:
  Thus Princes difcontent dooth honor fome,
  And others through their hates to credit come.
Without thy helpe the Soldier fhunnes the féeld:
You ftudeous Arts how fatall haps had you,
If difcontents did not fome fuccors yéeld ⸱
Oh fléeting Fame who could thy grace purfue:
  Did not my God fend emulations out
  To whet the wits and pens of *Pallas* rout,
How could the Heauens haue retrograde afpects
Without thy helpe ⸱ How might the Plannets finde
Their oppofitions, and their ftrange effects,
Vnleffe thy powre affifted euerie kinde ⸱
  The aire by thée at firft inuented voice,
  Which once reuerberate, ftraight yéelds a noice.
The pencile man that with a careles hand
Hath fhaddowed *Venus*, hates his flack regard;
And all amaz'd doth difcontented ftand,
And mends the fame that he before had mard:
  Who fées not then that it was *Difcontent*,
  That fight to eie, and perfect iudgement lent ⸱
The fchooleman that with héedleffe florifh writes,
Refines his fault, if thou direct his eie:
And then againe with wonder he endites
Such fwéete fententious lines, as neuer die:
  Loft in my felfe in praifing of thy might,
  My fpéech yéelds vp his office to delight.
This faid he fmil'd, and on his reftles bed
Repofde and toft his indifpofed lims:
A world of thoughts ftill hammerd in his head,
Now would he fléepe, and ftraight his couch he trims:
  And then he walkes, and therewith fits him downe:
  And faines to fing, yet endeth with a frowne.

D 3   I

33

The discontented Satyre.

I stood amaz'd and wondred at his words,
And sought to suck the soule from out his lips,
His rare discourse such wondrous ioye affords:
But vnawares, like lightfoote Fawne he trips
    Along the lawnes: and I with watch forespent,
    Drew home and vowde to honor *Discontent*.

FINIS.   *Thomas Lodge.*

Sundrie sweete Sonnets
written by the said
Gent.

In praise of the Countrey life.

M Ost *happie blest the man that midst his countrie bowers*
   Without suspect of hate, or dread of enuious tongue
May dwell among his owne: not dreading fortunes lowres,
Farre frõ those publique plagues that mightie men hath stoong:
   Whose libertie and peace is neuer sold for gaine,
   Whose words doo neuer sooth a wanton princes vaine.
Incertaine hopes, and vowes, doo neuer harme his thought,
And vaine desires doo shunne the place of his repose;
He weepes no yeares misspent, nor want of that he sought,
Nor reapes his gaine by words, nor builds vpon suppose:
   The stormes of troubled Sea do neuer force his fears, (ears,
   Nor Trumpets sound dooth chang his sleepes, or charme his
Ambitions neuer build within his constant minde,
A cunning coy deceipt his soule dooth not disguise,
His firme and constant faith corruptions neuer blind,
He neuer waits his weale from princes wandring eyes:
   But liuing well content with euerie kinde of thing,
   He is his proper court, his fauor, and his King.

His

Delectable Sonets.

His will (restraind by wit) is neuer forst awrie,
Vaine hopes, and fatall feares (the courtiers common foes)
(Afraid by his forefight) doo fhun his piercing eye:
And naught but true delight acquaints him where he goes,
No high attempts to winne; but humble thoughts and deeds.
The verie fruites and flowers that fpring from vertues feeds.
(O deities diuine) your Godheads I adore
That haunt the hils, the feelds, the forrests and the fprings,
That make my quiet thoughts contented with my ftore,
And fixe my hopes on heauen, and not on earthly things;
That driue me from defires, (in view of courtly ftrife,)
And drawe me to commend the fields and countrie life.
My thoughts are now enclofde within my proper land,
And if my bodie fleepe my minde dooth take his reft,
My fimple zeale and loue my dangers doo withftand,
The mornings pleafant ayer inuites me from my nest,
If wether wax too warme I feeke the filent fhade,
If frosts afflict, I ftriue for warmth by hunters trade.
Although my biding home be not imbost with gold,
And that with cunning skill my chambers are not drest,
(Whereas the curious eye my fundrie fights behold)
Yet feedes my quiet lookes on thoufand flowers at leaft,
The treafures of the plaine, the beauties of the fpring,
Made rich with Rofes fweete and euerie pleafant thing.
Amidst the pallace braue puft vp with wanton fhowes
Ambicions dwell, and there falfe fauors finde difguife,
There lodge confuming cares that hatch our common woes:
Amidst our painted feelds the pleafant Fayrie lies,—
And all thofe powers diuine that with vntruffed treffes,
Contentment, happie loue, and perfect fport profeffes.
So liuing, naught remaines my folace to betray;
I heare the pleafant birds record their facred ftraines,
When at the mornings rife they bleffe the fpringing day:
The murmuring fountains noife from out the marble vaines,
Are pleafing to mine eares: whilft with a gentill fall
They fleete from hie, and ferue to wet the meads withall.

What

Delectable Poems.

What sport may equall this, to see two prettie doues
When neb to neb they ioyne, in fluttering of their wings,
And in their roundelaies with kisses seale their loues?
Then wondering at the gifts which happie nature brings;
    What sport is it to sleepe and slumber by a well,
    Whose fleeting falls maks show, some louely tale to tell?
Oh what content to see amidst the darkesome night
(When as the setting sonne hath left the moone in place)
The Nimphes amidst the vales and groues to take delight,
To dance, to leap, to skip, with sweet and pleasant grace,
    To giue greene gownes in sport, and in their tripping make
    By force of footing all the springing grasse to quake.
Their daunces brought to end, I lift my lookes one hie
To see the horned moone, and deskant on her hew
Cleere siluer shining bright, and eftsoones then think I
Vpon that hapie chance the Latmian *shepheard knew:*
    Then doo I wish myselfe as faire a friend as she,
    But watching I desire she might disport with me.
Thus midst the silent night my selfe I doo content:
Then when as Phœbus *beames our* Hemisphere *enflames,*
A thousand change of sports for pleasure I inuent,
And feast my quiet thoughts with sundrie pleasant games,
    Now angle I awhile, then seek I for the chace,
    And straight my limerods catch the Sparrows on the place.
I like, and make some loue: but yet in such a sort
That naught but true delight my certaine sute pursues;
My libertie remaines, and yet I reape the sport,
Nor can the snares of loue my heedefull thoughts abuse:
    But when I would forgoe, I haue the power to flie,
    And stand aloofe and laugh, while others starue and die.
My sweete and tender flocks (my faithfull feeld compeers)
You forrests, hoults, and groues, you meads & mountaines hie,
Be you the witnesses of my contented yeares:
And you O sacred powers vouchsafe my humble crie,
    And during all my daies, doo not these ioyes estrange;
    But let them still remaine, and graunt no other change.

Finis.

In

Poems.

In commendation of a folitarie life.

NOt yet forfaken (gentle Mufe) draw neere,
And helpe to wearie out thefe worldly thoughts;
Goe fit thy methode to my moodie cheere,
For why fond pleafure now preuaileth noughts:
    Since where content and wealthie ftate declines,
    The heart dooth droope, and dolefull be the lines.
For thy (fond man) why reft I not at laft?
My wings of hope are clipte by foule difgrace:
The filuer downe of age now flocketh faft,
Like moffe on oake to dwell vpon my face:
    And what with thoght & time, through want & ruth:
    I challenge care for ioy, and age for youth.
What fruites of former labours doo I finde?
My ftudious pen dooth traffique for a fcorne:
My due deferts are but repaid with winde;
And what I earne, is nought but bitter mourne:
    In which accompt I reap but this aduife,
    To ceafe to clime, and liue contented wife.
But gentle Mufe, where boadeth this content?
The Princes Court is fraught with endleffe woes,
Corruptions flocke where honors doo frequent,
The Cities fwarme with plagues, with futes, with foes:
    High climing wits doo catch a fodein fall,
    With none of thefe Content lift dwell withall.
Ah beautie of the double topped hill,
Thou faddeft fifter of the facred nine,
What fruitfull pleafance followeth now my quill?
What wondrous beauties bleffe my drooping eine?
    Euen fuch as earft the fhepheard in the fhade
    Beheld, when he a Poet once was made.
Me thinkes I fee the deferts frefh arraid,
New mantled in their liueries of greene,
Whofe frolicke pride makes fmiling heauen a paid;
Wherein the Nymphs doo wearie out their teene,
    Wafhing their iuorie in thofe murmuring fprings,
    At whofe kinde fall, the birds with pleafure fings.

E   See

Poems.

See where the babes of memorie are laid
Vnder the ſhadow of *Apollos* tree,
That pleit their garlands freſh, and well apaid,
And breath foorth lines of daintie poecie:
> Ah world farewell, the ſight hereof dooth tell,
> That true content dooth in the deſert dwell.

See where a Caue preſents it ſelfe to eie,
By Natures hand enforſt in marble vaines;
Where climing Cedars with their ſhades denie,
The eye of day to ſee what there remaines:
> A couch of moſſe, a brooke of ſiluer cleere,
> And more, for foode a flocke of ſauage deere.

Then here (kinde Muſe) vouchſafe to dwell with me,
My veluet robe ſhalbe a weede of gray
And leaſt my heart by tongue betrayed be,
For idle talke I will goe faſt and pray:
> No ſooner ſaid and thought, but that my heart
> His true ſuppoſde content gan thus impart.

Sweete ſolitarie life thou true repoſe,
Wherein the wiſe contemplate heauen aright,
In thee no dread of warre or worldly foes,
In thee no pompe ſeduceth mortall ſight,
> In thee no wanton eares to win with words,
> Nor lurking toyes, which Citie life affoords.

At peepe of day when in her crimſon pride,
The Morne beſpreds with roſes all the waie
Where *Phœbus* coach with radiant courſe muſt glide,
The Hermit bends his humble knees to pray:
> Bleſsing that God, whoſe bountie did beſtow
> Such beauties on the earthly things below.

Whether with ſolace tripping on the trees
He ſees the citizens of Forreſt ſport,
Or midſt the withered oake beholds the Bees
Intend their labour with a kinde conſort:
> Downe drop his teares, to thinke how they agree,
> Where men alone with hate inflamed be.

Taſte

Poems.

Tafte he the fruites that fpring from *Tellus* woomb;
Or drinke he of the chriftall fprings that flowes:
He thankes his God, and fighes their curfed doomb
That fondly wealth in furfetting beftowes:
    And with Saint *Hierom* faith, *The Defert is*
    A paradife of folace, ioy, and blis.
Father of light, thou maker of the heauen,
From whom my being well, and being fprings:
Bring to effect this my defired fteauen,
That I may leaue the thought of worldly things:
    Then in my troubles will I bleffe the time,
    My Mufe vouchfafde me fuch a luckie rime.

Finis. T. L.

Beauties Lullabie.

Hos ego verficulos feci, tulit alter honores.

GEntlemen, I had thought to haue fuppreffed this *Lullabie* in filence,
amongft my other papers that lie buried in obliuion: but the impu-
dent arrogancie of fome more then infolent Poets haue altered my
purpofe in that refpect, and made me fet my name to my owne worke,
leaft fome other vaine glorious *Batillus* fhould preiudice my paines, by
fubfcribing his name to that which is none of his owne.

Non mefureè.

    Lullabie Beautie, fweet Beautie lullabie;
    To fuch kind of Infants fing lulla would I.

S Weet, fweet defire that made my pleafant wondring eyes
To gaze on fuch a blazing ftarre, as dims the ftate of skies:
Whofe feature while my Mufe doth now deuife vpon;
Sweet Beautie reft thee ftill awhile, I fhal haue done anon.
    Firft lulla to thofe lockes deriu'd from Phœbus *rayes,*
Which faften light in dimmeft lookes by vertue of their fprayes:
From whence her golden wiers Diana *borowed then,*
When with Arachne *at the loombe fhe ftroue amidft the fen.*

Poems.

Next lulla to the front where onlie fhrowdes the die,
Which ruddie Morrow borowed then when Thetis *fhe did fpie*
To hunt forbidden bed, whereas vermillion hue
Is ftaind in fight, and euery fenfe approues my cenfure true.

Next lulla to thofe ftatelie couerts of her eyes,
In which in Alablafter white dame Nature did deuife
A fubtil frame of fetled wiers, in fuch confufed art:
As thofe that looke but on that worke amazed doo depart.

Next lulla to thofe lamps, thofe twinckling ftemmes of ftate:
Wherof but one, doth dim the Sunne (both) Sunne & Moone *do*
On which while Ioue *doth prie, the ielous* Iuno *chides. (mate,*
Thus Gods & men admire at her in whom fuch beautie bides.

But he that doth but marke thofe rocks of marble white;
Frõ whẽce do fpring thofe fweet perfumes the fenfes that delight,
And fees with how great ftate the ruddie lippes they fhade,
Wil think the workmã more diuine that fuch a work hath made.

Now fee thofe crimfon cheekes, the mounts wherein do dwell
The golden fruit Æneas *fet from midft the mouth of hell,*
Bedect with driuen fnow, and pounft with Rubie red;
To which compare the ruddie rofe, and it wil feeme but dead.

Next praife thofe cherrie lips where rofe and lillie meete,
Enclofures of th' Egiptian *gems, frõ whence doth* Zephir *fweet*
Breath forth a blaft, and yeeld a noyfe like to Orpheus *lute,*
Which mou'd the craggie rocks to ruth, & ftird what fo was mute.

Yet in that dimpled chinne bedect with euery grace,
Where curious eye may eaflie fee the beautie of the face.
Admit but this, that Ganimede *the cuppe for* Ioue *did chufe:*
And if a man might drink with Gods, would I the fame might vfe.

Then bleffed be thofe mounts where Venus *fits and fings,*
With wanton Cupid *in her lappe, and from thofe ftatelie fprings*
Draws Nectar *forth to feed her fonne: which taft him fo beguild,*
That onlie for to fucke thofe teates, he ftill would be a child.

But looke a low (my Mufe) and fixe thy ftatelie view:
Behold a path like Dedalls *maze, wherein with azure clew*
A Thefeus *may the fecret cells of beautie there behold,*
More ftatelie than th' Egiptian *tombes, though reared all of gold.*

Next

Poems.

Next which of Alablaster *white a mountaine there doth rife,*
A mountaine faire of driuen fnowe, wherein incarued lies
A ftatelie tipe of Venus *vale: fome calls it* Cupids *couch;*
Whereas the God deulfing lies which part were beft to touch.

There fpies he earths Elizium, *where Nature fits and paints*
Th' impreffions of the fweeteft formes her fancie her acquaints:
In which one lulla I would rocke to Beautis grace,
And be a prentife during life to ferue her in that place.

Next lulla to thofe forts whereout doth fancie prie,
As one amaz'd to fee the ftarre is fixt before her eye.
A Crinite Comet *crisped faire which on thofe arches ftands*
Of Marble white enameled, and clofde with azure bands.

But he that fees thofe knees, whofe feature is fo faire.
As when they bend, all knees do bend below and midft the aire;
Whofe cords by compaffe knit, and nerues by Nature fet,
Bindes Art apprentife for fome yeres the patterne for to get.

Here refts not wonders yet: for why behold a lowe
Two rifing filuer coloured clowdes, which like to thofe doo fhewe,
As compaft in faire Phœbus *then, when in his midday prime*
He fported with Caffandra *faire, amidft the fommer time.*

Now Nature ftands amazd her felfe to looke on Beauties feete,
To fee thofe ioynts combinde in one, and fram'd of Amber fweete,
So fmall a pile fo great a waight, like Atlas *to vphold*
The bodie, as the mightie man to beare the heauens is bold.

But to behold thofe Gemini, *thofe filuer coloured armes,*
Whõ natiue bloud with blufhing ftreames in azure cõduits warmes,
Inuite the fence like violets, bepurfurated faire
With Floras *lillies, lillie white thefe louelie branches are.*

But whileft I gaze a low, and fee thofe palmes of peace,
Wherein the mappe of fortune refts and times difcents increafe:
From whence the branching fingers fpred betipt with iuorie,
The leaft impreffion whereof a marble mind might mollifie.

Makes me cõfeffe pen may not write, hart think, nor tung vnfold
The leaft effect in Beautie, where both iuorie, pearle, and gold,
Where purphure, Ebonie, white, and red, al colours ftained bee:
And if thou feeke for all thefe fwcetes, then feeke my fweet to fee.

Finis.

E 3

Sundrie

41

Sundrie sweete Sonnets
written by the same
Gent.

1

A Verie *Phœnix*, in her radiant eies
  I leaue mine age, and get my life againe;
True *Hesperus*, I watch her fall and rise:
And with my teares extinguish all my paine,
  My lips for shadowes shield her springing roses,
Mine eies for watchmen guard her while shee sleepeth,
My reasons serue to quite her faint supposes:
Her fancie, mine; my faith her fancie keepeth;
She flowre, I branch; her sweetes my sowres supporteth,
O happie Loue, where such delights conforteth.
                 Finis.

2

I *Vow but with some griefe henceforth to shunne the place,*
  Where beautie casts her scortching lookes to feed me with dis-
And since I was so fond to build on such a molde,   *(grace.*
As euery waue of vaine conceit the substance may vnfolde;
    I will repent with teares the errors of my mind,
      And leaue to tie my thoghts to like of wanton womankind.
Whose wayward wiles I spie how full of sleights they be,
The heart delights in others choise, the hand yet faunes on me,
And faine she would forsake, yet followes if I shunne,
And with her tung repents the time that ere the fact was done.
    And yet she will be thought as constant as the best;
      Yet scornes the mã that beareth faith & courage in his crest.
Whom if she list to knowe, his colour sable is;
A mournful colour meete for those whose eyes haue gaz'd amis:
His colour pale for woe, his courage all forlorne;
His hart confirm'd to shun the sex that holds his faith in scorne.
    Willing all men to learne, least they be forst to proue,
      That women alter with the wind, and haue no hold in loue.
                 Finis.
                    The

Sonnets.

3

THe heauens inclinde to change, are paſsing cleere,
  Their ſhowres reſtraind make billowes of mine eies,
Their windes made calme within my breaſt appeere,
Which dims the aire with ſighs and heauie cries.
My frozen loue hath laid the froſt adowne,
Theſe ſnowes reſtraind ſerue to congeale my heart,
This pleaſant ſpring my ſtormie ſorrowes frowne:
Goe lying bookes, ceaſe fooles to boaſt your art,
  And marke the cauſe: my Miſtres ſmiles and lowres
  Makes cleere the heauens, & clowdes my heart with
            Finis.   (ſhowers.

4

I *Will become a Hermit now,*
  and doo my penance ſtraight
For all the errors of mine eyes
  with fooliſh raſhnes fild:
My hermitage ſhall placed be,
  where mellancholies waight,
And none but loue alone ſhall knowe
  the bower I meane to build.
My daylie diet ſhall be care,
  made calme by no delight:
My dolefull drinke my drierie teares,
  amidſt the darkeſome place
The fire that burnes my heedles heart
  ſhall ſtand in ſtead of light,
And ſhall confume my wearie life
  mine errors to deface.
My gowne ſhall be of ſpreding gray
  to clad my limmes withall:
My late repent vpon my browe
  ſhall plainlie written be.
My tedious griefe and great remorſe
  that doth my ſoule enthrall,
Shall ſerue to plead my wearie paines

and

43

Sonnets.

and penſiue miſerie.
Of faintfull hope ſhall be my ſtaffe,
and daylie when I pray,
My miſtris picture plac't by loue
ſhall witnes what I ſay.

Finis.

5

I F that I ſeeke the ſhade, I ſodeinlie doo ſee
The God of Loue forſake his bow, and ſit me by:
If that I thinke to write, his Muſes pliant be:
If that I plaine my griefe, the wanton boy will crie.
  If I lament my cares, he dooth increaſe my paine:
If teares my cheeks attaint, his cheeks be moyſt with mone:
If I diſcloſe the wounds the which my heart hath ſlaine,
He takes his *Faſcia* off, and wipes them drie anone.
  If that I walke the woods, the woods are his delight:
If I my ſelfe torment, he bathes him in my blood:
He will my Souldier be if once I wend to fight:
If ſeas delight, he ſteeres my barke amid the floud:
    In briefe, the cruell God dooth neuer from me goe,
    But makes my laſting loue eternall by my woe.

Finis.

6

V V Earie am I to wearie Gods and men,
Wearie am I to weep ſo manie teares
without ſome ſuccor:
Wearie am I my wretched ſtate to ken,
Wearie am I to ſee my wofull yeares
conſume with dolor.
Theſe mounts, theſe fields, theſe rocks, theſe waues, theſe woods
Reſigne their ecchoes to my wofull cries,
too much diſdained:
Theſe lambes, theſe kidds, theſe bullockes, leaue their foods,
Theſe flowers, this graſſe, with mourning parched lies
to ſee me pained.
Naught vnder Sunne that hath not tasted change,

My

44

Sonnets.

My bitter griefe alone abideth ftill
without departure.
Accurft be Loue, that wrought this wonder ftrange,
Boading my forowes by my wanton will
that caufde my fmarting.
O quiet life forepaft, why haft thou left
The wofull fhepheard wearie of his paine
to feed on forrow?
Oh weeping eies of wonted ioyes bereft,
Why leaue you him whom luckleffe Loue hath flaine
to view the morrow?
My faintfull flocke dooth languifh and lament,
To fee their mafter mourning his mifchance
this iolly feafon:
My bagpip's broke, my roundelaies are blent,
My rebecke now my folace to aduance
accounts it geafon:
Yet not alone fheepe, lambes, kidds weep my woe:
But rockes for ruth, and birds for forow plaine
my wofull wending:
Then cruell Loue vouchfafe me to forgoe
My wretched life, the caufe of mickle paine,
and make mine ending.
The rockes their brookes with murmuring noyfe fhall weepe,
The birds their fongs with warbling notes fhall fing;
and full of pleafure
My flockes fhall feed, although their mafter fleep,
And to my graue their falling fleeces bring,
their natiue treafure.
Solace each where fhall raigne when I am dead,
No care, no woe, no forrow fhall preuaile:
but well contented
Poore I fhall fleep, when curfed Loue is fled,
That firft with furie did the fields affaile
where I frequented.

Finis.

F   The

45

Sonnets.

7

THe earth late choakt with fhowers
Is now araid in greene :
Her bofome fprings with flowers,
The aire diffolues her teene,
    The heauens laugh at her glorie :
    Yet bide I fad and forie.
The woods are deckt with leaues,
And trees are cloathed gaie,
And *Flora* crownd with fheues
With oaken boughs dooth play:
    Where I am clad in blacke,
    The token of my wracke.
The birds vpon the trees
Doo fing with pleafant voices,
And chaunt in their degrees
Their loues and luckie choices :
    When I, whilft they are finging,
    With fighs mine armes am wringing.
The Thrufhes feeke the fhade,
And I my fatall graue :
Their flight to heauen is made,
My walke on earth I haue :
    They free, I thrall : they iolly,
    I fad and penciue wholly.

8

WHen with aduice I weigh my yeares forepast,
    And count the courfe that in my youth I kept:
How my fond eies on garifh beautie plaft,
Dimde by defires in vaine opinion flept:
    For euerie looke and thought with teares I crie,
    I loath the faults and follies of mine eie.
By which my heart was burnt with fcorching flame,
Growing to head by ftealth of idle time,
Whom oft my lookes with blufhing red did blame;
But follie fixt before, it grew to prime:
    So for my wanton lookes with teares I crie,
    I loath the faults and follies of mine eie.
Oh wanton looks, yee foes of sad forecast,
That wept the teares of will, and not repent:
Now fee the end how fickle faire is past,

And

46

Sonnets.

And crimfon cheekes with crooked yeares are fpent:
And blame your felues, and helpe my carefull crie,
Who loath the faults and follies of mine eye.

Finis.

H And, heart, and eye, toucht, thought, and did behold   9
  A lock, a ioye, a looke of great delight,
Lookes fweet, ioyes rare, but lockes of beaten gold,
Hearts ioye, eyes lookes, hands touch fo pleafde my fight;
   That what I would, by eye, hand, heart I trie,
   And what I am, is but hand, heart, and eye.

Finis.

I *F hollowe eyes, if wan and wearifh face,*   10
 If fcalding fighes my fecret fuites bewray:
Loe (loue) thofe lookes that want their former grace,
And dying thoughts which fecret ioyes betray.
   And grant me this that either death may eafe,
   Or humble fuite my miftris wrath appeafe.
Whofe dire difdaine more pines my fainting heart,
Than Ætnaes flame that fumes both night and day:
Whofe wifedome when it meafures by defart,
Diffolues my doubts and driues my woes away:
   Whofe lookes if once they yeeld me beames of grace,
   Difcharge the furrowes that befret my face.
Twixt hope and happe my fhippe doth beare a faile,
The Seas are fighes, the Ancker flipper ioye;
Would Sea and Ancker both, and tacke might faile,
So land of loue were gain'd to foile annoye.
   I fay no more, the teare that laft did fall
   On latter line, can fhewe and open all.

Finis.

A Satyre fitting by a riuer fide,   11
  Foreworne with care that hardlie findes recure:
A ftraying Nymph in pafsion did deride
His teares, his care, her fmiles her fcornes affure:
   He wept, fhe wifht, and all their thoughts among,
   Fancie beheld and fung this carefull fong.

F 2   Perhaps

Sonnets.

Perhaps the furrowes in thy wrinckled face
Growne by thy griefe, abate thy wonted forme:
Perhaps her eye was formde to yeeld difgrace,
And blemifht that which wit may not reforme.
    Perhaps fhe will if fo thou lift to proue,
    Perhaps fhe likes, and yet fhe dares not loue.
But if (perhaps) thy fortune be fo faire,
Laugh Satyre then it proues a pretie prize:
And if thou wilt, fo liue to fhunne difpaire
As looking long thou keepe thy proper eyes.
    This faid fhe ceaft: the Nymph fhe fled away,
    And good perfwafion caufde the Satyre play.

12 *Faire* Phœbus *flowre vpon a fommer morne,*
    Gan proud with loue to fhewe her painted pride,
And gay with glorie with a curious fcorne,
Difdainde thofe buds that bloffom'd her befide.
    When Rofe and Lillies, Violets and Balme,
    (Scarce warm'd to worke their beauties to a flowre)
With enuious wrath neere to a water calme,
Beheld my Phillis *in a happie howre.*
    Not wak't nor wonne too much with folemne fleepe,
But fweetlie flombring they beheld my Saint,
The Rofe and Lillies both together creepe;
The one her lip, the next her cheeke did taint,
    And both they fpread: the Violet confum'd
To gentle ayre her amber breath fulfilled:
Apollo *feeling all the aire perfumde,*
With gentle beames into her eyes distilled.
    His flowre amaz'd, gaue Rofe and Lillies place,
The Sunne his fhine within her eyes containeth,
The Rofe her lips, the Lillies decke her face,
The Violet within her breath remaineth.

Lenuoy.

THen ceafe (fond men) henceforth to boaft your flowers,
    Since Rofes, Lillies, Violets are ours:
    And Phœbus *flowre doth homage to their powers,*
And Phillis *eye his glorious beames deuours.*

FINIS.

NOTE

As the only known copy of the Firſt Edition of "Roſalynde. Euphues Golden Legacie," 1590, is imperfeċt, the text of Sig. R (pp. 129-136), diſtinguiſhed by being encloſed within ſquare brackets, is reprinted from the Second Edition of 1592.

Rosalynde.

Euphues golden le-

gacie: found after his death
in his Cell at Si-
lexedra.

Bequeathed to Philautus sonnes
noursed vp with their
father in Eng-
land.

Fetcht from the Canaries.
By T. L. Gent.

LONDON,
Imprinted by *Thomas Orwin* for *T. G.*
and *John Busbie.*
1 5 9 0.

TO THE RIGHT HO-
nourable and his moſt eſteemed
Lord the Lord of Hunſdon, Lord
Chamberlaine of her Maieſties
houſhold, and Gouernor of her
Towne of Barwicke:
T.L.G. wiſheth increaſe
of all honourable ver-
tues.

*Vch* Romanes *(right Ho-*
nourable) as delighted in
martiall exploytes, attemp-
ted their actions in the ho-
nour of Auguſtus, *becauſe*
he was a Patron of ſouldi-
ers: and Virgil *dignified him with his poems,*
as a Mœcenas *of ſchollers; both ioyntly ad-*
uauncing his royaltie, as a Prince warlike and
learned. Such as *ſacrifice to* Pallas, *preſent*
her with bayes as ſhe is wiſe, and with armour
as ſhe is valiant; obſeruing herein that excel-
lent το πρεπον *which dedicateth honours accor-*
ding to the perfection of the perſon. VVhen *J*

A 2   *entred*

3

The Epiſtle

*entred (right honourable) with a deep inſight
into the conſideration of theſe premiſſes, ſeeing
your L. to be a Patron of all martiall men, and
a* Mœcenas *of ſuch as applie themſelues to ſtudie; wearing with* Pallas *both the launce and
the bay, and ayming with* Auguſtus *at the fauour of all, by the honourable vertues of your
minde: being my ſelfe first a Student, and after
falling from bookes to armes, euen vowed in all
my thoughts dutifully to affect your L. Hauing
with Capt:* Clarke *made a voyage to the Ʒ-
lands of* Terceras *& the* Canaries, *to beguile
the time with labour, Ʒ writ this booke; rough,
as hatcht in the ſtormes of the Ocean, and feathered in the ſurges of many perillous ſeas. But
as it is the worke of a ſouldier and a ſcholler, Ʒ
preſumed to ſhrowde it vnder your Honors patronage, as one that is the fautor and fauourer
of all vertuous actions; and whoſe honourable
Loues growen from the generall applauſe of the
whole Common wealth for your higher deſerts,
may keep it frō the mallice of euery bitter tung.
Other reaſons more particular (right Honorable) chalenge in me a ſpeciall affection to your L.
as being a ſcholler with your two noble ſonnes,*
Ma-

4

Dedicatorie.

Master Edmond Carew *& M.* Robert Carew, *(two ſiens worthie of ſo honorable a tree,
and a tree glorious in ſuch honourable fruite)
as alſo being ſcholler in the Vniuerſitie vnder
that learned and vertuous Knight Sir* Edward
Hobbie, *when he was Batcheler in Arts, a mā
as well lettered as well borne, and after the E-
tymologie of his name ſoaring as high as the
wings of knowledge can mount him, happie euerie way, & the more fortunate, as bleſſed in the
honor of ſo vertuous a Ladie. Thus (right honourable) the duetie that Ĵ owe to the ſonnes,
chargeth me that all my affection be placed on
the father; for where the braunches are ſo precious, the tree of force must be most excellent.
Commaunded and emboldened thus with the
conſideration of theſe forepaſſed reaſons, to preſent my Booke to your Lordſhip; I humbly intreate, your Honour will vouch of my labours,
and fauour a ſouldiers and a ſchollers pen with
your gracious acceptance; who anſweres in affection what he wants in eloquence; ſo deuoted
to your Honour, as his onely deſire is, to end his
life vnder the fauour of ſo martiall and learned a Patron.*

A 3   *Resting*

The Epiſtle

Resting thus in hope of your Lordſhips cour-
teſie, in deyning the Patronage of my worke, J
ceaſe: wiſhing you as many honourable for-
tunes as your Lordſhip can deſire, or I imagine.

Your Honours ſouldier
humbly affectionate:

Thomas Lodge.

To

To the Gentlemen Readers.

 Entlemen, look not here
to find anie fprigs of *Pal-
las* bay tree, nor to heare
the humour of any amo-
rous Lawreate, nor the
pleafing vaine of anie e-
loquent Orator: *Nolo altum fapere,* they be
matters aboue my capacitie; the Coblers
checke fhall neuer light on my head, *Ne fu-
tor vltra crepidam,* I will goe no further than
the latchet, and then all is well. Heere you
may perhaps find fom leaues of *Venus* mir-
tle, but heawen down by a fouldier with his
curtleaxe, not bought with the allurement
of a filed tongue. To be briefe Gentlemen,
roome for a fouldier, & a failer, that giues
you the fruits of his labors that he wrought
in the *Ocean,* when euerie line was wet with
a furge, & euerie humorous pafsion countercheckt with a ftorme. If you like it, fo:
and

To the Gentlemen Readers.

and yet I will be yours in duetie, if you bee mine in fauour. But if *Momus* or anie fquint-eied affe that hath mightie eares to con-ceiue with *Midas*, and yet little reafon to iudge; if hee come aboord our Barke to find fault with the tackling, when he knows not the fhrowdes, Ile downe into the hold, and fetch out a ruftie poliax, that fawe no funne this feauen yeare, and either well be baft him, or heaue the cockfcombe ouer boord to feede cods. But courteous Gen-tlemen that fauour moft, backbite none, & pardon what is ouerslipt, let fuch come & vvelcome, Ile into the Stevvards roome, & fetch them a kan of our beft beuradge. VVell Gentlemen, you haue *Euphues Lega-cie*. I fetcht it as farre as the Ilands of *Ter-ceras*, and therefore read it; cenfure vvith fauour, and farevvell.

Yours   T.L.

Rofa-

Rosalynd.

Here dwelled adioyning to the ci-
tie of *Bourdeaux* a Knight of moſt
honorable parentage, whom Fortune had graced with manie fauours, and Nature honored with
ſundrie exquiſite qualities, ſo beautified with the excellence of both,
as it was a queſtion whether Fortune or Nature were more prodi-
gall in deciphering the riches of their bounties. Wiſe hée
was, as holding in his head a ſupreme conceipt of policie,
reaching with NESTOR into the depth of all ciuill gouernment; and to make his wiſedome more gracious, he had
that *ſalem ingenij* and pleaſant eloquence that was ſo highlie commended in VLISSES: his valour was no leſſe than his
wit, nor the ſtroake of his Launce no leſſe forcible, than the
ſweetneſſe of his tongue was perſwaſiue: for he was for
his courage choſen the principall of all the Knights of *Malta*. This hardie Knight thus enricht with Vertue and Honour, ſurnamed Sir IOHN of *Bourdeaux*, hauing paſſed the
prime of his youth in ſundrie battailes againſt the *Turkes*,
at laſt (as the date of time hath his courſe) grew aged: his
haires were ſiluer hued, and the map of age was figured on
his forehead: Honour ſat in the furrowes of his face, and
many yeres were pourtraied in his wrinckled liniaments,
that all men might perceiue his glaſſe was runne, and that

B   Nature

Euphues

Nature of neceffity chalenged her due. Sir IOHN (that with the Phenix knewe the tearme of his life was now expyred, and could with the Swanne difcouer his end by her fongs) hauing three fonnes by his wife LYNIDA, the verie pride of all his forepaffed yeres, thought now (feeing death by conftraint would compell him to leaue them) to beftowe vpon them fuch a Legacie as might bewray his loue, and increafe their enfuing amitie. Calling therefore thefe yong Gentlemen before him in the prefence of all his fellowe Knights of *Malta*, he refolued to leaue them a memoriall of his fatherlie care, in fetting downe a methode of their brotherlie dueties. Hauing therefore death in his lookes to mooue them to pitie, and teares in his eyes to paint out the depth of his paffions, taking his eldeft fonne by the hand, hee began thus.

Sir Iohn of Bourdeaux Legacie he gaue to his Sonnes.

OH my Sonnes, you fee that Fate hath fet a period of my yeares, and Deftinies haue determined the finall ende of my daies: the Palme tree waxeth away ward, for he ftoopeth in his height, and my plumes are full of ficke feathers touched with age. I muft to my graue that difchargeth all cares, and leaue you to the world that encreafeth many forowes: my filuer haires conteineth great experience, and in the number of my yeares are pend downe the fubtilties of Fortune. Therefore as I leaue you fome fading pelfe to counterchecke pouertie, fo I will bequeath you infallible precepts that fhall leade you vnto vertue. Firft therefore vnto thée SALADYNE the eldeft, and therefore the chiefeft piller of my houfe, wherein fhould be ingrauen as well the excellence of thy fathers qualities, as the effentiall forme of his porportion, to thée I giue fouretéene ploughlands, with all my Mannor houfes and richeft plate. Next vnto FERNANDYNE I bequeath twelue ploughlands.

But

But vnto ROSADER the yongeſt I giue my Horſe, My Armour and my Launce, with ſixteene ploughlands: for if the inward thoughts be diſcouered by outward ſhadowes, ROSADER will excéed you all in bountie and honour. Thus (my Sonnes) haue I parted in your portions the ſubſtance of my wealth, wherein if you bee as prodigall to ſpend, as I haue béen carefull to get, your friends will grieue to ſee you more waſtfull than I was bountifull, and your foes ſmile that my fall did begin in your exceſſe. Let mine honour be the glaſſe of your actions, and the fame of my vertues the Loadſtarre to direct the courſe of your pilgrimage. Ayme your déedes by my honorable endeuours, and ſhewe your ſelues ſiens worthie of ſo floriſhing a trée: leaſt as the birds HALCYONES which excéede in whiteneſſe, I hatch yong ones that ſurpaſſe in blackneſſe. Climbe not my ſonnes; aſpiring pride is a vapour that aſcendeth hie, but ſoone turneth to a ſmoake: they which ſtare at the Starres, ſtumble vppon ſtones; and ſuch as gaze at the Sunne (vnleſſe they bee Eagle eyed) fall blinde. Soare not with the Hobbie, leaſt you fall with the Larke; nor attempt not with PHAETON, leaſt you drowne with ICARUS. Fortune when ſhe wils you to flie, tempers your plumes with waxe, and therefore either ſit ſtill and make no wing, or els beware the Sunne, and holde DEDALUS axiome authenticall (*medium tenere tutiſſimum*). Low ſhrubbes haue déepe rootes, and poore Cottages great patience. Fortune lookes euer vpward, and enuie aſpireth to neſtle with dignitie. Take héede my ſonnes, the meane is ſwéeteſt melodie; where ſtrings high ſtretcht, either ſoone cracke, or quicklie growe out of tune. Let your Countries care be your hearts content, and thinke that you are not borne for your ſelues, but to leuell your thoughts to be loyall to your Prince, carefull for the Common weale, and faithfull to your friends; ſo ſhall *France* ſay, theſe men are as excellent in vertues, as they be exquiſite in features. Oh my ſonnes, a friend is a precious Iewell, within whoſe boſome you may vnloade your ſorowes and vnfolde your

B 2 ſecrets,

Euphues

secretes, and hee either will releeue with counfaile, or perfwade with reafon: but take heede in the choyce, the outward fhew makes not the inward man, nor are the dimples
in the face the Calenders of trueth. When the Liquorice
leafe looketh moft drie, then it is moft wet. When the
fhoares of *Lepanthus* are moft quiet, then they forepoint a
ftorme. The Baaran leafe the more faire it lookes, the more
infectious it is, and in the fwéeteft words is oft hid the moft
trecherie. Therefore my fonnes, choofe a friend as the HI-
PERBOREI do the mettals, feuer them from the ore with fire,
& let them not bide the ftamp before they be currant; fo trie
and then truft, let time be touchftone of friendfhip, & then
friends faithfull lay them vp for Iewells. Be valiant my
fonnes, for cowardife is the enemie to honour; but not too
rafh, for that is an extreame. Fortitude is the meane, and
that is limitted within bonds, and prefcribed with circumftance. But aboue all, and with that he fetcht a deepe figh,
beware of Loue, for it is farre more perilous than pleafant,
and yet I tell you it allureth as ill as the SYRENS. Oh my
fonnes, fancie is a fickle thing, and beauties paintings are
trickt vp with times colours, which being fet to drie in the
Sunne, perifh with the fame. VENUS is a wanton, & though
her lawes pretend libertie, yet there is nothing but loffe and
gliftering miferie. CUPIDS wings are plumed with the feathers of vanitie, and his arrowes where they pearce, inforce
nothing but deadly defires: a womans eye as it is precious
to behold, fo it is preiudiciall to gaze vpon; for as it affoordeth delight, fo it fnareth vnto death. Truft not their faw-
ning fauours, for their loues are like the breath of a man
vpon fteele, which no fooner lighteth on but it leapeth of, and
their paffions are as momentarie as the colours of a Po-
lipe, which changeth at the fight of euerie obiect. My breath
waxeth fhort and mine eyes dimme, the houre is come and
I muft away: therefore let this fuffice, women are wantons, and yet men cannot want one: and therefore if you
loue, choofe her that hath her eyes of Adamant, that will
turne

turne only to one poynt; her heart of a Diamond, that will
receiue but one forme; her tongue of a Sethin leafe, that
neuer wagges but with a Southeaſt winde: and yet my
ſonnes, if ſhe haue all theſe qualities, to be chaſt, obedient,
and ſilent; yet for that ſhe is a woman, ſhalt thou finde in
her ſufficient vanities to counteruaile her vertues. Oh
now my ſonnes, euen now take theſe my laſt words as my
lateſt Legacie, for my thrid is ſponne, and my foote is in the
graue: keepe my precepts as memorialls of your fathers
counſailes, and let them bee lodged in the ſecrete of your
hearts; for wiſedome is better than wealth, and a golden
ſentence worth a world of treaſure. In my fall ſee & marke
my ſonnes the follie of man, that being duſt climbeth with
BIARES to reach at the Heauens, and readie euerie minute
to dye, yet hopeth for an age of pleaſures. Oh mans life
is like lightning that is but a flaſh, and the longeſt date of
his yeares but as a bauens blaze. Seeing then man is ſo
mortall, bée carefull that thy life bée vertuous, that thy
death may be full of admirable honours; ſo ſhalt thou challenge fame to bee thy fautor, and put obliuion to exile with
thine honorable actions. But my Sonnes, leaſt you ſhould
forget your fathers axiomes, take this ſcroule, wherein
reade what your father dying, wils you to execute liuing.
At this hee ſhrunke downe in his bed and gaue vp the
ghoſt.

IOHN of *Bourdeaux* being thus dead, was greatlie lamented of his Sonnes and bewayled of his friends, eſpe-
ciallie of his fellowe Knights of *Malta,* who attended on
his Funeralls, which were performed with great ſolemni-
tie. His Obſequies done, SALADYNE cauſed next his Epitaph the contents of the ſcroule to be pourtraied out, which
were to this effect.

B 3 The

Euphues

The contents of the fcedule which Sir Iohn of Bourdeaux gaue to his Sonnes.

M Y *Sonnes, behold what portion J doo giue;*
I leaue you goods, but they are quicklie lost;
J leaue aduice, to fchoole you how to liue;
I leaue you wit, but wonne with little cost:
But keepe it well; for counfaile ftill is one,
When Father, friends, and worldlie goods are gone.

In choice of thrift let honour be thy gaine,
Winne it by vertue and by manly might;
In dooing good esteeme thy toyle no paine,
Protect the fatherleffe and widowes right:
Fight for thy faith, thy Countrie and thy King,
For why? this thrift will prooue a blefsed thing.

In choice of wife, preferre the modeft chaft,
Lillies are faire in fhew, but foule in fmell;
The fweeteft lookes by age are foone defaft:
Then choofe thy wife by wit and liuing well.
Who brings thee wealth and many faults withall,
Prefents thee honie, mixt with bitter gall.

In choice of friends, beware of light beliefe,
A painted tongue may fhroud a fubtill heart;
The Syrens *teares doo threaten mickle griefe,*
Forefee my fonne, for feare of fodaine fmart:
Chufe in thy wants: and he that friends thee then,
When richer growne, befriend him thou agen.

Learne of the Ant *in fommer to prouide;*
Driue with the Bee the Droane from out thy hiue;
Builde like the Swallowe in the fommer tide;
Spare not too much (my fonne) but fparing thriue:

B.

Be poore in follie, rich in all but finne:
So by thy death thy glorie fhall beginne.

SALADINE hauing thus fet vp the Scedule, and hangd a-
bout his Fathers hearfe many paffionate Poems, that
France might fuppofe him to be paffing forrowfull, he clad
himfelfe and his Brothers all in black, & in fuch fable futes
difcourfed his griefe: but as the HIENA when fhe mournes
is then moft guilefull, fo SALADINE vnder this fhew of griefe
fhadowed a heart full of contented thoughtes: the TYGER
though hee hide his clawes, will at laft difcouer his rapine:
the LIONS lookes are not the mappes of his meaning, nor a
mans phifnomie is not the difplay of his fecrets. Fire cannot bee hid in the ftraw, nor the nature of man fo concealed,
but at laft it will haue his courfe: nourture and art may doo
much, but that *Natura naturaus* which by propagation is
ingrafted in the heart, will be at laft perforce predominant
according to the olde verfe.

Naturam expellas furca licet, tamen vfque recurret.
So fared it with SALADYNE, for after a months mourning
was paft, he fell to confideration of his Fathers teftament,
how he had bequeathed more to his younger brothers than
himfelfe, that ROSADER was his Fathers darling, but now
vnder his tuition, that as yet they were not come to yeres,
& he being their gardin, might (if not defraud them of their
due) yet make fuch hauock of their legacies and lands, as
they fhould be a great deale the lighter: whereupon hee began thus to meditate with himfelfe.

Saladynes meditation with himfelfe.

SALADYNE, how art thou difquieted in thy thoughts, &
perplexed with a world of reftleffe paffions, hauing
thy minde troubled with the tenour of thy Fathers teftament,

ftament, and thy heart fiered with the hope of prefent preferment ¶ by the one, thou art counfaild to content thee with
thy fortunes; by the other, perfwaded to afpire to higher
wealth. Riches (SALADYNE) is a great royalty, & there is no
fwéeter phifick thā ftore. AUICEN like a foole forgot in his A-
phorifmes to fay, that golde was the moft precious reftora-
tiue, and that treafure was the moft excellent medecine of
the minde. Oh SALADYNE, what were thy Fathers precepts
breathed into the winde? haft thou fo foone forgottē his principles? did he not warne thée from coueting without honor,
and climing without vertue ¶ did hee not forbid thee to
aime at any aćtion that fhould not be honourable ¶ and what
will bee more preiudiciall to thy credit, than the careleffe
ruine of thy brothers welfare ¶ why fhouldft not thou bee
the piller of thy brothers profperitie; and wilt thou become
the fubuerfion of their fortunes ¶ is there any fwéeter thing
than concord, or a more precious Iewel then amity? are you
not fons of one Father, fiens of one trée, birds of one neft ¶
and wilt thou become fo vnnaturall as to rob them, whome
thou fhouldft relieue ¶ No SALADYNE, intreate them with
fauours, and intertaine them with loue; fo fhalt thou haue
thy confcience cleare and thy renowne excellent. Tufh, what
words are thefe bafe foole; farre vnfit (if thou be wife) for thy
humour. What though thy Father at his death talked of
many friuolous matters, as one that doated for age, and ra-
ued in his fickneffe: fhal his words be axioms, and his talke
be fo authentical, that thou wilt (to obferue them) preiudice
thy felfe ¶ No no SALADYNE, fick mens wills that are pa-
role, and haue neither hand nor feale, are like the lawes of a
Citie written in duft; which are broken with the blaft of e-
uerie winde. What man thy Father is dead, and hee can
neither helpe thy fortunes, nor meafure thy aćtions: therefore burie his words with his carkaffe, and bee wife for thy
felfe. What, tis not fo olde as true:

Non fapit, qui fibi non fapit.

Thy Brother is young, keepe him now in awe, make him
not

not check mate with thy felfe: for

Nimia familiarit as contemptum parit.

Let him knowe little, fo fhall he not be able to execute much;
fuppreffe his wittes with a bafe eftate, and though hee be a
Gentleman by nature yet forme him a new, and make
him a peafant by nourture: fo fhalt thou keepe him as a
flaue, and raign thy felfe fole Lord ouer al thy Fathers poffeffions. As for FERNANDYNE thy middle brother he is a fcho-
ler, and hath no minde but on ARISTOTLE, let him reade on
GALEN while thou rifleft with gold, and pore on his booke til
thou dooft purchafe lands: wit is great wealth, if hee haue
learning it is enough; and fo let all reft.

In this humour was SALADYNE making his brother RO-
SADER his foote boy, for the fpace of two or three yeares, kéeping him in fuch feruile fubiection, as if hee had been the
fonne of any countrie vaffall. The yong Gentleman bare al
with patience, til on a day walking in the gardē by himfelf,
he began to confider how he was the fon of IOHN of *Bourdeaux*, a knight renowmed for many victories, & a Gentlemā
famozed for his vertues, how contrarie to the teftament of
his father, he was not only kept from his land, and intreated as a feruant, but fmothered in fuch fecret flauerie, as he
might not attaine to any honourable actions. Ah quoth
he to himfelfe (nature working thefe effectuall paffions)
why fhould I that am a Gentleman borne, paffe my time in
fuch vnnaturall drudgerie? were it not better either in *Paris*
to become a fcholler, or in the court a courtier, or in the field
a fouldier, than to liue a foote boy to my own brother: nature
hath lent me wit to cōceiue, but my brother denied me arte
to contemplate: I haue ftrength to performe any honorable exployte, but no libertie to accomplifh my vertuous indeuours: thofe good partes that God hath beftowed vpon
me, the enuie of my brother dooth fmother in obfcuritie: the
harder is my fortune, and the more his frowardneffe. With
that cafting vp his hand he felt haire on his face, and perceiuing his beard to bud, for choler hee began to blufh, and

C

fwore

Euphues

fwore to himfelfe he would bee no more fubiect to fuch flauerie. As thus he was ruminating of his melancholie paffions, in came SALADYNE with his men, and feeing his brother in a browne ftudie, and to forget his wonted reuerence, thought to fhake him out of his dumps thus. Sirha
(quoth hee) what is your heart on your halfe penie, or are
you faying a Dirge for your fathers foule? what is my
dinner readie ʃ At this queftion ROSADER turning his head
afcance, & bending his browes as if anger there had plough-
ed the furrowes of her wrath, with his eyes full of fire, he
made this replie. Doeft thou afke me (SALADYNE) for thy
Cates ʃ afke fome of thy Churles who are fit for fuch an
office: I am thine equall by nature, though not by birth;
and though thou haft more Cardes in the bunch, I haue
as many trumps in my hands as thy felfe. Let me queftion
with thee, why thou haft feld my Woods, fpoyled my Manner houfes, and made hauock of fuch vtenfals as my father
bequeathed vnto me ʃ I tell thee SALADYNE, either anfwere
me as a brother, or I will trouble thee as an enemie.

At this replie of ROSADERS, SALADYNE fmiled as laughing
at his prefumption, & frowned as checking his follie: hée
therefore tooke him vp thus fhortlie. What firha, well I fee
earlie prickes the tree that will prooue a thorne: hath my
familiar conuerfing with you made you coy, or my good
lookes drawne you to be thus contemptuous ʃ I can quickly
remedie fuch a fault, and I will bende the tree while it is a
wand: In faith (fir boy) I haue a fnaffle for fuch a headftrōg
colt. You firs lay holde on him and binde him, and then I
will giue him a cooling carde for his choller. This made RO-
SADER halfe mad, that ftepping to a great rake that ftood in
the garden, he laide fuch loade vpon his brothers men that
he hurt fome of them, and made the reft of them run away.
SALADYNE feeing ROSADER fo refolute, and with his refolution fo valiant, thought his héeles his beft fafetie, and tooke
him to a loaft adioyning to the garden, whether ROSADER
purfued him hotlie. SALADYNE afraide of his brothers furie,
cried

cried out to him thus. ROSADER bee not fo rafh, I am thy
brother and thine elder, and if I haue done thee wrong Ile
make thee amends: reuenge not anger in bloud, for fo fhalt
thou ftaine the vertue of olde Sir IOHN of *Bourdeaux:* fay
wherein thou art difcontent and thou fhalt be fatified. Brothers frownes ought not to be periods of wrath: what man
looke not fo fowerlie, I knowe we fhall be friends, and better friends than we haue béen. For, *Amantium iræ amoris
redint egratio eft.*

Thefe wordes appeafed the choller of ROSADER, (for hée
was of a milde and courteous nature) fo that he laide downe
his weapons, and vpon the faith of a Gentleman affured
his brother he would offer him no preiudice: wherevpon
SALADYNE came downe, and after a little parley they imbraced each other and became frends, and SALADYNE promifing
ROSADER the reftitution of al his lands, and what fauour els
(quoth he) any waies my abilitie or the nature of a brother
may performe. Vpon thefe fugred recōciliations they went
into the houfe arme in arme together, to the great content
of all the old feruants of Sir IOHN of *Bourdeaux.* Thus
continued the pad hidden in the ftrawe, till it chaunced that
TORISMOND King of *France* had appoynted for his pleafure
a day of Wraftling and of Tournament to bufie his Commons heads, leaft being idle their thoughts fhould runne
vpon more ferious matters, and call to remembrance their
old banifhed King; a Champion there was to ftand againft
all commers a NORMAN, a man of tall ftature and of great
ftrength; fo valiant, that in many fuch conflicts he alwaies
bare away the victorie, not onely ouerthrowing them which
he incountred, but often with the weight of his bodie kil-
ling them outright. SALADYNE hearing of this, thinking
now not to let the ball fall to the ground, but to take oportunitie by the forehead: firft by fecret meanes conuented
with the NORMAN, and procured him with rich rewards to
fweare, that if ROSADER came within his clawes he fhould
neuer more returne to quarrell with SALADYNE for his pof-
C 2   feffions.

19

Euphues

feffions. The NORMAN defirous of pelfe, as (*Quis nifi mentis inops oblatum refpuit aurum.*) taking great gifts for little Gods, tooke the crownes of SALADYNE to performe the ftratagem. Hauing thus the Champion tied to his vilanous determination by oath, he profecuted the intent of his purpofe thus. Hee went to young ROSADER, (who in all his thoughts reacht at honour, and gazed no lower than vertue commaunded him) and began to tell him of this Tournament and Wraftling, how the King fhould be there, and all the chiefe Péeres of *France*, with all the beautifull damofels of the Countrey: now brother (quoth he) for the honor of Sir IOHN of *Bourdeaux* our renowmed father, to famous that houfe that neuer hath béen found without men approoued in Cheualrie, fhewe thy refolution to be peremptorie. For my felfe thou knoweft though I am eldeft by birth, yet neuer hauing attempted any deedes of Armes, I am yongeft to performe any Martiall exploytes, knowing better how to furuey my lands, than to charge my Launce: my brother FERNANDYNE he is at *Paris* poring on a fewe papers, hauing more infight into Sophiftrie and principles of Philofophie, than any warlike indeuours: but thou ROSADER the youngeft in yeares, but the eldeft in valour, art a man of ftrength and dareft doo what honour allowes thee; take thou my fathers Launce, his Sword, and his Horfe, and hie thee to the Tournament, and either there valiantlie crack a fpeare, or trie with the NORMAN for the palme of actiuitie. The words of SALADYNE were but fpurres to a free horfe; for hee had fcarce vttered them, ere ROSADER tooke him in his armes, taking his proffer fo kindly, that he promifed in what he might to requite his courtefie. The next morowe was the day of the Tournament, and ROSADER was fo defirous to fhew his heroycall thoughts, that he paft the night with little fléepe: but affoone as PHŒBUS had vailed the Curteine of the night, and made AURORA blufh with giuing her the *bezoles labres* in her filuer Couch, he gat him vp; and taking his leaue of his brother, mounted
himfelfe

himfelfe towards the place appoynted, thinking euery mile
ten leagues till he came there.   But leauing him fo defirous
of the iourney: to TORISMOND the King of *France*, who
hauing by force banifhed GERISMOND their lawfull King
that liued as an outlaw in the Forreft of *Ardon*, fought now
by all meanes to kéepe the *French* bufied with all fportes
that might breed their content. Amongft the reft he had appointed this folemne Tournament, whereunto he in moft
folemne manner reforted, accompanied with the twelue
Péeres of *France*, who rather for feare than loue graced
him with the fhewe of their dutifull fauours: to feede their
eyes, and to make the beholders pleafed with the fight of
moft rare and gliftring obiects, he had appoynted his owne
daughter ALINDA to be there, & the faire ROSALYND daughter vnto GERISMOND, with all the beautifull damofels that
were famous for their features in all *France*.   Thus in that
place did Loue and Warre triumph in a fimpathie: for fuch
as were Martiall, might vfe their Launce to bee renowmed for the excellence of their Cheualrie; and fuch as
were amorous, might glut themfelues with gazing on
the beauties of moft heauenly creatures.   As euerie mans
eye had his feuerall furuey, and fancie was partiall in
their lookes, yet all in generall applauded the admirable
riches that Nature beftowed on the face of ROSALYND: for
vppon her cheekes there feemed a battaile betwéene the
Graces, who fhould beftow moft fauours to make her excellent.   The blufh that gloried LUNA when fhe kift the fhepheard on the hills of *Latmos* was not tainted with fuch a
pleafant dye, as the Vermilion flourifht on the filuer hue
of ROSALYNDS countenance; her eyes were like thofe lampes
that make the wealthie couert of the Heauens more gorgeous, fparkling fauour and difdaine; courteous and yet
coye, as if in them VENUS had placed all her amorets, and
DIANA all her chaftitie.   The tramells of her hayre, foul-
ded in a call of golde, fo farre furpaft the burnifht glifter
of the mettall, as the Sunne dooth the meaneft Starre

C 3   in

Euphues

in brightneſſe: the treſſes that foldes in the browes of A-
POLLO were not halfe ſo rich to the ſight; for in her haires it
ſéemed loue had laide her ſelfe in ambuſh, to intrappe the
proudeſt eye that durſt gaſe vppon their excellence: what
ſhould I néede to decipher her particular beauties, when
by the cenſure of all ſhe was the paragon of all earthly per-
feᶜtion. This ROSALYND ſat I ſay with ALINDA as a beholder
of theſe ſportes, and made the CAUALIERS crack their lances
with more courage: many deeds of Knighthoode that day
were performed, and many prizes were giuen according to
their ſeuerall deſerts: at laſt when the tournament ceaſed,
the wraſtling began; and the NORMAN preſented himſelfe
as a chalenger againſt all commers; but he looked like HER-
CULES when he aduaunſt himſelfe againſt ACHELOÜS; ſo that
the furie of his countenance amaſed all that durſt attempt
to incounter with him in any déede of actiuitie: till at laſt a
luſtie FRANCKLIN of the Countrie came with two tall men
that were his Sonnes of good lyniaments and comely perſonage: the eldeſt of theſe dooing his obeyſance to the King
entered the lyſt, and preſented himſelfe to the NORMAN,
who ſtraight coapt with him, and as a man that would
triumph in the glorie of his ſtrength, rouſed himſelfe with
ſuch furie, that not onely hee gaue him the fall, but killed
him with the weight of his corpulent perſonage: which
the younger brother ſeeing, lept preſently into the place, and
thirſtie after the reuenge, aſſayled the NORMAN with ſuch
valour, that at the firſt incounter hee brought him to his
knées: which repulſt ſo the NORMAN, that recouering himſelfe, feare of diſgrace doubling his ſtrength, hee ſtept ſo
ſtearnely to the young FRANCKLIN, that taking him vp in his
armes he threw him againſt the ground ſo violently, that
he broake his neck, and ſo ended his dayes with his brother.
At this vnlookt for maſſacre, the people murmured, and
were all in a déepe paſſion of pittie; but the FRANCKLIN, Father vnto theſe, neuer changed his countenance; but as a mā
of a couragious reſolution, tooke vp the bodies of his
Sonnes

Sonnes without any fhew of outward difcontent. All this
while ftoode ROSADER and fawe this tragedie: who noting
the vndoubted vertue of the FRANCKLINS minde, alighted of
from his horfe, and prefentlie fat downe on the graffe, and
commaunded his boy to pull off his bootes, making him
readie to trie the ftrength of this Champion; being furnifhed as he would, hee clapt the FRANCKLIN on the fhoulder
and faide thus. Bolde yeoman whofe fonnes haue ended
the tearme of their yeares with honour, for that I fée thou
fcorneft fortune with patience, and twharteft the iniurie of
fate with content, in brooking the death of thy Sonnes:
ftand a while and either fée mee make a third in their tragedie, or elfe reuenge their fall with an honourable triumph;
the FRANCKLIN féeing fo goodlie a Gentleman to giue him
fuch courteous comfort, gaue him hartie thankes, with promife to pray for his happie fucceffe. With that ROSADER vailed bonnet to the King, and lightlie lept within the lifts,
where noting more the companie than the combatant, hee
caft his eye vpon the troupe of Ladies that gliftered there
like the ftarres of heauen, but at laft Loue willing to make
him as amourous as he was valiant, prefented him with
the fight of ROSALYND, whofe admirable beautie fo inuea-
gled the eye of ROSADER, that forgetting himfelfe, he ftoode
and fed his lookes on the fauour of ROSALYNDS face, which
fhe perceiuing, blufht: which was fuch a doubling of her
beauteous excellence, that the bafhfull red of AURORA at the
fight of vnacquainted PHAETON was not halfe fo glorious:
The NORMAN féeing this young Gentleman fettered in
the lookes of the Ladies, draue him out of his *memento*
with a fhake by the fhoulder; ROSADER looking back with an
angrie frowne, as if he had been wakened from fome pleafant dreame, difcouered to all by the furie of his countenance that he was a man of fome high thoughts: but when
they all noted his youth, and the fwéeteneffe of his vifage,
with a generall applaufe of fauours, they grieued that fo
goodly a young man fhould venture in fo bafe an action: but

féeing

Euphues

féeing it were to his diſhonour to hinder him from his enterpriſe, they wiſht him to be graced with the palme of victorie. After ROSADER was thus called out of his *memento*
by the NORMAN, hee roughlie clapt to him with ſo fierce an
incounter, that they both fell to the ground, and with the
violence of the fall were forced to breathe: in which ſpace the
NORMAN called to minde by all tokens, that this was hee
whom SALADYNE had appoynted him to kil; which coniecture
made him ſtretch euerie limb, & trie euerie ſinew, that working his death he might recouer the golde, which ſo bounti-
fully was promiſed him. On the contrarie part, ROSADER
while he breathed was not idle, but ſtill caſt his eye vppon
ROSALYND, who to incourage him with a fauour, lent him
ſuch an amorous looke, as might haue made the moſt coward deſperate: which glance of ROSALYND ſo fiered the paſſionate deſires of ROSADER, that turning to the NORMAN hee
ran vpon him and braued him with a ſtrong encounter; the
NORMAN receiued him as valiantly, that there was a ſore
combat, hard to iudge on whoſe ſide fortune would be prodigall. At laſt ROSADER calling to minde the beautie of his
new Miſtreſſe, the fame of his Fathers honours, and the
diſgrace that ſhould fall to his houſe by his misfortune,
rouſed himſelfe and threw the NORMAN againſt the ground,
falling vpon his Cheſt with ſo willing a waight, that the
NORMAN yeelded nature her due, and ROSADER the victorie.
The death of this Champion; as it highlie contented the
FRANCKLIN, as a man ſatiffied with reuenge, ſo it drue
the King and all the Péeres into a great admiration, that
ſo young yeares and ſo beautifull a perſonage, ſhould con-
taine ſuch martiall excellence: but when they knew him to
be the yongeſt Sonne of Sir IOHN of *Bourdeaux*, the King
roſe from his ſeate and imbraced him, and the Péeres intreated him with al fauourable courteſie, commending both
his valour and his vertues, wiſhing him to goe forward in
ſuch haughtie déedes, that he might attaine to the glorie of
his Fathers honourable fortunes. As the King and Lordes
graced

graced him with embracing, fo the Ladies fauored him
with their lookes, efpecially ROSALYND, whome the beautie
and valour of ROSADER had alreadie touched; but fhe accounted loue a toye, and fancie a momentarie paffion, that as it
was taken in with a gaze, might bee fhaken off with a
winck; and therefore feared not to dallie in the flame, and to
make ROSADER knowe fhe affeéted him; tooke from hir neck
a Iewell, and fent it by a Page to the young Gentleman.
The Prize that VENUS gaue to PARIS was not halfe fo pleafing to the TROIAN, as this Iemme was to ROSADER: for if
fortune had fworne to make him fole Monark of the world,
he would rather haue refufed fuch dignitie, than haue loft
the iewell fent him by ROSALYND. To retourne her with the
like he was vnfurnifhed, and yet that hee might more than
in his lookes difcouer his affeétion, he ftept into a tent, and
taking pen and paper writ this fancie.

Two Sunnes at once from one faire heauen there fhinde,
Ten branches from two boughes tipt all with rofes,
Pure lockes more golden than is golde refinde,
Two pearled rowes that Natures pride inclofes:

Two mounts faire marble white, downe-foft and daintie,
A fnow died orbe; where loue increast by pleafure
Full wofull makes my heart, and bodie faintie:
Hir faire (my woe) exceedes all thought and meafure.

In lines confufde my luckleffe harme appeereth;
Whom forrow clowdes, whom pleafant fmiling cleereth.

This fonnet he fent to ROSALYND, which when fhe read,
fhe blufht, but with a fweete content in that fhe perceaued
loue had alotted her fo amorous a feruant. Leauing her to
her new intertayned fancies, againe to ROSADER; who triumphing in the glory of this conqueft, accompanied with a
troupe of young Gentlemen, that were defirous to be his

D fami-

familiars, went home to his brother SALADYNES, who was walking before the gates, to heare what fucceffe his brother ROSADER fhould haue, affuring him felf of his death, and deuifing how w^t diffimuled forrow, to celebrate his funeralls; as he was in this thought, hee caft vp his eye, & fawe where ROSADER returned with the garlande on his heade, as hauing won the prize, accompanied with a crew of boone companions; greeued at this, hee ftepped in and fhut the gate. ROSADER feeing this, and not looking for fuch vnkinde intertaynement, blufht at the difgrace, and yet fmothering his griefe with a fmile, he turned to the Gentlemen, and defired them to holde his brother excufed, for hee did not this vpon any malicious intent or niggardize, but being brought vp in the countrie, he abfented him felfe, as not finding his nature fit for fuch youthfull companie. Thus hee fought to fhadow abufes proffred him by his brother, but in vayne, for he could by no meanes be fuffered to enter: whereupon hee ran his foote againft the doore, and brake it open; drawing his fworde and entring bouldly into the Hall, where hee founde none (for all were fled) but one ADAM SPENCER an Englifh man, who had been an olde and truftie feruant to Sir IOHN of *Bourdeaux*: he for the loue he bare to his deceafed Maifter, fauored the part of ROSADER, and gaue him and his fuch intertaynement as he coulde. ROSADER gaue him thankes, and looking about, feeing the hall empty, faide, Gentlemen, you are welcome, frolicke and be merie, you fhall be fure to haue Wine enough, whatfoeuer your fare be, I tell you CAUALIERS my brother hath in his houfe, fiue tunne of wine, and as long as that lafteth, I befhrewe him that fpares his liquor. With that he burft open the butterie dore, and with the helpe of ADAM SPENCER, couered the Tables, and fet downe whatfoeuer he could finde in the houfe, but what they wanted in meate, ROSADER fupplied with drinke, yet had they royall cheere, and withall fuch a hartie welcome, as would haue made the courfeft meates, féeme delicates. After they had feafted and frolickt it twife

or

or thrife with an vpfey freeze, they all tooke their leaues of
ROSADER and departed. Affoone as they were gone ROSADER
growing impatient of the abufe, drewe his fworde, and
fwore to be reuenged on the difcuiteoua SALADYNE: yet by
the meanes of ADAM SPENCER, who fought to continue
friendfhip and amitie betwixt the brethren, and through the
flattering fubmiffion of SALADYNE, they were once agayne
reconciled, & put vp all fore paffed iniuries, with a peaceable
agreement, liuing together for a good fpace in fuch brotherly loue, as did not onely reioyce the feruants, but made all
the Gentlemen and bordring neighbours glad of fuch
friendlie concord. SALADYNE hiding fire in the ftraw, and
concealing a poyfoned hate in a peaceable countenance, yet
deferring the intent of his wrath till fitter opportunitie, he
fhewed him felfe a great fauorer of his brothers vertuous endeuours: where leauing them in this happie league,
let vs returne to ROSALYND.

ROSALYND returning home from the triumph, after fhe
waxed folitarie, loue prefented her with the IDEA of ROSA-
DERS perfection, and taking her at difcouert, ftrooke her fo
deepe, as fhe felt her felfe grow paffing paffionate: fhe began to call to minde the comelineffe of his perfon, the honor
of his parents, and the vertues that excelling both, made
him fo gracious in the eies of euerie one. Sucking in thus
the hony of loue, by imprinting in her thoughtes his rare
qualities, fhe began to furfit with the contemplation of his
vertuous conditions, but when fhe cald to remembrance
her prefent eftate, & the hardneffe of her fortunes, defire began to fhrink, & fancy to vale bonnet, that betwéene a *Chaos*
of confufed thoughtes, fhe began to debate with her felfe in
this manner.

Rofalynds pafsion.

INfortunate ROSALYND, whofe miffortunes are more than
thy yeeres, and whofe paffions are greater than thy pati-
D 2 ence.

ence. The bloffomes of thy youth, are mixt with the froftes
of enuie, and the hope of thy enfuing frutes, perifh in the
bud. Thy father is by TORISMOND banifht from the crowne,
& thou the vnhappie daughter of a King detained captiue,
liuing as difquieted in thy thoughts, as thy father difcontē
ted in his exile. Ah ROSALYND what cares wait vpō a crown,
what griefes are incident to dignitie? what forrowes haunt
royal Pallaces S The greateft feas haue the foreft ftormes,
the higheft birth fubiect to the moft bale, and of al trees the
Cedars fooneft fhake with the winde: fmall Currents are
euer calme, lowe valleyes not fcorcht in any lightnings, nor
bafe men tyed to anye balefull preiudice. Fortune flies,
& if fhe touch pouertie, it is with her heele, rather difdayning
their want with a frowne, than enuying their wealth with
difparagement. Oh ROSALYND, hadft thou been borne lowe,
thou hadft not fallen fo high; and yet being great of bloud,
thine honour is more, if thou brookeft miffortune with patience. Suppofe I contrary fortune with content, yet Fates
vnwilling to haue me any way happie, haue forced loue
to fet my thoughts on fire with fancie. Loue ROSALYND S becommeth it women in diftreffe to thinke of loue S Tufh, defire hath no refpect of perfons, CUPID is blinde and fhooteth
at randon, as foone hitting a rag, as a robe, and percing affoone the bofome of a Captiue, as the breaft of a Libertine.
Thou fpeakeft it poore ROSALYND by experience, for being
euerie way diftreft, furcharged with cares, and ouergrowne
with forrowes, yet amidft the heape of all thefe mifhaps,
loue hath lodged in thy hart the perfection of young ROSA-
DER, a man euery way abfolute as well for his inward life,
as for his outward lyniaments, able to content the eye with
beauty, and the eare with the report of his vertue. But confider ROSALIND his fortunes, and thy prefent eftate, thou art
poore and without patrimonie, and yet the daughter of a
Prince, he a younger brother, and voide of fuch poffeffions
as eyther might maintayne thy dignities, or reuenge thy
fathers iniuries. And haft thou not learned this of other Ladies

dies, that louers cannot liue by lookes; that womens eares
are fooner content with a dram of giue me, than a pound of
heare me; that gould is fweeter than eloquence; that loue is
a fire, & wealth is the fewell, that VENUS Coffers fhould be
euer full. Then ROSALYND, féeing ROSADER is poore, thinke
him leffe beautifull, becaufe he is in want, and account his
vertues but qualities of courfe, for that hee is not indued
with wealth. Doth not HORACE tell thee what methode is to
be vfed in loue,

Querenda pecunia primum, post nummos virtus.

Tufh ROSALYND, be not ouer rafh; leape not before thou
looke; eyther loue fuch a one as may with his landes purchafe thy liberty, or els loue not at all. Choofe not a fayre face
with an emptie purfe, but fay as moft women vfe to fay,

Si nihil attuleris, ibis Homere foras.

Why ROSALYND, can fuch bafe thoughtes harbour in fuch
high beauties ᶜ Can the degree of a Princes, the daughter of
GERISMOND harbour fuch feruile conceites, as to prize gold
more than honor, or to meafure a Gentleman by his wealth,
not by his vertues. No ROSALYND, blufh at thy bafe refolution, and fay if thou loueft, either ROSADER or none: and why ᶜ
becaufe ROSADER is both beautifull and vertuous. Smiling to her felfe to thinke of her new entertayned paffions,
taking vp her Lute that lay by her, fhe warbled out this
dittie.

Rofalynds Madrigal.

Loue in my bofome like a Bee
　　　doth fucke his fweete:
Now with his wings he playes with me,
　　　now with his feete.
Within mine eies he makes his neast,
His bed amidst my tender breast,
My kiffes are his daily feast;
And yet he robs me of my rest.
　　　Ah wanton, will ye?
　　　　D 3　　　　　　　*And*

Euphues

And if J sleepe, then pearcheth he
        with pretie flight,
And makes his pillow of my knee
        the liuelong night.
    Strike I my lute he tunes the string,
    He musicke playes if so I sing,
    He lends me euerie louelie thing;
    Yet cruell he my heart doth sting.
        Whift wanton still ye?

Els I with rofes euerie day
        will whip you hence;
And binde you when you long to play,
        for your offence.
    Ile shut mine eyes to keepe you in,
    Ile make you fast it for your finne,
    Ile count your power not worth a pinne;
    Ahlas what hereby shall I winne,
        Jf he gainfay me?

What if J beate the wanton boy
        with manie a rod?
He will repay me with annoy,
        becaufe a God.
    Then fit thou fafely on my knee,
    And let thy bowre my bofome be:
    Lurke in mine eyes J like of thee:
    Oh Cupid *fo thou pitie me.*
        Spare not but play thee.

Scarce had ROSALYNDE ended her Madrigale, before
TORISMOND came in with his daughter ALINDA, and manie
of the Péeres of *France*, who were enamoured of her beautie: which TORISMOND perceiuing, fearing leaft her perfection might be the beginning of his preiudice, and the hope
of his fruite ende in the beginning of her bloffomes, hee
                                   thought

thought to banifh her from the Court: for quoth he to him-felfe, her face is fo full of fauour, that it pleades pitie in the eye of euerie man; her beautie is fo heauenly and deuine, that fhe will prooue to me as HELEN did to PRIAM : fome one of the Péeres will ayme at her loue, ende the marriage, and then in his wiues right attempt the kingdome. To preuent therefore had I wift in all thefe actions, fhe tarries not about the Court, but fhall (as an exile) either wander to her father, or els féeke other fortunes. In this humour, with a ftearne countenance full of wrath, hee breathed out this cenfure vnto her before the Péeres, that charged her that that night fhee were not féene about the Court: for (quoth he) I haue heard of thy afpiring fpeaches, and inten-ded treafons. This doome was ftrange vnto ROSALYNDE, and prefently couered with the fhield of her innocence, fhee boldly brake out in reuerend tearmes to haue cleared her felfe: but TORISMOND would admit of no reafon, nor durft his Lordes plead for ROSALYNDE, although her beautie had made fome of them paffionate, féeing the figure of wrath portraied in his brow. Standing thus all mute, and ROSA-LYNDE amazed, ALINDA who loued her more than her felfe, with griefe in her heart, & teares in her eyes, falling downe on her knées, began to intreate her father thus:

Alindas oration to her father in defence of faire Rofalynde.

IF (mightie TORISMOND) I offende in pleading for my friend, let the law of amitie craue pardon for my boldnes; for where there is depth of affection, there friendfhip al-loweth a priuiledge. ROSALYNDE and I haue béene foftered vp from our infancies, and nurfed vnder the harbour of our conuerfing together with fuch priuate familiarities, that cuftome had wrought an vnion of our nature, and the fym-pathie of our affections fuch a fecrete loue, that we haue two bodies, and one foule. Then meruaile not (great TORIS-MOND)

Euphues

MOND) if feeing my friend diftreft, I finde my felfe perplexed with a thoufand forrowes: for her vertuous and honourable thoughts (which are the glories that maketh women
excellent) they be fuch, as may challenge loue, and race out
fufpition: her obedience to your Maieftie, I referre to the
cenfure of your owne eye, that fince her fathers exile hath
fmothered all griefes with patience, and in the abfence of
nature, hath honoured you with all dutie, as her owne Father by nouriture: not in word vttering anie difcontent, nor
in thought (as farre as coniecture may reach) hammering
on reuenge; onely in all her actions feeking to pleafe you, &
to winne my fauour. Her wifedome, filence, chaftitie, and
other fuch rich qualities, I néed not decypher: onely it refts
for me to conclude in one word, that fhe is innocent. If then,
Fortune who triumphs in varietie of miferies, hath prefented fome enuious perfon (as minifter of her intended ftratagem) to taint ROSALYNDE with anie furmife of treafon, let
him be brought to her face, and confirme his accufation by
witneffes; which prooued, let her die, and ALINDA will execute the maffacre. If none can auouch anie confirmed relation of her intent, vfe Iuftice my Lord, it is the glorie of a
King, and let her liue in your wonted fauour: for if you banifh her, my felfe as copartner of her hard fortunes, wil par-
ticipate in exile fome part of her extremities.

TORISMOND (at this fpeach of ALINDA) couered his face
with fuch a frowne, as Tyrannie feemed to fit triumphant
in his forehead, and checkt her vp with fuch taunts, as made
the Lords (that onlie were hearers) to tremble. Proude
girle (quoth he) hath my lookes made thee fo light of tung,
or my fauours incouraged thee to be fo forward, that thou
dareft prefume to preach after thy father? Hath not my
yeares more experience than thy youth, and the winter of
mine age deeper infight into ciuill policie, than the prime of
thy florifhing daies? The olde Lion auoides the toyles
where the yong one leapes into the net: the care of age is
prouident and forefees much: fufpition is a vertue, where
a man

a man holds his enemie in his bofome. Thou fonde girle meafureft all by prefent affeﬅion, & as thy heart loues thy thoughts cenfure: but if thou kneweft that in liking ROSA-LYND thou hatcheft vp a bird to pecke out thine owne eyes, thou wouldft intreate as much for her abfence, as now thou delighteft in her prefence. But why do I alleadge policie to thee ʃ fit you downe hufwife and fall to your needle: if idle-neffe make you fo wanton, or libertie fo malipert, I can quicklie tie you to a fharper tafke: and you (maide) this night be packing either into *Arden* to your father, or whe-ther beft it fhall content your humour, but in the Court you fhall not abide. This rigorous replie of TORISMOND nothing amazed ALINDA, for ftill fhe profecuted her plea in the de-fence of ROSALYND, wifhing her father (if his cenfure might not be reuerft) that he would appoint her partner of her ex-ile; which if he refufed to doo, either fhe would (by fome fe-cret meanes) fteale out and followe her, or els end her daies with fome defperate kinde of death. When TORISMOND heard his daughter fo refolute, his heart was fo hardned a-gainft her, that he fet downe a definitiue and peremptorie fentence that they fhould both be banifhed: which prefent-lie was done. The Tyrant rather choofing to hazard the loffe of his only child, than any waies to put in queftion the ftate of his kingdome: fo fufpicious and feareful is the con-fcience of an vfurper. Well, although his Lords perfwaded him to retaine his owne daughter, yet his refolution might not bee reuerft, but both of them muft away from the court without either more companie or delay. In he went with great melancholie, and left thefe two Ladies alone. ROSA-LYND waxed very fad, and fat downe and wept. ALINDA fhe fmiled, and fitting by her friende began thus to comfort her.

E   Alindas

Euphues

Alindas comfort to perplexed Rofalynd.

WHy how now ROSALYND, difmaide with a frowne of contrarie fortune? Haue I not oft heard thee fay that high minds were difcouered in fortunes contempt, and heroycall feene in the depth of extremities? Thou wert wont to tell others that complained of diftreffe, that the fwéeteft falue for miferie was patience; and the onlie medicine for want, that precious implaifter of content: being fuch a good Phifition to others, wilt thou not minifter receipts to thy felfe? But perchance thou wilt fay:

Confulenti nunquam caput doluit.

Why then, if the patients that are ficke of this difeafe can finde in themfelues neither reafon to perfwade, nor arte to cure; yet (ROSALYND) admit of the counfaile of a friend, and applie the falues that may appeafe thy paffions. If thou grieueft that beeing the daughter of a Prince, and enuie thwarteth thée with fuch hard exigents, thinke that royaltie is a faire marke; that Crownes haue croffes when mirth is in Cottages; that the fairer the Rofe is, the fooner it is bitten with Catterpillers; the more orient the Pearle is, the more apt to take a blemifh; and the greateft birth, as it hath moft honour, fo it hath much enuie. If then Fortune aimeth at the faireft, be patient ROSALYND; for firft by thine exile thou goeft to thy father; nature is higher prifed than wealth, & the loue of ones parents ought to bée more precious than all dignities: why then doth my ROSALYND grieue at the frowne of TORISMOND, who by offering her a preiudice, proffers her a greater pleafure? and more (mad laffe) to be melancholie, when thou haft with thee ALINDA a frend, who will be a faithfull copartner of al thy miffortunes, who hath left her father to followe thee, and choofeth rather to brooke all extremities than to forfake thy prefence. What ROSALYND:

Solamen

golden Legacie. 14

Solamen miferis focios habuiffe doloris.

Chéerelie woman, as wee haue been bedfellowes in royaltie, we will be fellowe mates in pouertie: I will euer bée
thy ALINDA, and thou fhalt euer reft to me ROSALYND: fo fhall
the world canonize our friendfhip, and fpeake of ROSALVND
and ALINDA, as they did of PILADES and ORESTES. And if euer
Fortune fmile and wee returne to our former honour, then
folding our felues in the fwéete of our friendfhip, wee fhall
merelie fay (calling to minde our forepaffed miferies),

Olim hæc meminiffe iuuabit.

At this ROSALYND began to comfort her; and after fhée
had wept a fewe kind teares in the bofome of her ALINDA,
fhe gaue her heartie thanks, and then they fat them downe
to confult how they fhould trauell. ALINDA grieued at nothing but that they might haue no man in their companie:
faying, it would be their greateft preiudice in that two women went wandring without either guide or attendant.
Tufh (quoth ROSALYND) art thou a woman, and haft not a
fodaine fhift to preuent a miffortune? I (thou feeft) am of
a tall ftature, and would very well become the perfon and
apparell of a page, thou fhalt bee my Miftris, and I will
play the man fo properly, that (truft me) in what company
fo euer I come I will not bee difcouered; I will buy mee a
fuite, and haue my rapier very handfomely at my fide, and
if any knaue offer wrong, your page wil fhew him the point
of his weapon. At this ALINDA fmiled, and vpon this they
agreed, and prefentlie gathered vp all their Iewels, which
they truffed vp in a Cafket, and ROSALYND in all haft prouided her of roabes, and ALINDA (from her royall weedes) put
her felfe in more homelie attire. Thus fitted to the purpofe,
away goe thefe two friends, hauing now changed their
names, ALINDA being called ALIENA, and ROSALYND GANI-
MEDE: they trauailed along the Vineyards, and by many
by-waies; at laft got to the Forreft fide, where they trauailed by the fpace of two or three daies without feeing a-
nie creature, being often in danger of wild beafts, and pay-

E 2   ned

Euphues

ned with many paffionate forrowes. Now the black Oxe
began to tread on their feete, and ALINDA thought of her
wonted royaltie: but when fhe caft her eyes on her ROSA-
LYND, fhe thought euerie danger a ftep to honour. Paffing
thus on along, about midday they came to a Fountaine,
compaft with a groue of Cipreffe trees, fo cunninglie and
curiouflie planted, as if fome Goddeffe had intreated Nature in that place to make her an Arbour. By this Fountaine fat ALIENA and her GANIMEDE, and foorth they pulled
fuch victualls as they had, and fed as merilie as if they had
béen in *Paris* with all the Kings delicates: ALIENA onely
grieuing that they could not fo much as meete with a fhepheard to difcourfe them the way to fome place where they
might make their aboade. At laft GANIMEDE cafting vp his
eye efpied where on a tree was ingrauen certaine verfes:
which affoone as he efpied, he cried out; bee of good cheere
Miftris, I fpie the figures of men; for here in thefe trées be
ingrauen certaine verfes of fhepheards, or fome other
fwaines that inhabite here about. With that ALIENA ftart
vp ioyfull to heare thefe newes; and looked, where they
found carued in the barke of a Pine trée this paffion.

Montanus pafsion.

Hᴀᴅ*ft thou been borne whereas perpetuall cold*
  Makes Tanais *hard, and mountaines filuer old:*
  Had I complain'd vnto a marble ftone;
Or to the flouds bewraide my bitter mone,
  I then could beare the burden of my griefe.
But euen the pride of Countries at thy birth,
Whil'ft heauens did fmile did new aray the earth
                    with flowers chiefe.
Yet thou the flower of beautie bleffed borne,
Haft pretie lookes, but all attir'd in fcorne.

Had

Had I the power to weepe sweet Mirrhas *teares;*
Or by my plaints to pearce repining eares;
Hadst thou the heart to smile at my complaint;
To scorne the woes that doth my heart attaint,
    I then could beare the burden of my griefe.
But not my teares, but truth with thee preuailes,
And seeming sowre my sorowes thee assailes:
                yet small reliefe.
For if thou wilt thou art of marble hard;
And if thou please my suite shall soone be heard.

No doubt (quoth ALIENA) this poesie is the passion of some perplexed shepheard, that being enamoured of some faire and beautifull Shepheardesse, suffered some sharpe repulse, and therefore complained of the crueltie of his Mistris. You may see (quoth GANIMEDE) what mad cattell you women be, whose hearts sometimes are made of Adamant that will touch with no impression; and sometime of waxe that is fit for euerie forme: they delight to be courted, and then they glorie to seeme coy; and when they are most desired then they freese with disdaine: and this fault is so common to the sex, that you see it painted out in the shepheards passions, who found his Mistris as froward as he was enamoured. And I pray you (quoth ALIENA) if your roabes were off, what mettall are you made of that you are so satyricall against women? Is it not a foule bird defiles the owne nest? Beware (GANIMEDE) that ROSADER heare you not; if he doo, perchance you will make him leape so far from loue, that he wil anger euery vain in your hart. Thus (quoth GANIMEDE) I keepe decorum, I speake now as I am ALIENAS page, not as I am GERISMONDS daughter: for put me but into a peticoate, and I will stand in defiance to the vttermost that women are courteous, constant, vertuous, and what not. Stay there (quoth ALIENA) and no more words; for yonder be Caraƈters grauen vpon the barke of the tall Béech trée: let vs see (quoth GANIMEDE): and with

E 3   that

Euphues

that they read a fancie written to this effect.

Firſt ſhall the heauens want ſtarrie light;
The ſeas be robbed of their waues;
The day want ſunne, and ſunne want bright;
The night want ſhade, the dead men graues;
    The Aprill, flowers and leafe and tree,
    Before I falſe my faith to thee.

Firſt ſhall the tops of higheſt hills
By humble plaines be ouerpride;
And Poets ſcorne the Muſes quills,
And fiſh forſake the water glide;
    And Iris *looſe her coloured weed,*
    Before I faile thee at thy need.

Firſt direfull hate ſhall turne to peace,
And loue relent in deepe diſdaine;
And death his fatall ſtroake ſhall ceaſe,
And enuie pitie euery paine;
    And pleaſure mourne, and ſorowe ſmile,
    Before I talke of any guile.

Firſt time ſhall ſtay his ſtayleſſe race,
And winter bleſſe his browes with corne;
And ſnow bemoysten Julies face;
And winter ſpring, and ſommer mourne,
    Before my pen by helpe of fame,
    Ceaſe to recite thy ſacred name.
            Montanus.

No doubt (quoth GANIMEDE) this proteſtation grewe from one full of paſſions. I am of that mind too (quoth A-LIENA) but ſee I pray, when poore women ſeeke to keepe themſelues chaſt, how men woo them with many fained promiſes, alluring with ſweet words as the SYRENS, and after

ter proouing as trothleffe as ÆNEAS. Thus promifed DE-
MOPHOON to his PHILLIS, but who at laſt grewe more falfe?
The reafon was (quoth GANIMEDE) that they were womens fonnes, and tooke that fault of their mother; for if
man had growen from man, as ADAM did from the earth,
men had neuer béen troubled with inconftancie. Leaue off
(quoth ALIENA) to taunt thus bitterly, or els Ile pul off your
pages apparell and whip you (as VENUS doth her wantons)
with nettles. So you will (quoth GANIMEDE) perfwade
me to flattrie, and that needs not: but come (féeing we haue
found heere by this Fount the trackt of Shepheards by
their Madrigals and Roundelaies) let vs forward; for ei·
ther we fhall finde fome foldes, fheepcoates, or els fome cottages wherein for a day or two to reſt. Cōtent (quoth ALIE-
NA) and with that they rofe vp, and marched forward till towards the euen: and then comming into a faire valley
(compaffed with mountaines, whereon grewe many pleafant fhrubbs) they might defcrie where two flocks of fhéepe
did feede. Then looking about, they might perceiue where
an old fhepheard fat (and with him a yong fwaine) vnder a
couert moſt pleafantlie fcituated. The ground where they
fat was diapred with FLORAS riches, as if fhe ment to wrap
TELLUS in the glorie of her veftments: round about in the
forme of an Amphitheater were moſt curiouſlie planted
Pine trees, interfeamed with Limons and Citrons, which
with the thickneffe of their boughes fo fhadowed the place,
that PHŒBUS could not prie into the fecret of that Arbour;
fo vnited were the tops with fo thicke a clofure, that VENUS
might there in her iollitie haue dallied vnfeene with her dée-
reſt paramour. Faſt by (to make the place more gorgeous)
was there a Fount fo Chriſtalline and cléere, that it feemed DIANA with her DRIADES and HEMADRIADES had that
fpring, as the fecrete of all their bathings. In this glorious
Arbour fat thefe two fhepheards (feeing their fhéepe feede)
playing on their pipes many pleafant tunes, and from mufick and melodie falling into much amorous chat: drawing
more

Euphues

more nigh wee might defcrie the countenance of the one to
be full of forowe, his face to be the verie pourtraiture of difcontent, and his eyes full of woes, that liuing he feemed to
dye: wee (to heare what thefe were) ftole priuilie behind the
thicke, where we ouerheard this difcourfe.

A pleafant Eglog betweene Montanus and Coridon.

Coridon.

Ay fhepheards boy, what makes thee greet fo fore?
Why leaues thy pipe his pleafure and delight?
Yong are thy yeares, thy cheekes with rofes dight:
Then fing for ioy (fweet fwaine) and figh no more.

This milke white Poppie and this climbing Pine
Both promife fhade; then fit thee downe and fing,
And make thefe woods with pleafant notes to ring,
Till Phœbus *daine all Westward to decline.*

Montanus.

*Ah (*Coridon*) vnmeet is melodie*
To him whom proud contempt hath ouerborne:
Slaine are my ioyes by Phœbes *bitter fcorne,*
Farre hence my weale and nere my ieopardie.

Loues burning brand is couched in my breft,
Making a Phœnix *of my faintfull hart:*
And though his furie doo inforce my fmart,
Ay blyth am I to honour his beheft.

Preparde to woes fince fo my Phœbe *wills,*
My lookes difmaid fince Phœbe *will difdaine:*
I banifh bliffe and welcome home my paine;
So ftreame my teares as fhowers from Alpine hills.

In

Jn errours maske I blindfolde iudgements eye,
J fetter reafon in the fnares of lust,
J feeme fecure, yet know not how to trust;
J liue by that, which makes me liuing die.

Deuoyd of rest, companion of distreffe,
Plague to myfelfe, confumed by my thought;
How may my voyce or pipe in tune be brought?
Since I am reft of folace and delight.

Coridon.

Ah Lorrell lad, what makes thee Herry loue?
A fugred harme, a poyfon full of pleafure,
A painted fhrine ful-fild with rotten treafure,
A heauen in fhew, a hell to them that proue.

Againe, in feeming fhadowed ftill with want,
A broken ftaffe which follie doth vpholde,
A flower that fades with euerie frostie colde,
An orient rofe fprong from a wythred plant.

A minutes ioy to gaine a world of greefe,
A fubtill net to fnare the idle minde,
A feeing Scorpion, yet in feeming blinde,
A poore reioyce, a plague without releefe.

For thy Montanus *follow mine arreede,*
(Whom age hath taught the traynes that fancie vfeth)
Leaue foolifh loue; for beautie wit abufeth,
And drownes (by follie) vertues fpringing feede.

Montanus.

So blames the childe the flame, becaufe it burnes;
And bird the fnare, becaufe it doth intrap;

F   *And*

Euphues

And fooles true loue, becaufe of forrie hap;
And faylers curffe the fhip that ouerturnes:

But would the childe forbeare to play with flame,
And birdes beware to trust the fowlers ginne,
And fooles forefee before they fall and finne,
And maifters guide their fhips in better frame;

The childe would praife the fire, becaufe it warmes;
And birds reioyce, to fee the fowler faile;
And fooles preuent, before their plagues preuaile;
And faylers bleffe the barke that faues from harmes.

Ah Coridon, *though manie be thy yeares,*
And crooked elde hath fome experience left;
Yet is thy minde of iudgement quite bereft
In view of loue, whofe power in me appeares.

The ploughman little wots to turne the pen,
Or bookeman skills to guide the ploughmans cart,
Nor can the cobler count the tearmes of Art,
Nor bafe men iudge the thoughts of mightie men;

Nor wythered age (vnmeete for beauties guide,
Vncapable of loues impreffion)
Difcourfe of that, whofe choyce poffeffion
May neuer to fo bafe a man be tied.

But I (whom nature makes of tender molde,
And youth most pliant yeeldes to fancies fire)
Doo builde my hauen and heauen on fweete defire,
On fweete defire more deere to me than golde.

Thinke I of loue, ô how my lines aspire?
How hast the Mufes to imbrace my browes,
And hem my temples in with lawrell bowes,

And

And fill my braines with chaſt and holy fire?

Then leaue my lines their homely equipage,
Mounted beyond the circle of the Sunne;
Amaz'd I read the ſtile when I haue done,
And Herry Loue that ſent that heauenly rage.

Of Phœbe *then, of* Phœbe *then I ſing,*
Drawing the puritie of all the ſpheares,
The pride of earth, or what in heauen appeares,
Her honoured face and fame to light to bring.

Jn fluent numbers and in pleaſant vaines,
J rob both ſea and earth of all their ſtate,
To praiſe her parts: I charme both time and fate,
To bleſse the Nymph that yeeldes me loue ſicke paines.

My ſheepe are turnd to thoughts, whom froward will
Guides in the restleſſe Laborynth of loue,
Feare lends them paſture whereſoere they moue,
And by their death their life renueth ſtill,

Hy ſheephooke is my pen, mine oaten reede
My paper, where my manie woes are written;
Thus ſilly ſwaine (with loue and fancie bitten)
J trace the plaines of paine in wofull weede.

Yet are my cares, my broken ſleepes, my teares,
My dreames, my doubts, for Phœbe *ſweete to me:*
Who wayteth heauen in ſorrowes vale must be,
And glorie ſhines where danger most appeares.

Then Coridon *although I blythe me not,*
Blame me not man, ſince ſorrow is my ſweete;
So willeth Loue, and Phœbe *thinkes it meete,*
And kinde Montanus *liketh well his lot.*

F 2

Coridon.

Euphues

Coridon.

Oh ſtayleſse youth, by errour ſo miſguided;
Where will preſcribeth lawes to perfeƈt wits,
Where reaſon mournes, and blame in triumph ſits,
And follie poyſoneth all that time prouided.

With wilfull blindneſſe bleard, preparde to ſhame,
Prone to negleƈt Occaſion when ſhe ſmiles:
Alas that Loue (by fond and froward guiles)
Should make thee traƈt the path to endleſſe blame.

Ah (my Montanus) *curſed is the charme*
That hath bewitched ſo thy youthfull eyes:
Leaue off in time to like theſe vanities;
Be forward to thy good, and fly thy harme.

As manie bees as Hibla *daily ſhields,*
As manie frie as fleete on Oceans *face,*
As manie heards as on the earth doo trace,
As manie flowres as decke the fragrant fields,

As manie ſtarres as glorious heauen containes,
As manie ſtormes as wayward winter weepes,
As manie plagues as hell incloſed keepes;
So manie greefes in loue, ſo manie paines.

Suſpitions, thoughts, deſires, opinions, praiers,
Miſlikes, miſdeedes, fond ioyes, and fained peace,
Ꝓlluſions, dreames, great paines, and ſmall increaſe,
Vowes, hopes, acceptance, ſcornes, and deepe deſpaires,

Truce, warre, and woe doo waite at beauties gate;
Time loſt, lament, reports, and priuie grudge,
And last, fierce Loue is but a partiall Iudge,

Who

44

Who yeeldes for feruice fhame, for friendfhip hate,

Montanus.

All Adder-like I ftop mine eares (fond fwaine)
So charme no more; for I will neuer change.
Call home thy flockes in time that ftragling range:
For loe, the Sunne declineth hence amaine.

Terentius.

Jn amore hæc omnia infunt vitia, induciæ, inimicitæ, bel-
lum, pax rurfum: incerta hæc fi tu postules, ratione cer-
ta fieri nihilo plus agas, quam fi des operam, vt cum ra-
tione infanias.

The fhepheards hauing thus ended their Eglogue, ALI-
ENA ftept with GANIMEDE from behinde the thicket: at
whofe fodaine fight the fhepheards arofe, and ALIENA faluted them thus; Shepheards all haile, (for fuch wee déeme
you by your flockes) and Louers, good lucke; (for fuch you
féeme by your paffions) our eyes being witneffe of the one,
and our eares of the other. Although not by Loue, yet by
Fortune, I am a diftreffed Gentlewoman, as forrowful as
you are paffionate, and as full of woes as you of perplexed
thoughts: wandring this way in a forreft vnknowen, onely
I and my Page, wearied with trauaile would faine haue
fome place of reft. May you appoint vs anie place of quiet
harbour, (be it neuer fo meane) I fhall be thankfull to you,
contented in my felfe, and gratefull to whofoeuer fhall bee
mine hofte. CORIDON hearing the Gentlewoman fpeak fo
courteoufly returned her mildly and reuerentlie this aunfwere.

Faire Miftres, we returne you as heartie a welcome, as
you gaue vs a courteous falute. A fhepheard I am, & this
a louer, as watchful to pleafe his wench, as to féed his fhéep:

full of fancies, and therefore (fay I) full of follies. Exhort
him I may, but perfwade him I cannot; for Loue admits
neither of counfaile, nor reafon. But leauing him to his
paffions, if you be diftreft, I am forrowfull fuch a faire creature is croft w^t calamitie: pray for you I may, but reléeue
you I cannot: marry, if you want lodging, if you vouch
to fhrowd your felues in a fhepheards cotage, my houfe (for
this night) fhalbe your harbour. ALIENA thankt CORIDON
greatly, and prefently fate her downe and GANIMEDE by
her. CORIDON looking earneftly vppon her, and with a curious furuey viewing all her perfections, applauded (in his
thought) her excellence, and pitying her diftreffe, was defirous to heare the caufe of her miffortunes, began to queftion with her thus.

If I fhould not (faire Damofell) occafionate offence, or
renue your griefes by rubbing the fcarre, I would faine
craue fo much fauour, as to know the caufe of your miffortune: and why, and whether you wander with your page in
fo dangerous a forreft. ALIENA (that was as courteous as
fhe was faire) made this reply; Shepheard, a friendlie demaund ought neuer to be offenfiue, and queftions of courtefie carrie priuiledged pardons in their forheads. Know therfore, to difcouer my fortunes were to renue my forrowes,
and I fhould by difcourfing my mifhaps, but rake fier out of
the cinders. Therefore let this fuffice (gentle fhepheard)
my diftreffe is as great as my trauell is dangerous, and I
wander in this forreft, to light on fome cottage where I and
my Page may dwell: for I meane to buy fome farme, and
a flocke of fheepe, and fo become a fhepheardeffe, meaning
to liue low, and content me with a countrey life: for I haue
heard the fwaynes fay, that they drunke without fufpition, &
flept without care. Marry Miftres (quoth CORIDON) if you
meane fo you came in a good time, for my landflord intends
to fell both the farme I till, and the flocke I keepe, & cheap
you may haue them for readie money: and for a fhepheards
life (oh Miftreffe) did you but liue a while in their content,

you

you would faye the Court were rather a place of forrowe, than of folace. Here (Miftreffe) fhall not Fortune thwart you, but in meane miffortunes, as the loffe of a few fheepe, which, as it breedes no beggerie, fo it can bee no extreame preiudice: the next yeare may mend al with a frefh increafe. Enuie ftirres not vs, wee couet not to climbe, our defires mount not aboue our degrees, nor our thoughts aboue our fortunes. Care cannot harbour in our cottages, nor doo our homely couches know broken flumbers: as we exceede not in diet, fo we haue inough to fatiffie: and Miftres I haue fo much Latin, *Satis est quod fufficit.*

By my troth fhepheard (quoth ALIENA) thou makeft me in loue with your countrey life, and therefore fende for thy Landflord, and I will buy thy farme and thy flockes, & thou fhalt ftill (vnder me) be ouerfeer of them both: onely for pleafurefake I and my Page wil ferue you, lead the flocks to the field, and folde them: thus will I liue quiet, vnkno- wen, and contented. This newes fo gladded the hart of CO- RIDON, that he fhould not be put out of his farme, that (put- ting off his fhepheards bonnet) he did her all the reuerence that he might. But all this while fate MONTANUS in a mufe thinking of the crueltie of his PHŒBE, whom he woed long, but was in no hope to winne. GANIMEDE who ftill had the remembrance of ROSADER in his thoughts, tooke delight to fee the poore fhepheard paffionate, laughing at loue that in all his actions was fo imperious. At laft when fhee had no- ted his teares that ftole downe his cheekes, and his fighes that broake from the center of his heart, pittying his la- ment, fhe demaunded of CORIDON why the young fhepheard looked fo forrowfull? Oh fir (quoth he) the boy is in loue. Why (quoth GANIMEDE) can fhepheards loue? I (quoth MONTANUS) and ouerloue, els fhouldft not thou fee mee fo penfiue. Loue (I tell thee) is as precious in a fhepheards eye as in the lookes of a King, and we countrey fwaynes intertain fancie with as great delight, as the proudeft cour- tier doth affection. Opportunitie (that is the fweeteft freind

to

Euphues

to VENUS) harboureth in our cottages, and loyaltie (the chiefeſt fealtie that CUPID requires) is found more among ſhepheards than higher degrees. Then aſke not if ſuch ſilly ſwaynes can loue? What is the cauſe then, quoth GANI-MEDE, that Loue being ſo ſweete to thee, thou lookeſt ſo ſorrowfull? Becauſe, quoth MONTANUS, the partie beloued is froward: and hauing courteſie in her lookes, holdeth diſ-daine in her tongues ende. What hath ſhe then quoth ALIE-NA, in her heart? Deſire (I hope Madame) quoth he: or els my hope loſt, deſpaire in Loue were death. As thus they chatted, the Sunne being readie to ſet, and they not ha-uing folded their ſheepe, CORIDON requeſted ſhe would ſit there with her Page, till MONTANUS and he lodged their ſheepe for that night. You ſhall goe quoth ALIENA, but firſt I will intreate MONTANUS to ſing ſome amorous Sonnet, that hee made when he hath been deeply paſſionate. That I will quoth MONTANUS: and with that he began thus.

Montanus Sonnet.

Phœbe ſate
Sweete ſhe ſate,
      Sweete ſate Phœbe when I ſaw her,
White her brow,
Coy her eye:
      Brow and eye how much you pleaſe me?
Words J ſpent,
Sighes J ſent,
      Sighes and words could neuer draw her.
Oh my loue
Thou art loſt,
      Since no ſight could euer eaſe thee.

Phœbe

48

Phœbe fat
By a fount;
>   *Sitting by a fount J fpide her:*
Sweet her touch,
Rare her voyce;
>   *Touch and voice what may distaine you?*
As fhe fung,
I did figh,
>   *And by fighs whilft that I tride her.*
Oh mine eyes
You did loofe
>   *Her firft fight whofe want did paine you.*

Phœbes flocks
White as wooll,
>   *Yet were* Phœbes *locks more whiter.*
Phœbes eyes
Douelike mild,
>   *Douelike eyes both mild and cruell.*
Montan fweares
In your lampes
>   *He will die for to delight her.*
Phœbe yeeld,
Or I die;
>   *Shall true hearts be fancies fuell?*

MONTANUS had no fooner ended his fonnet, but CORIDON with a lowe courtefie rofe vp and went with his fellow and fhut their fheepe in the foldes: and after returning to A-LIENA and GANIMEDE, conducted them home wearie to his poore Cottage. By the way there was much good chat with MONTANUS about his loues; he refoluing ALIENA that PHŒ-BE was the faireft Shepherdice in all FRANCE, and that in his eye her beautie was equall with the Nimphs. But (quoth hee) as of all ftones the Diamond is moft cléereft, and yet moft hard for the Lapidory to cut; as of all flowers
G   the

the Rofe is the faireft, and yet guarded with the fharpeft
prickles: fo of all our Countrey Laffes PHŒBE is the
brighteft, but the moft coy of all to ftoope vnto defire. But
let her take héede quoth he, I haue heard of NARCISSUS, who
for his high difdaine againft Loue, perifhed in the follie of
his owne loue. With this they were at CORIDONS cotage,
where MONTANUS parted from them, and they went in to
reft. ALINDA and GANIMEDE glad of fo contented a fhelter,
made merrie with the poore fwayne: and though they had
but countrey fare and courfe lodging, yet their welcome
was fo great, and their cares fo litle, that they counted their
diet delicate, and flept as foundly as if they had béen in the
court of TORISMOND. The next morne they lay long in bed,
as wearied with the toyle of vnaccuftomed trauaile: but
affoone as they got vp, ALIENA refolued there to fet vp her
reft, and by the helpe of CORIDON fwept a barga ne with his
Landflord, and fo became Miftres of the farme & the flocke:
her felfe putting on the attire of a fhepheardeffe, and GANI-
MEDE of a yong fwaine: euerie day leading foorth her flocks
with fuch delight, that fhe held her exile happie, and thought
no content to the bliffe of a Countrey cottage. Leauing her
thus famous amongft the fhepheards of *Arden*, againe to
SALADYNE.

When SALADYNE had a long while concealed a fecret refolution of reuenge, and could no longer hide fire in the flax,
nor oyle in the flame; (for enuie is like lightning, that will
appeare in the darkeft fogge). It chaunced on a morning
verie early he calde vp certaine of his feruaunts, and went
with them to the chamber of ROSADER, which being open,
he entred with his crue, and furprifed his brother beeing a
fleepe, and bound him in fetters, and in the midft of his hall
chained him to a poaft. ROSADER amazed at this ftraunge
chaunce, began to reafon with his brother about the caufe of
this fodaine extremitie, wherein he had wrongd ꝗ and what
fault he had committed worthie fo fharpe a penaunce. SALA-
DYNE anfwered him onely with a looke of difdaine, & went
his

his way, leauing poore ROSADER in a deepe perplexitie. Who
(thus abufed) fell into fundrie paffions, but no meanes of
releefe could be had: wherevpon (for anger) he grew into
a difcontented melancholy. In which humour he continued
two or thrée dayes without meate: infomuch, that feeing his
brother would giue him no foode, he fell into defpaire of his
life. Which ADAM SPENCER the olde feruaunt of Sir IOHN
of *Bourdeaux* feeing, touched with the duetie and loue he
ought to his olde Mafter, felt a remorfe in his confcience of
his fonnes mifhap: and therefore, although SALADYNE had
giuen a generall charge to his feruaunts, that none of them
vppon paine of death fhoulde giue either meate or drinke to
ROSADER, yet ADAM SPENCER in the night arofe fecretely,
and brought him fuch victualls as hee could prouide, and vnlockt him and fet him at libertie. After ROSADER had well
feafted himfelfe, and felt he was loofe, ftraight his thoughts
aymed at reuenge, and now (all being a fleepe) hee woulde
haue quit SALADYNE with the methode of his owne mifchief.
But ADAM SPENCER perfwaded him to the contrarie, with
thefe reafons; Sir quoth he, be content, for this night go a-
gaine into your olde fetters, fo fhall you trie the faith of
friends, and faue the life of an olde feruant. To morrowe
hath your brother inuited al your kindred and allyes to a folempne breakfaft, onely to fee you, telling them all, that you
are mad, & faine to be tied to a poaft. Affone as they come,
make complaint to them of the abufe profered you by SALA-
DYNE. If they redreffe you, why fo: but if they paffe ouer
your plaints *ficco pede*, and holde with the violence of your
brother before your innocence, then thus: I will leaue you
vnlockt that you may breake out at your pleafure, and at the
ende of the hall fhall you fee ftand a couple of good pollaxes,
one for you, and another for me. When I giue you a wink,
fhake off your chaynes, and let vs play the men, and make
hauocke amongft them, driue them out of the houfe and
maintaine poffeffion by force of armes, till the King hath
made a redreffe of your abufes. Thefe wordes of ADAM

G 2   SPENCER

Euphues

SPENCER fo perfwaded ROSADER, that he went to the place of his punifhment, and ftood there while the next morning. About the time appoynted, came all the guefts bidden by SALADYNE, whom he intreated with courteous and curious intertainment, as they al perceiued their welcome to be great. The tables in the hal where ROSADER was tyed, were couered, and SALADYNE bringing in his guefts together, fhewed them where his brother was bound, and was inchainde as a man lunaticke. ROSADER made replie, and with fome inuectiues made complaints of the wrongs proffered him by SALADYNE, defiring they would in pitie feeke fome meanes for his reliefe. But in vaine, they had ftopt their eares with VLISSES, that were his words neuer fo forceable, he breathed onely his paffions into the winde. They careleffe, fat down with SALADYNE to dinner, being verie frolicke and pleafant, wafhing their heads well with wine. At laft, when the fume of the grape had entred peale meale into their braines, they began in fatyrical fpeaches to raile againft ROSADER: which ADAM SPENCER no longer brooking, gaue the figne, and ROSADER fhaking off his chaines got a pollax in his hand, and flew amongft them with fuch violence and fury, that he hurt manie, flew fome, and draue his brother and all the reft quite out of the houfe. Seeing the coaft cleare, he fhut the doores, and being fore an hungred, and feeing fuch good victuals, he fate him downe with ADAM SPENCER and fuch good fellows as he knew were honeft men, and there feafted themfelues with fuch prouifion as SALADYNE had prepared for his friēds. After they had taken their repaft, ROSADER rampierd vp the houfe, leaft vpon a fodaine his brother fhould raife fome crue of his tenaunts, and furprife them vnawares. But SALADYNE tooke a contrarie courfe, and went to the Sheriffe of the fhyre and made complaint of ROSADER, who giuing credite to SALADYNE, in a determined refolution to reuenge the Gentlemans wrongs, tooke with him fiue and twentie tall men, and made a vowe, either to breake into the houfe and take ROSADER, or els to coope him in till he made him yéelde

by

by famine. In this determination, gathering a crue together he went forward to fet SALADYNE in his former eftate.
Newes of this was brought vnto ROSADER, who fmiling at
the cowardize of his brother, brookt all the iniuries of Fortune with patience, expecting the comming of the Sheriffe.
As he walkt vpon the battlements of the houfe, he defcryed
where SALADYNE and he drew neare, with a troupe of luftie
gallants. At this he fmilde, and calde vp ADAM SPENCER,
and fhewed him the enuious treacherie of his brother, and
the folly of the Sheriffe to bee fo credulous: now ADAM,
quoth he, what fhall I doo? It refts for me, either to yéelde
vp the houfe to my brother and feeke a reconcilement, or els
iffue out, and breake through the companie with courage,
for coopt in like a coward I will not bee. If I fubmit (ah
ADAM) I difhonour my felfe, and that is worfe than death;
for by fuch open difgraces the fame of men growes odious:
if I iffue out amongft them, fortune may fauour me, and I
may efcape with life; but fuppofe the worft: if I be flaine,
then my death fhall be honourable to me, and fo inequall a
reuenge infamous to SALADYNE. Why then Mafter forward
and feare not, out amongft them, they bee but faint hearted
lozells, and for ADAM SPENCER, if he die not at your foote, fay
he is a daftard. Thefe words chéered vp fo the hart of yong
ROSADER, that he thought himfelfe fufficient for them all, &
therefore prepared weapons for him and ADAM SPENCER,
and were readie to intertaine the Sheriffe: for no fooner
came SALADYNE and he to the gates, but ROSADER vnlookt for
leapt out and affailed them, wounded manie of them, and
caufed the reft to giue backe, fo that ADAM and hee broke
through the preafe in defpite of them all, and tooke theyr
way towards the forreft of *Arden*. This repulfe fo fet the
Sheriffes heart on fire to reuenge, that he ftraight rayfed al
the countrey, and made Hue and Crie after them. But RO-
SADER and ADAM knowing full well the fecrete wayes that
led through the vineyards, ftole away priuely through the
prouince of *Bourdeaux*, & efcaped fafe to the forreft of *Ar-*

den. Being come thether, they were glad they had fo good a
harbour: but Fortune *(*who is like the Camelion*)* variable with euerie obieᴄt, & conftant in nothing but inconftãcie,
thought to make them myrrours of her mutabilitie, and
therefore ftill croft them thus contrarily.   Thinking ftill to
paffe on by the bywaies to get to *Lions,* they chaunced on a
path that led into the thicke of the forreft, where they wandred fiue or fixe dayes without meat, that they were almoft
famifhed, finding neither fhepheard nor cottage to relieue
them: and hunger growing on fo extreame, ADAM SPEN-
CER (being olde) began firft to faint, and fitting him downe
on a hill, and looking about him, efpied where ROSADER laye
as féeble and as ill perplexed: which fight made him fhedde
teares, and to fall into thefe bitter tearmes.

Adam Spencers fpeach.

OH how the life of man may well be compared to the
ftate of the Ocean feas, that for euerie calme hath a
thoufand ftormes: refembling the Rofe trée, that
for a few faire flowers, hath a multitude of fharpe prickles:
all our pleafures ende in paine, and our higheft delights, are
croffed with déepeft difcontents.   The ioyes of man, as they
are few, fo are they momentarie, fcarce ripe before they are
rotten; and wythering in the bloffome, either parched with
the heate of enuie, or fortune.   Fortune, oh inconftant friend,
that in all thy déedes are froward and fickle, delighting in
the pouertie of the loweft, and the ouerthrow of the higheft,
to decypher thy inconftancie.   Thou ftandft vpon a gloabe,
and thy wings are plumed with times feathers, that thou
maift euer be reftleffe; thou art double faced like IANUS, ca-
rying frownes in the one to threaten, and fmiles in the other
to betray; thou profffereft an Eele, and perfourmeft a Scorpion; and where thy greateft fauours be, there is the feare
of the extreameft miffortunes; fo variable are all thy aᴄti-
ons,

ons. But why ADAM dooft thou exclaime againft fortune?
fhe laughs at the plaints of the diftreffed; and there is nothing more pleafing vnto her, than to heare fooles boaft in
her fading allurements, or forrowfull men to difcouer the fo-
wer of their paffions. Glut her not ADAM then with content, but thwart her with brooking all mifhappes with patience. For there is no greater checke to the pride of fortune,
than with a refolute courage to paffe ouer her croffes without care. Thou art olde ADAM, and thy haires wax white,
the Palme trée is alreadie full of bloomes, and in the furrowes of thy face appeares the Kalenders of death? Wert
thou bleffed by fortune thy yeares could not be manie, nor
the date of thy life long: then fith Nature muft haue her
due, what is it for thée to refigne her debt a little before the
day. Ah, it is not this which grieueth mee: nor doo I care
what mifhaps Fortune can wage againft me: but the fight
of ROSADER, that galleth vnto the quicke. When I remember the worfhips of his houfe, the honour of his fathers, and
the vertues of himfelfe; then doo I fay, that fortune and the
fates are moft iniurious, to cenfure fo hard extreames, a-
gainft a youth of fo great hope. Oh ROSADER, thou art in the
flower of thine age, and in the pride of thy yeares, buxfome
and full of May. Nature hath prodigally inricht thée with
her fauours, and vertue made thee the myrrour of her excellence: and now through the decree of the vniuft ftarres, to
haue all thefe good partes nipped in the blade, and blemifht
by the inconftancie of Fortune. Ah ROSADER, could I helpe
thee, my griefe were the leffe, and happie fhould my death
be, if it might be the beginning of thy reliefe: but feeing we
perifh both in one extreame, it is a double forrowe. What
fhall I do? preuent the fight of his further miffortune, with a
prefent difpatch of mine owne life. Ah, defpaire is a mercileffe finne.

As he was readie to go forward in his paffion, he looked
earneftly on ROSADER, and feeing him change colour, he rife
vp and went to him, and holding his temples, faide, What
                                                    cheere

Euphues

cheere mafter? though all faile, let not the heart faint: the courage of a man is fhewed in the refolution of his death. At thefe words ROSADER lifted vp his eye, and looking on A-DAM SPENCER began to weepe. Ah ADAM quoth he, I forrowe not to die, but I grieue at the manner of my death. Might I with my launce encounter the enemie, and fo die in the field, it were honour, and content: might I (ADAM) combat with fome wilde beaft, and perifh as his pray, I wer fatiffied; but to die with hunger, O ADAM, it is the extreameft of all extreames. Mafter (quoth hee) you fee wee are both in one predicament, and long I cannot liue without meate, feeing therefore we can find no foode, let the death of the one preferue the life of the other. I am olde, and ouerworne with age, you are young, and are the hope of many honours: let me then die, I will prefently cut my veynes, & mafter with the warme bloud relieue your fainting fpirits: fucke on that till I ende, and you be comforted. With that *A*DAM SPENCER was readie to pull out his knife, when RO-SADER full of courage (though verie faint) rofe vp, and wifht *A*DAM SPENCER to fit there till his retourne: for my minde giues me quoth he, I fhall bring thee meate. With that, like a mad man he rofe vp, and ranged vp and downe the woods, feeking to encounter fome wilde beaft with his rapier, that either he might carrie his friend *A*DAM food, or els pledge his life in pawne of his loyaltie. It chaunced that day, that GERISMOND the lawfull king of *France* banifhed by TORIS-MOND, who with a luftie crue of Outlawes liued in that foreft, that day in honour of his Birth made a Feaft to all his bolde yeomen, and frolickt it with ftore of wine and venifon, fitting all at a long table vnder the fhadowe of lymon trees. To that place by chance Fortune conducted ROSADER, who feeing fuch a crue of braue men hauing ftore of that, for want of which he and *A*DAM perifhed, he ftept boldly to the boords end, and faluted the companie thus.

Whatfoere thou bee that art mafter of thefe luftie fquiers, I falute thee as gracioufly, as a man in extreame diftreffe

ftreffe may; knowe that I and a fellow friend of mine, are héere famifhed in the forreft for want of foode: perifh we muft vnleffe relieued by thy fauours. Therefore if thou be a Gentleman, giue meate to men, and to fuch men as are euerie way worthie of life; let the proudeft fquire that fittes at thy table, rife & incounter with me in anie honourable point of actiuitie what foeuer, and if he and thou proue me not a man, fend me a way comfortleffe. If thou refufe this, as a niggard of thy cates, I will haue amongft you with my fword; for rather will I die valiantly, than perifh with fo cowardly an extreame. GERISMOND looking him earneftly in the face, and féeing fo proper a Gentleman in fo bitter a paffion, was mooued with fo great pitie; that rifing from the table, he tooke him by the hand and bad him welcome, willing him to fit downe in his place, and in his roome not onely to eate his fill, but be Lord of the feaft. Gramercie fir (quoth ROSADER) but I haue a féeble friend that lies heereby famifhed almoft for food, aged and therfore leffe able to abide the extremitie of hunger than my felfe, and difhonour it were for me to tafte one crum, before I made him partner of my fortunes: therefore I will runne and fetch him, and then I will gratefully accept of your proffer. Away hies ROSADER to ADAM SPENCER, and tells him the newes, who was glad of fo happie fortune, but fo feeble he was that hee could not goe: whereupon ROSADER got him vp on his backe, and brought him to the place. Which when GERISMOND & his men faw, they greatly applauded their league of friendfhip; & ROSADER hauing GERISMONDS place affigned him, would not fit there himfelfe, but fet downe ADAM SPENCER. Well to be fhort, thofe hungrie fquires fell to their victualls, and feafted themfelues with good delicates, and great ftore of wine. Affoone as they had taken their repaft, GERISMOND (defirous to heare what hard fortune draue them into thofe bitter extreames) requefted ROSADER to difcourfe, (if it wer not anie way preiudiciall vnto him) the caufe of his trauell. ROSADER (defirous anie way to fatiffie the courtefie of his

H   fauou-

fauourable hoſt, (firſt beginning his *exordium* with a volley of ſighes, and a few luke warme teares) proſecuted his
diſcourſe, & told him frō point to point all his fortunes; how
he was the yongeſt Sonne of Sir IOHN of *Bourdeaux*, his
name ROSADER, how his brother ſundrie times had wronged
him, and laſtly, how for beating the Sheriffe, and hurting
his men, he fled; and this olde man (quoth he) whome I ſo
much loue and honour, is ſurnamed ADAM SPENCER, an old
ſeruant of my fathers, and one (that for his loue) neuer fay-
led me in all my miſfortunes.   When GERISMOND hearde
this, hee fell on the necke of ROSADER, and next diſcourſing
vnto him, how he was GERISMOND their lawfull King exiled by TORISMOND, what familiaritie had euer béen betwixt
his father Sir IOHN of *Bourdeaux* and him, how faithful a
ſubieᴄt he liued, and how honourable he died; promiſing (for
his ſake) to giue both him and his friend ſuch courteous intertainment, as his preſent eſtate could miniſter: and vpon
this made him one of his forreſters.   ROSADER ſeeing it was
the King, craude pardon for his boldneſſe, in that he did not
doo him due reuerence, and humbly gaue him thankes for
his fauourable courteſie.   GERISMOND not ſatiffied yet with
newes, began to enquire if he had béen lately in the court of
TORISMOND, and whether he had ſeene his daughter ROSA-
LYNDE, or no ꞓ At this, ROSADER fetcht a deep ſigh, and ſhed-
ding manie teares, could not anſwere: yet at laſt, gathering his ſpirites together, hee reuealed vnto the King, how
ROSALYNDE was baniſhed, and how there was ſuch a ſimpa-
thie of affeᴄtions betweene ALINDA and her, that ſhee choſe
rather to be partaker of her exile, than to part fellowſhippe:
whereupon the vnnaturall King baniſhed them both; and
now they are wandred none knowes whether, neither could
anie learne ſince their departure, the place of their abode.
This newes driue the King into a great melancholy, that
preſently he aroſe from all the companie, and went into his
priuie chamber, ſo ſecret as the harbor of the woods would
allow him.   The companie was all daſht at theſe tidings, &
ROSADER

ROSADER and ADAM SPENCER hauing fuch opportunitie, went to take their reſt. Where we leaue them, and returne againe to TORISMOND.

The flight of ROSADER came to the eares of TORISMOND, who hearing that SALADYNE was fole heire of the landes of Sir IOHN of *Bourdeaux*, defirous to poſſeſſe fuch faire reuenewes, found iuſt occafion to quarrell with SALADYNE, about the wrongs hee proffred to his brother: and therefore difpatching a Herehault, hee fent for SALADYNE in all poaſt haſt. Who meruailing what the matter fhould be, began to examine his owne confcience, wherein he had offended his Highneſſe: but imboldened with his innocence, hee boldly went with the Herehault vnto the Court. Where aſſoone as hee came, hee was not admitted into the prefence of the King, but prefently fent to prifon. This greatly amazed SALADYNE, chiefly in that the Iayler had a ſtraight charge ouer him, to fee that he fhould be clofe prifoner. Manie paffionate thoughts came in his head, till at laſt he began to fall into confideration of his former follies, & to meditate with himfelfe. Leaning his head on his hand, and his elbowe on his knee, full of forrow, griefe and difquieted paffions, he refolued into thefe tearmes.

Saladynes complaint.

VNhappie SALADYNE, whome folly hath led to thefe miſfortunes, and wanton defires wrapt within the laborinth of thefe calamities. Are not the heauens doomers of mens deedes Ϛ And holdes not God a ballaunce in his fiſt, to reward with fauour, and reuenge with iuſtice? Oh SALADYNE, the faults of thy youth, as they were fond, fo were they foule; and not onely difcouering little nourture, but blemiſhing the excellence of nature. Whelpes of one lytter are euer moſt louing, and brothers that are fonnes of one father, fhould liue in friendſhip without iarre. Oh SALADYNE, fo it fhould bee: but thou haſt with the deere fedde againſt the winde, with the Crab ſtroue againſt the ſtreame, and fought to peruert Nature by vnkindneſſe. ROSADERS wrongs, the wrongs of ROSADER (SALADYNE) cries for reuenge, his youth pleades to God to inflict ſome penaunce vpon thée, his vertues are pleas that inforce writs of diſpleaſure to croſſe thee: thou haſt highly abuſed thy kinde & naturall brother, and the heauens cannot ſpare to quite thee with puniſhment. There is no ſting to the worme of conſcience, no hell to a minde toucht with guilt. Euerie wrong I offered him (called now to remembrance) wringeth a drop of bloud from my heart, euerie bad looke, euerie frowne pincheth me at the quicke, and ſayes SALADYNE thou haſt find againſt ROSADER. Be penitent, and aſſigne thy ſelfe ſome penaunce to diſcouer thy ſorrow, and pacifie his wrath.

In the depth of his paſſion, he was ſent for to the King: who with a looke that threatned death entertained him, and demaunded of him where his brother was? SALADYNE made aunſwere, that vpon ſome ryot made againſt the Sheriffe of the ſhyre, he was fled from *Bourdeaux*, but he knew not whether. Nay villain (quoth he) I haue heard of the wrongs thou haſt proffered thy brother ſince the death of thy father, and by thy meanes haue I loſt a moſt braue and reſolute Cheualier. Therefore, in Iuſtice to puniſh thee, I ſpare thy life for thy fathers ſake, but baniſh thee for euer from the Court and Countrey of *France*, and ſee thy departure bee within tenne dayes, els truſt me thou ſhalt looſe thy head, & with that the King flew away in a rage, and left poore SALADYNE greatly perplexed. Who grieuing at his exile, yet determined to beare it with patience, and in penaunce of his former follies to trauell abroade in euerie Coaſt, till hee had founde out his Brother ROSADER. With whom now I begin.

ROSADER beeing thus preferred to the place of a Foreſter by GERISMOND, rooted out the remembrance of his brothers vnkindnes by continual exerciſe, trauerſing the groues and wilde Forreſts: partly to heare the melodie of the ſweete birdes

birdes which recorded, and partly to fhewe his diligent in-
deauour in his mafters behalfe.   Yet whatfoeuer he did, or
howfoeuer he walked, the liuely Image of ROSALYNDE remained in memorie: on her fwéete perfections he fedde his
thoughts, proouing himfelfe like the Eagle a true bornc
bird, fince as the one is knowen by beholding the Sunne:
fo was he by regarding excellent beautie.   One day among
the reft, finding a fit oportunitie and place conuenient, defirous to difcouer his woes to the woodes, hee engraued with
his knife on the barke of a Myrtle tree, this pretie eftimate
of his Miftres perfection.

Sonnetto.

Of all chast birdes the Phœnix doth excell,
Of all ftrong beasts the Lion beares the bell,
Of all fweete flowers the Rofe doth fweetest fmell,
Of all faire maides my Rofalynde *is fairest.*

Of all pure mettals golde is onely purest,
Of all high trees the Pine hath highest crest,
Of all foft fweetes J like my Mistres brest,
Of all chast thoughts my Mistres thoughts are rarest.

Of all proud birds the Ægle pleafeth Ioue,
Of pretie fowles kinde Venus *likes the Doue,*
Of trees Minerua *doth the Oliue loue,*
Of all fweete Nimphes I honour Rofalynde.

Of all her gifts her wifedome pleafeth most,
Of all her graces vertue fhe doth boast:
For all thefe giftes my life and ioy is lost,
If Rofalynde *proue cruell and vnkinde.*

   In thefe and fuch like paffions, ROSADER did euerie daye
eternize the name of his ROSALYNDE: and this day efpecial-

lie when ALIENA and GANIMEDE *(*inforced by the heate of
the Sunne to féeke for fhelter*)* by good fortune arriued in
that place, where this amorous forrefter regiftred his melancholy paffions; they faw the fodaine change of his looks,
his folded armes, his paffionate fighes; they heard him often
abruptly call on ROSALYNDE: who (poore foule) was as
hotly burned as himfelfe, but that fhe fhrouded her paines in
the cinders of honorable modeftie. Whereupon, (geffing
him to be in loue, and according to the nature of their fexe,
being pitifull in that behalfe) they fodainly brake off his melancholy by their approach: and GANIMEDE fhooke him out
of his dumpes thus.

What newes Forrefter ﹖ haft thou wounded fome deere,
and loft him in the fall ﹖ Care not man for fo fmall a loffe,
thy fées was but the fkinne, the fhoulder, and the hornes: tis
hunters lucke, to ayme faire and miffe: and a woodmans
fortune to ftrike and yet goe without the game.

Thou art beyond the marke GANIMEDE, quoth ALIENA,
his paffions are greater, and his fighs difcouers more loffe;
perhaps in trauerfing thefe thickets, he hath feen fome beautifull Nymph, and is growen amorous. It maye bee fo
(quoth GANIMEDE) for heere he hath newly ingrauen fome
fonnet: come and fee the difcourfe of the Forefters poems.
Reading the fonnet ouer, and hearing him name ROSALYND,
ALIENA lookt on GANIMEDE and laught, and GANIMEDE
looking backe on the Forrefter, and feeing it was ROSADER
blufht, yet thinking to fhroud all vnder hir pages apparell,
fhe boldly returned to ROSADER, and began thus.

I pray thee tell me Forrefter, what is this ROSALYNDE,
for whom thou pineft away in fuch paffions? Is fhee fome
Nymph that waites vpon DIANAES traine, whofe chaftitie
thou haft decyphred in fuch Epethites ﹖ Or is fhee fome
fhepheardeffe, that haunts thefe plaines, whofe beautie hath
fo bewitched thy fancie, whofe name thou fhaddoweft in couert vnder the figure of ROSALYNDE, as OUID did IULIA vnder the name of CORINNA? Or fay mee for footh, is it that
ROSA-

ROSALYNDE, of whome we fhepheards haue heard talke, fhee Forrefter, that is the Daughter of GERISMOND, that once was King, and now an Outlaw in this Forreft of *Arden*. At this ROSADER fetcht a deepe figh, and faid, It is fhee, O gentle fwayne, it is fhe, that Saint it is whom I ferue, that Goddeffe at whofe fhrine I doo bend all my deuotions: the moft faireft of all faires, the Phenix of all that fexe, and the puritie of all earthly perfeftion. And why (gentle Forrefter) if fhe bee fo beautifull and thou fo amorous, is there fuch a difagreement in thy thoughts? Happely fhe refembleth the rofe, that is fweete but full of prickles? or the ferpent REGIUS that hath fcales as glorious as the Sunne, & a breath as infeftious as the *Aconitum* is deadly? So thy ROSALYNDE, may be moft amiable, and yet vnkinde: full of fauour, and yet froward: coy without wit, and difdainefull without reafon.

O fhepheard (quoth ROSADER) kneweft thou her perfonage graced with the excellence of all perfeftion, beeing a harbour wherein the Graces fhroude their vertues: thou wouldft not breathe out fuch blafphemie againft the beauteous ROSALYNDE. She is a Diamond, bright but not hard, yet of moft chaft operation: a pearle fo orient, that it can be ftained with no blemifh: a rofe without prickles, and a Princeffe abfolute afwell in beautie, as in vertue. But I, vnhappie I, haue let mine eye foare with the Eagle againft fo bright a Sunne, that I am quite blinde; I haue with A-POLLO enamoured my felfe of a DAPHNE, not (as fhee) difdainfull, but farre more chaft than DAPHNE; I haue with IXION laide my loue on IUNO, and fhall (I feare) embrace nought but a clowde. Ah fhepheard, I haue reacht at a ftar, my defires haue mounted aboue my degree, & my thoughts aboue my fortunes. I being a peafant haue ventred to gaze on a Princeffe, whofe honors are too high to vouchfafe fuch bafe loues.

Why Forrefter (quoth GANIMEDE) comfort thy felfe: be blythe and frolicke man, Loue fowfeth as low as fhe foa-
reth

reth high: CUPIDE fhootes at a ragge affoone as at a roabe, and VENUS eye that was fo curious fparkled fauor on pole footed VULCAN. Feare not man, womens lookes are not tied to dignities feathers, nor make they curious efteeme, where the ftone is found, but what is the vertue. Feare not Forrefter, faint heart neuer wonne faire Ladie. But where liues ROSALYNDE now, at the Court?

Oh no (quoth ROSADER) fhe liues I knowe not where, and that is my forrow; banifht by TORISMOND, and that is my hell: for might I but finde her facred perfonage, & plead before the barre of her pitie the plaint of my paffions, hope tells mee fhee would grace me with fome fauour; and that woulde fuffice as a recompence of all my former miferies. Much haue I heard of thy Miftres excellence, and I know Forrefter thou canft defcribe her at the full, as one that haft furuayd all her parts with a curious eye: then doo me that fauour, to tell mee what her perfections bee. That I will (quoth ROSADER) for I glorie to make all eares wonder at my Miftres excellence. And with that he pulde a paper forth his bofome, wherein he read this.

Rofalyndes defcription.

Like to the cleere in higest fpheare
Where all imperiall glorie fhines,
Of felfe fame colour is her haire
Whether vnfolded or in twines:
            Heigh ho faire Rofalynde.
Her eyes are Saphires fet in fnow,
Refining heauen by euerie winke;
The Gods doo feare when as they glow,
And I doo tremble when I thinke.
            Heigh ho, would fhe were mine.

                                        Her

Her cheekes are like the blu∫hing clowde
That beaute∫ies Auroraes *face,*
Or like the ∫iluer crim∫on ∫hrowde
That Phœbus *∫miling lookes doth grace:*
          Heigh ho, faire Ro∫alynde.
Her lippes are like two budded ro∫es,
Whom rankes of lillies neighbour nie,
Within which bounds ∫he balme inclo∫es,
Apt to intice a Deitie:
          Heigh ho, would ∫he were mine.

Her necke like to a ∫tately towre,
Where Loue him∫elfe impri∫oned lies,
To watch for glaunces euerie howre,
From her deuine and ∫acred eyes,
          Heigh ho, faire Ro∫alynde.
Her pappes are centers of delight,
Her pappes are orbes of heauenlie frame,
Where Nature moldes the deaw of light,
To feede perfection with the ∫ame:
          Heigh ho, would ∫he were mine.

With orient pearle, with rubie red,
With marble white, with ∫aphire blew,
Her bodie euerie way is fed;
Yet ∫oft in touch, and ∫weete in view:
          Heigh ho, faire Ro∫alynde.
Nature her ∫elfe her ∫hape admires,
The Gods are wounded in her ∫ight,
And Loue for∫akes his heauenly fires,
And at her eyes his brand doth light:
          Heigh ho, would ∫he were mine.

Then mu∫e not Nymphes though I bemoane
The ab∫ence of faire Ro∫alynde:
          J   *Since*

Euphues

Since for her faire there is fairer none,
Nor for her vertues fo deuine.
Heigh ho faire Rofalynde:
Heigh ho my heart, would God that fhe were mine.

Perijt, quia deperibat.

Beléeue me (quoth GANIMEDE) either the Forrefter is
an exquifite painter, or ROSALYNDE faire aboue wonder: fo
it makes me blufh, to heare how women fhould be fo excellent, and pages fo vnperfect.

ROSADER beholding her earneftly, anfwered thus.   Truly *(*gentle page*)* thou haft caufe to complaine thée, wert
thou the fubftance: but refembling the fhadow, content thy
felfe: for it is excellence inough to be like the excellence of
Nature.   He hath aunfwered you GANIMEDE (quoth ALIE-
NA) it is inough for pages to waite on beautifull Ladies, &
not to be beautifull themfelues.   Oh Miftres (quoth GANI-
MEDE) holde you your peace, for you are partiall: Who
knowes not, but that all women haue defire to tie fouerein-
to their peticoats, and afcribe beautie to themfelues, where
if boyes might put on their garments, perhaps they would
prooue as comely; if not as comely, it may be more curteous.   But tell mee Forrefter, (and with that fhee turnde to
ROSADER) vnder whom maintaineft thou thy walke⸗   Gentle fwaine vnder the King of Outlawes faid he, the vnfortunate GERISMOND: who hauing loft his kingdome, crowneth
his thoughts with content, accompting it better to gouern
among poore men in peace, than great men in daunger.   But
haft thou not faid fhe, (hauing fo melancholie opportunities
as this Forreft affoordeth thee) written more Sonnets in
commendations of thy Miftres?   I haue gentle Swayne
quoth he, but they be not about me: to morrow by dawne of
daye, if your flockes feede in thefe paftures, I will bring
them you: wherein you fhall reade my paffions, whileft I
féele them; iudge my patience when you read it; till when

I

I bid farewell. So giuing both GANIMEDE and ALIENA a gentle good night, he reforted to his lodge: leauing ALIENA and GANIMEDE to their prittle prattle. So GANIMEDE (faid ALIENA, the Forrefter beeing gone) you are mightely belo-ued, men make ditties in your praife, fpend fighes for your fake, make an Idoll of your beautie: beleeue me it greeues mee not a little, to fee the poore man fo penfiue, and you fo pittileffe.

Ah ALIENA (quoth fhe) be not peremptorie in your iudg-ments, I heare ROSALYNDE praifde as I am GANIMEDE, but were I ROSALYNDE, I could anfwere the Forrefter: If hee mourne for loue, there are medicines for loue: ROSALYNDE cannot be faire and vnkinde. And fo Madame you fée it is time to folde our flockes, or els CORIDON will frowne, and fay you will neuer prooue good hufwife. With that they put their Sheepe into the coates, and went home to her friend CORIDONS cottage, ALIENA as merrie as might be, that fhe was thus in the companie of her ROSALYNDE: but fhee poore foule, that had Loue her load ftarre, and her thoughts fet on fire with the flame of fancie, coulde take no reft, but being alone beganne to confider what paffionate penaunce poore ROSADER was enioyned to by loue and fortune: that at laft fhe fell into this humour with her felfe.

Rofalynde pafsionate alone.

AH ROSALYNDE, how the Fates haue fet downe in their Synode to make thee vnhappie: for when Fortune hath done her worft, then Loue comes in to begin a new tragedie; fhee feekes to lodge her fonne in thine eyes, and to kindle her fires in thy bofome. Beware fonde girle, he is an vnruly gueft to harbour; for cutting in by intreats he will not be thruft out by force, and her fires are fed with fuch fuell, as no water is able to quench. Seeft thou not how VENUS feekes to wrap thee in her Laborynth, wherein is pleafure at the entrance, but within, forrowes, cares, and

I 2   difcon-

Euphues

difcontent: fhe is a SYREN, ftop thine eares at her melodie; and a Bafilifcke, fhut thine eyes, and gaze not at her leaft thou perifh. Thou art nowe placed in the Countrey content, where are heauenly thoughts, and meane defires: in thofe Lawnes where thy flockes feede DIANA haunts: bee as her Nymphes, chafte, and enemie to Loue: for there is no greater honour to a Maide, than to accompt of fancie, as a mortall foe to their fexe. DAPHNE that bonny wench was not tourned into a Bay tree, as the Poets faine: but for her chaftitie her fame was immortall, refembling the Lawrell that is euer greene. Follow thou her fteps ROSALYNDE, and the rather, for that thou art an exile, and banifhed from the Court: whofe diftreffe, as it is appeafed with patience, fo it woulde bee renewed with amorous paffions. Haue minde on thy forepaffed fortunes, feare the worft, and intangle not thy felfe with prefent fancies: leaft louing in haft thou repent thee at leafure. Ah but yet ROSALYNDE, it is ROSADER that courts thee; one, who as hee is beautifull, fo he is vertuous, and harboureth in his minde as manie good qualities, as his face is fhadowed with gracious fauours: and therefore ROSALYNDE ftoope to Loue, leaft beeing either too coy, or too cruell, VENUS waxe wrothe, and plague thee with the reward of difdaine.

ROSALYNDE thus paffionate, was wakened from her dumpes by ALIENA, who faide it was time to goe to bedde. CORIDON fwore that was true, for CHARLES Wayne was rifen in the North. Whereuppon each taking leaue of other, went to their reft all, but the poore ROSALYNDE: who was fo full of paffions, that fhee coulde not poffeffe anie content. Well, leauing her to her broken flumbers, expect what was perfourmed by them the nexte morning.

The Sunne was no fooner ftept from the bed of AURORA, but ALIENA was wakened by GANIMEDE: who reftleffe all night had toffed in her paffions: faying it was then time to goe to the field to vnfold their fheepe. ALIENA (that fpied where

where the hare was by the hounds, and could fée day at a little hole) thought to be pleafant with her GANIMEDE, & therfore replied thus; What wanton? the Sun is but new vp, & as yet IRIS riches lies folded in the bofome of FLORA, PHŒBUS hath not dried vp the pearled deaw, & fo long CORIDON hath taught me, it is not fit to lead the fhéepe abroad: leaft the deaw being vnwholefome, they get the rot: but now fée I the old prouerbe true, he is in haft whom the diuel driues, & where loue prickes forward, there is no worfe death than delay. Ah my good page, is there fancie in thine eie, and paffions in thy heart ç What, haft thou wrapt loue in thy looks ç and fet all thy thoughts on fire by affeçtion ç I tell thee, it is a flame as hard to be quencht as that of ÆTNA. But nature muft haue her courfe, womens eyes haue facultie attraçtiue like the ieat, and retentiue like the diamond: they dallie in the delight of faire obieçts, til gazing on the Panthers beautifull fkinne, repenting experience tell them hee hath a deuouring paunch. Come on (quoth GANIMEDE) this fermon of yours is but a fubtiltie to lie ftill a bed, becaufe either you thinke the morning colde, or els I being gone, you would fteale a nappe: this fhifte carries no paulme, and therefore vp and away. And for Loue let me alone, Ile whip him away with nettles, and fet difdaine as a charme to withftand his forces: and therefore looke you to your felfe, be not too bolde, for VENUS can make you bend; nor too coy, for CUPID hath a piercing dart, that will make you crie *Peccaui*. And that is it (quoth ALIENA) that hath rayfed you fo early this morning. And with that fhe flipt on her peticoate, and ftart vp: and affoone as fhe had made her readie, and taken her breakfaft, away goe thefe two with their bagge and bottles to the field, in more pleafant content of mind, than euer they were in the Court of TORISMOND. They came no fooner nigh the foldes, but they might fee where their difcontented Forrefter was walking in his melancholy. Affoone as ALIENA faw him, fhe fmiled, and fayd to GANIMEDE; wipe your eyes fweeting: for yonder is your fweet hart this morning

I 3 in

Euphues

in déepe praiers no doubt to VENUS, that fhe may make you as pitifull as hee is paffionate. Come on GANIMEDE, I pray thee lets haue a little fport with him. Content (quoth GANIMEDE) and with that, to waken him out of his deepe *memento*, he began thus.

Forrefter, good fortune to thy thoughts, and eafe to thy paffions, what makes you fo early abroad this morne, in cō- templation, no doubt of your ROSALYNDE. Take heede Fo- refter, ftep not too farre, the foord may be deepe, and you flip ouer the fhooes: I tell thee, flies haue their fpleene, the ants choller, the leaft haires fhadowes, & the fmalleft loues great defires. Tis good (Forrefter) to loue, but not to ouer- loue: leaft in louing her that likes not thee, thou folde thy felfe in an endleffe Laborynth. ROSADER feeing the fayre fhepheardeffe and her pretie fwayne, in whofe companie he hee felt the greateft eafe of his care, he returned them a fa- lute on this manner.

Gentle fhepheards, all haile, and as healthfull bee your flockes, as you happie in content. Loue is reftleffe, and my bedde is but the cell of my bane, in that there I finde bufie thoughtes and broken flumbers: heere (although euerie where paffionate) yet I brooke loue with more patience, in that euerie obiect feedes mine eye with varietie of fancies; when I looke on FLORAES beauteous tapeftrie, checkered with the pride of all her treafure, I call to minde the fayre face of ROSALYNDE, whofe heauenly hiew exceedes the Rofe and the Lilly in their higheft excellence; the brightneffe of PHŒBUS fhine, puts me in minde to thinke of the fparkling flames that flew from her eies, and fet my heart firft on fire; the fweet harmonie of the birds, puts me in remembrance of the rare melodie of her voyce, which like the SYREN en- chaunteth the eares of the hearer. Thus in contemplation I falue my forrowes, with applying the perfection of eue- rie obiect to the excellence of her qualities.

She is much beholding vnto you (quoth ALIENA) and fo much, that I haue oft wifht with my felfe, that if I fhould e-
uer

uer prooue as amorous as OENONE, I might finde as faithfull a PARIS as your felfe.

How fay you by this *Item* Forefter, (quoth GANIMEDE)
the faire fhepheardeffe fauours you, who is miftreffe of fo
manie flockes. Leaue of man the fuppofition of ROSALYNDS
loue, when as watching at her, you roue beyond the Moone;
and caft your lookes vpon my Miftres, who no doubt is as
faire though not fo royall; one birde in the hande is woorth
two in the wood; better poffeffe the loue of ALIENA, than
catch friuououfly at the fhadow of ROSALYNDE.

Ile tell thee boy (quoth GANIMEDE) fo is my fancie fixed on my ROSALYNDE, that were thy Miftres as faire as LÆ-
DA or DANAE, whome IOUE courted in tranfformed fhapes,
mine eyes would not vouch to intertaine their beauties: and
fo hath Loue lockt mee in her perfections, that I had rather
onely contemplate in her beauties, than abfolutely poffeffe
the excellence of anie other. VENUS is too blame (Forrefter) if hauing fo true a feruant of you, fhe reward you not
with ROSALYNDE, if ROSALYNDE were more fairer than her
felfe. But leauing this prattle, nowe Ile put you in
minde of your promife, about thofe fonnets which you faide
were at home in your lodge. I haue them about me (quoth
ROSADER) let vs fit downe, and then you fhall heare what a
Poeticall furie Loue will infufe into a man: with that they
fate downe vpon a greene bank, fhadowed with figge trees,
and ROSADER, fetching a deepe figh read them this Sonnet.

Rofaders Sonnet.

In forrowes cell I laid me downe to fleepe:
But waking woes were iealous of mine eyes,
They made them watch, and bend themfelues to weepe:
But weeping teares their want could not fuffice:
    Yet fince for her they wept who guides my hart,
    They weeping fmile, and triumph in their fmart.

                                            Of

Euphues

Of thefe my teares a fountaine fiercely fprings,
Where Venus *baynes her felfe incenst with loue;*
Where Cupid *bowfeth his faire feathred wings:*
But I behold what paines I muft approue.
  Care drinkes it drie: but when on her ʒ thinke,
  Loue makes me weepe it full vnto the brinke.

Meane while my fighes yeeld truce vnto my teares,
By them the windes increast and fiercely blow:
Yet when ʒ figh the flame more plaine appeares,
And by their force with greater power doth glow:
  Amids thefe paines, all Phœnix like I thriue,
  Since Loue that yeelds me death, may life reuiue.

Rofader en efperance.

Now furely Forrefter (quoth ALIENA) when thou madeft this fonnet, thou wert in fome amorous quandarie, neither too fearfull, as defpairing of thy Miftres fauours: nor too gleefome, as hoping in thy fortunes. I can fmile (quoth GANIMEDE) at the Sonettoes, Canzones, Madrigales, rounds and roundelayes, that thefe penfiue patients powre out, when their eyes are more ful of wantonneffe, than their hearts of paffions. Then, as the fifhers put the fweeteft baite to the faireft fifh: fo thefe OUIDIANS (holding *Amo* in their tongues, when their thoughtes come at hap hazarde, write that they be wrapt in an endleffe laborynth of forrow, when walking in the large leas of libertie, they onely haue their humours in their inckpot. If they finde women fo fond, that they will with fuch painted lures come to theyr luft, then they triumph till they be full gorgde with plea-fures: and then fly they away (like ramage kytes) to their owne content, leauing the tame foole their Miftres full of fancie, yet without euer a feather. If they miffe (as dealing with fome wary wanton, that wāts not fuch a one as them-felues, but fpies their fubtiltie) they ende their amors with
                                        a few

72

a few fained fighes: and fo there excufe is, their Miftres is cruell, and they fmoother paffions with patience. Such gentle Forrefter we may deeme you to bee, that rather paffe away the time héere in thefe Woods with writing amorets, than to bee déepely enamoured (as you faye) of your ROSA-LYNDE. If you bee fuch a one, then I pray God, when you thinke your fortunes at the higheft, and your defires to bee moft excellent, then that you may with IXION embrace IU-NO in a clowde, and haue nothing but a marble Miftres to releafe your martyrdome: but if you be true and truftie, eypaind and hart ficke, then accurfed bee ROSALYNDE if fhee prooue cruell: for Forrefter (I flatter not) thou art woorthie of as faire as fhee. ALIENA fpying the ftorme by the winde, fmiled to fee how GANIMEDE flew to the fift without anie call: but ROSADER who tooke him flat for a fhepheards Swayne made him this anfwere.

Truft me Swayne (quoth ROSADER) but my Canzon was written in no fuch humour: for mine eye & my heart are relatiues, the one drawing fancie by fight, the other entertaining her by forrowe. If thou faweft my ROSALYNDE, with what beauties Nature hath fauoured her, with what perfection the heauens hath graced her, with what qualities the Gods haue endued her; then wouldft thou fay, there is none fo fickle that could be fléeting vnto her. If fhe had ben AENEAS DIDO, had VENUS and IUNO both fcolded him from *Carthage*, yet her excellence defpite of them, woulde haue detained him at *Tyre*. If PHILLIS had béen as beauteous, or ARIADNE as vertuous, or both as honourable and excellent as fhe; neither had the Philbert trée forrowed in the death of defpairing PHILLIS, nor the ftarres haue been graced with ARIADNE: but DEMOPHOON and THESEUS had been truftie to their Paragons. I will tell thee Swaine, if with a deepe infight thou couldft pearce into the fecrete of my loues, and fee what deepe impreffions of her IDEA affeftion hath made in my heart: then wouldft thou confeffe I were paffing paffionate, and no leffe indued with admirable patience. Why

K   (quoth

Euphues

(quoth ALIENA) needes there patience in Loue? Or els in nothing (quoth ROSADER) for it is a reftleffe foare, that hath no eafe, a cankar that ftill frets, a difeafe that taketh awaie all hope of fleepe. If then fo manie forrowes, fodain ioies, momentarie pleafures, continuall feares, daylie griefes, and nightly woes be found in Loue, then is not he to be accompted patient, that fmoothers all thefe paffions with filence? Thou fpeakeft by experience (quoth GANIMEDE) and therefore wee holde all thy words for Axiomes: but is Loue fuch a lingring maladie? It is (quoth he) either extreame or meane, according to the minde of the partie that entertaines it: for as the weedes growe longer vntouchte than the pretie flowers, and the flint lies fafe in the quarrie, when the Emeraulde is fuffering the Lapidaries toole: fo meane men are fréeed from VENUS iniuries, when kings are enuyroned with a laborynth of her cares. The whiter the Lawne is, the deeper is the moale, the more purer the chryfolite the fooner ftained; and fuch as haue their hearts ful of honour, haue their loues full of the greateft forrowes. But in whomfoeuer (quoth ROSADER) he fixeth his dart, hee neuer leaueth to affault him, till either hee hath wonne him to follie or fancie: for as the Moone neuer goes without the ftarre LUNISEQUA, fo a Louer neuer goeth without the vnreft of his thoughts. For proofe you fhall heare another fancie of my making. Now doo gentle Forrefter (quoth GANIMEDE) and with that he read ouer this *Sonetto*.

Rofaders fecond Sonetto.

Turne I my lookes vnto the Skies,
Loue with his arrowes wounds mine eies:
Jf fo I gaze vpon the ground,
Loue then in euerie flower is found.

Search

Search J the ſhade to flie my paine,
He meetes me in the ſhade againe:
Wend J to walke in ſecrete groue,
Euen there I meete with ſacred Loue.
Jf ſo I bayne me in the ſpring,
Euen on the brinke I heare him ſing:
Jf ſo I meditate alone,
He will be partner of my moane.
Jf ſo I mourne, he weepes with mee,
And where I am, there will he bee.
When as I talke of Roſalynde,
The God from coyneſſe waxeth kinde,
And ſeemes in ſelfe ſame flames to frie,
Becauſe he loues as well as I.
Sweete Roſalynde *for pitie rue,*
For why, then Loue I am more true:
He if he ſpeede will quicklie flie,
But in thy loue I liue and die.

How like you this Sonnet, quoth ROSADER? Marrie
quoth GANIMEDE, for the penne well, for the paſſion ill: for
as I praiſe the one; I pitie the other, in that thou ſhouldeſt
hunt after a clowde, and loue either without rewarde or regarde. Tis not her frowardneſſe, quoth ROSADER, but my
hard fortunes, whoſe Deſtenies haue croſt me with her abfence: for did ſhee feele my loues, ſhe would not let me lin-
ger in theſe ſorrowes. Women, as they are faire, ſo they
reſpect faith, and eſtimate more (if they be honourable) the
wil than the wealth, hauing loyaltie the obiect whereat they
ayme their fancies. But leauing off theſe interparleyes,
you ſhall heare my laſt *Sonnetto,* and then you haue heard
all my Poetrie: and with that he ſight out this.

K 2   Roſa-

Euphues

Rofaders third Sonnet.

Of vertuous Loue my felfe may boast alone,
Since no fuspeƐt my feruice may attaint:
For perfeƐt faire fhee is the onely one,
Whom I esteeme for my beloued Saint:
    Thus for my faith Ɉ onely beare the bell,
    And for her faire fhe onely doth excell.

Then let fond Petrarch *fhrowde his* Lawraes *praife,*
And Taffo *ceafe to publifh his affeƐt;*
Since mine the faith confirmde at all affaies,
And hers the faire, which all men doo respeƐt:
    My lines her faire, her faire my faith affures;
    Thus Ɉ by Loue, and Loue by me endures.

Thus quoth ROSADER, heere is an ende of my Poems, but for all this no releafe of my paffions: fo that I refemble him, that in the deapth of his diftreffe hath none but the Eccho to aunfwere him. GANIMEDE pittying her ROSA-DER, thinking to driue him out of this amorous melancholie, faid, that now the Sunne was in his Meridionall heat, and that it was high noone, therefore we fhepheards fay, tis time to goe to dinner: for the Sunne and our ftomackes, are Shepheards dialls. Therefore Forrefter, if thou wilt take fuch fare as comes out of our homely fcrippes, welcome fhall aunfwere whatfoeuer thou wantft in delicates. ALIENA tooke the entertainment by the ende, and told RO-SADER he fhould be her gueft. He thankt them heartely, and fate with them downe to dinner: where they had fuch cates as Countrey ftate did allow them, fawft with fuch content, and fuch fweete prattle, as it feemed farre more fweete, than all their Courtly iunckets.

Affoone as they had taken their repaft, ROSADER giuing them thankes for his good cheere, would haue been gone: but

but GANIMEDE, that was loath to let him paffe out of her prefence, began thus; Nay Forrefter quoth he, if thy bufines be not the greater, feeing thou faift thou art fo deeply in loue, let me fee how thou canft wooe: I will reprefent ROSALYNDE, and thou fhalt bee as thou art ROSADER; fee in fome amorous Eglogue, how if ROSALYNDE were prefent, how thou couldft court her: and while we fing of Loue, ALIENA fhall tune her pipe, and playe vs melodie. Content, quoth ROSADER. And ALIENA, fhee to fhew her willingneffe, drewe foorth a recorder, and began to winde it. Then the louing Forrefter began thus.

The wooing Eglogue betwixt Rofalynde and Rofader.

Rofader.

J pray thee Nymph by all the working words,
By all the teares and fighes that Louers know,
Or what or thoughts or faltring tongue affords,
J craue for mine in ripping vp my woe.
Sweete Rofalynd *my loue (would God my loue)*
My life (would God my life) ay pitie me;
Thy lips are kinde, and humble like the doue,
And but with beautie pitie will not be.
Looke on mine eyes made red with rufull teares,
From whence the raine of true remorfe defcendeth,
All pale in lookes, and J though young in yeares,
And nought but loue or death my daies befrendeth.
Oh let no ftormie rigour knit thy browes,
Which Loue appointed for his mercie feate:
The tallest tree by Boreas *breath it bowes,*
The yron yeelds with hammer, and to heate.
    Oh Rofalynde *then be thou pittifull,*
    For Rofalynde *is onely beautifull.*

Euphues

Rosalynde.

Loues wantons arme their traitrous sutes with teares,
With vowes, with oathes, with lookes, with showers of golde:
But when the fruite of their affects appeares,
The simple heart by subtill sleights is solde.
Thus suckes the yeelding eare the poysoned bait,
Thus feedes the hart vpon his endlesse harmes,
Thus glut the thoughts themselues on selfe deceipt,
Thus blinde the eyes their sight by subtill charmes.
The louely lookes, the sighs that storme so sore,
The deaw of deepe dissembled doublenesse:
These may attempt, but are of power no more,
Where beautie leanes to wit and soothfastnesse.
> *Oh* Rosader *then be thou wittifull,*
> *For* Rosalynde *scornes foolish pitifull.*

Rosader.

I pray thee Rosalynde *by those sweete eyes*
That staine the Sunne in shine, the morne in cleare;
By those sweete cheekes where Loue incamped lies
To kisse the roses of the springing yeare.
I tempt thee Rosalynde *by ruthfull plaints,*
Not seasoned with deceit or fraudfull guile,
But firme in paine, farre more than tongue depaints,
Sweete Nymph be kinde, and grace me with a smile.
So may the heauens preserue from hurtfull food
Thy harmelesse flockes, so may the Summer yeeld
The pride of all her riches and her good,
To fat thy sheepe (the Citizens of field).
Oh leaue to arme thy louely browes with scorne:
The birds their beake, the Lion hath his taile,
And Louers nought but sighes and bitter mourne,
The spotlesse fort of fancie to assaile.
> *Oh* Rosalynde *then be thou pitifull:*
> *For* Rosalynde *is onely beautifull.*

Rosa-

78

Rofalynde.

The hardned fteele by fire is brought in frame:

Rofader.

And Rofalynde *my loue than anie wooll more fofter;*
And fhall not fighes her tender heart inflame?

Rofalynde.

Were Louers true, maides would beleeue them ofter.

Rofader.

Truth and regard, and honour guide my loue.

Rofalynde.

Faine would I trust, but yet I dare not trie.

Rofader.

Oh pitie me fweete Nymph, and doo but proue.

Rofalynde.

I would refist, but yet I know not why.

Rofader.

Oh Rofalynde *be kinde, for times will change,*
Thy lookes ay nill be faire as now they be,
Thine age from beautie may thy lookes eftrange:
Ah yeelde in time fweete Nymph, and pitie me.

Rofalynde.

Oh Rofalynde *thou must be pitifull.*
For Rofader *is yong and beautifull.*

Rofader.

Oh gaine more great than kingdomes, or a crowne.

Rofalynde.

Oh trust betraid if Rofader *abufe me.*

Rofader.

First let the heauens conspire to pull me downe,
And heauen and earth as abiect quite refufe me.
Let forrowes ftreame about my hatefull bower,
And restleffe horror hatch within my breast,
Let beauties eye afflict me with a lowre,
Let deepe despaire purfue me without rest;

Ere

Euphues

Ere Rofalynde *my loyaltie disproue,*
Ere Rofalynde *accufe me for vnkinde.*
       Rofalynde.
Then Rofalynde *will grace thee with her loue,*
Then Rofalynde *will haue thee ftill in minde.*
       Rofader.
Then let me triumph more than Tithons *deere,*
Since Rofalynde *will* Rofader *respeƈt:*
Then let my face exile his forrie cheere,
And frolicke in the comfort of affeƈt:
    And fay that Rofalynde *is onely pitifull,*
    Since Rofalynde *is onely beautifull.*

When thus they had finifhed their courting Eglogue in fuch a familiar claufe, GANIMEDE as Augure of fome good fortunes to light vpon their affeƈtions, beganne to be thus pleafant; How now Forrefter, haue I not fitted your turn ᶜ haue I not plaide the woman handfomely, and fhewed my felfe as coy in graunts, as courteous in defires, and béen as full of fufpition, as men of flatterie ᶜ And yet to falue all, iumpt I not all vp with the fweete vnion of loue? Did not ROSALYNDE content her ROSADER? The Forrefter at this fmiling, fhooke his head, and folding his armes made this merrie replie.

Truth gentle Swaine, ROSADER hath his ROSALYNDE: but as IXION had IUNO, who thinking to poffeffe a goddeffe, onely imbraced a clowde: in thefe imaginarie fruitions of fancie, I refemble the birds that fed themfelues with ZEU-XIS painted grapes; but they grewe fo leane with pecking at fhaddowes, that they were glad with AESOPS Cocke to fcrape for a barley cornell: fo fareth it with me, who to féede my felfe with the hope of my Miftres fauours, footh my felf in thy futes, and onely in conceipt reape a wifhed for con-tent: but if my food be no better than fuch amorous dreames, VENUS at the yeares ende, fhall finde mee but a leane louer. Yet doo I take thefe follies for high fortunes, and hope thefe fained

fained affections doo deuine fome vnfained ende of enfuing
fancies. And thereupon (quoth ALIENA) Ile play the prieft,
from this day forth GANIMEDE fhall call thée hufband, and
thou fhalt call GANIMEDE wife, and fo wéele haue a marriage. Content (quoth ROSADER) and laught. Content (quoth
GANIMEDE) and changed as redde as a rofe: and fo with a
fmile and a blufh, they made vp this iefting match, that after prooude to a marriage in earneft; ROSADER full little
thinking he had wooed and wonne his ROSALYNDE. But all
was well, hope is a fwéete ftring to harpe on: and therefore
let the Forrefter a while fhape himfelfe to his fhaddow, and
tarrie Fortunes leafure, till fhe may make a Metamorphofis fit for his purpofe. I digreffe, and therefore to ALIENA:
who faid, the wedding was not worth a pinne, vnles there
were fome cheere, nor that bargaine well made that was
not ftriken vp with a cuppe of wine: and therefore fhe wild
GANIMEDE to fet out fuch cates as they had, and to drawe
out her bottle, charging the Forrefter as hee had imagined
his loues, fo to conceipt thefe cates to be a moft fumptuous
banquet, and to take a Mazer of wine and to drinke to his
ROSALYNDE: which ROSADER did; and fo they paffed awaye
the day in manie pleafant deuices. Till at laft ALIENA perceiued time would tarrie no man, and that the Sunne waxed verie lowe, readie to fet: which made her fhorten their a-
morous prattle, and ende the Banquet with a frefh Car-
rowfe; which done, they all three rofe, and ALIENA broke
off thus.

Now Forrefter, PHŒBUS that all this while hath been
partaker of our fports; feeing euerie Woodman more fortunate in his loues, than hee in his fancies; feeing thou haft
wonne ROSALYNDE, when he could not wooe DAPHNE, hides
his head for fhame, and bids vs adiew in a clowde; our fheep
they poore wantons wander towards their foldes, as taught
by Nature their due times of reft: which tells vs Forrefter,
we muft depart. Marrie, though there were a marriage,
yet I muft carrie (this night) the Bryde with me, and to

L   mor-

Euphues

morrow morning if you meete vs heere, Ile promife to deliuer her as good a maide as I finde her.   Content quoth RO-
SADER, tis enough for me in the night to dreame on loue, that
in the day am fo fond to doate on loue: and fo till to morrow
you to your Foldes, and I will to my Lodge; and thus the
Forrefter and they parted.   He was no fooner gone, but A-
LIENA and GANIMEDE went and folded their flockes, and taking vp their hookes, their bagges, and their bottles, hied
homeward.   By the waye, ALIENA to make the time feeme
fhort, began to prattle with GANIMEDE thus; I haue heard
them fay, that what the Fates forepoint, that Fortune pricketh downe with a period, that the ftarres are fticklers in
VENUS Court, and defire hangs at the heele of Deftenie;
if it be fo, then by all probable coniectures, this match will
be a marriage: for if Augurifme be authenticall, or the de-
uines doomes principles, it cannot bee but fuch a fhaddowe
portends the iffue of a fubftaunce, for to that ende did the
Gods force the conceipt of this Eglogue, that they might
difcouer the enfuing confent of your affections: fo that
eare it bee long, I hope (in earneft) to daunce at your
Wedding.

Tufh (quoth GANIMEDE) al is not malte that is caft on
the kill, there goes more words to a bargaine than one, loue
feeles no footing in the aire, and fancie holdes it flipperie
harbour to neftle in the tongue: the match is not yet fo furely made but he may miffe of his market; but if Fortune be
his friend, I will not be his foe: and fo I pray you (gentle
Miftreffe ALIENA) take it.   I take all things well (quoth
fhee) that is your content, and am glad ROSADER is yours:
for now I hope your thoughts will be at quiet; your eye that
euer looked at Loue, will nowe lende a glaunce on your
Lambes: and then they will proue more buxfome and you
more blythe, for the eyes of the Mafter feedes the Cattle.
As thus they were in chat, they fpied olde CORIDON where
hee came plodding to meete them: who tolde them fupper
was readie: which newes made them fpeede them home.
Where

Where we leaue them to the next morrow, and returne to
SALADYNE.

All this while did poore SALADYNE (banifhed from *Bourdeaux* and the Court of *France* by TORISMOND) wander
vp and downe in the Forreft of *Arden*, thinking to get to
Lions, and fo trauell through *Germanie* into *Italy:* but
the Forreft being full of by-pathes, and he vnfkilfull of the
Countrey coaft, flipt out of the way, and chaunced vp into
the Defart, not farre from the place where GERISMOND
was, and his brother ROSADER. SALADYNE wearie with wandring vp and downe, and hungrie with long fafting; finding a little caue by the fide of a thicket, eating fuch frute as
the Forreft did affoord, and contenting himfelfe with fuch
drinke as Nature had prouided, and thirft made delicate, after his repaft he fell in a dead fleepe. As thus he lay, a hungrie Lion came hunting downe the edge of the groue for
pray, and efpying SALADYNE began to ceaze vpon him: but
feeing he lay ftill without anie motion, he left to touch him,
for that Lions hate to pray on dead carkaffes: and yet defirous to haue fome foode, the Lion lay downe and watcht to
fee if hee would ftirre. While thus SALADYNE flept fecure,
fortune that was careful ouer her champion, began to fmile,
and brought it fo to paffe, that ROSADER (hauing ftriken a
Deere that but lightly hurt fled through the thicket) came
pacing downe by the groue with a Boare fpeare in his hand
in great haft, he fpied where a man lay a fleepe, and a Lion
faft by him: amazed at this fight, as hee ftood gazing, his
nofe on the fodaine bled; which made him coniecture it was
fome friend of his. Whereuppon drawing more nigh, hee
might eafely difcerne his vifage, and perceiued by his phifnomie that it was his brother SALADYNE: which draue RO-
SADER into a deepe paffion, as a man perplexed at the fight
of fo vnexpected a chaunce, maruelling what fhoulde driue
his brother to trauerfe thofe fecrete Defarts without anie
companie in fuch diftreffe and forlorne fort. But the prefent
time craued no fuch doubting ambages: for either he muft

L 2　　　　　　refolue

refolue to hazard his life for his reliefe, or els fteale awaye, and leaue him to the crueltie of the Lion. In which doubt, he thus briefly debated with himfelfe.

Rofaders meditation.

Now ROSADER, Fortune that long hath whipt thee with nettles, meanes to falue thee with rofes; and hauing croft thee with manie frownes, now fhe prefents thee with the brightneffe of her fauours. Thou that didft count thy felfe the moft diftreffed of all men, maift accompt thy felfe now the moft fortunate amongft men; if fortune can make men happie, or fweete reuenge be wrapt in a pleafing content. Thou feeft SALADYNE thine enemie, the worker of thy miffortunes, and the efficient caufe of thine exile, fubieét to the crueltie of a mercileffe Lion: brought into this miferie by the Gods, that they might feeme iuft in reuenging his rigour, and thy iniuries. Seeft thou not how the ftarres are in a fauourable afpeét, the plannets in fome pleafing coniunétion, the fates agreeable to thy thoughtes, and the deftenies perfourmers of thy defires, in that SALADYNE fhall die, and thou free of his bloud; he receiue meede for his amiffe, and thou ereét his Tombe with innocent hands. Now ROSADER fhalt thou returne to *Bourdeaux*, and enioye thy poffeffions by birth, and his reuenewes by inheritaunce: now maift thou triumph in loue, and hang Fortunes Altares with garlandes. For when ROSALYNDE heares of thy wealth, it will make her loue thee more willingly: for womens eyes are made of Chrifecoll, that is euer vnperfeét vnleffe tempred with golde: and IUPITER fooneft enioyed DANAE, becaufe he came to her in fo rich a fhower. Thus fhall this Lion (ROSADER) end the life of a miferable man, and from diftreffe raife thee to bee moft fortunate. And with that cafting his Boare fpeare on his neck, away he began to trudge. But hee had not ftept backe two

or

or thrée paces, but a new motion ftroke him to the very hart,
that refting his Boare fpeare againft his breaft, hee fell into
this paffionate humour.

Ah ROSADER, wert thou the fonne of Sir IOHN of *Bourdeaux*, whofe vertues exceeded his valour, and yet the moft
hardieft Knight in all *Europe?* Should the honour of the
father fhine in the actions of the fonne? and wilt thou difhonour thy parentage, in forgetting the nature of a Gentleman? Did not thy father at his laft gafpe breathe out this
golden principle; Brothers amitie is like the drops of *Bal-
famum*, that falueth the moft dangerous fores? Did hee
make a large exhort vnto concord, and wilt thou fhewe thy
felfe carelefle? Oh ROSADER, what though SALADYNE hath
wronged thee, and made thee liue an exile in the Forreft?
fhall thy nature be fo cruell, or thy nurture fo crooked, or thy
thoughts fo fauage, as to fuffer fo difmall a reuenge? what,
to let him be deuoured by wilde beafts? *Non fapit, qui non
fibi fapit* is fondly fpoken in fuch bitter extreames. Loofe
not his life ROSADER to winne a world of treafure: for in hauing him thou haft a brother, and by hazarding for his life,
thou getteft a friend, and reconcileft an enemie: and more
honour fhalt thou purchafe by pleafuring a foe, than reuenging a thoufand iniuries.

With that his Brother began to ftirre, and the Lion to
rowfe himfelfe: whereupon ROSADER fodainely charged him
with the Boare fpeare, and wounded the Lion verie fore at
the firft ftroake. The beaft féeling himfelfe to haue a mortall hurt, leapt at ROSADER, and with his pawes gaue him a
fore pinch on the breaft that he had almoft faln: yet as a man
moft valiant, in whom the fparkes of Sir IOHN of *Bourdeaux* remained, he recouered himfelfe, and in fhort combat
flew the Lion: who at his death roared fo lowde, that SALA-
DYNE awaked, and ftarting vp was amazed at the fodayne
fight of fo monftrous a beaft lie flaine by him, and fo fweete
a Gentleman wounded. He prefently (as hee was of a ripe
conceipt) began to coniecture, that the Gentleman had flain

L 3

him

Euphues

him in his defence. Whereuppon (as a man in a traunce) he ftood ftaring on them both a good while, not knowing his Brother beeing in that difguife: at laft hee burft into thefe tearmes.

Sir whatfoeuer thou bee, (as full of honour thou muft needs be, by the view of thy prefent valure) I perceiue thou haft redreft my fortunes by thy courage, and faued my life with thine owne loffe: which ties me to be thine in all humble feruice. Thankes thou fhalt haue as thy due, and more thou canft not haue: for my abilitie denies to perfourme a déeper debt. But if anie wayes it pleafe thee to commaund me, vfe me as farre as the power of a poore Gentleman may ftretch.

ROSADER féeing hee was vnknowen to his brother, wondred to heare fuch courteous words come from his crabbed nature; but glad of fuch reformed nourture, hee made this aunfwere. I am fir (whatfoeuer thou art) a Forrefter and Ranger of thefe walkes: who following my Deere to the fall, was conducted hether by fome affenting Fate, that I might faue thee, and difparage my felfe. For comming into this place, I fawe thee a fleepe, and the Lion watching thy awake, that at thy rifing hee might prey vppon thy carkaffe. At the firft fight, I coniectured thee a Gentleman, (for all mens thoughts ought to be fauourable in imagination) and I counted it the hart of a refolute man to purchafe a ftrangers reliefe, though with the loffe of his owne bloud: which I haue perfourmed (thou feeft) to mine owne preiudice. If therefore thou be a man of fuch worth as I valew thee by thy exteriour liniaments, make difcourfe vnto mee what is the caufe of thy prefent fortunes. For by the furrowes in thy face thou feemeft to be croft with her frowns: but whatfoeuer or howfoeuer, let me craue that fauour, to heare the tragicke caufe of thy eftate. SALADYNE fitting downe, and fetching a deepe figh, began thus.

Sala-

Saladynes difcourfe to Rofader
vnknowen.

Lthough the difcourfe of my fortunes, be the renew-
ing of my forrowes, and the rubbing of the fcar, will
open a frefh wound; yet that I may not prooue ingratefull to fo courteous a Gentleman, I will rather fitte
downe and figh out my eftate, than giue anie offence by
fmoothering my griefe with filence.   Know therefore (fir)
that I am of *Bourdeaux*, and the fonne and heire of Syr
IOHN of *Bourdeaux*, a man for his vertues and valour fo
famous, that I cannot thinke, but the fame of his honours,
hath reacht farther than the knowledge of his Perfonage.
The infortunate fonne of fo fortunate a Knight am I, my
name SALADYNE: Who fucceeding my Father in poffeffions but not in qualities, hauing two Brethren committed
by my Father at his death to my charge, with fuch golden
principles of brotherly concord, as might haue pierft like
the SYRENS melodie into anie humane eare.   But I (with
VLYSSES became deafe againft his Philofophicall harmony,
and made more value of profite than of vertue, efteeming
golde fufficient honour, and wealth the fitteft title for a gentlemans dignitie: I fet my middle brother to the Vniuerfitie to be a Scholler, counting it enough if he might pore on
a booke, while I fed vpon his reuenewes: and for the yongeft (which was my fathers ioye) yong ROSADER.   And with
that, naming of ROSADER, SALADYNE fate him downe and
wept.

Nay forward man (quoth the Forrefter) teares are the
vnfitteft falue that anie man can applie for to cure forowes,
and therefore ceafe from fuch feminine follies, as fhoulde
droppe out of a Womans eye to deceiue, not out of a
Gentlemans looke to difcouer his thoughts, and forward
with thy difcourfe.

                                                              Oh

Oh fir (quoth SALADYNE) this ROSADER that wringes teares from mine eyes, and bloud from my heart, was like my father in exteriour perfonage and in inward qualities: for in the prime of his yeares he aimed all his acts at honor, and coueted rather to die, than to brooke anie iniurie vnworthie a Gentlemans credite. I, whom enuie had made blinde, and couetoufneffe mafked with the vaile of felfe loue, feeing the Palme tree grow ftraight, thought to fuppreffe it being a twig: but Nature will haue her courfe, the Cedar will be tall, the Diamond bright, the Carbuncle gliftering, and vertue will fhine though it be neuer fo much obfcured. For I kept ROSADER as a flane, and vfed him as one of my feruile hindes, vntil age grew on, and a fecrete infight of my abufe entred into his minde: infomuch, that hee could not brooke it, but coueted to haue what his father left him, and to liue of himfelfe. To be fhort fir, I repined at his fortunes, and he countercheckt me not with abilitie but valour, vntill at laft by my friends and aid of fuch as followed golde more than right or vertue, I banifht him from *Bourdeaux*, and he pore Gentleman liues no man knowes where in fome diftreffed difcontent. The Gods not able to fuffer fuch impietie vnreuenged, fo wrought, that the King pickt a caufeles quarrell againft me, in hope to haue my lands, and fo hath exiled me out of *France* for euer. Thus, thus fir, am I the moft miferable of all men, as hauing a blemifh in my thoughtes for the wrongs I proffered ROSADER, and a touche in my ftate to be throwen from my proper poffeffions by iniuftice. Paffionate thus with manie griefes, in penaunce of my former follies, I goe thus pilgrime like to feeke out my Brother, that I may reconcile my felfe to him in all fubmiffion, and afterward wend to the holy Land, to ende my yeares in as manie vertues, as I haue fpent my youth in wicked vanities.

ROSADER hearing the refolution of his brother SALADYNE began to compaffionate his forrowes, and not able to fmother the fparkes of Nature with fained fecrecie, he burft into
to

to thefe louing fpeaches. Then know SALADYNE (quoth he) that thou haft met with ROSADER; who grieues as much to fee thy diftreffe, as thy felfe to féele the burden of thy mife- rie. SALADYNE cafting vp his eye, and noting well the phif- nomie of the Forrefter, knew that it was his brother ROSA- DER: which made him fo bafh and blufh at the firft méeting, that ROSADER was faine to recomfort him. Which he did in fuch fort, yᵗ he fhewed how highly he held reuenge in fcorne. Much a doo there was betwéene thefe two Brethren, SALA- DYNE in crauing pardon, and ROSADER in forgiuing and for- getting all former iniuries; the one fubmiffe, the other cur- teous; SALADYNE penitent and paffionate, ROSADER kinde & louing; that at length Nature working an vnion of theyr thoughts, they earneftly embraced, and fell from matters of vnkindneffe, to talke of the Countrey life, which ROSADER fo highly commended, that his brother began to haue a de- fire to tafte of that homely content. In this humour RO- SADER conducted him to GERISMONDS Lodge, and prefented his brother to the King; difcourfing the whole matter how all had happened betwixt them. The King looking vppon SALADYNE, found him a man of a moft beautifull perfonage, and faw in his face fufficient fparkes of enfuing honours, gaue him great entertainment, and glad of their friendly reconcilement, promifed fuch fauour as the pouertie of his eftate might affoord: which SALADYNE gratefully accepted. And fo GERISMOND fell to queftion of TORISMONDS life? SALADYNE briefly difcourft vnto him his iniuftice and tyran- nies: with fuch modeftie (although hee had wronged him) that GERISMOND greatly praifed the fparing fpeach of the yong Gentleman.

Manie queftions paft, but at laft GERISMOND began with a deepe figh, to inquire if there were anie newes of the wel- fare of ALINDA or his daughter ROSALYNDE? None fir quoth SALADYNE, for fince their departure they were neuer heard of. Iniurious Fortune (quoth the King) that to double the Fathers miferie, wrongft the Daughter with miffortunes.

M   And

Euphues

And with that (furcharged with forrowes) he went into his
Cel, & left SALADYNE and ROSADER, whom ROSADER ftreight
conducted to the fight of ADAM SPENCER. Who féeing SA-
LADYNE in that eftate, was in a browne ftudie: but when hée
heard the whole matter, although he grieued for the exile of
his Mafter, yet hee ioyed that banifhment had fo reformed
him, that from a lafciuious youth hee was prooued a vertuous Gentleman. Looking a longer while, and feeing what
familiaritie paft betweene them, and what fauours were in-
terchanged with brotherly affection, he faid thus; I marrie,
thus fhould it be, this was the concord that olde Sir IOHN
of *Bourdeaux* wifht betwixt you. Now fulfill you thofe
precepts he breathed out at his death, and in obferuing them,
looke to liue fortunate, and die honourable. Wel faid ADAM
SPENCER quoth ROSADER, but haft anie victualls in ftore for
vs ¶ A peece of a red Deere (quoth he) and a bottle of wine.
Tis Forrefters fare brother, quoth ROSADER: and fo they
fate downe and fell to their cates. Affoone as they had taken their repaft, and had well dined, ROSADER tooke his brother SALADYNE by the hand, and fhewed him the pleafures of
the Forreft, and what content they enioyed in that meane e-
ftate. Thus for two or three dayes he walked vp and down
with his brother, to fhewe him all the commodities that belonged to his Walke. In which time hee was mift of his
GANIMEDE, who mufed greatly (with ALIENA) what fhould
become of their Forefter. Some while they thought he had
taken fome word vnkindly, and had taken the pet: then they
imagined fome new loue had withdrawen his fancie, or happely that he was ficke, or detained by fome great bufineffe of
GERISMONDS, or that he had made a reconcilement with his
brother, and fo returned to *Bourdeaux*. Thefe coniectures
did they caft in their heads, but efpecially GANIMEDE: who
hauing Loue in her heart prooued reftleffe, and halfe without patience, that ROSADER wronged hir with fo long abfence: for Loue meafures euerie minute, and thinkes how-
ers to be dayes, and dayes to be months, till they feed their
eyes

eyes with the fight of their defired obiect. Thus perplexed
liued poore GANIMEDE: while on a day fitting with ALIENA
in a great dumpe, fhe caft vp her eye, and faw where ROSA-
DER came pacing towards them with his forreft bill on his
necke. At that fight her colour chaungde, and fhe faid to A-
LIENA; See Miftreffe where our iolly Forrefter comes.
And you are not a little glad thereof (quoth ALIENA) your
nofe bewrayes what porredge you loue, the winde can not
bee tied within his quarter, the Sunne fhaddowed with a
vaile, Oyle hidden in water, nor Loue kept out of a Womans lookes: but no more of that, *Lupus est in fabula.* As
foone as ROSADER was come within the reach of her tungs
ende, ALIENA began thus: Why how now gentle Forrefter, what winde hath kept you from hence? that beeing fo
newly married, you haue no more care of your ROSALYNDE,
but to abfent your felfe fo manie dayes? Are thefe the paffions you painted out fo in your Sonnets and roundelaies?
I fee well hote loue is foone colde, and that the fancie of
men, is like to a loofe feather that wandreth in the aire with
the blaft of euerie winde. You are deceiued Miftres quoth
ROSADER, twas a coppie of vnkindneffe that kept me hence,
in that I being married, you carried away the Bryde: but
if I haue giuen anie occafion of offence by abfenting my
felfe thefe three dayes, I humblie fue for pardon: which
you muft graunt of courfe, in that the fault is fo friendly
confeft with penaunce. But to tell you the truth (faire Miftreffe, and my good ROSALYNDE) my eldeft Brother by the
iniurie of TORISMOND is banifhed from *Bourdeaux*, and by
chaunce hee and I met in the Forreft. And heere ROSADER
difcourft vnto them what had hapned betwixt them: which
reconcilement made them gladde, efpecially GANIMEDE.
But ALIENA hearing of the tyrannie of her Father, grieued
inwardly, and yet fmothred all things with fuch fecrecie,
that the concealing was more forrow than the conceipt: yet
that her eftate might be hid ftill, fhee made faire weather of
it, and fo let all paffe.

M 2

For-

Euphues

Fortune, that fawe how thefe parties valued not her Deitie, but helde her power in fcorne, thought to haue about with them, and brought the matter to paffe thus. Certaine Rafcalls that liued by prowling in the Forreft, who for feare of the Prouoft Marfhall had caues in the groues and thickets, to fhrowde themfelues from his traines; hearing of the beautie of this faire Shepheardeffe ALIENA, thought to fteale her away, and to giue her to the King for a prefent; hoping, becaufe the King was a great lechour, by fuch a gift to purchafe all their pardons: and therfore came to take her and her Page away. Thus refolued, while ALIENA and GANIMEDE were in this fad talk, they came rufhing in, and laid violent hands vpon ALIENA and her Page, which made them crie out to ROSADER: who hauing the valour of his father ftamped in his heart, thought rather to die in defence of his friends, than anie way be toucht with the leaft blemifh of difhonour; and therfore dealt fuch blowes amongft them with his weapon, as he did witneffe well vpon their carcaffes, that he was no coward. But as *Ne Hercules quidem contra duos*, fo ROSADER could not refift a multitude, hauing none to backe him; fo that hee was not onely rebatted, but fore wounded, and ALIENA and GANIMEDE had been quite carried away by thefe Rafcalls, had not Fortune (that ment to turne her frowne into a fauour) brought SALADYNE that way by chaunce; who wandring to finde out his Brothers Walke, encountred this crue: and feeing not onely a fhepheardeffe and her boy forced, but his brother wounded, hee heaued vp a forreft bill he had on his necke, and the firft hee ftroke had neuer after more neede of the Phifition: redoubling his blowes with fuch courage, that the flaues were amazed at his valour.

ROSADER efpying his brother fo fortunately arriued, and feeing how valiantly he behaued himfelfe, though fore woūded, rufhed amongft them, and laid on fuch load, that fome of the crue were flaine, and the reft fled, leauing ALIENA & GANIMEDE in the poffeffion of ROSADER and SALADYNE.

ALIENA

ALIENA after fhe had breathed a while and was come to her
felfe from this feare, lookt about her, and faw where GANI-
MEDE was bufie dreffing vp the wounds of the Forrefter:
but fhe caft her eye vpon this courteous champion that had
made fo hote a refcue, and that with fuch affection, that fhee
began to meafure euerie part of him with fauour, and in her
felfe to commend his perfonage and his vertue, holding him
for a refolute man, that durft affaile fuch a troupe of vnbridled villaines. At laft gathering her fpirites together, fhe
returned him thefe thankes.

Gentle fir, whatfoeuer you be that haue aduentured your
flefh to relieue our fortunes, as we holde you valiant, fo we
efteeme you courteous, and to haue as manie hidden vertues, as you haue manifeft refolutions. Wee poore Shepheards haue no wealth but our flockes, and therefore can
we not make requitall with anie great treafures: but our
recompence is thankes, and our rewardes to our friendes
without faining. For ranfome therefore of this our refcue,
you muft content your felfe to take fuch a kinde gramercie,
as a poore Shepheardeffe and her Page may giue: with promife (in what wee may) neuer to prooue ingratefull. For
this Gentleman that is hurt, yong ROSADER, he is our good
neighbour and familiar acquaintance, weele pay him with
fmiles, and feede him with loue-lookes: and though he bee
neuer the fatter at the yeares ende, yet wele fo hamper him
that he fhall holde himfelfe fatiffied.

SALADYNE hearing this Shepheardeffe fpeake fo wifely
began more narrowly to prie into her perfection, and to furuey all her liniaments with a curious infight; fo long dallying in the flame of her beautie, that to his coft he found her
to be moft excellent: for Loue that lurked in all thefe broiles
to haue a blowe or two, feeing the parties at the gaze, encountred them both with fuch a venie, that the ftroke pierft
to the heart fo deepe, as it could neuer after be raced out. At
laft after he had looked fo long, till ALIENA waxt red, he returned her this anfwere.

M 3   Faire

Euphues

Faire Shepheardeffe, if Fortune graced mee with fuch good hap, as to doo you anie fauour, I holde my felfe as contented, as if I had gotten a great conqueft: for the reliefe of diftreffed women is the fpeciall point, that Gentlemen are tied vnto by honour: féeing then my hazarde to refcue your harmes, was rather dutie than curtefie, thāks is more than belongs to the requitall of fuch a fauour. But leaft I might féeme either too coye or too careleffe of a Gentlewomans proffer, I wil take your kinde gramercie for a recompence. All this while that he fpake, GANIMEDE lookt earneftly vpon him, and faid; Trulie ROSADER, this Gentleman fauours you much in the feature of your face. No meruaile (quoth hee, gentle Swaine) for tis my eldeft brother SALADYNE. Your brother quoth ALIENA? (& with that fhe blufht) he is the more welcome, and I holde myfelfe the more his debter: and for that he hath in my behalfe done fuch a peece of feruice, if it pleafe him to doo me that honour, I will call him feruant, and he fhall call me Miftreffe. Content fweet Miftreffe quoth SALADYNE, and when I forget to call you fo, I will be vnmindfull of mine owne felfe. Away with thefe quirkes and quiddities of loue quoth ROSADER, and giue me fome drinke, for I am paffing thirftie, and then wil I home for my wounds bleede fore, and I will haue them dreft. GANIMEDE had teares in her eyes, and paffions in her heart to fee her ROSADER fo pained, and therefore ftept haftely to the bottle, and filling out fome wine in a Mazer, fhee fpiced it with fuch comfortable drugs as fhe hàd about her, and gaue it him; which did comfort ROSADER: that rifing (with the helpe of his brother) he tooke his leaue of them, and went to his Lodge. GANIMEDE affoone as they were out of fight ledde his flockes downe to a vale, and there vnder the fhaddow of a Beech tree fate downe, and began to mourne the miffortunes of her fweete heart.

And ALIENA (as a woman paffing difcontent) feuering her felfe from her GANIMEDE, fitting vnder a Lymon tree, began to figh out the paffions of her newe Loue, and to meditate

ditate with her felfe on this manner.

Alienaes meditation.

AY me, now I fee, and forrowing figh to fee that DI-
ANAES Lawrells are harbours for VENUS Doues,
that there trace as well through the Lawnes, wantons as chaft ones; that CALISTO be fhe neuer fo charie, will
caft one amorous eye at courting IOUE: that DIANA her felf
will change her fhape, but fhee will honour Loue in a fhaddow: that maidens eyes be they as hard as Diamonds, yet
CUPIDE hath drugs to make them more pliable than waxe.
See ALINDA, howe Fortune and Loue haue interleagued
themfelues to be thy foes: and to make thee their fubiect or
els an abiect, haue inueigled thy fight with a moft beautiful
obiect. Alate thou didft holde VENUS for a giglot, not a goddeffe; and now thou fhalt be forft to fue fuppliant to her Deitie. CUPIDE was a boy and blinde, but alas his eye had aime
inough to pierce thee to the heart. While I liued in the
Court, I helde Loue in contempt, and in high feates I had
fmall defires. I knewe not affection while I liued in dignitie, nor could VENUS counterchecke me, as long as my fortune was maieftie, and my thoughtes honour: and fhall I
nowe bee high in defires, when I am made lowe by Deftenie?

I haue hearde them faye, that Loue lookes not at low
cottages, that VENUS iettes in Roabes not in ragges,
that CUPIDE flyes fo high, that hee fcornes to touche
pouertie with his heele. Tufh ALINDA, thefe are but olde
wiues tales, and neither authenticall precepts, nor infallible principles: for Experience tells thee, that Pea-
faunts haue theyr paffions, as well as Princes, that
Swaynes as they haue their labours, fo they haue theyr
amours, and Loue lurkes affoone about a Sheepcoate, as
a Pallaice.

Ah

Euphues

Ah ALINDA, this day in auoiding a preiudice thou art fallen
into a deeper mifchiefe; being refcued from the robbers, thou
art become captiue to SALADYNE: and what then? Women
muft loue, or they muft ceafe to liue: and therefore did Nature frame them faire, that they might be fubiects to fancie.
But perhaps SALADYNES eye is leuelde vpon a more feeme-
lier Saint. If it be fo, beare thy paffions with patience, fay
Loue hath wrongd thee, that hath not wroong him; and if he
be proud in contempt, bee thou rich in content; and rather
die than difcouer anie defire: for there is nothing more precious in a woman, than to conceale Loue, and to die modeft.
He is the fonne and heire of Sir IOHN of *Bourdeaux*, a
youth comely enough: oh ALINDA, too comely, els hadft not
thou been thus difcontent; valiant, and that fettered thine
eye; wife, els hadft thou not been nowe wonne: but for all
thefe vertues, banifhed by thy father; and therefore if hee
know thy parentage, he will hate the fruite for the tree, and
condempne the yong fien for the olde ftocke. Well, howfoeuer, I muft loue: and whomfoeuer, I will: and whatfoeuer betide, ALIENA will thinke well of SALADYNE: fuppofe he of me as he pleafe. And with that fetching a deepe
figh, fhe rife vp, and went to GANIMEDE: who all this while
fate in a great dumpe, fearing the imminent danger of her
friend ROSADER; but now ALIENA began to comfort her, her
felfe beeing ouer growen with forrowes, and to recall her
from her melancholie with manie pleafaunt perfwafions.
GANIMEDE tooke all in the beft part, and fo they went home
together after they had folded their flockes, fupping with
olde CORIDON, who had prouided there cates. He after fupper, to paffe away the night while bedde time, began a long
difcourfe, how MONTANUS the yong Shepheard that was
in loue with PHŒBE, could by no meanes obtaine anie fauour at her hands: but ftill pained in reftleffe paffions, remained a hopeleffe and perplexed Louer. I would I might
(quoth ALIENA) once fee that PHŒBE, is fhee fo faire, that
fhe thinkes no fhepheard worthie of her beautie: or fo froward,

ward that no loue nor loyaltie will content hir: or fo coye,
that fhe requires a long time to be wooed: or fo foolifh that
fhe forgets, that like a fop fhe muft haue a large harueft for
a little corne ?

I cannot diftinguifh (quoth CORIDON) of thefe nice qualities: but one of thefe dayes Ile bring MONTANUS and her
downe, that you may both fee their perfons, and note theyr
paffions: and then where the blame is, there let it reft. But
this I am fure quoth CORIDON, if all maidens were of her
minde, the world would growe to a madde paffe; for there
would be great ftore of wooing and little wedding, manie
words and little worfhip, much follie and no faith. At this
fad fentence of CORIDON fo folempnlie brought foorth, ALI-
ENA fmiled: and becaufe it waxt late, fhe and her page went
to bed, both of them hauing fleas in their eares to kéep thē
awake, GANIMEDE for the hurt of her ROSADER, and ALIE-
NA for the affeċtion fhe bore to SALADYNE. In this difcontented humor they paft away the time, til falling on fleep, their
fenfes at reft, Loue left them to their quiet flumbers: which
were not long. For affoone as PHŒBUS rofe from his Au-
RORA, and began to mount him in the Skie, fummoning the
Plough-fwaines to their handie labour, ALIENA arofe; and
going to the couche where GANIMEDE laye, awakened her
page, and faid the morning was farre fpent, the deaw fmal,
and time called them awaye to their foldes. Ah, ah, (quoth
GANIMEDE) is the winde in that doore ? then in faith I perceiue that there is no Diamond fo harde but will yéelde to
the file, no Cedar fo ftrong but the winde will fhake, nor
anie minde fó chafte but Loue will change. Well ALIENA,
muft SALADYNE be the man, and will it be a match ? Truft
me he is faire and valiant, the fonne of a worthie Knight;
whome if hee imitate in perfeċtion as hee reprefents him in
proportion, he is worthie of no leffe than ALIENA. But he is
an exile: what then? I hope my Miftres refpeċts the vertues not the wealth, and meafures the qualities not the fubftance. Thofe dames that are like DANAE, that like loue in

N   no

no fhape but in a fhower of golde; I wifh them hufbandes
with much wealth and little wit; that the want of the one
may blemifh the abundance of the other. It fhould (my A-
LIENA) ftaine the honour of a Shepheardes life to fet the end
of paffions vpon pelfe. Loues eyes looks not fo low as gold,
there is no fées to be paid in CUPIDS Courtes: and in elder
time (as CORIDON hath tolde me) the Shepheards Loue-
gifts were apples and cheftnuts, & then their defires were
loyall and their thoughts conftant. But now

> *Quærenda pecunia primum, post nummos virtus.*

And the time is growen to that which HORACE in his Sa-
tyres wrote on:

> *omnis enim res*
> *Virtus-fama decus diuina humanáque pulchris*
> *Diuitijs parent: quas qui-constrinxerit ille*
> *Clarus erit, fortis, iustus, fapiens, etiam & rex*
> *Et quic quid volet—*

But ALIENA let it not be fo with thee in thy fancies, but
refpeét his faith, and there an ende. ALIENA hearing GA-
NIMEDE thus forward to further SALADYNE in his affeétions,
thought fhe kift the childe for the nurfes fake, and wooed for
him that fhe might pleafe ROSADER, made this replie; Why
GANIMEDE, whereof growes this perfwafion? Haft thou
féene Loue in my lookes? Or are mine eyes grown fo a-
morous, that they difcouer fome new entertained fancies?
If thou meafureft my thoughtes by my countenance, thou
maift prooue as ill a Phifiognomer as the Lapidarie, that
aymes at the fecrete vertues of the Topace, by the exterior
fhadow of the ftone. The operation of the Agate is not knowen by the ftrakes, nor the Diamond prized by his brightneffe, but by his hardneffe. The Carbuncle that fhineth
moft, is not euer the moft precious: and the Apothecaries
choofe not flowers for their coulours, but for their vertues.
Womens faces are not alwaies Kalenders of fancie, nor
doo their thoughtes and their lookes euer agree: for when
their eyes are fulleft of fauors, then they are oft moft emptie

tie of defire: and when they feeme to frown at difdaine, then are they moft forwarde to affection. If I bee melancholie, then GANIMEDE tis not a confequence that I am entangled with the perfection of SALADYNE. But feeing fire cannot be hid in the ftraw, nor Loue kept fo couert but it will bee fpied, what fhould friends conceale fancies ¶ Know my GA-NIMEDE, the beautie and valour, the wit and proweffe of SA-LADYNE hath fettered ALIENA fo farre, as there is no obiect pleafing to her eyes, but the fight of SALADYNE: and if loue haue done me iuftice, to wrap his thoughts in the foldes of my fare, and that he be as deeply enamoured as I am paffi-onate; I tell thee GANIMEDE, there fhall not be much woo-ing, for fhe is alreadie wonne, and what néedes a longer bat-terie. I am glad quoth GANIMEDE that it fhall be thus pro-portioned, you to match with SALADYNE, and I with ROSA-DER: thus haue the Deftenies fauoured vs with fome plea-fing afpect, that haue made vs as priuate in our loues, as fa-miliar in our fortunes.

With this GANIMEDE ftart vp, made her readie, & went into the fields with ALIENA: where vnfolding their flockes, they fate them downe vnder an Oliue trée, both of them a-morous, and yet diuerflie affected; ALIENA ioying in the ex-cellence of SALADYNE, and GANIMEDE forrowing for the wounds of her ROSADER, not quiet in thought till fhe might heare of his health. As thus both of them fate in theyr dumpes, they might efpie where CORIDON came running towards them (almoft out of breath with his haft). What newes with you (quoth ALIENA) that you come in fuch poft ¶ Oh Miftres (quoth CORIDON) you haue a long time defi-red to fee PHŒBE the faire Shepheardeffe whom MONTA-NUS loues: fo nowe if it pleafe you and GANIMEDE but to walke with me to yonder thicket, there fhall you fee MON-TANUS and her fitting by a Fountaine; he courting with his Countrey ditties, and fhe as coye as if fhe helde Loue in difdaine.

The newes were fo welcome to the two Louers, that

vp they rofe, and went with CORIDON. Affoone as they drew nigh the thicket, they might efpie where PHŒBE fate, (the faireft Shepheardeffe in all *Arden*, and he the frolickft Swaine in the whole Forreft) fhe in a peticoate of fcarlet, couered with a greene mantle; and to fhrowde her from the Sunne, a chaplet of rofes: from vnder which appeared a face full of Natures excellence, and two fuch eyes as might haue amated a greater man than MONTANUS. At gaze vp-pon this gorgeous Nymph fat the Shepheard, feeding his eyes with her fauours, wooing with fuch piteous lookes, & courting with fuch deep ftraind fighs, as would haue made DIANA her felfe to haue been compaffionate. At laft, fixing his lookes on the riches of her face, his head on his hande, and his elbow on his knee, he fung this mournefull Dittie.

Montanus Sonnet.

A Turtle fate vpon a leaueleffe tree,
  Mourning her abfent pheare
  With fad and forrie cheare:
  About her wondring ftood
  The citizens of Wood,
  And whileft her plumes fhe rents
  And for her loue laments,
  The ftately trees complaine them,
  The birdes with forrow paine them:
  Each one that doth her view
  Her paine and forrowes rue.
  But were the forrowes knowen
  That me hath ouerthrowen,
Oh how would Phœbe *figh, if fhe did looke on me?*

The loue ficke Polypheme *that could not fee,*
  Who on the barraine fhore
  His fortunes doth deplore,

And

And melteth all in mone
For Galatea *gone:*
And with his piteous cries
Afflicts both earth and Skies:
And to his woe betooke
Doth breake both pipe and hooke;
For whome complaines the Morne,
For whom the Sea Nymphs mourne.
Alas his paine is nought:
For were my woe but thought,
Oh how would Phœbe *figh, if fhe did looke on mee?*

> *Beyond compare my paine*
> *yet glad am I,*
> *If gentle* Phœbe *daine*
> *to fee her* Montan *die.*

After this, MONTANUS felt his paffions fo extreame, that he fell into this exclamation againft the iniuftice of Loue.

Helas Tirant plein de rigueur,
Modere vn peu ta violence:
Que te fert fi grande defpenfe?
C'eft trop de flammes pour vn cueur.
Efparguez en vne eftin celle,
Puis fay ton effort d'efmoûoir,
La fiere qui ne veut point voir,
En quel fu je brufle pour elle.
Execute Amour ce deffein,
Et rabaiffe vn peu fon audace,
Son cuer ne doit eftre de glace.
Bien que elle ait de Niege le fein.

Euphues

MONTANUS ended his Sonet with such a volley of sighs, and such a streame of teares, as might haue mooued any but PHŒBE to haue graunted him fauour. But she measuring all his passions with a coye disdaine, and triumphing in the poore Shepheardes patheticall humours, smiling at his martyrdome, as though loue had been no maladie, scornefully warbled out this Sonnet.

Phœbes Sonnet a replie to Montanus passion.

Downe a downe.
    Thus Phillis *sung*
        by fancie once distressed:
Who so by foolish Loue are stung,
       are worthely oppressed.
           And so sing I. With a downe, downe, &c.

      When Loue was first begot,
      And by the moouers will
      Did fall to humane lot
      His solace to fulfill.
      Deuoid of all deceipt,
      A chast and holy fire
      Did quicken mans conceipt,
      And womens breast inspire.
      The Gods that saw the good
      That mortalls did approue,
      With kinde and holy mood
      Began to talke of Loue.
            Downe a downe,
        Thus Phillis *sung*
           by fancie once distressed, &c.

But

But during this accord,
A wonder ſtrange to heare:
Whilest Loue in deed and word
Most faithfull did appeare.
Falſe ſemblance came in place
By iealozie attended,
And with a doubleface
Both loue and fancie blended.
Which made the Gods forſake,
And men from fancie flie,
And maidens ſcorne a make;
Forſooth and ſo will I.
Downe a downe.
Thus Phillis *ſung*
by fancie once distreſſed;
Who ſo by fooliſh Loue are ſtung
are worthely oppreſſed.
And ſo ſing I.
with downe a downe, adowne downe, a-
(downe a,

MONTANUS hearing the cruel reſolution of PHŒBE, was
ſo ouergrowen with paſſions, that from amorous Ditties
he fell flat into theſe tearmes; Ah PHŒBE quoth he, whereof art thou made, that thou regardeſt not my maladie? Am
I ſo hatefull an obieᶜt, that thine eyes condempne me for an
abieᶜt? or ſo baſe, that thy deſires cannot ſtoope ſo lowe as to
lende mee a gracious looke⸴ My paſſions are manie, my
loues more, my thoughts loyaltie, and my fancie faith: all
deuoted in humble deuoire to the ſeruice of PHŒBE: & ſhal
I reape no reward for ſuch fealties. The Swaines daylie
labours is quit with the euenings hire, the Ploughmans
toyle is eaſed with the hope of corne, what the Oxe ſweates
out at the plough he fatneth at the cribbe: but infortunate
MONTANUS hath no ſalue for his ſorrowes, nor anie hope of
recom-

recōpence for the hazard of his perplexed paſſions. If PHŒ-
BE, time may plead the proofe of my truth, twice ſeuen winters haue I loued faire PHŒBE: if conſtancie bee a cauſe to
farther my ſute, MONTANUS thoughtes haue beene ſealed
in the ſweete of PHŒBES excellence, as farre from chaunge
as ſhe from loue: if outward paſſions may diſcouer inward
affeCtions, the furrowes in my face may decypher the ſorrowes of my heart, and the mappe of my lookes the griefes
of my minde.   Thou féeſt (PHŒBE) the teares of deſpayre
haue made my cheekes full of wrinkles, and my ſcalding
ſighes haue made the aire Eccho her pitie conceiued in my
plaints: PHILOMELE hearing my paſſions, hath left her
mournfull tunes to liſten to the diſcourſe of my miſeries.   I
haue pourtraied in euerie tree the beautie of my Miſtreſſe, &
the deſpaire of my loues.   What is it in the woods cannot
witnes my woes? and who is it would not pitie my plaints ꝇ
Onely POŒBE.   And why?   Becauſe I am MONTANUS, and
ſhe PHŒBE; I a worthleſſe Swaine and ſhee the moſt excellent of all faires.   Beautifull PHŒBE, oh might I ſay
pitifull, then happie were I though I taſted but one minute
of that good hap.   Meaſure MONTANUS not by his fortunes
but by his loues; and ballaunce not his wealthe, but his
deſires, and lend but one gracious looke to cure a heape of
diſquieted cares: if not, ah if PHŒBE can not loue, let a
ſtorme of frownes ende the diſcontent of my thoughts, and
ſo let me periſh in my deſires, becauſe they are aboue my
deſerts: onely at my death this fauour cannot be denied me,
that all ſhall ſay, MONTANUS died for loue of harde hearted
PHŒBE.   At theſe words ſhe fild her face full of frownes, and
made him this ſhort and ſharpe replie.

Importunate Shepheard, whoſe loues are lawleſſe, becauſe reſtleſſe: are thy paſſions ſo extreame that thou canſt
not conceale them with patience ꝇ   Or art thou ſo folly-ſick,
that thou muſt needes be fancie-ſicke ꝇ and in thy affeCtion
tied to ſuch an exigent, as none ſerues but PHŒBE.   Well
ſir, if your market may be made no where els, home again,
for

for your Mart is at the faireſt. PHŒBE is no lettice for your lippes, and her grapes hangs ſo high, that gaze at them you may, but touch them you cannot. Yet MONTANUS I ſpeake not this in pride, but in diſdaine; not that I ſcorne thee, but that I hate Loue: for I count it as great honour to triumph ouer Fancie, as ouer Fortune. Reſt thée content therefore MONTANUS, ceaſe from thy loues, and bridle thy lookes; quench the ſparkles before they grow to a further flame: for in louing me thou ſhalt liue by loſſe, & what thou vttereſt in words, are all written in the winde. Wert thou (MONTA-NUS) as faire as PARIS, as hardie as HECTOR, as conſtant as TROYLUS, as louing as LEANDER; PHŒBE could not loue, be-cauſe ſhe cannot loue at all: and therefore if thou purſue me with PHŒBUS, I muſt flie with DAPHNE.

GANIMEDE ouer-hearing all theſe paſſions of MONTA-NUS, could not brooke the crueltie of PHŒBE, but ſtarting from behinde the buſh ſaid; And if Damzell you fled from me, I would tranſforme you as DAPHNE to a bay, and then in contempt trample your branches vnder my féete. PHŒBE at this ſodaine replie was amazed, eſpecially when ſhe ſaw ſo faire a Swaine as GANIMEDE; bluſhing therefore, ſhee would haue béen gone: but that he held her by the hand, and proſecuted his replie thus. What Shepheardeſſe, ſo fayre and ſo cruell? Diſdaine beſeemes not cottages, nor coynes maides: for either they be condempned to bee too proude, or too froward. Take heede (faire Nymph) that in deſpiſing Loue, you be not ouer-reacht with Loue, and in ſhaking off all, ſhape your ſelfe to your own ſhaddow: and ſo with NAR-CISSUS prooue paſſionate & yet vnpitied. Oft haue I heard, and ſometimes haue I ſeene, high diſdaine turnd to hot de-ſires. Becauſe thou art beautifull, be not ſo coye: as there is nothing more faire, ſo there is nothing more fading, as momentary as the ſhadowes which growes from a clowdie Sunne. Such (my faire Shepheardeſſe) as diſdaine in youth deſire in age, and then are they hated in the winter, that might haue béen loued in the prime. A wrinkled maide

O   is

is like to a parched Rofe, that is caft vp in coffers to pleafe
the fmell, not worne in the hand to content the eye. There
is no follie in Loue to had I wift: and therefore be rulde by
me, Loue while thou art young, leaft thou be difdained when
thou art olde. Beautie nor time cannot bee recalde, and if
thou loue, like of MONTAUNS: for as his defires are manie,
fo his deferts are great.

PHŒBE all this while gazed on the perfection of GANI-
MEDE, as deeplie enamoured on his perfection, as MONTA-
NUS inueigled with hers: for her eye made furuey of his excellent feature, which fhe found fo rare, that fhe thought the
ghoft of ADONIS had been leapt from ELIZIUM in the fhape
of a Swaine. When fhe blufht at her owne follie to looke
fo long on a ftranger, fhe mildlie made aunfwere to GANI-
MEDE thus. I cannot denie fir but I haue heard of Loue,
though I neuer felt Loue; and haue read of fuch a Goddeffe as VENUS, though I neuer faw anie but her picture: &
perhaps, and with that fhe waxed red and bafhful, and with
all filent: which GANIMEDE perceiuing, commended in her
felfe the bafhfulneffe of the maide, and defired her to goe forward. And perhaps fir (quoth fhe) mine eye hath ben more
prodigall to day than euer before: and with that fhe ftaid a-
gaine, as one greatly paffionate and perplexed. ALIENA feeing the hare through the maze, bade her forwarde with her
prattle: but in vaine, for at this abrupt periode fhe broke off,
and with her eyes full of teares, and her face couered with a
vermillion die, fhe fate downe and fightht. Whereuppon,
ALIENA and GANIMEDE feeing the Shepheardeffe in fuch
a ftrange plight, left PHŒBE with her MONTANUS, wifhing
her friendly that fhee would be more pliant to Loue, leaft
in penaunce VENUS ioyned her to fome fharpe repentaunce.
PHŒBE made no replie, but fetcht fuch a figh, that Eccho
made relation of her plaint: giuing GANIMEDE fuch an a-
dieu with a piercing glaunce, that the amorous Girle-boye
perceiued PHŒBE was pincht by the heele.

But leauing PHŒBE to the follies of her new fancie, and
MONTA-

MONTANUS to attend vpon her; to SALADYNE, who all this laſt night could not reſt for the remembrance of ALIENA: infomuch that he framed afweete conceipted ſonnet to content his humour, which he put in his boſome: being requeſted by his brother ROSADER to go to ALIENA and GANIMEDE, to ſignifie vnto them that his wounds were not daungerous. A more happie meſſage could not happen to SALADYNE, that taking his Forreſt bil on his necke, he trudgeth in all haſt towards the plaines, where ALIENAES flockes did feede: comming iuſt to the place when they returned from MONTANUS and PHŒBE. Fortune ſo conducted this iollie Forreſter, that he encountred them and CORIDON, whom he preſently faluted in this manner.

Faire Shepheardeſſe, and too faire, vnleſſe your beautie be tempred with courteſie, & the liniaments of the face graced with the lowlineſſe of minde: as manie good fortunes to you and your Page, as your ſelues can deſire, or I imagine. My brother ROSADER (in the griefe of his greene wounds) ſtill mindfull of his friends, hath ſent me to you with a kind ſalute, to ſhew that he brookes his paines with the more patience, in that he holds the parties precious in whoſe defence he receiued the preiudice. The report of your welfare, will bee a great comfort to his diſtempered bodie and diſtreſſed thoughts, and therefore he ſent mee with a ſtrict charge to viſite you. And you (quoth ALIENA) are the more welcome in that you are meſſenger from ſo kind a Gentleman, whoſe paines we compaſſionate with as great ſorrowe, as hee brookes them with griefe; and his wounds breedes in vs as manie paſſions, as in him extremities: ſo that what diſquiet hee feeles in bodie, wee partake in heart. Wiſhing (if wee might) that our miſhap might ſalue his maladie. But ſeeing our wills yeelds him little eaſe, our orizons are neuer idle to the Gods for his recouerie. I pray youth (quoth GANIMEDE with teares in his eies) when the Surgeon ſearcht him, helde he his wounds dangerous? Dangerous (quoth SALADYNE) but not mortall: and the ſooner to be cured, in

O 2   that

Euphues

that his patient is not impatient of anie paines: whereupon my brother hopes within thefe ten dayes to walke abroad and vifite you himfelfe.   In the meane time (quoth GANIMEDE) fay his ROSALYNDE commends her to him and bids him be of good cheere.   I know not (quoth SALADYNE) who that ROSALYNDE is, but whatfoeuer fhe is, her name is neuer out of his mouth: but amidft the deepeft of his paffions he vfeth ROSALYNDE as a charme to appeafe all forrows with patience.   Infomuch that I conieĉture my brother is in loue, and fhe fome Paragon that holdes his hart perplexed: whofe name he oft records with fighs, fometimes with teares, ftraight with ioy, then with fmiles; as if in one perfon Loue had lodged a Chaos of confufed paffions.   Wherein I haue noted the variable difpofition of fancie, that like the POLYPE in colours, fo it changeth into fundrie humours: being as it fhould feeme a combate mixt with difquiet, and a bitter pleafure wrapt in a fweete preiudice, like to the SINOPLE tree, whofe bloffomes delight the fmell, and whofe fruite infeĉts the taft.   By my faith (quoth ALIENA) fir, you are deepe read in loue, or growes your infight into affeĉtion by experience?   Howfoeuer, you are a great Philofopher in VENUS principles, els could you not difcouer her fecrete aphorifmes.   But fir our countrey amours are not like your courtly fancies, nor is our wooing like your fuing: for poore fhepheards neuer plaine them till Loue paine them, where the Courtiers eyes is full of paffions when his heart is moft free from affeĉtion: they court to difcouer their eloquence, we wooe to eafe our forrowes: euerie faire face with them muft haue a new fancie fealed with a forefinger kiffe and a farre fetcht figh; we heere loue one, and liue to that one fo lōg as life can maintain loue, vfing few ceremonies becaufe we know fewe fubtilties, and little eloquence for that wee lightly accompt of flatterie: only faith and troth thats fhepfheards wooing, and fir howe like you of this?   So (quoth SALADYNE) as I could tie my felfe to fuch loue.   What, and looke fo low as a Shepheardeffe, being the Sonne of Sir
IOHN

IOHN of *Bourdeaux*: such desires were a disgrace to your
honours. And with that surueying exquisitely euerie part of
him, as vttering all these words in a déepe passion, she espi-
ed the paper in his bosome: whereupon growing iealous
that it was some amorous Sonnet, shee sodainly snatcht it
out of his bosome, and asked if it were any secret? She was
bashfull, and SALADYNE blusht: which she perceiuing sayd;
Nay then sir, if you waxe redde, my life for yours tis some
Loue matter: I will see your Mistresse name, her praises,
and your passions. And with that she lookt on it: which was
written to this effect.

Saladynes Sonnet.

If it be true that heauens eternall course
With restlesse sway and ceaselesse turning glides,
If aire inconstant be, and swelling sourse
Turne and returnes with many fluent tides,
*   If earth in winter summers pride estrange,*
*   And Nature seemeth onely faire in change.*

If it be true that our immortall spright
Deriude from heauenly pure, in wandring still
In noueltie and strangenesse doth delight,
And by discouerent power discerneth ill,
*   And if the bodie for to worke his best*
*   Doth with the seasons change his place of rest:*

Whence comes it that (inforst by furious Skies)
I change both place and soyle, but not my hart?
Yet salue not in this change my maladies?
Whence growes it that each obiect workes my smart?
*   Alas I see my faith procures my misse,*
*   And change in loue against my nature is.*
    Et florida pungunt.

O 3	ALI-

Euphues

ALIENA hauing read ouer his fonnet, began thus plefant-
ly to defcant vpon it.   I fee SALADYNE *(*quoth fhee*)* that as
the Sunne is no Sunne without his brightneffe, nor the diamond accounted for precious vnleffe it be hard: fo men are
not men vnleffe they be in loue; and their honours are meafured by their amours not their labours, counting it more
commendable for a Gentleman to be full of fancie, than full
of vertue.   I had thought

Otia fi tollas periere Cupidinis arcus,
Contemptæq iacent, & fine luce faces:

But I fee OUIDS axiome is not authenticall, for euen labor
hath her loues, and extremitie is no pumice ftone to race out
fancie.   Your felfe exiled from your wealth, friends & countrey by TORISMOND, *(*forrowes enough to fuppreffe affections*)* yet amidft the depth of thefe extreamities, Loue will
be Lord, and fhew his power to bee more predominant than
Fortune.   But I pray you fir (if without offence I maye
craue it) are they fome new thoughts, or fome olde defires?
SALADYNE (that now faw opportunitie pleafaunt) thought
to ftrike while the yron was hote, and therefore taking ALI-
ENA by the hand fate downe by her; and GANIMEDE to giue
them leaue to their Loues, founde her felfe bufie about
the foldes, whileft SALADYNE fell into this prattle with A-
LIENA.

Faire Miftres, if I bee blunt in difcouering my affections, and vfe little eloquence in leuelling out my loues: I
appeale for pardon to your owne principles that fay, Shepheards vfe few ceremonies, for that they acquaint thēfelues
with fewe fubtilties: to frame my felfe therefore to your
countrey fafhion with much faith and little flatterie, knowe
beautifull Shepheardeffe, that whileft I liued in the court
I knew not Loues cumber, but I held affection as a toy, not
as a maladie; vfing fancie as the HIPERBOREI do their flowers, which they weare in their bofome all day, and caft them
in the fire for fuell all night.   I liked al becaufe I loued none,
and who was moft faire on her I fed mine eye: but as charely

rely as the Bee, that affoone as fhee hath fuckt honnie from the rofe, flies ftraight to the next Marigold. Liuing thus at mine owne lift, I wondred at fuch as were in loue, & when I read their paffions, I tooke them only for poems that flowed from the quickneffe of the wit not the forrowes of the heart. But nowe (faire Nymph) fince I became a Forrefter, Loue hath taught me fuch a leffon that I muft confeffe his deitie and dignitie, and faye as there is nothing fo precious as beautie, fo there is nothing more piercing than fancie. For fince firft I arriued in this place, and mine eie tooke a curious furuey of your excellence, I haue been fo fettered with your beautie and vertue, as (fweet ALIENA) SALADYNE without further circumftance loues ALIENA. I coulde paint out my defires with long ambages, but feeing in manie words lies miftruft, and that trueth is euer naked; let this fuffice for a countrey wooing, SALADYNE loues ALIENA, and none but ALIENA.

Although thefe words were moft heauenly harmonie in the eares of the Shepheardeffe: yet to feeme coye at the firft courting, and to difdaine Loue howfoeuer fhee defired Loue, fhe made this replie.

Ah SALADYNE, though I feeme fimple, yet I am more fubtile than to fwallow the hook becaufe it hath a painted bait: as men are wilie fo women are warie, efpecially if they haue that wit by others harmes to beware. Doo wee not knowe SALADYNE, that mens tongues are like MERCURIES pipe, that can inchaunt ARGUS with an hundred eies; and their words as preiudiciall as the charmes of CIRCES, that tranffourme men into monfters. If fuch SYRENS fing, wee poore Women had neede ftoppe our eares, leaft in hearing we proue fo foolifh hardie as to beleeue them, and fo perrifh in trufting much, and fufpecting little. SALADYNE, *Pifcator ictus fapit*, he that hath been once poyfoned & afterwards feares not to bowfe of euerie potion, is woorthie to fuffer double pennaunce. Giue me leaue then to miftruft, though I doo not condempne. SALADYNE is now in loue with ALIENA, he

a

Euphues

a Gentleman of great Parentage, fhe a Shepheardeffe of meane Parents; he honourable, and fhee poore? Can Loue confift of contrarieties? Will the Fawlcon pearch with the Kiftreffe, the Lion harbour with the Woolfe? Will VENUS ioyne roabes and rags together? Or can there be a fimpathie betweene a King and a begger. Then SALADYNE how can I beléeue thée that loue fhould vnite our thoughts, when Fortune hath fet fuch a difference betweene our degrees? But fuppofe thou likeft of ALIENAES beautie, men in their fancie refemble the wafpe, which fcornes that flower from which fhe hath fetcht her waxe; playing like the inhabitants of the Ilande *Tenerifa*, who when they haue gathered the fweete fpices, vfe the trees for fuel: fo men when they haue glutted themfelues with the faire of womens faces, holde them for neceffarie euills; and wearied with that which they feemed fo much to loue, caft away fancie as children doo their rattles; and loathing that which fo deepelie before they likte, efpecially fuch as take loue in a minute, & haue their eyes attractiue like ieate apt to entertaine anie obiect, are as readie to let it flip againe. SALADYNE hearing howe ALIENA harpt ftill vppon one ftring, which was the doubt of mens conftancie, hee broke off her fharp inuectiue thus.

I graunt ALIENA (quoth hee) manie men haue doone amiffe in proouing foone ripe and foone rotten, but particular inftances inferre no generall conclufions: and therefore I hope what others haue faulted in fhall not preiudice my fauours. I will not vfe fophiftrie to confirme my loue, for that is fubtiltie; nor long difcourfes, leaft my words might bee thought more than my faith: but if this will fuffice, that by the honour of a Gentleman I loue ALIENA, and wooe ALIENA not to crop the bloffomes and reiect the tree, but to confummate my faithfull defires, in the honourable ende of marriage.

At this word marriage: ALIENA ftood in a maze what to anfwere: fearing that if fhe were too coye to driue him away

with

with her difdaine; and if fhe were too courteous to difcouer
the heate of her defires. In a dilemma thus what to doo, at
laft this fhe faid. SALADYNE euer fince I faw thée, I fauoured thée, I cannot diffemble my defires, becaufe I fée thou
dooft faithfully manifeft thy thoughtes, and in liking thee
I loue thee fo farre as mine honour holdes fancie ftill in fufpence: but if I knew thee as vertuous as thy father, or as
well qualified as thy brother ROSADER, the doubt fhoulde be
quicklie decided: but for this time to giue thee an anfwere,
affure thy felfe this, I will either marrie with SALADYNE, or
ftill liue a virgine: and with this they ftrained one anothers
hand. Which GANIMEDE efpying, thinking he had had his
Miftres long enough at fhrift, faid; what, a match or no?
A match (quoth ALIENA) or els it were an ill market. I am
glad (quoth GANIMEDE) I would ROSADER were well here
to make vp a meffe. Well remembred (quoth SALADYNE)
I forgot I left my brother ROSADER alone: and therefore
leaft being folitarie he fhould increafe his forrowes I will
haft me to him. May it pleafe you then to commaund me a-
nie feruice to him, I am readie to be a duetifull meffenger.
Onely at this time commend me to him (quoth ALIENA) &
tell him, though wee cannot pleafure him we pray for him.
And forget not (quoth GANIMEDE) my commendations:
but fay to him that ROSALYNDE fheds as manie teares from
her heart, as he drops of bloud from his wounds, for the forrow of his misfortunes; feathering all her thoughtes with
difquiet, till his welfare procure her content: fay thus (good
SALADYNE) and fo farewell. He hauing his meffage, gaue a
courteous adieu to them both, efpecially to ALIENA: and fo
playing loath to depart, went to his brother. But ALIENA,
fhe perplexed and yet ioyfull, paft away the day pleafauntly
ftill praifing the perfection of SALADYNE, not ceafing to chat
of her new Loue, till euening drew on; and then they folding their fheepe, went home to bed. Where we leaue them
and returne to PHŒBE.

P   PHŒ-

Euphues

PHŒBE fiered with the vncouth flame of loue, returned
to her fathers houfe; fo galled with reftleffe paffions, as
now fhe began to acknowledge, that as there was no flower
fo frefh but might bee parched with the Sunne, no tree fo
ftrong but might bee fhaken with a ftorme; fo there was no
thought fo chaft, but Time armde with Loue could make a-
morous: for fhee that helde DIANA for the Goddeffe of her
deuotion, was now faine to flie to the Altare of VENUS; as
fuppliant now with prayers, as fhe was froward afore with
difdaine.   As fhe lay in her bed, fhe called to minde the feuerall beauties of yong GANIMED, firft his locks, which being
amber hued, paffeth the wreathe that PHŒBUS puts on to
make his front glorious; his browe of yuorie, was like the
feate where Loue and Maieftie fits inthronde to enchayne
Fancie; his eyes as bright as the burnifhing of the heauen,
darting foorth frownes with difdaine, and fmiles with fauor,
lightning fuch lookes as would enflame defire; were fhee
wrapt in the Circle of the frozen Zoane; in his cheekes the
vermilion teinture of the Rofe flourifhed vpon naturall A-
labafter, the blufh of the Morne and LUNAES filuer fhowe
were fo liuely portrayed, that the TROYAN that fils out wine
to IUPITER was not halfe fo beautifull; his face was full of
pleafance, and all the reft of his liniaments proportioned
with fuch excellence, as PHŒBE was fettred in the fweetnes
of his feature.   The IDEA of thefe perfections tumbling in
her minde, made the poore Shepheardffe fo perplexed, as
feeling a pleafure tempred with intollerable paines, and yet
a difquiet mixed with a content, fhe rather wifhed to die, than
to liue in this amorous anguifh.   But wifhing is little worth
in fuch extreames, and therefore was fhe forft to pine in her
maladie, without anie falue for her forrowes. Reueale it fhe
durft not, as daring in fuch matters to make none her fecre-
tarie; and to conceale it, why it doubled her griefe: for as
fire fuppreft growes to the greater flame, and the Current
ftopt to the more violent ftreame; fo Loue fmothred wrings
the heart with the déeper paffions.

Per-

Perplexed thus with fundrie agonies, her foode began to
faile, and the difquiet of her minde began to worke a diftem-
perature of her bodie, that to be fhort PHŒBE fell extreame
ficke, and fo ficke, as there was almoſt left no recouerie of
health. Her father feeing his faire PHŒBE thus diftreft,
fent for his friends, who fought by medicine to cure, and by
counfaile to pacifie, but all in vaine: for although her bodie
was feeble through long fafting, yet fhe did *magis agrotare
animo quàm corpore.* Which her friends perceiued and forrowed at, but falue it they could not.

The newes of her fickneffe was bruted abroad thorough
all the Forreft: which no fooner came to MONTANUS eare,
but he like a madde man came to vifite PHŒBE. Where fitting by her bedde fide, he began his Exordium with fo manie teares and fighes, that fhe perceiuing the extremitie of
his forrowes, began now as a louer to pitie them, although
GANIMEDE helde her from redreffing them. MONTANUS
craued to knowe the caufe of her fickneffe, tempred with fecrete plaints: but fhe aunfwered him (as the reft) with filence, hauing ftill the forme of GANIMEDE in her minde, &
coniecturing how fhee might reueale her loues. To vtter it
in words fhe found herfelfe too bafhfull, to difcourfe by anie
friend fhee would not truft anie in her amours, to remayne
thus perplexed ftill and conceale all, it was a double death.
Whereuppon for her laft refuge fhe refolued to write vnto
GANIMEDE: and therefore defired MONTANUS to abfent him
felfe a while, but not to depart: for fhe would fee if fhe could
fteale a nappe. He was no fooner gone out of the chamber,
but reaching to her ftandifh, fhe tooke penne and paper, and
wrote a letter to this effect.

P 2　　　PHŒBE

Euphues

Phœbe to Ganimede wiſheth what ſhe
wants her ſelfe.

F Aire Shepheard (and therefore is PHŒBE infortunate
becauſe thou art ſo faire) although hetherto mine eies
were adamants to refiſt Loue, yet I no ſooner ſaw thy
face but they became amorous to intertaine Loue: more deuoted to fancie than before they were repugnant to affection, addicted to the one by Nature, and drawne to the other
by beautie; which being rare, and made the more excellent
by manie vertues, hath ſo ſnared the freedome of PHŒBE,
as ſhe reſts at thy mercie, either to bee made the moſt fortunate of all Maidens, or the moſt miſerable of all Women.
Meaſure not GANIMEDE my loues by my wealth, nor my
deſires by my degrees: but thinke my thoughts are as full
of faith, as thy face of amiable fauours.   Then as thou knoweſt thy ſelfe moſt beautifull, ſuppoſe me moſt conſtant.   If
thou deemeſt me hardhearted becauſe I hated MONTANUS,
thinke I was forſt to it by Fate: if thou ſaiſt I am kinde
hearted becauſe ſo lightly I loue thee at the firſt looke, thinke
I was driuen to it by Deſtenie, whoſe influence as it is
mightie, ſo it is not to be refiſted.   If my fortunes were a-
nie thing but infortunate Loue, I woulde ſtriue with Fortune: but he that wreſts againſt the will of VENUS, ſeekes
to quench fire with oyle, and to thruſt out one thorne by putting in another.   If then GANIMEDE, Loue enters at the eie,
harbours in the heart, and will neither bee driuen out with
Phiſicke nor reaſon: pitie me, as one whoſe maladie hath
no ſalue but from thy ſweete ſelfe, whoſe griefe hath no eaſe
but through thy graunt, and thinke I am a Virgine, who
is deepely wrongd, when I am forſt to wooe: and coniecture Loue to bee ſtrong, that is more forceable than Nature.
   Thus diſtreſſed vnleſſe by thee eaſed, I expect either to
liue

liue fortunate by thy fauour, or die miferable by thy deniall.
Liuing in hope. Farewell.

She that muft be thine, or
not be at all.

Phœbe.

To this Letter fhe annexed this Sonnet.

Sonnetto.

My boate doth paffe the ftraights
  of feas incenft with fire,
Filde with forgetfulneffe:
  amidst the winters night,
A blinde and careleffe boy
  (brought vp by fonde defire)
Doth guide me in the fea
  of forrow and defpight.

For euerie oare, he fets
  a ranke of foolifh thoughts,
And cuts (in ftead of waue)
  a hope without diftreffe;
The windes of my deepe fighs
  (that thunder ftill for noughts)
Haue fplit my fayles with feare,
  with care, with heauineffe.

A mightie ftorme of teares,
  a blacke and hideous cloude,
A thoufand fierce difdaines
  dooo flacke the haleyards oft:

P 3   *Till*

Euphues

Till ignorance doo pull
and errour hale the ſhrowdes,
No ſtarre for ſafetie ſhines,
no Phœbe *from aloft.*
Time hath ſubdued arte,
and ioy is ſlaue to woe:
Alas (Loues guide) be kinde;
what ſhall I periſh ſo?

This Letter and the Sonnet being ended, ſhe could find no fitte meſſenger to ſende it by; and therefore ſhee called in MONTANUS, and intreated him to carrie it to GANIMEDE. Although poore MONTANUS ſaw day at a little hole, and did perceiue what paſſion pincht her: yet (that he might ſéeme dutifull to his Miſtres in all ſeruice) he diſſembled the matter, and became a willing meſſenger of his owne Martyrdome. And ſo (taking the letter) went the next morne verie early to the Plaines where ALIENA fed her flockes, and there hee found GANIMEDE ſitting vnder a Pomegranade trée ſorrowing for the hard fortunes of her ROSADER. MONTANUS ſaluted him, and according to his charge deliuered GANIMEDE the letters, which (he ſaid) came from PHŒBE. At this the wanton bluſht, as beeing abaſht to thinke what newes ſhould come from an vnknowen Shepheardeſſe, but taking the letters vuript the ſeales, and read ouer the diſcourſe of PHŒBES fancies. When ſhee had read and ouerread them, GANIMEDE began to ſmile, & looking on MONTANNS fell into a great laughter: and with that called ALIENA, to whom ſhe ſhewed the writings. Who hauing peruſed them, conceipted them verie pleaſantly, and ſmiled to ſée how Loue had yoakt her, who before diſdained to ſtoupe to the lure, ALIENA whiſpering GANIMEDE in the eare, and ſaying; Knewe PHŒBE what want there were in thée to perfourme her will, and how vnfit thy kinde is to bee kinde to her, ſhe would be more wiſe and leſſe enamoured: but leauing

uing

uing that, I pray thée let vs fport with this Swaine. At
that worde, GANIMEDE tourning to MONTANUS, began to
glaunce at him thus.

I pray thee tell me Shepheard, by thofe fweet thoughts
and pleafing fighes that grow from my Miftreffe fauours,
art thou in loue with PHŒBE? Oh my Youth, quoth MON-
TANUS, were PHŒBE fo farre in loue with me, my Flockes
would be more fat and their Mafter more quiet: for through
the forrowes of my difcontent growes the leanneffe of my
fheepe. Alas poore Swaine quoth GANIMEDE, are thy paffions fo extreame or thy fancie fo refolute, that no reafon
will blemifh the pride of thy affeftion, and race out that
which thou ftrlueft for without hope? Nothing can make
me forget PHŒBE, while MONTANUS forget himfelfe: for
thofe charafters which true Loue hath ftamped, neither the
enuie of Time nor Fortune can wipe awaye. Why but
MONTANUS qnoth GANIMEDE, enter with a deepe infight
into the defpaire of thy fancies, and thou fhalt fee the depth
of thine owne follies: for (poore man) thy progreffe in
loue is a regreffe to loffe, fwimming againft the ftreame
with the Crab, and flying with APIS INDICA againft winde
and weather. Thou feekeft with PHŒBUS to winne DAPH-
NE, and fhee flies fafter than thou canft followe: thy defires
foare with the Hobbie, but her difdaine reacheth higher than
thou canft make wing. I tell thee MONTANUS, in courting
PHŒBE thou barkeft with the Wolues of *Syria* againft the
Moone, and roaueft at fuch a marke with thy thoughtes, as
is beyond the pitch of thy bow, praying to Loue when Loue
is pitileffe, and thy maladie remedileffe. For proofe MON-
TANUS read thefe letters, wherein thou fhalt fee thy great
follies and little hope.

With that MONTANUS tooke them and perufed them, but
with fuch forrow in his lookes, as they bewrayed a fourfe of
confufed paffions, in his heart: at euerie line his coulour
changed, and euerie fentence was ended with a periode of
fighes.

At

Euphues

At laſt, noting PHŒBES extreame deſire toward GA-
NIMEDE, and her diſdaine towards him, giuing GANIMEDE
the letter, the Shepheard ſtoode as though hee had neither
wonne nor loſt. Which GANIMEDE perceiuing, wakened
him out his dreame thus; Now MONTANUS, dooſt thou ſee
thou voweſt great ſeruice and obteineſt but little reward:
but in lieu of thy loyaltie, ſhe maketh thee as BELLEPHORON
carrie thine owne bane. Then drinke not willinglie of that
potion wherein thou knoweſt is poyſon, creepe not to her
that cares not for thee. What MONTANUS, there are manie
as faire as PHŒBE, but moſt of all more courteous than
PHŒBE. I tell thee Shepheard, fauour is Loues fuell:
then ſince thou canſt not get that, let the flame vaniſh into
ſmoake, and rather ſorrow for a while than repent thee for
euer.

I tell thee GANIMEDE (quoth MONTANUS) as they which
are ſtung with the Scorpion, cannot be recoured but by
the Scorpion, nor hee that was wounded with ACHILLES
lance be cured but with the ſame trunchion: ſo APOLLO was
faine to crie out, that Loue was onely eaſed with Loue, and
fancie healed by no medecin but fauor. PHŒBUS had hearbs
to heale all hurts but this paſſion, CYRCES had charmes for
all chaunces but for affeᶜtion, and MERCURIE ſubtill reaſons
to refell all griefes but Loue. Perſwaſions are bootleſſe,
Reaſon lendes no remedie, Counſaile no comfort, to ſuch
whome Fancie hath made reſolute: and therefore though
PHŒBE loues GANIMEDE, yet MONTANUS muſt honor none
but PHŒBE.

Then quoth GANIMEDE, may I rightly tearme thee a
deſpayring Louer, that liueſt without ioy, & loueſt without
hope: but what ſhall I doo MONTANUS to pleaſure thee?
Shall I deſpiſe PHŒBE as ſhe diſdaines thee? Oh (quoth
MONTANUS) that were to renew my griefes, and double my
ſorrowes: for the ſight of her diſcontent were the cenſure
of my death. Alas GANIMEDE, though I periſh in my
thoughtes, let not her die in her deſires. Of all paſſions,
Loue

Loue is moſt impatient: then let not ſo faire a creature as
PHŒBE ſinke vnder the burden of ſo déepe a diſtreſſe. Being
loue ſicke ſhe is prooued heart ſicke, and all for the beautie
of GANIMEDE. Thy proportion hath entangled her affection, and ſhe is ſnared in the beautie of thy excellence. Then
ſith ſhe loues thée ſo déere, miſlike not her deadly. Bee thou
paramour to ſuch a paragon: ſhee hath beautie to content
thine eye, and flockes to enrich thy ſtore. Thou canſt not
wiſh for more than thou ſhalt winne by her: for ſhe is beautifull, vertuous and wealthie, three deepe perſwaſions to
make loue frolicke. ALIENA ſeeing MONTANUS cut it againſt
the haire, and plead that GANIMEDE ought to loue PHŒBE,
when his onely life was the loue of PHŒBE: anſwered him
thus. Why MONTANUS dooſt thou further this motion ﹖ ſeeing if GANIMEDE marrie PHŒBE thy market is clean mard.
Ah Miſtres (quoth he) ſo hath Loue taught mee to honour
PHŒBE, that I would preiudice my life to pleaſure her, and
die in deſpaire rather than ſhe ſhould periſh for want. It ſhal
ſuffice me to ſee him contented, and to feed mine eye on her
fauour. If ſhe marrie though it be my Martyrdome: yet if
ſhee bee pleaſed I will brooke it with patience, and triumph
in mine owne ſtarres to ſee her deſircs ſatiſſied. Therefore
if GANIMEDE bee as courteous as hee is beautifull, let him
ſhew his vertues, in redreſſing PHŒBES miſeries. And this
MONTANUS pronounſt with ſuch an aſſured countenance, that
it amazed both ALIENA and GANIMEDE to ſee the reſolution
of his loues: ſo that they pitied his paſſions and commended his patience; deuiſing how they might by anie ſubtiltie,
get MONTANUS the fauour of PHŒBE. Straight (as Womens heads are full of wyles) GANIMEDE had a fetch to force
PHŒBE to fancie the Shepheard MALGRADO the reſolution
of her minde hee proſecuted his policie thus. MONTANUS
(quoth he) ſeeing PHŒBE is ſo forlorne leaſt I might bee
couuted vnkinde, in not ſaluing ſo faire a creature, I will
goe with thee to PHŒBE, and there heare her ſelfe in worde
vtter that which ſhe hath diſcourſt with her penne, and then

Q   as

Euphues

as Loue wills me, I will fet downe my cenfure. I will
home by our houfe, and fend CORIDON to accompanie ALIE-
NA. MONTANUS féemed glad of this determination, and a-
way they goe towards the houfe of PHŒBE. When they
drew nigh to the Cottage, MONTANUS ranne afore, & went
in and tolde PHŒBE that GANIMEDE was at the dore. This
word GANIMEDE founding in the eares of PHŒBE, draue her
into fuch an extafie for ioy, that rifing vp in her bed fhe was
halfe reuiued, and her wan colour began to waxe red: and
with that came GANIMEDE in, who faluted PHŒBE with
fuch a curteous looke, that it was halfe a falue to her forrowes. Sitting him downe by her bed fide, hee queftioned
about her difeafe, and where the paine chiefly helde her?
PHŒBE looking as louely as VENUS in her night geere,
tainting her face with as ruddie a blufh as CLITIA did when
when fhee bewrayed her Loues to PHŒBUS: taking GA-
NIMEDE by the hand began thus. Faire fhepheard, if loue
were not more ftrong then nature, or fancie the fharpeft extreame; my immodefty were the more, and my vertues the
leffe: for nature hath framed womens eyes bafhfull, their
hearts full of feare, and their tongues full of filence: But
Loue, that imperious Loue, where his power is predominant, then he peruerts all and wrefteth the wealth of nature
to his owne will: an Inftance in my felfe fayre GANIMEDE,
for fuch afire hath hee kindled in my thoughts, that to finde
eafe for the flame, I was forced to paffe the bounds of modeftie and feeke a falue at thy handes for my fecret harmes:
blame mee not if I bee ouer bolde for it is thy beautie, and
if I be too forward it is fancie, & the deepe infight into thy
vertues that makes me thus fond. For let me fay in a word,
what may be contayned in a volume, PHŒBE loues GANI-
MEDE: at this fhe held downe her head and wept, and GANI-
MEDE rofe as one that would fuffer no fifh to hang on his fingers made this replie. Water not thy plants PHŒBE, for
I doe pitie thy plaintes, nor feeke not to difcouer thy Loues

in

122

in teares: for I coniecture thy trueth by thy paffions: forrow is no falue for loues, nor fighes no remedie for affection. Therefore frolick PHŒBE, for if GANIMEDE can cure
thée, doubt not of recoueric. Yet this let me fay without
offence, that it gréeues me to thwart MONTANUS in his fancies, féeing his defires haue ben fo refolute, and his thoughts
fo loyall: But thou alleadgeft that thou art forft from him
by fate; fo I tell thee PHŒBE either fome ftarre or elfe fome
deftinie fits my minde rather with ADONIS to die in chafe,
than be counted a wanton in VENUS knee. Although I pittie thy martyrdome, yet I can grant no mariage; for though
I held thee faire, yet mine eye is not fettered, Loue growes
not like the hearb Spattanna to his perfection in one night
but creepes with the fnaile, and yet at laft attaines to the
top *Feftina Lente* efpecially in Loue: for momentarie
fancies are oft times the fruites of follies: If PHŒBE I
fhould like thee as the HIPERBOREI do their Dates, which
banquet with them in the morning and throw them awaie
at night, my folly fhould be great, and thy repentance more,
Therefore I will haue time to turne my thoughts, and my
Loues fhall growe vp as the water *Creffes*, flowly but with
a deepe roote. Thus PHŒBE thou maift fee I difdaine not
though I defire not, remaining indifferent till time and
loue makes me refolute. Therefore PHŒBE feeke not to
fuppreffe affection, and with the Loue of MONTANUS quench
the remembrance of GANIMEDE, ftriue thou to hate me as
I feeke to like of thee, and euer haue the duties of MON-
TANUS in thy minde, for I promife thee thou mayft haue
one more welthie but not more loyall. Thefe wordes
were corafiues to the perplexed PHŒBE, that fobbing out
fighes and ftrayning out teares fhee blubbered out thefe
wordes.

And fhall I then haue no falue of GANIMEDE, but fufpence, no hope but a doubtfull hazard, no comfort, but bee
pofted off to the will of time ? iuftly haue the Gods ballanft

Q 2   my

my fortunes, who beeing cruell to MONTANUS found GANI-
MEDE, as vnkinde to my felfe: fo in forcing him perifh for
loue, I fhall die my felfe with ouermuch loue. I am glad
(quoth GANIMEDE) you looke into your owne faults, and fee
where your fhooe wrings you, meafuring now the paines of
MONTANNS by your owne paffions. Truth quoth PHŒBE,
and fo deeply I repent me of my frowardneffe toward the
Shepheard, that could I ceafe to loue GANIMEDE, I would
refolue to like MONTANUS. What if I can with reafon perfwade PHŒBE to miflike of GANIMEDE, will fhe then fauour
MONTANUS? When reafon (quoth fhe) doth quench that loue
that I owe to thee, then will I fancie him: conditionallie,
that if my loue can bee fuppreft with no reafon, as beeing
without reafon, GANIMEDE wil onely wed himfelfe to PHŒ-
BE. I graunt it faire Shepheardeffe quoth he: and to feede
thee with the fweetneffe of hope, this refolue on: I will neuer marrie my felfe to woman but vnto thy felfe: and with
that GANIMEDE gaue PHŒBE a fruiteleffe kiffe & fuch words
of comfort, that before GANIMEDE departed fhe arofe out of
her bed, and made him and MONTANUS fuch cheere, as could
be found in fuch a Countrey cottage. GANIMEDE in the
midft of their banquet rehearfing the promifes of either in
MONTANUS fauour, which highly pleafed the Shephearde.
Thus all three content, and foothed vp in hope, GANIMEDE
tooke his leaue of his PHŒBE & departed, leauing her a contented woman, and MONTANUS highly pleafed. But poore
GANIMEDE, who had her thoughtes on her ROSADER, when
fhe calde to remembrance his wounds, filde her eyes full of
teares, and her heart full of forrowes, plodded to finde A-
LIENA at the Foldes, thinking with her prefence to driue a-
way her paffions. As fhe came on the Plaines, fhe might e-
fpie where ROSADER and SALADYNE fate with ALIENA vnder
the fhade: which fight was a falue to her griefe, and fuch a
cordiall vnto her heart, that fhe tript alongft the Lawnes
full of ioy.

At laft CORIDON who was with them fpied GANIMEDE,
and

and with that the Clowne rofe, and running to méete him
cried, Oh firha, a match, a match, our Miftres fhall be ma-
ried on Sunday. Thus the poore peafant frolickt it before
GANIMEDE, who comming to the crue faluted them all, and
efpecially ROSADER, faying that hee was glad to fee him fo
well recouered of his wounds. I had not gone abroade fo
foone quoth ROSADER, but that I am bidden to a marriage,
which on Sunday next muft bee folempnized betweene my
brother and ALIENA. I fee well where Loue leades delay is
loathfome, and that fmall wooing ferues, where both the
parties are willing. Truth quoth GANIMEDE: but a happie day fhould it be, if ROSADER that day might be married
to ROSALYNDE. Ah good GANIMEDE (quoth he) by naming
ROSALYNDE renue not my forrowes: for the thought of her
perfections, is the thrall of my miferies. Tufh, bee of good
cheere man quoth GANIMEDE, I haue a friend that is deeply experienft in Negromancie and Magicke, what arte can
doo fhall bee acted for thine aduantage: I will caufe him to
bring in ROSALYNDE, if either *France* or anie bordering Nation harbour her; and vppon that take the faith of a young
Shepheard. ALIENA fmilde to fee how ROSADER frownde,
thinking that GANIMEDE had iefted with him. But breaking off from thofe matters, the Page (fomewhat pleafant)
began to difcourfe vnto them what had paft betweene him
and PHŒBE: which as they laught, fo they wondred at; all
confeffing, that there is none fo chaft but Loue will change.
Thus they paft away the day in chat, and when the Sunne
began to fet, they tooke their leaues and departed: ALIENA
prouiding for their marriage day fuch folempne cheere and
handfome roabes as fitted their countrey eftate, & yet fomewhat the better, in that ROSADER had promifed to bring GE-
RISMOND thether as a gueft. GANIMEDE (who then meant
to difcouer her felfe before her father, had made her a gowne
of greene, and a kirtle of the fineft fendall, in fuch fort that
fhe feemed fome heauenly Nymph harboured in Countrey
attire.

Q 3   SA-

Euphues

SALADYNE was not behind in care to fet out the nuptials, nor ROSADER vnmindfull to bid guefts, who inuited GERISMOND and all his Followers to the Feaft: who willinglye graunted; fo that there was nothing but the daye wanting to this marriage. In the meaue while, PHŒBE being a bidden gueft, made her felfe as gorgeous as might be to pleafe the eye of GANIMEDE; and MONTANUS futed himfelfe with the coft of many of his flocks to be gallant againft that day; for then was GANIMEDE to giue PHŒBE an anfwere of her loues, and MONTANUS either to heare the doome of his miferie, or the cenfure of his happineffe. But while this geare was a bruing, PHŒBE paft not one day without vifiting hir GANIMEDE, fo farre was fhee wrapt in the beauties of this louely Swaine. Much prattle they had, and the difcourfe of manie paffions, PHŒBE wifhing for the daye (as fhee thought) of her welfare, and GANIMEDE fmiling to thinke what vnexpected euents would fall out at the wedding. In thefe humours the weeke went away, that at laft Sundaye came.

No fooner did PHŒBUS Hench man appeare in the Skie, to giue warning that his mafters horfes fhoulde bee trapt in his glorious couch, but CORIDON in his holiday fute meruailous féemely, in a ruffet iacket welted with the fame, and faced with red worfted, hauing a paire of blew chamlet fleeues, bound at the wrefts with foure yeolow laces, clofed afore verie richly with a doffen of pewter buttons: his hofe was of gray karfie, with a large flop bard ouerthwart the pocket holes with three fair gards, ftitcht of either fide with red thred, his ftock was of the own fewed clofe to his breech, and for to beautefie his hofe, he had truft himfelf round with a dofen of new thredden points of medley coulour: his bonnet was greene whereon ftood a copper brooch with the picture of SAINT DENIS: and to want nothing that might make him amorous in his olde dayes, he had a fayre fhyrt band of fine lockram, whipt ouer with Couentrey blew, of no fmall coft.

Thus

Thus attired, CORIDON beftird himfelfe as chiefe ftickler in
thefe actions, and had ftrowed all the houfe with flowers,
that it feemed rather fome of FLORAES choyce bowers, than
anie Countrey cottage.

Thether repaired PHŒBE with all the maides of the forreft to fet out the bride in the moft feemelieft fort that might
be: but howfoeuer fhe helpt to pranke out ALIENA, yet her
eye was ftill on GANIMEDE, who was fo neate in a fute of
gray, that he feemed ENDYMION when hee won LUNA with
his lookes, or PARIS when he plaide the Swaine to get the
beautie of the Nymph OENONE. GANIMEDE like a prettie
Page waited on his Miftreffe ALIENA, and ouerlookt that al
was in a readineffe againft the Bridegroome fhoulde come.
Who attired in a Forrefters fute came accompanied with
GERISMOND and his brother ROSADER early in the morning;
where arriued, they were folempnlie entertained by ALIENA
and the reft of the Countrey Swaines, GERISMOND verie
highly commending the fortunate choyce of SALADYNE, in
that had chofen a Shepheardeffe, whofe vertues appeared
in her outward beauties, being no leffe faire than feeming
modeft.

GANIMEDE comming in and feeing her Father began to
blufh, Nature working affects by her fecret effects: fcarce
could fhe abftaine from teares to fee her Father in fo lowe
fortunes: he that was wont to fit in his royall Pallaice, attended on by twelue noble peeres, now to be contented with
a fimple Cottage, and a troupe of reuelling Woodmen
for his traine. The confideration of his fall, made GANI-
MEDE full of forrowes: yet that fhee might triumph ouer
Fortune with patience, and not anie way dafh that merrie
day with her dumpes, fhee fmothered her melancholy with
a fhaddow of mirth: and verie reuerently welcommed the
King, not according to his former degree, but to his prefent eftate, with fuch diligence, as GERISMOND began to
commend the Page for his exquifite perfon, and excellent
qualities.

As

Euphues

As thus the King with his Forrefters frolickt it among
the fhepheards, CORIDON came in with a faire mazer full of
Sidar, and prefented it to GERISMOND with fuch a clown-
ifh falute, that he began to fmile, and tooke it of the old fhepheard verie kindly, drinking to ALIENA and the reft of her
faire maides, amongft whom PHŒBE was the formoft. ALI-
ENA pledged the King, and drunke to ROSADER: fo the car-
rowfe went round from him to PHŒBE, &c. As they were
thus drinking and readie to goe to Church, came in MON-
TANUS apparailed all in tawney, to fignifie that he was forfaken; on his head he wore a garland of willowe, his bottle
hanged by his fide wheron was painted defpaire, and on his
fheephooke hung two fonnets as labels of his loues & fortunes.

Thus attired came MONTANUS in, with his face as
full of griefe, as his heart was of forrowes, fhewing in his
countenance the map of extremities. Affoone as the Shepheards faw him, they did him all the honour they could, as
being the flower of all the Swaines in *Arden*: for a bonni-
er boy was there not feene fince the wanton Wag of *Troy*
that kept fheep in *Ida*. He feeing the king, and geffing it to
be GERISMOND, did him all the reuerence his countrey curtefie could affoord. Infomuch that the King wondring at his
attire, began to queftion what he was. MONTANUS ouer-
hearing him made this replie.

I am fir quoth he Loues Swaine, as full of inward difcontents as I feeme fraught with outward follies. Mine
eyes like Bees delight in fweete flowers, but fucking their
full on the faire of beautie, they carrie home to the Hiue of
my heart farre more gall than honnie, and for one droppe of
pure deaw, a tunne full of deadly *Aconiton*. I hunt with
the Flie to purfue the Eagle, that flying too nigh the
Sunne, I perifh with the Sunne: my thoughts are aboue
my reach, and my defires more than my fortunes; yet neither greater than my Loues. But daring with PHAETON,
I fall with IRARUS, and feeking to paffe the meane, I dye
for

[for being fo mean, my night fleeps are waking flombers, as full of forrowes as they be far from reft, & my dayes labors are fruitleffe amors, ftaring at a ftar & ftombling at a ftraw, leauing reafon to follow after repentance: yet euery paffion is a pleafure thogh it pinch, becaufe loue hides his worme-feed in figs, his poyfons in fweet potions, & fhadows preiu-dize with the mafke of pleafure. The wifeft counfellers are my deep difcontents, and I hate that which fhould falue my harm, like the patient which ftung with the *Tarantula* loaths mufick, and yet the difeafe incurable but by melody. Thus (Sir) reftleffe I hold my felfe remediles, as louing without either reward or regard, and yet louing, bicaufe there is none worthy to be loued, but the miftreffe of my thoughts. And that I am as full of paffions as I haue difcourft in my plaintes, Sir if you pleafe fee my Sonnets, and by them cenfure of my forrowes.

Thefe wordes of MONTANUS brought the king into a great wonder, amazed as much at his wit as his attire: infomuch that he tooke the papers off his hooke, and read them to this effect.

Montanus firft Sonnet.

Alas how wander I amidft thefe woods,
Whereas no day bright fhine doth finde acceffe:
But where the melancholy fleeting floods
(Darke as the night) my night of woes expreffe,
Difarmde of reafon, fpoilde of natures goods,
Without redreffe to falue my heauineffe
    I walke, whilest thought (too cruell to my harmes)
    With endles grief my heedles iudgement charmes.

My filent tongue affailde by fecret feare,
My traitrous eyes imprifoned in their ioy,

R

My

Euphues

My fatall peace deuourd in fained cheare,
My heart inforſt to harbour in annoy,
My reaſon robde of power by yeelding eare,
My fond opinions ſlaue to euery toy.
  Oh Loue thou guide in my vncertaine way,
  Woe to thy bow, thy fire, the cauſe of my decay.
    Et florida pungunt.

When the King had read this Sonnet, he highly commended the deuice of the ſhepheard, that could ſo wittily wrap his paſſions in a ſhaddow, and ſo couertly conceale that which bred his chiefeſt diſcontent: affirming, that as the leaſt ſhrubs haue their tops, the ſmalleſt haires their ſhadowes: ſo the meaneſt ſwaines had their fancies, and in their kynde were as charie of Loue as a King. Whetted on with this deuice, he tooke the ſecond and read it: the effects were theſe.

Montanus ſecond Sonnet.

When the Dog
Full of rage,
    With his irefull eyes
    Frownes amidſt the skies
The Shepheard to aſſwage
    The fury of the heat,
    Himſelfe doth ſafely ſeat
By a fount
Full of faire,
    Where a gentle breath
    (Mounting from beneath)
Tempreth the aire.

                                        There

There his flocks
Drinke their fill,
 And with eafe repofe
 Whilest fweet fleep doth clofe
Eyes from toylfome ill.
But I burne
Without reft,
 No defenfiue power
 Shields from Phoebes *lower:*
Sorrow is my best.
Gentle Loue
Lowre no more,
 If thou wilt inuade,
 In the fecret fhade,
Labour not fo fore.
I *my felfe*
A*nd my flocks*
 They their loue to pleafe,
 I my felfe to eafe,
Both leaue the fhadie oakes:
 Content to burne in fire
 Saith Loue doth fo defire.
   Et florida pungunt.

GERISMOND feeing the pithy vaine of thofe Sonets, began
to make further enquiry what hee was? Whereupon RO-
SADER difcourft vnto him the loue of MONTANUS to PHOEBE,
his great loialtie & her deep crueltie: and how in reuenge
the Gods had made the curious Nymph amorous of yoong
GANIMEDE. Vpon this difcourfe, yᵉ king was defirous to
fee PHOEBE: who being broght before GERISMOND by RO-
SADER, fhadowed the beauty of her face with fuch a vermilion teinture, that the Kings eyes began to dazle at the
   R 2   puritie

puritie of her excellence. After GERISMOND had fed his lookes a while vpon her faire, he queftioned with her, why fhe rewarded MONTANUS loue with fo little regard, feeing his defertes were many, and his paffions extreame. PHOEBE to make reply to the Kings demaund, anfwered thus: Loue (fir) is charitie in his lawes, and whatfoeuer hee fets downe for iuftice (bee it neuer fo vniuft) the fentence cannot be reuerft: womens fancies lende fauours not euer by defert, but as they are inforft by their defires: for fancy is tied to the wings of Fate, & what the ftarres decree, ftands for an infallible doome. I know MONTANUS is wife, & womens ears are greatly delighted with wit, as hardly efcaping the charme of a pleafant toong, as VLISSES the melody of the SYRENS. MONTANUS is bewtifull, and womens eyes are fnared in the excellence of obiects, as defirous to feede their lookes with a faire face, as the Bee to fuck on a fweet floure. MONTANUS is welthy, & an ounce of giue me perfwades a woman more than a pound of heare me. DANAE was won with a golden fhower, when fhe could not be gotten with all the intreaties of IUPITER: I tell you fir, the ftring of a womans heart reacheth to the pulfe of her hand, and let a man rub that with gold, & tis hard but fhe wil prooue his hearts gold. MONTANUS is yoong, a great claufe in fancies court: MONTANUS is vertuous, the richeft argument that Loue yeelds: & yet knowing all thefe perfections I praife them, and wonder at them, louing the qualities, but not affecting the perfon, becaufe the Deftenies haue fet downe a contrary cenfure. Yet VENUS to ad reuenge, hath giuē me wine of yᵉ fame grape, a fip of the fame fauce, & firing me with the like paffiō, hath croft me with as il a penance: for I am in loue with a fhepheards fwaine, as coy to mee as I am cruel to MONTANUS, as peremptory in difdain as I was peruerfe in defire, & that is (quoth fhe) ALIENAES page, yong GANIMEDE.

GERISMOND defirous to profecute the ende of thefe paffions, called in GANIMEDE: who knowing the cafe, came in graced with

golden Legacie. 63

with fuch a blufh, as beautified the Chriftall of his face with
a ruddie brightneffe. The King noting well the phifnomy
of GANIMEDE, began by his fauours to cal to mind the face
of his ROSALYND, and with that fetcht a deepe figh. RO-
SADER that was paffing familiar with GERISMOND, demanded
of him why he fighed fo fore ¶ Becaufe ROSADER (quoth
hee) the fauour of GANIMEDE puts mee in minde of ROSA-
LYNDE. At this word, ROSADER fight fo deepely as though
his heart would haue burft. And whats the matter (quoth
GERISMOND) that you quite mee with fuch a figh ¶ Pardon
mee fir (quoth ROSADER) becaufe I loue none but ROSA-
LYND. And vpon that condition (quoth GERISMOND) that
ROSALYND were here, I would this day make vp a marriage
betwixt her and thee. At this ALIENA turnd her head and
fmilde vpon GANIMEDE, and fhee could fcarce keep countenance. Yet fhee falued all with fecrecie, and GERISMOND
to driue away fuch dumpes, queftioned with GANIMEDE,
what the reafon was he regarded not PHŒBES loue, feeing
fhe was as faire as the wantō that brought *Troy* to ruine.
GANIMEDE mildly anfwered, If I fhuld affeᵭ the fair PHOEBE,
I fhould offer poore MONTANUS great wrong to winne that
from him in a moment, that hee hath labored for fo many
monthes. Yet haue I promifed to the bewtiful fhepheardeffe,
to wed my felf neuer to woman except vnto her: but with
this promife, yᵗ if I can by reafon fuppreffe PHOEBES loue
towards me, fhe fhall like of none but of MONTANUS. To
yᵗ q. PHOEBE I ftand, for my loue is fo far beyond reafon, as
it wil admit no perfuafion of reafon. For iuftice q. he, I
appeale to GERISMOND: and to his cenfure wil I ftand q.
PHOEBE. And in your viᵭory q. MONTANUS ftands the hazard
of my fortunes: for if GANYMEDE go away with conqueft,
MONTANUS is in conceit loues Monarch, if PHOEBE winne,
then am I in effeᵭ moft miferable. We wil fee this con-
trouerfie q. GERISMŌD, & then we will to church: therefore
GANIMEDE let vs heare your argument. Nay, pardon my
abfence a while (quoth fhee) and you fhall fee one in ftore.

R 3   In

Euphues

In went GANIMEDE and dreſt her ſelf in womans attire, hauing on a gowne of greene, with kirtle of rich ſandall, ſo quaint, that ſhe ſeemed DIANA triumphing in the Forreſt: vpon her head ſhe wore a chaplet of Roſes, which gaue her ſuch a grace, yᵗ ſhe looked like FLORA pearkt in the pride of all hir floures. Thus attired came *R*OSALIND in, & preſented her ſelf at her fathers feete, with her eyes full of teares, crauing his bleſſing, & diſcourſing vnto him all her fortunes, how ſhee was baniſhed by TORISMOND, and how euer ſince ſhe liued in that country diſguiſed.

GERISMOND ſeeing his daughter, roſe from his ſeat & fel vpon her necke, vttering the paſſions of his ioy in watry plaints driuen into ſuch an extaſie of content, that hee could not vtter one word. At this ſight, if *R*OSADER was both amazed & ioyfull, I refer my ſelfe to the iudgement of ſuch as haue experience in loue, ſeeing his ROSALYND before his face whom ſo long and deeply he had affeſted. At laſt GERISMOND recouered his ſpirites, and in moſt fatherly tearmes entertained his daughter *R*OSALYND, after many queſtions demanding of her what had paſt betweene her and *R*OSADER. So much ſir (quoth ſhe) as there wants nothing but your Grace to make vp the marriage. Why then (quoth GERISMOND) *R*OSADER take her, ſhee is thine, and let this day ſolemnize both thy brothers and thy nuptials, *R*OSADER beyond meaſure cōtent, humbly thanked the king, & imbraced his ROSALYNDE, who turning to PHOEBE, demanded if ſhe had ſhewen ſufficient reaſon to ſuppreſſe the force of her loues. Yea quoth PHŒBE, & ſo great a perſwaſiue, that if it pleaſe you Madame and ALIENA to giue vs leaue, MONTANUS and I will make this day the thirde couple in marriage. She had no ſooner ſpake this word, but MONTANUS, threw away his garland of willow, his bottle, where was painted diſpaire, & caſt his ſonnets in the fire, ſhewing himſelfe as frolicke as PARIS when he hanſeled his loue with HELENA. At this GERISMOND and the reſt ſmiled, and concluded that MONTANUS and PHOEBE ſhould

keepe

golden Legacie.   64

keepe their wedding with the two brethren. ALIENA feeing
SALADYNE ftand in a dumpe, to wake him from his dreame
began thus. Why how now my SALADYNE, all a mort,
what melancholy man at the day of marriage? perchaunce
thou art forrowfull to thinke on thy brothers high fortunes,
and thyne owne bafe defires to chufe fo meane a fhepheardize.
Cheare vp thy hart man, for this day thou fhalt bee married
to the daughter of a King: for know SALADYNE, I am not
ALIENA, but ALINDA the daughter of thy mortal enemie
TORISMOND. At this all the company was amazed,
efpecially GERISMOND, who rifing vp, tooke ALINDA in his
armes, and faid to ROSALYND: is this that faire ALINDA
famous for fo many vertues, that forfoke her fathers court
to liue with thee exilde in the country? The fame q. ROSA-
LYNDE. Then quoth GERISMOND, turning to SALADINE,
iolly Forrefter be frolick, for thy fortunes are great, & thy
defires excellent, thou haft got a princeffe as famous for her
perfection, as exceeding in proportion. And fhe hath with
her beauty won (quoth SALADYNE) an humble feruant, as
full of faith, as fhe of amiable fauour. While euery one
was amazed with thefe Comicall euentes, CORIDON came fkip-
ping in, & told them that the Prieft was at Church and
tarried for their comming. With that GERISMOND led the
way, & the reft followed, where to the admiration of all
the countrey fwains in *Arden*, their mariages were folemnly
folemnized. As foone as the Prieft had finifhed, home they
went with ALINDA, where CORIDON had made all things in
readines. Dinner was prouided, & the tables being fpread,
and the Brides fet downe by GERISMOND, ROSADER, SALA-
DYNE, & MONTANUS that day were feruitors: homely cheare
thay had, fuch as their country could affoord: but to mend
their fare they had mickle good chat, and many difcourfes
of their loues and fortunes. About mid dinner, to make
them mery CORIDON came in with an old crowd, and plaid
them a fit of mirth, to which he fung this pleafant fong.

Cori-

Euphues

Coridons Song.

A blyth and bonny country Laſſe,
   heigh ho the bonny Laſſe:
Sate ſighing on the tender graſſe,
   and weeping ſaid, will none come woo mee?
A ſmicker boy, a lyther Swaine,
   heigh ho a ſmicker Swaine:
That in his Loue was wanton faine,
   with ſmiling looks ſtraight came vnto her.

When as the wanton wench eſpide,
   heigh ho when ſhe eſpide
The meanes to make her ſelfe a bride,
   ſhe ſimpred ſmooth like bonny bell:
The Swaine that ſaw her ſquint eied kind
   heigh ho ſquint eyed kind,
His armes about her body twind,
   and faire Laſſe, how fare ye, well?

The country kit ſaid well forſooth,
   heigh ho well forſooth,
But that I haue a longing tooth,
   a longing tooth that makes me crie:
Alas ſaid he what garres thy griefe?
   heigh ho what garres thy griefe?
A wound quoth ſhe without reliefe,
   I feare a maid that I ſhall die.

If that be all the ſhepheard ſaid
   heigh ho the ſhepheard ſaid,

Ile]

Ile make thee wiue it gentle maide,
And fo recure thy maladie.
Hereon they kist with manie a oath,
heigh ho with manie a oath,
And fore God Pan *did plight their troath,*
and to the Church they hied them fast.

And God fend euerie pretie peate
heigh ho the pretie peate
That feares to die of this conceate,
fo kinde a friend to helpe at last.

CORIDON hauing thus made them merrie: as they were
in the midft of all their iollitie, word was brought in to SA-
LADYNE and ROSADER, that a brother of theirs, one FERNAN-
DYNE was arriued, and defired to fpeake with them. GERIS-
MOND ouer hearing this newes, demaunded who it was?
It is fir (quoth ROSADER) our middle brother, that lyues a
Scholler in *Paris:* but what fortune hath driuen him to féek
vs out I know not. With that SALADYNE went and met his
brother, whom he welcommed with all curtefie, and ROSA-
DER gaue him no leffe friendly entertainment: brought hee
was by his two brothers into the parlour where they al fate
at dinner. FERNANDYNE as one that knewe as manie manners as he could points of fophiftrie, & was afwell brought
vp as well lettered, faluted them all. But when hee efpied
GERISMOND, knéeling on his knée he did him what reuerence
belonged to his eftate: and with that burft foorth into thefe
fpeaches. Although (right mightie Prince) this day of my
brothers mariage be a day of mirth, yet time craues another
courfe: and therefore from daintie cates rife to fharpe weapons. And you the fonnes of Sir IOHN of *Bourdeaux,* leaue
off your amors & fall to armes, change your loues into lances, and now this day fhewe your felues as valiant, as he-
thertoo you haue been paffionate. For know GERISMOND,
that hard by at the edge of this forreft the twelue Peeres of

S   *France*

Euphues

France are vp in Armes to recouer thy right; and TORIS-
MOND troupt with a crue of defperate runnagates is ready
to bid them battaile. The Armies are readie to ioyne: therfore fhew thy felfe in the field to encourage thy fubiects; and
you SALADYNE & ROSADER mount you, and fhewe your felues
as hardie fouldiers as you haue been heartie louers: fo fhall
you for the benefite of your Countrey, difcouer the IDEA of
your fathers vertues to bee ftamped in your thoughts, and
proue children worthie of fo honourable a parent. At this
alarum giuen by FERNANDYNE, GERISMOND leapt from the
boord, and SALADYNE and ROSADER betook themfelues to their
weapons. Nay quoth GERISMOND, goe with me I haue
horfe and armour for vs all, and then being well mounted,
let vs fhew that we carrie reuenge and honour at our faw-
chions points. Thus they leaue the Brides full of forrow,
efpecially ALINDA, who defired GERISMŌD to be good to her
father: he not returning a word becaufe his haft was great,
hied him home to his Lodge, where he deliuered SALADYNE
and ROSADER horfe and armour, and himfelfe armed royally
led the way: not hauing ridden two leagues before they difcouered where in a Valley both the battailes were ioyned.
GERISMOND féeing the wing wherein the Peeres fought,
thruft in there, and cried SAINT DENIS, GERISMOND laying on fuch loade vppon his enemies, that hee fhewed how
highly he did eftimate of a Crowne. When the Peeres perceiued that their lawfull King was there, they grewe more
eager: and SALADYNE and ROSADER fo behaued themfelues,
that none durft ftend in their way, nor abide the furie of their
weapons. To be fhort, the Peeres were conquerours, TO-
RISMONDS armie put to flight, & himfelfe flaine in battaile.
The Peeres then gathered themfelues together, and falu-
ting their king, conducted him royallie into *Paris*, where he
was receiued with great ioy of all the citizens. Affoone as
all was quiet and he had receiued againe the Crowne, hee
fent for ALINDA and ROSALYNDE to the Court, ALINDA being
verie paffionate for the death of her father: yet brooking it
with

with the more patience, in that fhe was contented with the welfare of her SALADYNE. Well, affoone as they were come to *Paris*, GERISMOND made a royall Feaft for the Peeres and Lords of his Lande, which continued thirtie dayes, in which time fummoning a Parliament, by the confent of his Nobles he created ROSADER heire apparant to the kingdom he reftored SALADYNE to all his fathers lande, and gaue him the Dukedome of *Nameurs*, he made FERNANDYNE principall Secretarie to himfelfe: and that Fortune might euerie way feeme frolicke, he made MONTANUS Lord ouer all the Forreft of *Arden:* ADAM SPENCER Captaine of the Kings Gard, and CORIDON Mafter of ALINDAS Flocks.

H Eere Gentlemen may you fee in EUPHUES GOLDEN LE-GACIE, that fuch as negleɛt their fathers precepts, incurre much preiudice; that diuifion in Nature as it is a blemifh in nurture, fo tis a breach of good fortunes; that vertue is not meafured by birth but by aɛtion; that yonger brethren though inferiour in yeares, yet may be fuperiour to honours; that concord is the fweeteft conclufion, and amitie betwixt brothers more forceable than fortune. If you gather any frutes by this Legacie, fpeake well of EUPHUES for writing it, and me for fetching it. If you grace me with that fauour, you encourage me to be more forward: and affoone as I haue o-uerlookt my labours, expeɛt the SAILERS KALENDER.

T. Lodge.

FINIS.